The Ecological Augury in
the Works of JRR Tolkien

Liam Campbell

The Ecological Augury in the Works of JRR Tolkien

2011

Cormarë Series No. 21

Series Editors: Peter Buchs • Thomas Honegger • Andrew Moglestue • Johanna Schön

Editor responsible for this volume: Thomas Honegger

Library of Congress Cataloging-in-Publication Data

Campbell, Liam:
The Ecological Augury in the Works of JRR Tolkien
ISBN 978-3-905703-18-4

Subject headings:
Tolkien, J.R.R. (John Ronald Reuel), 1892-1973 – Criticism and interpretation
Tolkien, J.R.R. (John Ronald Reuel), 1892-1973 – Language
Middle-earth (Imaginary place)
Literature, Comparative
Ecocriticism.

Cormarë Series No. 21

First published 2011

© Walking Tree Publishers, Zurich and Jena, 2011

All rights reserved. No portion of this book may be reproduced, by any process or technique, without the express written consent of the publisher

Cover illustration: "JRR Tolkien, Portrait by Pamela Chandler".
Copyright to the photo held by Diana Willson.

Set in Adobe Garamond Pro and Shannon by Walking Tree Publishers
Printed by Lightning Source in the United Kingdom and United States

For my dad

Carl Campbell

(1941-2004)

BOARD OF ADVISORS

ACADEMIC ADVISORS

Douglas A. Anderson (independent scholar)

Dieter Bachmann (Universität Zürich)

Patrick Curry (independent scholar)

Michael D.C. Drout (Wheaton College)

Vincent Ferré (Université de Paris 13)

Thomas Fornet-Ponse (Rheinische Friedrich-Wilhelms-Universität Bonn)

Verlyn Flieger (University of Maryland)

Christopher Garbowski (University of Lublin, Poland)

Mark T. Hooker (Indiana University)

Andrew James Johnston (Freie Universität Berlin)

Rainer Nagel (Johannes-Gutenberg-Universität Mainz)

Helmut W. Pesch (independent scholar)

Tom Shippey (Saint Louis University)

Allan Turner (Friedrich-Schiller-Universität Jena)

Frank Weinreich (independent scholar)

GENERAL READERS

Johan Boots

Jean Chausse

Johan Vanhecke (Letterenhuis, Antwerp)

Patrick Van den hole

Friedhelm Schneidewind

Acknowledgments

There are many kind hearts and generous souls that I wish to thank for their selfless advice, guidance and insight related to the research and realisation of this book. I offer such thanks humbly and somewhat randomly since all assistance and support was, and is, appreciated equally.

I am indebted to all at Walking Tree Publishers for their support and faith in the development of this study. I could not have reached the point of publication without the professionalism, expertise and patience of Prof. Dr. Thomas Honegger, editor of the Cormarë Series – I thank Thomas sincerely.

I also owe a huge debt of gratitude to my friends at the University of Ulster: Professor John Gillespie and Dr. Paul Davies whose collective advice has been invaluable to me throughout my research. I thank also Professor Jan Jędrzejewski whose clear seeing was (and is) always a light in the dark. Further thanks are also respectfully and humbly offered to Dr. Frank Sewell and Dr. Andrew Keanie whose words of wisdom and encouragement were a constant inspiration. Thanks also to Dr. Stanley Black for professional assistance.

I acknowledge also the guidance and professionalism of Professor Trevor Hart of St Andrews University, and wish to pay tribute to the advice offered by Tolkien illustrator, Ted Nasmith. I extend further kind thoughts and thanks to Diana Willson and her husband Barry for the chats about Tolkien, and for permitting me to include a journal entry in this book from Diana's sister, Pamela Chandler, related to her memories of Tolkien, and for the release of the image of Professor Tolkien, taken by Pamela, which adorns the cover of this book.

I humbly acknowledge the unconditional support of my family, especially Liz and Jordan, who were with me throughout and had to put up with the research, the writing, the long absences and the coffee-filled evenings. I wish to extend a special thanks to my mother Maeve and brother Carl for continued encouragement and support, and offer the work herein to the memory of my late father Carl. Finally I want to thank J.R.R. Tolkien for creating such extraordinary works of fiction and for effectively setting the wheels of this book in motion.

About the author

Liam Campbell is an independent writer and scholar from Northern Ireland who holds a PhD in English literature. Liam has lectured in English literature for the University of Ulster, published previously on Tolkien and environmentalism, and given many talks across Europe and America on Tolkien, ecocriticism and contemporary literature.

Contents

Introduction	1
Chapter One Rage against the Machine	27
Chapter Two Contrasting Environmental Personas in *The Lord of the Rings*: Tom Bombadil and Saruman	73
Chapter Three Contrasting Environmental Personas in *The Lord of the Rings*: Gandalf and Sauron	109
Chapter Four Seeing the World through Elvish Eyes: An Examination of the Human & Non-Human in Tolkien's Fiction	153
Chapter Five Tales That Grew in the Telling	201
Conclusion Mirrors of the Golden Wood	243
Afterword Trouble with the Trees	255
Bibliography	273
Index	285

Series Editor's Preface

As series editor at Walking Tree Publishers one has the pleasure of being close to the most recent developments in Tolkien studies. Some topics, such as Tolkien and Wagner, have been 'in the air' for several years but have not yet received any in-depth, extended critical attention. So the time has been obviously ripe for a study on that topic – two studies actually. They have been conceived independently of each other and have come to our attention only recently and are now scheduled for publication in 2012.

Tolkien and Ecocriticism/Green Studies/Environmentalism is somewhat different. It has been, ever since Patrick Curry's seminal *Defending Middle-earth* (1997), one of the topics to receive regularly at least some critical attention. Yet it took some years until the first book-length study on the subject appeared, which was Dickerson and Evans' *Ents, Elves, and Eriador* (2006). Five years later, Liam Campbell presents the second monograph paying close attention to the environmental vision of J.R.R. Tolkien, and it may be justified to speak of an 'emerging tradition' in matters of 'green Tolkien studies'. Campbell's *The Ecological Augury in the Works of JRR Tolkien* not only takes up, critically evaluates and engages with the studies and ideas of his predecessors, but also opens up new territories inside and outside Tolkien studies proper. All of this, I may point out, in a clear and reader-friendly language.

Seeing this engaging study from manuscript into print has been a rewarding experience – and has been made possible by Liam's untiring effort of striving for the best text possible, by the support of my co-series-editors, by the members of the Board of Advisors who evaluated the initial project submission, and the students who served part of their internship as proofreaders and layouters for WTP. I would like to thank all of them and mention only two of the latter by name, Stefanie Busch and Madline Seiler, who each proofread the entire manuscript.

I wish, in the name of WTP, an enjoyable and engrossing reading!

Thomas Honegger
Jena, July 2011

"the withering of all woods may be drawing near"

The Lord of the Rings: The Two Towers

Introduction

In a letter to Milton Waldman, editor of Collins Books, a few years before the publication of *The Lord of the Rings*, Tolkien states that his Middle-earth writings were 'mainly concerned with Fall, Mortality and the Machine.'[1] As a devout Catholic Tolkien believed that, since humanity had fallen from Grace, '[t]here [could not] be any 'story' without a fall.'[2] Mortality as a major theme in his work, of course, also has theological and philosophical roots, and Tolkien on more than one occasion declared that questions related to death and deathlessness were central to the thematic grounding of his *legendarium*. Attempting to clarify to Waldman what he meant by the third term, Tolkien explains that by 'the Machine' he is referring not only to the development and use of 'external plans or devices (apparatus)' – in other words technologies, engines, industries and their related regimes – but also a worldview that only deals in self-aggrandisement and 'the corrupted motive of dominating: bulldozing the real world, or coercing other wills.'[3] For Tolkien one of the victims of regimes or worldviews that bulldozed 'other wills' (and the imagery he uses is not co-incidental) included nature itself. It is under the umbrella of this major thematic concern that much of this study's matters are discussed. Of course readers of Tolkien for decades have made the implicit connection between his fiction and ecological issues pertaining to the primary world. For me the realization that such issues were a major concern of Tolkien's fiction came somewhat out of the blue, and has led, albeit by a winding path, to the writing of this book.

(I) A Green Reading

A few (too many) years back whilst visiting a particularly picturesque part of Donegal in Ireland, I was sitting in an unfamiliar chair by a window that looked out upon a clear blue sky, an expanse of wood and the distant peak of Mount Errigal, the most majestic of the Derryveagh Mountains. I was deeply immersed in reading *The Lord of the Rings*, but I found my attention distracted by the lure of the landscape that beckoned from the window. In the book I had reached Fangorn Forest, as Pippin and Merry first encounter Treebeard

---

1 J.R.R. Tolkien, *The Letters of J.R.R. Tolkien,* edited by Humphrey Carpenter, London: HarperCollins, 2006, p.145.
2 Tolkien, *Letters*, p.184.
3 Tolkien, *Letters*, p.146.

and the ents – and to them my attention returned. I settled as best I could into the chair and began again to read. Treebeard, his voice thundering in my imagination, bellowed, 'the withering of all woods may be drawing near.'[4] I glanced momentarily at the wood and trees revealed by my window and then read on. Speaking of Saruman's love of machines and disregard for the natural world Treebeard was saying, '[Saruman] is plotting to become a Power. He has a mind of metal and wheels; and he does not care for growing things, except as far as they serve him for the moment.'[5] Treebeard's voice seemed to sadden as he lamented upon how the forest had suffered under the apparatus of Saruman's assault: 'there are wastes of stump and bramble where once there were singing groves. I have been idle.'[6] My notice was drawn irresistibly back to the landscape that reached from my window to the wild horizon beyond. And, remembering Galdor's words at the Council of Elrond: 'Sauron can torture and destroy the very hills',[7] it suddenly occurred to me that the War of the Ring and the struggle of the free peoples of Middle-earth against the rising shadows in Mordor and Isengard amounted to more than a struggle against tyranny and enslavement – that behind the fight for freedom lay a struggle to resist powers (sometimes cloaked in wisdom) which threatened the very land itself. Middle-earth and the waking force of nature that sustained 'her' were at stake. And as I perused my view of a wild country unspoiled by 'metal and wheels', I reflected upon how the peril facing Tolkien's created world of Middle-earth seemed so curiously to resemble the real world: the troubled and tainted planet upon which we live, the environmental problems that surround us and the irreverent, indiscriminate power-lusts that preside over our fate.

Since first visiting the Third Age of Middle-earth as a reader I have found myself increasingly drawn to the environmental dimension of Tolkien's work. Writing prior to the advent of any 'organised' green agenda, before the literary birth of words such as ecotheology or ecocriticism, Tolkien's ecological worldview is surprisingly developed in terms of its consonance with much of what we now understand as environmentalism. The key concern of this study is to assert that Tolkien was a writer who adhered, throughout his work, to a consistent

---

4 J.R.R. Tolkien, *The Two Towers*, London: HarperCollins, 1997, p.461.
5 Tolkien, *Two Towers*, p.462.
6 Tolkien, *Two Towers*, p.563.
7 J.R.R. Tolkien, *The Fellowship of the Ring*, London: HarperCollins, 1997, p.259.

and systematic representation of ecological themes, threads and motifs which together amount to an augury against the dangers of ecological apathy and the pursuit of progress and technological advancement in the absence of an environmental conscience. I contend that there is a clearly observable ecologically themed undercurrent to Tolkien's fiction that reflects, consciously or not, his environmental anxieties for a world he believed was too readily embracing the machine age.

Nature, the ennoblement of the non-human, and environmental concerns lie just below the surface of Tolkien's narratives. In the analysis of Tolkien's green themes I seek to show that behind the self-declared myth-maker, the philologist and the storyteller we may find a visionary environmentalist who, as Ralph C. Wood comments, was 'an unapologetic defender of nature before environmentalism had yet been made into a cause.'[8] That is, of course, not to presume to offer Tolkien as an environmentalist first and a storyteller second. Tolkien was first and foremost a teller of tales, but his tales: those of the passing Ages of Middle-earth as well as his unrelated short stories and narrative poems display a profound and multifaceted embrace of and concern for the natural world.

Indeed, aside from his fiction, this study will consider Tolkien's essays, private papers and letters, and reveal a man who was a vociferous and passionate champion of the natural world. The study seeks to offer that Tolkien, who once declared '[e]very tree has its enemy, few have an advocate',[9] deeply mistrusted the rise of the machine and the industrial age, under the hand of misuse, to such an extent that he anticipated the scale of the environmental crisis that was yet to dawn. Interlaced with these considerations this book will also concern itself with the interconnection of Tolkien's environmental ideals and his deeply held theological beliefs.

It should also be noted that Tolkien's literature contains a complexity of themes of which the ecological dimension is but one. But, given the emergence and rise to prominence of environmental issues throughout the last century and the ecological problems now facing modern generations, I have no doubt that

---

8 Ralph C. Wood, *The Gospel According to Tolkien: Visions of the Kingdom in Middle-earth*, Louisville: Westminster John Knox Press, 2003, p.28.
9 Tolkien, *Letters*, p.321.

the green threads that run through Tolkien's work have played a major part in its enduring appeal. Indeed before proceeding, I wish to take a moment to consider the popularity of Tolkien's major work *The Lord of the Rings*, which continues, thanks in part to the phenomenal global success of Peter Jackson's film adaptation of the story, to feature prominently on best seller lists worldwide, in contrast to the often hostile critical reception the work has received. As Joseph Pearce states in *Tolkien Man and Myth*, '[r]arely has a book caused such controversy and rarely has the vitriol of the critics highlighted to such an extent the cultural schism between the literary illuminati and the views of the reading public.'[10]

(II) The War of the Words: Tolkien and the Critics

When Tolkien's *The Lord of the Rings* began to find favour among the book-buying public, a host of detractors were all too ready to categorise such popularity as being down to the 'don't-know-any-better' purchasing habits of an accumulation of capricious, ill-informed readers. Many self-declared 'know-better' (or 'in-the-know') literary commentators classed the early commercial success of Tolkien's major work as the product of a transient phase that would soon fade and be forgotten. Philip Toynbee, writing with perceptible hostility (and perhaps even glee) in the *Observer* in 1961, announced that Tolkien's fiction had 'passed into merciful oblivion'[11] – a remark that has proven to be as short-sighted as it was inaccurate. Like the denigrating tone evident in Toynbee's words, open hostility often marked the critical attacks on Tolkien as esteemed forces from within the literary establishment moved to dismiss his fiction as puerile and second rate. Edmund Wilson the then pre-eminent American literary critic, in an article for *The Nation* entitled 'Oo, Those Awful Orcs', dated April 1956, categorised *The Lord of the Rings* as 'a children's book which has somehow got out of hand.' Abandoning any pretence of reasoned argument, he referred to it simply as 'balderdash'. Wilson was particularly vitriolic in his dismissal of Tolkien's major work: 'the poverty of invention displayed [is] almost pathetic' he wrote, adding that he believed Tolkien suffered from '[a]n impotence of imagination.' As was soon to become a common trait of Tolkien detractors (one

---

10 Joseph Pearce, *Tolkien: Man and Myth*, London: HarperCollins, 1998, p.2.
11 Philip Toynbee, 'Dissension among the Judges' in the *Observer* (6th August 1961).

which persists even today), Wilson also directed his scorn towards anyone who declared admiration for Tolkien's literature.

One of Tolkien's more ardent supporters in those first years after the publication of *The Lord of the Rings* was prominent poet and critic W.H. Auden[12] who, in a review of *The Fellowship of the Ring* for the *New York Times* in 1954, wrote: '[n]o fiction I have read in the last five years has given me more joy.' Wilson, emphasising that Auden's critical credentials were earned as a commentator of verse and not prose, and essentially writing off his judgement as an objective critic, declared that Auden 'so overrates *The Lord of the Rings* because he reads into it something that he means to write himself'. By anyone's standards the claim to have what amounts to telepathic insight into the creative imagination of another writer and critic could hardly qualify Wilson's remarks as valid or rational commentary. Moreover Wilson was prepared to proffer another theory as to why any tributes at all should exist for Tolkien's work, or why any would seek to extol its virtues: 'the answer' he proclaimed, with all the surety of a scientist offering incontrovertible test results, 'is that certain people – especially, perhaps, in Britain – have a lifelong appetite for juvenile trash.'[13] This condescending, elitist and essentially jaundiced position characterised (to one degree or another) much of the anti-Tolkien rhetoric that followed the release (and subsequent commercial success) of *The Lord of the Rings*. Indeed Peter Green's commentary in the *Daily Telegraph* dated 27th August 1954, which included the rather blunt remark: 'I presume [*The Lord of the Rings*] is meant to be taken seriously, and am apprehensive that I can find no adequate reasons for doing

---

12 Auden was among the first serious critics to recognise and proclaim the literary worth of Tolkien's fiction. He had studied under Tolkien at Oxford and in later life occasionally corresponded with his old professor. Although a vociferous champion of Tolkien's fiction, Auden stated that Tolkien's influence upon him was as a philologist rather than as an author. Describing a lecture given by Tolkien on *Beowulf* in which part of the poem was recited, Auden states: 'I was spellbound. This poetry, I knew was going to be my dish' (W.H. Auden, *The Dyer's Hand and other Essays*, New York: Vintage, 1968, pp.41-42). Each later went on to honour the other in verse form, with Tolkien writing an Anglo-Saxon poem 'For W.H.A.' on the occasion of Auden's 60th birthday, and Auden praising Tolkien in the closing lines of his poem 'A Short Ode to a Philologist'. Both men died in the same year: 1973. For a more detailed insight into Tolkien and Auden's friendship and exchanges see Rod Jellema 'Auden, W.H.: Influence of' in Michael D.C. Drout (ed.), *J.R.R. Tolkien Encyclopedia: Scholarship and Critical Assessment*, New York: Routledge, 2006, pp.41-42.
13 Edmund Wilson, 'Oo, Those Awful Orcs' in *The Nation* 182:15 (14th April 1956).

so',[14] caused Tolkien to wonder if Green's remarks were motivated by more than professional disapproval: 'he is so rude as to make one suspect malice.'[15]

Of course Tolkien had his share of favourable reviews and critical defenders, even among the first waves of reaction to *The Lord of the Rings*. Alongside the aforementioned W.H. Auden, A.E. Cherryman commenting in *Truth* three weeks before Green's broadside, was convinced of the profundity of Tolkien's work: '[i]t's an amazing piece of work [...Tolkien] has added something, not only to the world's literature, but to its history.'[16] H. l'A. Fawcett in the *Manchester Guardian*, August 20th 1954, rejected the claim that *The Lord of the Rings* was a book for children but rather asserted that Tolkien's skill as 'one of those born storytellers' left his adult readership 'as wide-eyed as children for more.'[17] Other critics such as Howard Spring in *Country Life* (26th August 1954) and Donald Barr in the *New York Times* (1st May 1955) were enthused by the grand sweep of Tolkien's narrative. Spring stated categorically '[t]his is a work of art [...], a profound parable of man's everlasting struggle against evil.'[18] Barr, acknowledging that Tolkien's work was traceable along the line of an 'epic tradition' that 'disappear[ed] in the mists of Germanic history', added 'his style is full of joy, the joy that follows the making of a perfect gesture. But more than this [...] his story has a kind of echoing depth behind it.'[19] Perhaps Tolkien's most strident advocate, however, was his old friend, fellow 'Inkling'[20] and Oxford colleague C.S. Lewis, who had helped in the gestation and publishing of Tolkien's work. Lewis, who himself attracted derision from critics for his 'Narnia' series, extolled Tolkien's praises on the dust cover of the first edition of *The Fellowship of the Ring*:

> If Ariosto rivalled it in invention (in fact he did not) he would still lack its heroic seriousness. No imaginary world has been projected which is at once multifarious and so true to its own inner laws; none so seemingly objective, so

---

14 Peter Green, 'Review of *The Fellowship of the Ring*' in the *Daily Telegraph* (27th August 1954).
15 Tolkien, *Letters*, p.184.
16 A.E. Cherryman in *Truth* (6th August 1954).
17 H. l'A. Fawcett in the *Manchester Guardian* (20th August 1954).
18 Howard Spring, 'Review of *The Fellowship of the Ring*' in *Country Life* (26th August 1954).
19 Donald Barr, 'Review of *The Two Towers*' in the *New York Times* (1st May 1955).
20 'The Inklings' were a group of writers and friends that included Tolkien, C.S. Lewis, Charles Williams and Owen Barfield. The group would often meet around the Oxford area, settling eventually in 'The Eagle and Child' pub (known locally as 'The Bird and Baby'). The group of friends would drink ale, smoke tobacco, and read out, in turn, their creative works in progress. They would also engage in (sometimes) heated conversation about philosophical, literary and even everyday matters.

disinfected from the taint of an author's merely individual psychology; none so relevant to the actual human situation.[21]

Lewis' favourable comparison of Tolkien to Ariosto,[22] a widely celebrated narrative poet from the Italian Renaissance period, only served to further aggravate certain sectors of the literary establishment. Lewis had warned Tolkien after he had been approached by Stanley Unwin to put together a few words for the cover, that, in terms of his own critical standing, he was 'an increasingly, hated man, whose name might do [Tolkien] more harm than good.'[23] These words proved to have more substance than Tolkien could have imagined as critics, in turn, sneered at both the audacity of Lewis' comparison and the fact that it had been Lewis in particular who had made it.[24] Of course we should note that Lewis did himself (and Tolkien) no favours (given Tolkien's fledgling reputation as an author and the well-known friendship of the two) by evoking comparison with a canonised figure such as Ariosto – despite the honesty of his sentiments.[25] But, in the same manner as critics of Tolkien were often extreme and even malicious in their condemnation of his work, supporters like Lewis and Auden were, more-often-than-not, equally extreme and passionate in their praise. Indeed Auden, during an interview regarding *The Lord of the Rings* for radio on 16th November 1954, caused further fury among the *literati*, by proclaiming '[i]f someone dislikes it I shall never trust their literary judgement about anything again.'[26] Two years later in an article for the *New York Times* entitled 'At the End of the Quest, Victory', Auden, acknowledging a degree of impartiality in his own views, addressed the question of polarised opinions related to *The Lord of the Rings*:

---

21 Lewis had been asked by Stanley Unwin to provide a few words of endorsement for the dust jacket of *The Fellowship of the Ring*. Lewis obliged but warned Tolkien that he may have done more harm than good given his own critical reception.
22 Ludovico Ariosto's most famous work *Orlando Furioso*, an epic narrative poem he worked on for a large period of his life, was considered by many critics to be the greatest work of its kind in print.
23 Quoted in Humphrey Carpenter, *J.R.R. Tolkien: A Biography*, London: George Allen & Unwin, 1977, p.222.
24 One such 'sneering' critic was Edwin Muir who, in the *Observer* on 22nd of August 1954, alluded to Lewis' dust cover eulogy of Tolkien, and offered sardonically: '[t]his remarkable book makes its appearance at a disadvantage. Nothing but a great masterpiece could survive the bombardment of praise directed at it from the blurb.'
25 Referring to Lewis' blurb, Tolkien, in a letter to Unwin dated 9th September 1954, remarks that whilst he believed reviews had been 'better than [he had] feared' they 'might have been better still, if we had not quoted the Ariosto remark' (Tolkien, *Letters*, p.184).
26 Quoted in Carpenter, *Biography*, p.229.

> I rarely remember a book about which I have had such violent arguments. Nobody seems to have a moderate opinion: either, like myself, people find it a masterpiece of its genre or they cannot abide it, and among the hostile there are some, I must confess, for whose literary judgment I have great respect. A few of these may have been put off by the first forty pages of the first chapter of the first volume in which the daily life of the hobbits is described; this is light comedy and light comedy is not Mr. Tolkien's forte. In most cases, however, the objection must go far deeper. I can only suppose that some people object to Heroic Quests and Imaginary Worlds on principle; such, they feel, cannot be anything but light "escapist" reading. That a man like Mr. Tolkien, the English philologist who teaches at Oxford, should lavish such incredible pains upon a genre which is, for them, trifling by definition, is, therefore, very shocking.[27]

This passage by Auden (especially in his opening remarks) goes a long way to capturing the nature of the critical reception afforded to Tolkien. In terms of critical viewpoint, middle ground for the tales of Middle-earth was (and is) hard to come by. Unfortunately for supporters of Tolkien, however, among those who as Auden put it 'cannot abide' his work were a significant number of prominent literary commentators who, wilfully or not, began a trend that would see Tolkien cast to the margins of critically acknowledged twentieth-century writers.

In the years after the initial release of *The Lord of the Rings* interest in and sales of Tolkien's work increased steadily despite the critical storm it attracted. In particular his books found a new audience among American college students of the mid 1960s who were beginning to embrace and ignite the anti-establishment themed counter-culture movement. These students detected, as we shall discuss later, much common ground with aspects of Tolkien's work, and by the end of 1966, in what Humphrey Carpenter describes as a 'campus cult',[28] *The Lord of the Rings* had usurped the popularity of J.D. Salinger's *The Catcher in the Rye* and William Golding's *Lord of the Flies* among the book buying studentship of institutions such as Yale and Harvard.[29]

---

27 W.H. Auden, 'At the End of the Quest, Victory' in the *New York Times* (22nd January 1956).
28 Carpenter, *Biography*, p.229.
29 This sudden popularity of *The Lord of the Rings* in American colleges was also due in part to a complicated legal dispute that Tolkien himself played a prominent role in diffusing. In 1965 an American publishing house, Ace Books, announced that they planned to produce an unauthorised edition of *The Lord of the Rings* despite vociferous opposition from Tolkien's official American publishers, Houghton Mifflin. Ace claimed that their edition was valid, even though they had no official authorisation and indeed no intention of forwarding any of the money made from the venture to Tolkien. Houghton Mifflin, in association with Ballantine Books, moved swiftly to counter the unofficial release with an authorised version. They decided a few hurried revisions to the original

The counter-culture philosophy soon made its way across the Atlantic and began to find favour among the British university population, who, inheriting an inclination for the accompanying literature, delved into *The Lord of the Rings* with renewed vigour and increased its (and its author's) public profile as a result. The surge of interest in Tolkien's fiction, precipitated by the counter-culture trends of some of the younger generation of the 1960s, was evidence enough for some critics that Tolkien was an author who was defined by trends and fashions rather than a writer whose work should be afforded serious academic consideration. One such critic, Nigel Walmsley, in a particularly deprecatory essay 'Tolkien and the Sixties' declared '[t]he popularity of *The Lord of the Rings* has to be understood in the context of the group which most surely guaranteed its reputation, the young, disaffected section of the Western industrial middle class of the mid 1960s.' Walmsley, framing Tolkien's appeal against the backdrop of a fleeting sub-cultural trend, goes on (somewhat puzzlingly) to describe his work as 'an artifact as commercially enticing as a Bob Dylan record.' Walmsley, attempting to underline his point that Tolkien's work has no claim to serious critical or scholarly acclaim, also cites an exchange of correspondence in *The Times* newspaper where British university lecturers expressed their concern 'at what they saw as a sign of the collapse of their students' critical judgement in embracing Middle-earth.'[30] Walmsley concludes by proclaiming that 'a sharp change in cultural attitude [...] was effectively to end Tolkien's brief period of coruscating contemporary relevance', adding that any semblance of success for *The Lord of the Rings* was down to 'its radically imaginative appeal to a transient sub-cultural atavism'.

---

narrative (and to that of *The Hobbit*) would allow them to issue their books as 'new' editions, thereby undermining the Ace publications. Rayner Unwin explained the situation to Tolkien who eventually made the necessary revisions. It was, however, Tolkien's proclivity for answering his fan mail (a lot of which came from America) and correspondence in general (sometimes as the preferred activity to actually making revisions) that led to an organised campaign to boycott the Ace edition. Aware that Ace were intent in keeping all profits related to the sale of his work, Tolkien began adding a postscript to his letters informing his correspondents of the situation. Word spread quickly amongst Tolkien devotees and eventually bodies such as the Science Fiction Writers of America got involved. Ace, now under considerable pressure, agreed to pay Tolkien his dues and to cease publication of his works after the current run. Of course the upshot of all this was greatly increased publicity in America related to Tolkien's work and two publishing houses distributing his work in large volume – for by the time a truce had been reached with Ace, Houghton Mifflin had released authorised versions of *The Lord of the Rings* and *The Hobbit*. For a more detailed account of the legal wrangle described above see 'Cash or Kudos' in Carpenter, *Biography*, pp.219-232.

30 Quoted in Robert Giddings (ed.), *J.R.R. Tolkien: This Far Land*, London: Vision and Barnes & Noble, 1983, p.73.

Such was the perceptible scorn in Walmsley's essay for both the counter-culture movement and its embrace of Tolkien's work that at one point he declares Tolkien's 'mainstream international popularity' was down in part to 'hallucinogenic hedonism.'[31] Joseph Pearce in *Tolkien: Man and Myth*, referring to the extreme and sometimes ranting nature of Walmsley's commentary, declares with equal scorn '[o]ne wonders if 'Nigel Walmsley' is really a pseudonym of John Cleese, and his essay 'Tolkien and the Sixties' a Pythonesque pastiche.' Pearce goes on, quite rightly, to point to the fact that after the 1960s had come and gone Tolkien's work continued to have growing appeal, 'culminating in his emergence as the most popular writer of the century in several nationwide polls.'[32] The polls to which Pearce alludes were commissioned among large sections of the book buying public in Britain and elsewhere towards the end of the century and the results were to re-ignite the touch paper of polarised opinion on Tolkien, and bring open hostility against his work back into the public arena.

(III) Tolkien: Author of the Century?

Both Pearce (in *Tolkien: Man and Myth*) and Shippey (in *J.R.R. Tolkien: Author of the Century*) have offered more extensive commentary and analysis on the critical storm engendered by these end of century polls, but in what follows I will briefly cover the ground. In 1997 Waterstone's chain of book stores and the Channel Four programme *Book Choice* together sponsored a 'reader's poll' to establish (as the century was drawing to a close) the five books that could be considered to be 'the greatest of the century'. After a polling return that ran to around 26,000 replies, Waterstone's marketing manager Gordon Kerr, declared that *The Lord of the Rings* had finished as the runaway favourite in almost all of the 105 UK branches – only in Wales did it fail to top the overall regional poll, losing out to James Joyce's *Ulysses*. When the results were announced there was a general outcry of disgust among literary commentators, professional critics, journalists and those who would consider themselves to be guardians of literary taste. The *Times Literary Supplement* (24th January 1997) called the result 'horrifying'[33] and the *Guardian* (4th March 1997) suggested

---

31 Quoted in Giddings, *This Far Land*, pp.82-83.
32 Pearce, *Man and Myth*, p.141.
33 *Times Literary Supplement* (24th Jan 1997).

that contrary to misguided public opinion *The Lord of the Rings* was in fact 'by any reckoning one of the worst books ever written.'[34] Susan Jefferys of the *Sunday Times* (26th January 1997) reported that the reaction of a colleague upon hearing that Tolkien had topped the poll was to say, 'Oh hell! Has it? Oh my God. Oh dear oh dear.' This reaction according to Jefferys was 'echoed up and down the country wherever one or two[35] literati gathered together.' Jefferys went on to offer her own thoughts on the matter pronouncing that it was 'a depressing thought that the votes for the world's best 20th-century book should have come from those burrowing an escape into a nonexistent world.'[36] Indeed a chorus of voices rose to pour scorn and register consternation at the survey's result. Writer Howard Jacobson was especially venomous in his condemnation declaring that Tolkien appealed to 'the adult slow', and that such a result was proof of 'the folly of teaching people to read.' He concluded his somewhat pompous tirade by fuming '[c]lose all the libraries [...] It's another black day for British culture.'[37] Germaine Greer commenting in Waterstone's literary journal *W Magazine* was equally vitriolic in her reaction, 'it has been my nightmare', she writes 'that Tolkien would turn out to be the most influential writer of the twentieth century. The bad dream has materialised.' Despite conceding rather gracelessly the influence of Tolkien on twentieth-century readers, Greer goes on to dismiss *The Lord of the Rings* and 'books that come in Tolkien's train' as 'flight[s] from reality' implying that in the absence of 'a recognisable place' and 'a recognisable time'[38] such work holds little relevance for the modern world.

Barbed criticism aside, however, disgruntled cultural and literary commentators, in their outrage at Tolkien's success in the poll, began to question the validity of the result itself. Allegations began to surface that the Tolkien Society, a fan-based group formed in appreciation of all things Tolkien, had canvassed its membership to vote en masse thus 'hijacking' the poll and 'fixing' the outcome. Such reservations began to be expressed and repeated across various media outlets and the Waterstone's/*Book Choice* poll was soon tainted with the slur of

---

34 *Guardian* (4th March 1997).
35 Shippey with rather cutting wit observed that Jefferys must have meant 'two or three literati' as opposed to 'one or two', 'unless the literati talk only to themselves (a thought that does occur)' (Tom Shippey, *J.R.R. Tolkien: Author of the Century*, London: HarperCollins, 2000, p.xxi).
36 Susan Jefferys, *Sunday Times* (26th Jan 1997).
37 Howard Jacobson quoted by Susan Jefferys, in *Sunday Times* (26th Jan 1997).
38 Germaine Greer, *W Magazine* (Winter/Spring 1997).

unreliability. These allegations, however, were short-lived as other polls were set in motion: the readership of the *Daily Telegraph* in a similarly constructed survey to that of Waterstone's voted *The Lord of the Rings* as the book of the century, and the Folio society also canvassed its entire membership of fifty thousand to name their ten favourite books of any era. Well over a fifth of their members responded voting *The Lord of the Rings* as the unrivalled choice. When the Director of the Folio Society Sue Bradbury confirmed that only members had been permitted to take part, suspicions surrounding 'anorak-clad troops'[39] of the Tolkien Society ambushing the surveys were shown to be unfounded. A further poll commissioned by the BBC's *Bookworm* programme, in which around fifty thousand respondents were estimated to have taken part, returned the same result. *The Lord of the Rings* was eventually, if grudgingly, accepted as the nation's favourite book of the last century. In a later Mori poll carried out in 1999 and set up to determine the greatest book of any era, Tolkien's major work was finally beaten into second place – the winner? The Bible.

Although the suspicions of 'vote-fixing' have subsided and the popularity of *The Lord of the Rings* as Britain's 'book of the century' (as asserted through these polls) has now been corroborated, the outpouring of venom from mainstream literary criticism against Tolkien has continued unabated. And, in a practice initiated in Wilson's early criticisms of Tolkien in the mid-1950s, dissenters of Tolkien have continually felt the need to attack those who would praise, celebrate or defend him with equal venom as they would the author himself. Indeed Shippey's study *J.R.R. Tolkien: Author of the Century*, a study published on the turn of the Millennium, which alluded, in the title, to Tolkien's aforementioned success in the polls, was met with as much ridicule as the author it sought to defend. Andrew Rissik writing in the *Guardian* (2nd September 2000), refers to Shippey's defence of Tolkien as 'a belligerently argued piece of fan-magazine polemic.' 'Almost no-one', Rissik assures his readers, 'accepts Tolkien as one of the greatest writers of the last century [...] except the hard-core Tolkien addicts who've elevated his books to the status of a cult.' Certain critical positions, it seems, have moved little from the early anti-Tolkien tirades. Yet given

---

39 Quoted in Pearce, *Man and Myth*, p.3. Surprisingly this remark was made by Tolkien's biographer Humphrey Carpenter who himself suspected that the Tolkien Society, through 'covert' Internet orchestration, had played a part in the result of the original poll.

the growing wealth of serious, objective Tolkien study, and the ever-growing number of respected academics (Professor Shippey is certainly one) who consider Tolkien's fiction to be among the most influential and noteworthy of the twentieth century, the suggestion that anyone who would confer such praise on Tolkien must, by definition, be suffering from some sense-banishing addiction is perhaps evidence enough that a less than objective viewpoint persists.

Indeed, all in all, perhaps I could have saved myself some precious time and space amid these introductory words if I had merely submitted to W. H. Auden's assertion that 'people [either] find [*The Lord of the Rings*] a masterpiece of its genre or they cannot abide it'[40] and left it at that. In other words if we accept the premise that defenders and critics of Tolkien are marked by the polarised opinions they have of his work, what function does it serve to lay these criticisms out? Furthermore one might say that the *literati* and the denizens of academia such as they are, are quite right to dismiss popularity and poll-topping as any claim to greatness (even if they do tend to defend their position in terms of their 'distaste' for Tolkien with anything but professional detachment). So, questions must be asked: why offer a select and brief history of pro and anti-Tolkien commentary at all? Why present poll results in a scholarly discourse if they are no guide to an objective analysis of the author and his work, or perhaps more pertinent to this study, if they would seem to have little bearing on an examination of green themes in Tolkien's work?

Apart from historical critical context, and a wish to draw attention to the partisan and sometimes malicious nature of anti-Tolkien sentiment from certain quarters (who would ironically claim the higher ground of literary criticism) the rationale behind presenting a cross-section of Tolkien criticism and documenting controversy surrounding the poll results is to address one of the key underlying concerns of this study – namely the re-evaluation of Tolkien as an author whose work reflects the times and the anxieties of his age: an author, as Thomas Honegger and Frank Weinreich put it, 'whose literary creations can be seen as a response to the challenges of the modern world.'[41]

---

40 W.H. Auden, 'At the End of the Quest, Victory' in *The New York Times* (22nd January 1956).
41 Thomas Honegger & Frank Weinreich, 'Introduction' in Thomas Honegger & Frank Weinreich (eds.), *Tolkien and Modernity* 2, Zurich and Berne: Walking Tree Publishers, 2006, p.i.

In terms of the poll results, I am certainly not offering that widespread popular appeal is justification alone for critics of Tolkien to rethink or re-script their appraisals of his work, but rather that these results confirm that on some level and upon some virtue, Tolkien's literature has spoken to, has influenced, has moved and has enthralled a significant number of modern readers. Moreover, as evidenced in the growing and continued popularity of Tolkien's major work from the middle of the last century onwards (despite, as we have noted, frequent ill-judged critical associations of the book with changing literary trends and cults) Tolkien's literature has passed the test of time and has spoken to *generations* of twentieth-century readers. In the face of such facts, rather than merely offering contemptuous, sneering and dismissive remarks, one would imagine, or even expect, that mainstream literary criticism would at least seek to ask 'Why?' Shippey is similarly puzzled by the critics' response:

> It remains perfectly sensible, of course, to say that popular polls are no guide to literary value, any more than sales figures, and indeed both statements are no doubt true. The figures ought however to have produced some sort of considered response, even explanation, from professional critics of literature, rather than the nettled outrage they got.[42]

Indeed it would be no exaggeration to say that mainstream critical opinion, in its rush to relegate Tolkien's work to the periphery of literary history, has singularly failed to take account of the fact that the popularity of Tolkien's writings on Middle-earth represents a key cultural phenomenon in the later part of the twentieth century and on into the twenty-first. Moreover, as we have seen, the thrust of anti-Tolkien criticism has been levelled primarily on ideological grounds[43]– the majority of mainstream critics simply don't like his method of expression, and despite the evidence of his major work's enduring and widespread appeal, they continue to insist that the continu-

---

42 Shippey, *Author of the Century*, p.xxii.
43 There are certainly aspects of Tolkien's fiction that could be criticised. The 'biblical' and arguably stifled tone of some of his First Age writings for example, whilst an intentional component of the tone of the works, could be said to be somewhat self-indulgent – sacrificing tale for tone. The narrative structure of *The Lord of the Rings*, on occasion, demands a lot of patience from its readership. As readers we are forced to leave one plotline aside for pages on end whilst we pursue another. The Frodo and Sam plotline versus the Strider, Legolas, Gimli plotline is a case in point. Tolkien, however, trusted (correctly) that his readers would 'buy into' his narrative divisions. Rather than offer cohesive critical arguments based on aspects of his fiction such as those mentioned above, however, the majority of anti-Tolkien criticism has centred on ideological dismissals of his mode of expression or general elitist derision of his work.

ing popularity of *The Lord of the Rings* is explainable as the result of either a (long overdue to end) passing phase or the ill-informed reading habits of 'the great unwashed'.

In terms of the poll, it should be noted however, that those works which repeatedly finished just below *The Lord of the Rings*, works such as Orwell's *Nineteen Eighty-Four* and *Animal Farm*, James Joyce's *Ulysses*, J.D. Salinger's *Catcher in the Rye*, Harper Lee's *To Kill a Mockingbird* and John Steinbeck's *The Grapes of Wrath* are all works which are deeply engrained in the education system and frequently presented as set texts in various school and university curricula. And, as the *Times Educational Supplement* noted in reference to the Waterstone's accumulated final listings, the results had obviously reflected 'the formative influence of school set texts on a nation's reading habits'.[44] *The Lord of the Rings*, a considerably longer book that requires a much greater investment of time than the majority of those noted above, however, is generally shunned by the education system and thus must be a work that has accumulated, and captured the imagination of its admirers independent of any institutionalised instruction or recommendation. Indeed Auberon Waugh, editor of the *Literary Review*, suggested that the high placement of *Ulysses* on the Waterstone's list (arguably the only work that could rival Tolkien's in terms of reader time investment) was due to either the participation of English literature students or those who were 'showing off' their knowledge of academically renowned fiction.

(IV) A Man of his Times: Tolkien and the Twentieth Century

The central thrust of this discourse asserts that Tolkien's work is infused, intentionally or not, with environmental themes that may be read as a warning for our own times. The crucial phrase here is – for our own times. A green reading or analysis of Tolkien is, by its very nature, a reading that seeks to draw parallels between the primary world of external reality and the presentation of the alternate reality of Tolkien's *legendarium* and wider fiction. The wealth of criticism against Tolkien and his fiction, as we have noted however, asserts that he has little relevance as an author for the modern world. Indeed the greater part

---

44 Quoted in Shippey, *Author of the Century*, p.xxiii.

of anti-Tolkien sentiment has accused his work of being fundamentally escapist. Pearce states that, "'escapism' is probably the most persistently recurring label to be attached to *The Lord of the Rings* by critics desperate to find a 'pigeon-hole' for it.'[45] Heidi Krueger in her essay 'The Shaping of 'Reality' in Tolkien's Works' also acknowledges that the 'accusation of escapism' has been pejoratively used 'in the judgement of Tolkien's works'. Krueger, however, contends that 'this accusation is shared with many other authors since the Enlightenment who did not serve the mainstream.'[46] It may well be true that other authors have felt the scourge of the 'escapist' tag but few have been so severely criticised for what they are (apparently) escaping into.

Other criticisms dismiss Tolkien's work as being irrelevant, puerile or overly nostalgic. And of course all of these four 'categories': escapism, irrelevancy, puerility and nostalgia are inherently linked in that they all imply that Tolkien was turning away from a serious contemplation of the reality in which he lived and worked – that at best he had nothing of worth to say about the century in which he spent 73 of his 81 years, and at worst, that he created his fiction in order that he could withdraw *from* it like a frightened child hiding his head under the bedcovers. Let us allow a brief calling to mind of some of the criticisms levelled at Tolkien's work that make such a charge. We recall that Susan Jefferys of the *Sunday Times* accused Tolkien *and* his readers of 'burrowing an escape into a nonexistent world',[47] and Greer complained that Tolkien's work represented 'a flight from reality'[48] – or fiction without an externally identifiable place and time. Mockingly listing the 'horrors' which threaten the people and landscapes of Middle-earth, Wilson in his 1956 commentary on *The Lord of the Rings* states, '[w]hat one misses in all these terrors is any trace of concrete reality.'[49] Rissik, in his more recent criticism of both Shippey and Tolkien characterises Tolkien's fiction as existing in a 'never-never land' where 'there is never any remotely convincing treatment of those fundamental human concerns through which all societies ultimately define themselves – religion, philosophy, politics and the

---

45 Pearce, *Man and Myth*, p.144.
46 Heidi Krueger, 'The Shaping of Reality in Tolkien's Works' in Honegger & Weinreich (eds.), *Tolkien and Modernity* 2, p.235.
47 Susan Jefferys, *Sunday Times* (26th Jan 1997).
48 Germaine Greer in *W Magazine* (Winter/Spring 1997).
49 Wilson, 'Oo, Those awful Orcs'.

conduct of sexual relationships.'⁵⁰ Tolkien's works could certainly not be held up by even the most forthright of Tolkien defenders as being possessed of insightful journeys into the nature of sexual relationships⁵¹ (although, as is the case with Arwen and Aragorn, and Beren and Lúthien, relationships between the sexes are explored), but the suggestions above that Tolkien's works have essentially nothing of worth to say about (or to) the modern world, and that as such his fiction is escapist in essence are bordering on the blinkered. This, however, is an area of contention that is beginning to be redressed. More and more commentators on Tolkien are making parallels between his works and the issues and events which governed the twentieth century. John Garth's *Tolkien and the Great War* is a study which ably unfolds textual allusions in Tolkien's work to his experiences serving in the trenches of the First World War. Shippey's study *J.R.R. Tolkien: Author of the Century*, although cleverly drawing the results of the various polls (and the attendant controversy) into his field of reference, is a work that seeks to establish Tolkien's credentials as a contemporary writer. In the 'Foreword' of his book Shippey points out that his title is *J.R.R. Tolkien: Author of the Century* and not *J.R.R. Tolkien: [The] Author of the Century*, in other words Shippey's study is concerned with establishing Tolkien's credentials as an author whose work addresses the defining issues of the twentieth century. Alluding specifically to Tolkien's best known works Shippey comments:

---

50 Andrew Rissik, 'Middle-earth, Middlebrow' in *The Guardian* (2nd September 2000).
51 Edwin Muir writing in the *Observer* on November 27th 1955 also attacked Tolkien within the parameters of his portrayal (or lack of it) of sexual matters. Charging him with creating characters and heroes that were 'boys masquerading as adult heroes' Muir declares, 'hardly one of them knows anything about women.' Muir's comment irritated Tolkien to such an extent that he addressed the charge in a letter to his publisher dated December 8th of the same year: 'It might do [Muir] good to hear what women think of his 'knowing about women', especially as a test of being mentally adult' (Tolkien, *Letters*, p.230).
   In a similar critique of the lack of 'sexual chemistry' in the mythology of Middle-earth, John Carey as part of a review of Carpenter's biography of Tolkien described Tolkien's female characters as 'perfectly sexless' (John Carey 'Hobbit-forming: A Review of Humphrey Carpenter *J.R.R. Tolkien: A Biography*' in *The Listener*, Vol. 97 (May 12th 1977) p. 631). Joseph Pearce in his study *Tolkien: Man and Myth* replied many years later by commenting '[p]erhaps it says something of Carey's prurience that he neglects to mention that the men in Tolkien's mythology are also 'perfectly sexless', at least in the sense Carey intends.' Although I would venture that Pearce has read a little too much into Carey's focus on a specific gender, his point nonetheless exposes a similar bias of interest in Muir's earlier remark. Pearce goes on to add, 'Tolkien's characters are certainly not sexless in the sense of being asexual but, on the contrary, are archetypically and stereotypically sexual' (Pearce, *Man and Myth*, p.48). Indeed, as Pearce points out, a more explicit or 'gritty' rendering of sexuality in Middle-earth would only have served to undermine the nature of the work. For a more expansive view of Tolkien's attitude to the relationship between men and women, sex and love, see Brian Rosebury, *Tolkien: A Critical Assessment*, London: St Martin's Press, 1992, p.158 and Tolkien, *Letters*, p.60, pp.48-49 & pp.51-52.

> *The Lord of the Rings* and *The Hobbit* have said something important, and meant something important, to a high proportion of their many millions of readers. [...Tolkien] needs to be looked at and interpreted within his own time, as an 'author of the century', the twentieth century, responding to the issues and anxieties of that century.[52]

Brian Rosebury in *Tolkien: A Critical Assessment* also addresses the question of Tolkien's relevance to the modern world, not only in terms of his fiction holding up a mirror to the twentieth century, but also in terms of the significance of his mode of writing set against the dominant trends of the age. Speaking specifically of Tolkien's relevance as a contemporary writer Rosebury states: 'Tolkien's 'life and times' spanned almost three-quarters of the twentieth century: if we dispassionately reflect upon them, the grounds of his modernity, as well as his anti-modernity, may gradually come into view'.[53] Indeed the two world wars, the disillusionment with old truths and new lies, the incessant rise of industry and the machine at the expense of the natural world – all of these things are undoubtedly reflected and played out across the panorama of Tolkien's tales – not in the sense that specific aspects of his work can only be understood if they are related explicitly and directly to alleged real world counterparts, (Sauron equals Hitler/The One Ring equals nuclear power for example) but rather that the turbulent modern world of the twentieth century, in which Tolkien lived and worked, appears reflected in the mirror of his fiction. Rosebury takes up the point: '[t]he modernity of Tolkien's work, from the point of view of its content, lies not in the coded reference to specific contemporary events or phenomena but in the absorption of experiences and attitudes which Tolkien would scarcely have acquired had he not been a man of the twentieth century.'[54]

Tolkien, therefore, is not escaping from but rather facing the turmoil of the twentieth century – the desolation of once idyllic landscapes, the struggles of his various races to deal with the crisis in their midst, the machinations of magic-wielding, power-hungry technocrats, meddling in genetic engineering, creating machines of war and destruction, which ravage the natural world are but reflections of the age. As Roger Sale points out:

---

52 Shippey, *Author of the Century*, p.xxvii.
53 Rosebury, *Tolkien*, pp.122-23.
54 Rosebury, *Tolkien*, pp.145-46.

Technically the central action of *The Lord of the Rings* is a quest, and we know quite well that there are no modern quests, but in fact the central action more closely resembles a descent into hell. Tolkien could not have done this without displacing his story into the fairyland of Middle-earth, without using many ritual details of quest literature, but that does not change in any significant way the fact that at its best the trilogy is modern literature.[55]

The Lord of the Rings is a commentary on the modern world, every bit as valid as the fragmentation of modernity as presented in T.S. Eliot's *The Waste Land* or Joyce's *Ulysses*. Each of these three works returns to myth and fantasy in an attempt to make sense of or represent the twentieth-century world. Likewise Tolkien's fantastical mode of expression does not signify a turning away from reality but rather a re-conceptualization of it. In his now famous essay 'On Fairy-stories' Tolkien specifically addresses the question of escape when used to criticise the fantasy mode of expression:

> I have claimed that Escape is one of the main functions of fairy-stories, and since I do not disapprove of them, it is plain that I do not accept the tone of scorn or pity with which "Escape" is now so often used: a tone for which the uses of the word outside literary criticism give no warrant at all. In what the misusers are fond of calling Real Life, Escape is evidently as a rule very practical, and may even be heroic. In real life it is difficult to blame it, unless it fails; in criticism it would seem to be the worse the better it succeeds. Evidently we are faced by a misuse of words, and also by a confusion of thought. Why should a man be scorned, if, finding himself in prison, he tries to get out and go home? Or if, when he cannot do so, he thinks and talks about other topics than jailers and prison-walls? The world outside has not become less real because the prisoner cannot see it. In using Escape in this way the critics have chosen the wrong word, and, what is more, they are confusing, not always by sincere error, the Escape of the Prisoner with the Flight of the Deserter.[56]

Tolkien subverts the pejorative understanding of escapism and re-asserts that fantasy can provide a re-conceptualisation of primary reality that allows the 'escapee' to re-discover the world, and, pertinent to this discourse, the natural world anew. Tolkien refers to this re-discovery as 'Recovery' – this idea of recovery is a theory I return to in more detail at various points throughout this book (chapter five in particular). Indeed, as I point out below, understanding what Tolkien means by recovery is linked to the

---

55 Roger Sale, *Modern Heroisms: Essays on D.H. Lawrence, William Empson and J.R.R. Tolkien*, Berkeley and Los Angeles: University of California Press, 1973, pp.198-99.
56 J.R.R. Tolkien, *The Tolkien Reader*, New York: Ballantine, 1966, p.79.

ecological augury which I contend is evident in his work, and it is key to understanding his views on the power of literature and fantasy literature in particular.

(V) In the Green Corner

This study is not the only work to look at the environmental dimension of Tolkien's fiction. Amid the growing number of serious Tolkien scholars who have attempted to examine his work from differing philosophical, theological, linguistic and biographical angles, a select few have addressed, and thrown some light upon, what modern ecocritics would term his green themes. Some prominent Tolkien commentators have acknowledged the presence of ecological themes in his work without engaging in any dedicated or involved green reading. Shippey has on more than one occasion offered insights and thoughts on what he refers to in *J.R.R. Tolkien: Author of the Century* as 'Tolkien's 'Green' ideologies'.[57] Rosebury, as part of a wider study that seeks to establish Tolkien's importance as a modern author, refers to representations of 'industrial pollution', and regimes of power in Tolkien's work that 'actually pollute the soil, poison watercourses, pour smoke into the atmosphere, cut down trees, [and] create deserts where grass once grew.'[58] Others like Humphrey Carpenter, Jane Chance and Paul H. Kocher have acknowledged, or mentioned in passing, aspects of Tolkien's fiction that could be determined to be environmental in nature. More drawn-out and involved considerations of Tolkien's ecological themes have been undertaken in the form of dedicated essays, chapters and monograph sections by Don D. Elgin, Patrick Curry, Verlyn Flieger and Andrew Light. My work shares, in differing degrees, conceptual and critical common ground with aspects of each of these works. Primarily, of course, despite the disparaging views discussed above of those self-styled literary *illuminati* who would proclaim to the contrary, we all agree that Tolkien's fiction is addressing green issues arising from real world concerns. My study, however, seeking to move beyond the selective focus of these discourses, not only presents an analysis of the wider canon of Tolkien's fiction from an environmental perspective, but it also examines Tolkien's theories related to the nature, power and purpose of fantasy, and relates them to his ecological

---

57 Shippey, *Author of the Century*, p.89.
58 Rosebury, *Tolkien*, p.50.

worldview and his belief that, through our engagement with secondary worlds, we can rediscover the wonder of the primary world. I contend that this notion of recovery provides a basis and a rationale from which all of the green themes observable in Tolkien's tales emerge. Indeed the ecological augury, which I argue is the most representative way of characterising the nature of the green dimension of Tolkien's fiction, calls for a recovery of environmental values and a reconnection with nature in the hope that the modern world – in Tolkien's view, too immersed in, and too ready to embrace the machine age – may turn away from a path that may ultimately lead to a planetary home more akin to Mordor than Lothlórien. These key aspects of Tolkien's environmentalism: recovery and augury are, I contend, two sides of the same coin.

Aside from extended essays and the like, there has, to date, been one other complete study on environmental themes in Tolkien: *Ents, Elves and Eriador: The Environmental Vision of J.R.R. Tolkien* (2006) written by Mathew Dickerson and Jonathan Evans. The fundamental premise of Dickerson and Evans' work is that Tolkien's environmental worldview, his embrace and defence of (and thus his anxiety for) the natural world was defined and governed by religious doctrine and his Christian belief. Whilst I agree that Tolkien's faith was a prime mover in all his thoughts concerning the world in which he lived and worked, I contend that a close analysis of environmentally themed aspects of his philosophies and writings reveals that the principles upon which Tolkien expresses and founds his attitude to the natural world are not wholly consistent with conventional Christian attitudes to the relationship between the human and non-human, and cannot be defined in terms of being governed by Christian doctrine. In other words – I contend that although Tolkien's environmental themes would support a view that humanity is charged with taking care of God's green Earth, nonetheless, as evidenced in the narrative structure of his fiction, the environmental perspectives forwarded by some of his main characters, and the particulars of his documented thoughts on, what he once referred to as, the 'community of living things',[59] his environmentalism is not consistent with an understanding that humanity has some pre-eminence over nature. Whilst Tolkien's Catholicism is a fundamental part of all his philosophies – my study proposes that his fiction and aspects of his environmental worldview contain

---

59 Tolkien, *Letters*, p.400.

elements that move beyond traditional Christian understandings of humanity's relationship with the natural world. Alongside a consideration of the reconciliation of Tolkien's environmental and theological philosophies, however, this study differs from the others on a few major points of focus.

In the opening chapter, through an analysis of Tolkien's papers and letters, I explore and document Tolkien's environmental conscience, his ecological worldview and his profound love of things that grow – particularly trees. I focus also on Tolkien's apprehensions related to what he saw as the dawn of the machine age. In the two chapters which follow I consider some of Tolkien's major characters from an environmental perspective. Arguably Tolkien's greatest gift as a storyteller was his ability to create unforgettable and highly distinctive characters to populate the landscapes of his secondary worlds and convincingly carry the narrative strain of his unfolding tales. For Tolkien the creation of memorable and compelling characters was vital to the success of any story regardless of depth or weight of theme. Referring to the atmosphere of war and the presence of 'dark and threatening' powers that seek dominion over the lands and peoples of Middle-earth in *The Lord of the Rings*, Tolkien commented 'but that is mainly 'a setting' for characters to show themselves'.[60] With this in mind, and focusing on his major work, I argue that Tolkien, in the presentation of his individual characters, creates what I have termed 'cultures of opposition': positive and negative environmental models whose contrasting portrayals reflect the struggle for Middle-earth itself. I offer these 'cultures of opposition' in the form of Tom Bombadil and Saruman, and subsequently Gandalf and Sauron.

Perhaps Tolkien's most enigmatic character creation and perhaps even his most noteworthy representation of nature or natural forces is Tom Bombadil. As part of my analysis of Tolkien's 'cultures of opposition', I examine (the much overlooked) Bombadil's character in terms of how he may represent not just nature, but nature under threat – or nature in retreat when facing the destructive force of power hungry, machine-wielding, technocratic enemies. Indeed I will show that, in terms of point-for-point inverse mirroring, Bombadil's nega-

---

60 Tolkien, *Letters*, p.246.

tive counterpart was strictly Saruman – in word, deed and intention. Also, as part of this comparative analysis, I will address the question of Tom's origins and proffer a new detailed theory related to the much-touted enquiry: 'Who is Tom Bombadil?'

Following on from the Bombadil and Saruman chapter, I offer a similar comparative treatment of Gandalf and Sauron. Gandalf, in particular, is a guiding light in the darkest hour of Middle-earth. The shadow which rises across the landscape of the Third Age is, of course, set in motion and perpetuated primarily by the machinations of Sauron. This chapter, amongst other considerations, examines how Gandalf, who is described in *Unfinished Tales* as a force 'coëval and equal'[61] to the Dark Lord, offers hope, guidance and protection for every aspect of creation in direct comparison to the war on nature and freedom that is waged by Sauron, who seeks to secure absolute control of Middle-earth, enslave all manifestations of life (including nature itself) and impose his iron grip on creation.

Chapter four examines the centrality of the elves in Tolkien's mythology and offers an analysis of their metaphysical association with the earth and their interrelationship with the power of nature. The wider concerns of this chapter will assert that Tolkien, in the elevation of the non-human aspects of his fiction, creates his own ecosphere of interconnected life (of which humanity is but one component part) where the actions and fate of one aspect of creation impacts upon and fashions those of another. This understanding of the interconnectedness of life and the inherent value of all creation (reflected in the worldviews of Gandalf and Tom Bombadil) is considered in the wake of the totalitarian, supremacist outlooks previously observed in the regimes of Morgoth, Sauron and Saruman.

In the closing of the work, acknowledging that this entire study is essentially an ecocritical or green reading of Tolkien, I explore Tolkien the writer and Tolkien the literary theorist against some of the principal ideologies, tropes and works of ecocriticism, and propose that, given his engagement with literary theory and his views on literature, Tolkien may have anticipated the emergence of

---

61 J.R.R.Tolkien, *Unfinished Tales of Númenor and Middle-earth*, edited by Christopher Tolkien, London: HarperCollins, 1998, p.395.

green studies as a literary discipline. Indeed all of the above will be considered in the light of (and set against) the thoughts, theories and works of prominent ecologists, ecocritics and environmental commentators such as Jonathan Bate, Barry Commoner, Cheryl Glotfelty, Bill McKibben, William Rueckert and Paul B. Sears. The book will focus, in the main, on Tolkien's Middle-earth writings since it is within these works that his environmental themes are most prominently observed, but there are also considerations of his wider prose and some of his lesser known verse.

(VI) Applicability Not Allegory

In closing this introduction I should add that whilst attempting to offer Tolkien's work from an environmental perspective and whilst endeavouring to understand and analyse Tolkien's writing in terms of its ecocritical and contemporary significance, I am not, in any sense, trying to impose an exclusive meaning upon his work. To consider a green reading of Tolkien's work as definitive or to suggest that Tolkien was creating fiction in order to document allegorically his environmental anxieties would be to commit, as Patrick Curry suggests 'the violence of reductionism'.[62] Tolkien on many occasions voiced his displeasure at allegorical interpretations of his work that claimed to hold the key to meaning or intention. In his foreword to the second edition of *The Lord of the Rings* he writes:

> I cordially dislike allegory in all its manifestations, and always have done so since I grew old and wary enough to detect its presence. I much prefer history true or feigned, with its varied applicability to the thought and experience of the readers. I think that many confuse 'applicability' with 'allegory'; but one resides in the freedom of the reader, and the other in the purposed domination of the author.[63]

In keeping with Tolkien's own views regarding such things I make no definitive claim over Tolkien's work but instead invoke 'the freedom of the reader' and offer that, as I gaze into the 'Galadriel's Mirror' of Tolkien's fiction, I see reflected there, more than anything else, the spirit of an ecologically threatened Earth. Indeed in 'The Mirror of Galadriel' we may find the very essence of, or

---

62 Patrick Curry, *Defending Middle-earth. Tolkien: Myth and Modernity*, London: HarperCollins, 1997, p.18.
63 Tolkien, *Fellowship*, p.xv.

a defining symbol for, the ecological augury which I contend radiates from the pages of Tolkien's fiction. The mirror shows, like aspects of Tolkien's work, how the world may appear if the crisis of the age is not addressed, but as Galadriel points out, everything reflected there may not come to pass. Galadriel says to Frodo and Sam 'What will you see if you leave the Mirror free to work? I cannot tell. For it shows things that were, and things that are, and things that yet may be.'[64]

I will concede the last words of this introductory section to one of Tolkien's oldest defenders, W.H. Auden, who, writing in 1954 (his sentiments are equally valid today), also considers that Tolkien's fiction, despite its overtly fantastical nature, may be read and understood as a reflection of and a warning to the modern world:

> however superficially unlike the world we live in its characters and events may be, [*The Lord of the Rings*] nevertheless holds up the mirror to the only nature we know, our own; in this, too, Mr. Tolkien has succeeded superbly, and what happened in the year of the Shire 1418 in the Third Age of Middle Earth is not only fascinating in A.D. 1954 but also a warning and an inspiration.[65]

---

64 Tolkien, *Fellowship*, p.352.
65 W.H. Auden, 'The Hero is a Hobbit' in *The New York Times* (31st October 1954).

Chapter One

Rage against the Machine

As a boy J.R.R. Tolkien was plagued by a terrible recurring dream in which a vast, unstoppable tide 'advancing ineluctably' threatened to overwhelm him and the natural world of 'trees and green fields'[1] all around him. This apocalyptic vision, which was to trouble him well into his adult life, later became manifest in Tolkien's fiction as the Atlantis-themed description of the destruction of the island kingdom of Númenor which was swallowed up by an angry sea.

The account of the island kingdom of Númenor is an example of how Tolkien would take events, memories and anxieties from reality and absorb them into his fiction. Tolkien's tales are of course first and foremost just that – wonderfully creative and beautifully written tales, but, as with all stories, they are also reflections of and windows on external reality. Tolkien's greatest gift was no doubt his astonishing imagination, and this gift of imagination allowed him to re-discover the external world in his mind's eye – to reconstruct and re-create his anxieties, beliefs and passions in fictional form in the same way as he transformed his recurring nightmare into myth. Indeed Tolkien once said of his most famous work *The Lord of the Rings* 'it is written in my life-blood.'[2] In this sense Tolkien's works are mirrors that reflect the times in which he lived and the anxieties he felt, as the twentieth-century welcomed, with open arms, the age of the machine. That is not to say, of course, that in writing his fiction he had 'covert intentions' as Brian Rosebury puts it. Such an assertion would only serve to diminish or in Rosebury's words 'abolish the imaginative distinctness'[3] of Tolkien's fiction. Nonetheless we may observe clear threads of thematic concern that inevitably hold a mirror up to our own reality.

---

1 Humphrey Carpenter, *J.R.R. Tolkien: A Biography*, London: George Allen & Unwin, 1977, p.23.
2 J.R.R. Tolkien, *The Letters of J.R.R. Tolkien*, edited by Humphrey Carpenter, London: HarperCollins, 2006, p.122.
3 Brian Rosebury, *Tolkien: A Critical Assessment*, New York: St. Martin's Press, 1992, p.144.

Although what follows focuses on the ecological warnings and perspectives that arise out of Tolkien's apprehensions concerning the rise of machines and industry (both in his fiction and his private papers) it is important to note that Tolkien was not in any sense a Luddite who placed the blame for humanity's ills solely on the rise of technology and new machines. Like William Blake before him, however, he distrusted machine-wielders and builders, and trailblazing engineers who seemed indifferent to the ecological cost of their endeavours.[4] Indeed for Tolkien, machines rolling off mass production lines was the very negation of life and nature as he understood it. The passage below taken from 'On Fairy-stories' accurately sums up Tolkien's attitude to emergent (and to his mind sterile and environmentally unsound) industry:

> Not long ago – incredible though it may seem – I heard a clerk of Oxenford declare that he 'welcomed' the proximity of mass-production robot factories, and the roar of self-obstructive mechanical traffic, because it brought his university into 'contact with real life' [...] The notion that motor-cars are more 'alive' than, say, centaurs or dragons is curious; that they are more 'real' than, say, horses is pathetically absurd. How real, how startlingly alive is a factory chimney compared with an elm-tree.[5]

There is a clear point of tension in the passage above that centres on the embrace of machines and the accompanying displacement or decentring of nature in the common consciousness. This was a concern that manifests itself continually throughout Tolkien's fiction in his portrayals of literary creations such as Mordor, Isengard and the first Dark Lord, Morgoth. These aspects of Tolkien's fiction are considered below. I will also offer a detailed analysis of 'The Scouring of the Shire' as a representation of (although not a direct allegory of) the ecologically damaging potential of modern industry. Before such considerations, however, I examine how Tolkien's early years spent in the heart of the English countryside under the attentive eye of his mother Mabel may have helped to forge part of his creative imagination and deepen his reverence

---

4 Blake's environmental anxieties (mixed with his concerns for the exploitation of children and the poor) are deeply engrained in works such as his poem 'London' (1794) which, according to James C. McKusick, 'evokes the bleak, polluted urban environment [and] the unchecked growth of industrial capitalism with its attendant wage-slavery, the "mind-forg'd manacles" that bind the laborer [sic] to an inhuman machine' (James C. McKusick, *Green Writing: Romanticism and Ecology*, New York: St. Martin's Press, 2000, pp.96-97). For a further analysis of Blake's concerns regarding the rise of industry and the machine see Saree Makdisi, *William Blake and the Impossible History of the 1790s*, Chicago: University of Chicago Press, 2003.

5 J.R.R. Tolkien, *The Tolkien Reader*, New York: Ballatine Publishing, 1966, pp.80-81.

for both the natural world and later the Catholic faith – binding each in his mind. I also, through an analysis of his correspondence and private papers, document Tolkien's singular regard for trees and the natural world, setting up, as it were, his own environmental worldview and offering that he predated much of what now constitutes the Green Movement in terms of his environmental ethics. Indeed in a very real sense the green themes which radiate from the pages of Tolkien's work pick up the reins of Romantic writers such as William Blake, John Clare and William Wordsworth, and their celebration of natural phenomena, although it could be said that Tolkien was much more in alignment with Blake in terms of both the mythic quality of his work, and their shared anxiety for the green face of the Earth set against the rise of humanity's reliance on industry and the machine.

I will begin by travelling back to Tolkien's childhood, to 1896 when on a return visit to England, news reaches Tolkien's mother that her husband, and Tolkien's father Arthur, has died in South Africa.

(I) In the Garden of Nature

After the immediate disarray surrounding the unexpected death of his father, the young Tolkien moved with his mother and brother Hilary out of the urban surroundings of Birmingham[6] and into the more pastoral and idyllic hamlet of Sarehole, situated just outside the southern boundaries of the city. This relocation from cityscape to rural landscape was to significantly impact Tolkien's creative imagination or, as Humphrey Carpenter puts it, 'the effect of this move on Tolkien was deep and permanent. Just at an age when his imagination was opening out, he found himself in the English countryside.'[7]

Indeed the landmarks and characters that Tolkien encountered around the Sarehole area during these formative years provided the environment for the first flexing of his imaginative muscles. Just over a meadow from the new Tolkien family home stood Sarehole Mill, an impressive 'old world' construction with a huge chimney that resembled a tower. The old miller and his son who worked

---

[6] Mabel and the boys had stayed previously in Birmingham in a rather overcrowded house, under the benevolent, but nonetheless somewhat suffocating, presence of her own family – the Suffields.
[7] Carpenter, *Biography*, p.20.

there would become covered in a fine layer of white dust caused by the grinding of bones to produce fertilizer (or bone meal). The miller's son would often catch the boys, Tolkien (Ronald) and Hilary, peeking from clandestine vantage points and chase them off. Because of his fierce features, disagreeable manner and strange otherworldly appearance (caused by the covering of the white dust), young Tolkien named him 'the White Ogre'. Further up the hill lived an old farmer who had chased Tolkien off his land for stealing mushrooms in an episode strikingly similar to Tolkien's later telling of Farmer Maggot's pursuit of Frodo for the same offence. Tolkien referred to this farmer as 'the Black Ogre'. The influence of these childhood days on Tolkien cannot be overstated, not only in terms of the influence they exercised over the formation of his creative imagination, but also in how the happiness experienced by both the boys was directly related to being with their mother amid the idyllic surroundings of country life and away from the cut and thrust of a congested cityscape. Hilary Tolkien in old age recalled to Carpenter:

> We spent lovely summers just picking flowers and trespassing. The black Ogre used to take people's shoes and stockings from the bank where they'd left them to paddle, and run away with them, make them go and ask for them. And then he'd thrash them! The white Ogre wasn't quite so bad. But in order to get to the place where we used to blackberry (called the Dell) we had to go through the white one's land, and he didn't like us very much because the path was narrow through his field, and we traipsed off after corn-cockles and other pretty things. My mother got us lunch to have in this lovely place, but when she arrived she made a deep voice, and we both ran![8]

Brian Rosebury in *Tolkien: A Critical Assessment* contends that these years and in particular the bucolic and tranquil setting of Sarehole were to be a major influence in the creation of elements of the Shire: 'Sarehole, with its nearby farms, its mills by the riverside, its willow trees, its pool with swans, its dell with blackberries, was a serene, quasi-rural enclave, [and] an obvious model-to-be for certain aspects of Hobbiton and the Shire.' The serenity and rustic ambience of Sarehole was perhaps all the more vivid because it was, as Rosebury notes, 'only four miles from the industrial centre of Birmingham.'[9] Indeed in 1956 in a letter to Michael Straight, editor of the *New Republic*, Tolkien, whilst stating that '[t]here is no special reference to England in the 'Shire'' adds

---

8 Carpenter, *Biography*, p.21.
9 Rosebury, *Tolkien*, p.121.

'except of course as an Englishman brought up in an 'almost rural' village of Warwickshire on the edge of the prosperous bourgeoisie of Birmingham (about the time of the Diamond Jubilee!) I take my models like anyone else – from such 'life' as I know.'[10]

Whilst the rural surroundings of Sarehole provided a stimulating environment for the playful imagination of Tolkien, this was not just a time of play. Mabel Tolkien also endeavoured to provide instruction for her boys. Tolkien responded with great enthusiasm to his mother's able tuition, displaying an exceptional aptitude for learning. It was his mother who first introduced him to the interests that were to dominate his life. It was she who first stirred in him an appreciation of language:[11] her early instruction in first Latin and later French provided the foundation upon which Tolkien was to pursue an interest in philology. In correspondence related to an interview for the *Daily Telegraph Magazine*, Tolkien writes: 'my interest in languages was derived solely from my mother.'[12]

Mabel also at this time first introduced young Tolkien to tales, legends and adventures set in imaginary and mythical lands. Tolkien was particularly fond of the *Red Fairy Book*, one in a series of books by Andrew Lang[13] in which dragons with strange names such as Fafnir threatened the safety of all. But more pertinent to this discourse, it was his mother too who first fostered in Tolkien an appreciation of the natural world and things that grow. She would give him instruction in botany and developed in him a profound respect for the wonders of nature and in particular trees, which he was now beginning to sketch (again under his mother's tuition) with remarkable accuracy and attention to detail for one so young.[14]

---

10 Tolkien, *Letters*, p.235.
11 Tolkien inherited not only a curiosity for language from his mother but also a flair for calligraphy, a talent that Mabel had learned from her father.
12 Tolkien, *Letters*, p.377.
13 Tolkien was later to deliver the Andrew Lang Lecture on the nature of 'fairy stories' at the University of St. Andrews, in March 1939. This lecture gave rise to Tolkien's famed essay 'On Fairy-stories'.
14 Tolkien's interest in and flair for drawing trees calls to mind the character of Niggle in his short story 'Leaf by Niggle', who also shows a remarkable capacity and penchant for the drawing of leaves and trees – discussed in more detail in chapter five of this study.

(II) Every Tree has its Enemy

Tolkien's respect for trees developed quickly into an abiding love for them. He would climb upon them, seek solace among them and on occasion talk to them. In short, as Carpenter puts it, 'he liked most of all to be *with* trees' (emphasis in original).[15] It was as a boy, also, that Tolkien first began to become awakened to the threat humanity posed to nature in general and trees in particular. He began to understand that trees had their 'enemies', and that not everyone, like he, viewed trees and growing things as worthy of respect and affection. Looking back to his childhood days Tolkien below recalls how the felling of one particular tree, on whose branches he used to climb as a boy, had a profound effect upon him: '[t]here was a willow hanging over the mill-pool and I learned to climb it. It belonged to a butcher on the Stratford Road, I think. One day they cut it down. They didn't do anything with it: the log just lay there. I never forgot that.'[16] It is worthy of note perhaps that remembered from a time when young Tolkien was first learning about the usage and meaning of language, his older self should recall that the felled tree belonged to a 'butcher'. Indeed, as we shall see, such memories were later to become manifest in his fiction.

Tolkien in later years was to freely admit his love for trees: he viewed them very much as a beleaguered noble race set upon by an indifferent humanity and the rise of modernity. In the following passage, taken from a letter written to his aunt Jane Neave[17] in 1962, Tolkien shows that his love for trees ran to the extent of worrying for them:

> There was a great tree – a huge poplar with vast limbs – visible through my window even as I lay in bed. I loved it, and was anxious about it. It had been savagely mutilated some years before, but had gallantly grown new limbs – though of course not with the unblemished grace of its former natural self; and now a foolish neighbour was agitating to have it felled. Every tree has its enemy, few have an advocate. (Too often the hate is irrational, a fear of anything large and alive, and not easily tamed or destroyed, though it may clothe

---

15 Carpenter, *Biography*, p.22.
16 Carpenter, *Biography*, p.22.
17 Tolkien's aunt Jane Neave owned a farm in Dormston, Worcestershire. The farm was at the bottom of a lane (or cul-de-sac) and the locals referred to it as Bag End. The literal translation of cul-de-sac is bottom of the bag or bag end. Andrew H. Morton & John Hayes in *Tolkien's Gedling 1914: The Birth of a Legend* (Studley, Warwickshire: Brewin Books, 2008) speculate that Jane Neave, indisputably a major influence in Tolkien's life, may have been the inspiration and model for the character of Gandalf – with her brimmed hat, long cloak and sometimes fearsome, but always fair, nature.

> itself in pseudo-rational terms.) This fool said that it cut off the sun from her house and garden, and that she feared for her house if it should crash in a high wind. It stood due *east* of her front door, across a wide road, at a distance nearly *thrice* its total height. Thus only about the equinox would it even cast a shadow in her direction [...] and any wind that could have uprooted it and hurled it on her house, would have demolished her and her house without any assistance from the tree.

Interestingly Tolkien goes on in the letter to say 'I believe [the tree] still stands where it did',[18] but just a few years later in the introduction to an early publication of *Tree and Leaf*, Tolkien, citing the human assault on this particular tree as part inspiration for the writing of 'Leaf by Niggle' confirms that the 'agitating' enemies of the tree had finally had it felled: '[i]t is cut down now, a less barbarous punishment for any crime it may have been accused of, such as being large and alive. I do not think it had any friends, or any mourners except myself and a pair of owls.'[19] There is a suggestion in Tolkien's somewhat ironic comment regarding the trees' 'mourners' that the 'pair of owls' are representatives of the natural world, lamenting, in their wisdom, the passing of a great tree. There is a further suggestion that the owls have been directly affected by the loss of the tree, evoking Barry Commoner's first law of ecology: 'everything is connected to everything else',[20] and the now widely accepted premise that the destruction of one aspect of nature will affect many others and eventually humanity itself. Modern ecological concerns related to an understanding of these interconnections have warned of an ever-increasing loss of biodiversity as a direct result of deforestation. T. C. Whitmore and J. A. Sayer, in *Tropical Deforestation and Species Extinction*, make such a connection with regard to tropical rainforests: '[p]erhaps the single greatest cause for concern over the loss of tropical forests is that there is a considerable body of evidence to suggest that it is leading to the unprecedented loss of the biological diversity that these forests contain.'[21]

---

18 Tolkien, *Letters*, p.321.
19 J.R.R. Tolkien, *Tree and Leaf*, London: Unwin, 1964, p.5.
20 Barry Commoner, *The Closing Circle: Confronting the Environmental Crisis*, London: Cape, 1972, p.44.
21 T. C. Whitmore & J. A. Sayer, 'Deforestation and Species Extinction in Tropical Moist Forests' in T. C. Whitmore & J. A. Sayer (eds.), *Tropical Deforestation and Species Extinction*, London: Chapman & Hall, 1992, p.1.

Is it a stretching of the point to suggest that Tolkien's remarks about owls and the passing of a single poplar tree is evidence that he was a visionary environmentalist? Perhaps it is. Tolkien's articulation, however, that this particular tree was not damaged but 'savagely mutilated' demonstrates to what extent he viewed the tree as a living thing worthy of consideration. Indeed much like a defence lawyer, Tolkien here is actively taking the part of a tree against what he describes as an 'irrational' and 'agitating' 'enemy',[22] ascribing the tree, as it were, the right to life. This notion of defending the rights of nature against the human 'enemy' was indeed visionary, and such considerations of the non-human were later to become central in the ideas of many Green and environmentally active groupings such as 'Friends of the Earth' and 'Greenpeace'. Writing in 1978, William Rueckert, in the essay that arguably coined the term ecocriticism says:

> The idea that nature should also be protected by human laws, that trees (dolphins and whales, hawks and whooping cranes) should have lawyers to articulate and defend their rights is one of the most marvellous and characteristic parts of the ecological vision.[23]

Tolkien's proclivity to claim quasi-human rights for trees is further exemplified in a letter written to the *Daily Telegraph* (responding to a reference adversely connecting the trees of Middle-earth to those of the Forestry Commission): '[N]othing [the Forestry Commission] has done that is stupid compares with the destruction, torture and murder of trees perpetrated by private individuals and minor official bodies.'[24] Some of the words Tolkien has chosen to use here, 'torture and murder', are extremely powerful and emotive; they express a view that, to Tolkien's mind, the needless devastation of trees amounts to nothing less than a violation of life. In another letter to his American publishers Houghton Mifflin dated 1955 Tolkien, widening his declaration of love for natural phenomena to include plant life, draws a distinct parallel between the harming of trees and cruelty against animals: 'I am (obviously) much in love with plants

---

22 Tolkien, *Letters*, p.321.
23 William Rueckert, 'Literature and Ecology: An Experiment in Ecocriticism' in Cheryll Glotfelty & Harold Fromm (eds.), *The Ecocriticism Reader: Landmarks in Literary Ecology*, Athens and London: University of Georgia Press, 1996, p.108.
24 Tolkien, *Letters*, p.420.

and above all trees and always have been; and I find human maltreatment of them as hard to bear as some find ill-treatment of animals.'[25]

Given the years that some of these letters were written: 1962 (to Jane Neave) and 1955 (to Houghton Mifflin), Tolkien's ecologically focused viewpoint would no doubt have been considered radical. For some it would appear radical even now, certainly in terms of the language Tolkien has chosen to use. Indeed a worldview, such as the one espoused by Tolkien, that considers the unwarranted felling of trees to be 'murder' presupposes that the life of a tree (like that of a cherished pet or another human) has intrinsic worth as of itself, as opposed to worth that is determined only in relation to how a tree may serve the needs of humanity. In modern ecological terms this worldview has very clear parallels with aspects of Deep Ecology – a term first coined by Norwegian eco-activist and philosopher Arne Næss in 1973 to describe a philosophical position that elevates and promotes the intrinsic value of non-human life forms, in turn placing no great pre-eminence on the value of human life or indeed human affairs.[26] In 1984 Næss, along with George Sessions, attempted to summarise and place the central ideas of the Deep Ecology Movement into fifteen principle tenets, the first of which appears clearly to echo the views expressed by Tolkien:

> The well-being and flourishing of human and nonhuman Life on Earth have value in themselves (synonyms: intrinsic value, inherent value). These values are independent of the usefulness of the non-human world for human purposes.[27]

Although it would be obtuse (and a blatant disregard of his Christian values) to deem Tolkien to be a deep ecologist (for one thing Deep Ecology advocates active measures which may reduce the human population[28]) nonetheless (as evidenced in his correspondence and elsewhere) Tolkien's emergent environmentalism embraced a worldview that considered non-human life, even plant life, valuable beyond its use for the human race.

---

25 Tolkien, *Letters*, p.220.
26 For a fuller explanation and understanding of Deep Ecology see Arne Næss, 'The Shallow and the Deep, Long-Range Ecology Movement' in Alan Drengson & Yuichi Inoue (eds.), *The Deep Ecology Movement: An Introductory Anthology*, Berkeley: North Atlantic Books, 1995, pp.3-10.
27 Arne Næss & George Sessions, 'Platform Principles of the Deep Ecology Movement' in Alan Drengson & Yuichi Inoue (eds.), *The Deep Ecology Movement: An Introductory Anthology*, Berkeley: North Atlantic Books, 1995, p.49.
28 This is principle 4 as laid out by Næss & Sessions: 'The flourishing of human life and cultures is compatible with a substantial decrease in the human population. The flourishing of nonhuman life requires such a decrease.' Arne Næss & George Sessions 'Platform Principles', p.49.

(III.1) Shadows on the Landscape

The above examples of what we may term Tolkien's environmental ethics pertain to events and situations occurring in the primary world. In the response he offers to the *Daily Telegraph* concerning the Forestry Commission, however, it is crucial to note that Tolkien in the letter declares that his propensity to defend trees against an 'agitating' 'enemy' extends not only to the real world but also to the entire canon of his fiction:

> In all my works I take the part of trees as against all their enemies. Lothlórien is beautiful because there the trees were loved; elsewhere forests are represented as awakening to consciousness of themselves. The Old Forest was hostile to two-legged creatures because of the memory of many injuries. Fangorn Forest was old and beautiful, but at the time of the story tense with hostility because it was threatened by a machine-loving enemy.[29]

It is clear from the above admission that there appears to be little distance between Tolkien the writer of fiction who 'in all [his] work take[s] the part of trees as against all their enemies' and Tolkien the twentieth-century man who was 'in love with plants', who 'was anxious about' the needless destruction of trees (and by extension nature itself), and who believed that '[e]very tree has its enemy, few have an advocate.'[30] We recall that Tolkien took inspiration for 'Leaf by Niggle' from the felling of a real tree, and that he states in relation to the creation of his fiction, 'I take my models like anyone else – from such 'life' as I know'[31] and he further states in relation to *The Lord of the Rings*: 'it is written in my life-blood.'[32] Indeed although the frame of reference in the above correspondence to the *Daily Telegraph* begins in the secondary world with Lothlórien, the Old Forest and Fangorn Forest, and the allusion to 'a machine-loving enemy' is clearly meant to denote a threat coming from within Middle-earth, Tolkien ends the short letter by adding, '[t]he savage sound of the electric saw is never silent wherever trees are still found growing.'[33] This is obviously meant to refer to a real threat facing real trees in the primary world since there is no electricity and thus no

---

29 Tolkien, *Letters*, p.420 – Verlyn Flieger has contended that Tolkien, in his presentation of, in particular, Old Man Willow as a villainous character has failed to always take the part of trees. Technically, we could say that Willow-man may not be tree; it is more likely he is a huorn (an ent-like being with a more malicious disposition). See 'Afterword' in this book for more on this.
30 Tolkien, *Letters*, p.321.
31 Tolkien, *Letters*, p.220.
32 Tolkien, *Letters*, p.122.
33 Tolkien, *Letters*, p.420.

'electric saw[s]' in Middle-earth. As I will examine repeatedly throughout this discourse, on many occasions Tolkien held up aspects of his fiction to reflect issues pertaining to the primary world. Referring to his dislike of government appointed 'planners' for example, Tolkien associated them and (as he viewed) their ill-judged decisions with 'the spirit' of his fictional bringers of evil: 'the spirit of "Isengard", if not of Mordor, is of course always cropping up. The present design of destroying Oxford in order to accommodate motor-cars is a case.'[34]

When we read of the crisis facing, not only the peoples, but also the natural world of Middle-earth, when we encounter imagined trees, grasslands and flowing waters which are 'threatened by a machine-loving enemy' bereft of an environmental conscience, when we find ourselves in fictional locations where the healing force of nature has been corrupted or cast out, it is no great leap of faith, using 'applicability' as our watchword, to see the environmental crisis facing our own reality reflected. Indeed when we make such connections, ecological warnings for our own times arise out of Tolkien's texts like steam from heated water.

(III.2) The Destructive Power of the Dark Towers: Mordor and Isengard

Nowhere in Tolkien's fiction is the warning against an absence of environmental conscience so pronounced as it is in his depictions of Mordor and Isengard. In his presentation of these sinister and forbidding places, Tolkien offers us two related (yet distinct) portrayals of what may befall the entire landscape of Middle-earth if defeat is visited upon those who oppose the power of Sauron and Saruman. Mordor, a land blighted and twisted by the malevolent will of Sauron, is described as a lifeless abomination of nature:

> Here nothing lived, not even the leprous growths that feed on rottenness. The gasping pools were choked with ash and crawling muds, sickly white and grey, as if the mountains had vomited the filth of their entrails upon the lands about. High mounds of crushed and powdered rock, great cones of earth fire-blasted and poison-stained, stood like an obscene graveyard in the endless rows, slowly revealed in the reluctant light.[35]

---

34 Tolkien, *Letters*, p.235.
35 J.R.R. Tolkien, *The Two Towers*, London: HarperColline, 1997, p.617.

This is a place where the waking force of nature faces attack from a malignant, frenzied will that seeks only dominion and power. Perhaps one of the most chilling aspects of Tolkien's desolation of Mordor is that it is presented as a kind of 'graveyard' – a scene of death. The implication is that a part of nature has been murdered and in death can never reawaken. The parallels with our own reality here are blatant, where human activities have brought about the extinction of countless species and wrought irreversible devastation to wildlife habitats and woodland regions.

Later in the same passage we are told that this 'graveyard' land of Mordor is a 'lasting monument to the dark labour of its slaves that should endure when all their purposes were made void.'[36] Tolkien might be read as warning us that if we sacrifice our environmental conscience in the pursuit of short-term ends, then our legacy to future generations can only be a world scarred by misdeeds.

In Isengard too we are given a clear example of how short-term thinking based on power and ambition, independent of any ecological ethic, may impact directly upon the landscape. We recall that Treebeard, in effect a voice of nature in *The Lord of the Rings*, refers to Saruman as having 'a mind of metal and wheels'[37] and as the expanse of Isengard is revealed to us we see that the land has become a manifestation of Saruman's will: 'iron wheels revolved there endlessly, and hammers thudded. At night plumes of vapour steamed from the vents.'[38] Reading this description, one cannot help but draw parallels between Isengard and some huge steelworks or rows of smokestacks in an industrial heartland. Tolkien of course drew on his perception of the environmental havoc visited upon Birmingham and what came to be known as 'The Black Country' with the onset of the industrial age. Passing through Sarehole and the scene of his childhood, Tolkien, aged forty-one, notes in his diary that the idyllic landscape he once knew has 'become a huge tram-ridden meaningless suburb.' He further records: 'how I envy those whose precious early scenery has not been exposed to such violent and peculiarly hideous change.'[39]

---

36 Tolkien, *Two Towers*, p.617.
37 Tolkien, *Two Towers*, p.462.
38 Tolkien, *Two Towers*, p.451.
39 Carpenter, *Biography*, p.125.

It is perhaps all too easy to view Tolkien (as many have) as an old-fashioned romantic trying desperately to resist the onset of modernity whilst lamenting the passing of a pre-industrial age. Tolkien, however, in portraying Isengard and indeed Saruman as representative of the ecologically destructive face of industry and technology is touching upon emotions greater than those of simple nostalgia. In setting up an opposition between the naturally sustained landscape of Middle-earth and the power of Isengard, which is propagated by machines, engines, breeding experiments and furnace fires, Tolkien is in effect describing for us a war between nature and human society. In drawing up these battle-lines Tolkien joins distinguished company, not all of it nostalgic or sentimentalist.

Jonathan Bate's *The Song of the Earth* tells us 'a battle between the country (customarily regarded as the sign of nature) and the city (the sign of civilization) has been fought almost since literature began.'[40] And just as this war between nature and civilization resonates with what has gone before – for as Tolkien said of *The Lord of the Rings* 'as the story grew it put down roots (into the past)'[41] – so also it seems to speak of things to come. When Saruman, served by his unnatural creations and poised for his moment of glory, falls, it is primarily at the hands of the ents, who are arguably Tolkien's most conspicuous portrayal of conscious natural forces. Indeed the ent attack on Isengard, precipitated by Saruman's relentless destruction of the surrounding natural world, has discernible parallels with modern ecological theories concerning the potential destructive power of an environmentally imbalanced and fragile planet.[42]

---

40 Jonathan Bate, *The Song of the Earth*, London: Picador, 2000, p.3.
41 J.R.R.Tolkien, *The Fellowship of the Ring*, London: HarperCollins, 1997, p.xiv.
42 Richard Mathews in his work *Fantasy: The Liberation of Imagination* also contends that the mobilisation of the ents against Saruman (and Sauron) is representative of 'set-upon' and reactive natural forces in conflict with technology. Mathews believes that alongside the technologically themed towers of Orthanc and Barad-dûr, the orcs (a unifying factor in Saruman and Sauron's regime) are also a symbolic representation of what he calls 'dark technology'. He states: 'their very existence was contrived through technological manipulation of other living creatures [… Orcs] are extensions of the dark technology of The Two Towers. Resembling the sorceress's towers, the Ents and the trees they guard tower over the earth in their trunks but are clearly in harmony with it. […] the Orcs are weighed against the Ents – technology is weighed against nature' (Richard Mathews, *Fantasy: The Liberation of Imagination*, New York: Routledge, 2002, p.74). Mathews further suggests that aspects of Tolkien's portrayal of orcs cast them as machine-like in contrast to the more naturally conceived ents: 'In their abduction of Merry and Pippin, the Orcs run tirelessly for hours as if they were machines: Tolkien even describes them as being made of 'wire and horn'. The Ents on the other hand, move agonizingly slowly and their every aspect, from their appearance to their mission of tree herding

In *Making Peace with the Planet* pioneering ecologist Barry Commoner discusses the notion of a 'wounded' earth striking back. Commoner says humanity has created what he has called the 'technosphere' – a human-made counterpart of the ecosphere (or biosphere). The 'technosphere', if deprived of ecological ethics, endures and grows stronger because as things stand there is no will, no environmental counterforce, strong enough to oppose it. Whilst the Green movement seeks this change in will (or global mindset), the ecosphere continues to endure attack, and as the balance of the planet's fragile support system is thrown out of kilter, so humanity begins to feel the first tremors of a catastrophic environmental backlash – or as Commoner concisely puts it 'the human attack on the ecosphere[43] has instigated an ecological counterattack. The two worlds are at war.'[44]

The balance of human politics is at present in a conflicted relationship with environmental ethics and thus humanity, in this light, risks being cast as the

---

associates them with natural rather than technological images' (Mathews, *Fantasy*, pp.73-74).

43 The circumstances of the ent attack on Isengard also recalls aspects of James Lovelock's Gaia theory which asserts that the Earth may be viewed as a unified, single organism, integrating every conceivable component, element and system of life within the constructive make-up of the planet. The Gaia theory suggested that the Earth, as a 'single-organism' or biomass entity is capable of self-regulation, and that this self-regulatory process ultimately provides the conditions for life – seeking optimum balance between received energy and the reaction of all matter that makes up the planet. As the Gaia theory relates to any and all points of matter and energy upon the planet (organic or synthetic) including the lithosphere, atmosphere, hydrosphere, cryosphere and biosphere, it also relates to what Commoner would refer to as the technosphere – and all human activity and production.

How the reaction of Tolkien's ents relates to all of this lies in outreach theories related to Gaia which suggest that, since the Earth system of self-regulation seeks to maintain optimum balance – simply put – it will take account of human activities which alter conditions on a global scale (across time) creating a change in the system which may prove irreversible and less hospitable to human life. Considering Gaia (or such an Earth system of regulation) as the Earth looking after itself by striking back or re-dressing that which unsettles the natural balance, the ent (nature) attack on Isengard (ecologically damaging human activity) comes into view. In a work of fantasy the idea of nature (or natural forces) rising up and striking back at a representation of ecologically unsound technology is a premise that does contain an ecological warning for the human race. To what extent Tolkien anticipated such conditions or such real world theories can only be conjecture – the fact remains that the concept is clearly evident in his work.

The theory itself is certainly not all fantasy – part of the theory's supporting evidence points to the Earth's ability to regulate global scale factors such as surface temperature and atmospheric composition over the history of the planet, despite significant increases in levels of received energy from the sun. Indeed since first proposed by Lovelock as the Gaia hypothesis (or the Earth feedback hypothesis), some of his assertions have been supported by scientific studies – nonetheless his theory has always been controversial and has attracted severe criticism from biologists and scientists, who would consider the theory to be more metaphorical than scientific. For a starting point for more in-depth study related to the Gaia theory see James Lovelock, *Gaia: A New Look at Life on Earth*, Oxford: Oxford University Press, 1979; and James Lovelock, *The Revenge of Gaia: Why the Earth Is Fighting Back – and How We Can Still Save Humanity*, London: Penguin, 2006.

44 Barry Commoner, *Making Peace with the Planet*, London: Gollancz, 1990. p.4.

Dark Lord of the 'technosphere' – a Dark Lord that now has become so powerful and dangerous that the very existence of life on earth is threatened, just as Sauron and Saruman threaten all living things in Middle-earth. Applying this idea further, one is drawn to articulate the resemblances between the One Ring (that devours all who try to wield it)[45] and the human desire to be master of all things, which may yet lead us to our own undoing through the progressive destruction of the life support systems of the planet (if not through nuclear war). The only way that humanity may be stopped in this needless devastation of the natural world is to destroy the will or global mindset that permits it to continue. And just as the One Ring may only be destroyed in the fire where it was first forged, so, there is only one place in which a will, or mindset may be destroyed, and that is in the mind in which it was created.

We shall revisit the twisted landscapes of Mordor and Isengard again in the chapters to come. For now, as part of my discussion on what I have termed the 'Shadows on the Landscape(s)' of Tolkien's major works, I turn to what many commentators consider to be Tolkien's most explicit critique of the modern, industrialised world: 'The Scouring of the Shire', as Saruman, in the guise of Sharkey, brings environmental ruination to the homelands of the hobbits.

(III.3) The Coming of Sharkey and the 'The Scouring of the Shire'

Frodo, Sam, Merry and Pippin, returning from their various adventures and trials with wizards, wars, Balrogs, Barrow-wights, Necromancers and Nazgûl, and believing that they had, for the most part, seen off the darkest forces which threatened the people and lands of Middle-earth, are soon brought face to face with an unexpected but all too familiar evil. Arriving again in the land of their birth and youth, they find that the Shire is not as they remember: a land where '[e]verything looked fresh' and where 'the new green of Spring [...]

---

45 The One Ring proves to be the undoing even of Sauron in the end. He cannot perceive of anyone destroying the One Ring and thus it becomes his weakness. Elrond says of the Ring at the Council in Rivendell 'as long as it is in the world it will be a danger even to the Wise' (Tolkien, *Fellowship*, p.261). Only Tom Bombadil remains unaffected by the destructive allure of the One Ring (although Galadriel and Sam Gamgee also resist it). See also Patrick Curry, 'The Ring as Megamachine' in *Defending Middle-earth. Tolkien: Myth and Modernity*, London: HarperCollins, 1997.

shimmer[ed] in the fields and on the tips of the trees' fingers',[46] but rather it has become what Andrew Light in his essay 'Tolkien's Green Time' describes as 'a nineteenth-century industrial wasteland (a kind of Middle-earth version of turn-of-the-century Manchester or Pittsburgh).'[47] And as the hobbits view the full extent of industrialised change that has been visited upon their home, the scene of desolation unfolds to both reader and returning hobbit alike:

> The pleasant row of old hobbit-holes in the bank on the north side of the Pool were deserted, and their little gardens that used to run down bright to the water's edge were rank with weeds [...] an avenue of trees had stood there. They were all gone. And looking with dismay up the road towards Bag End they saw a tall chimney of brick in the distance. It was pouring out black smoke into the distance.[48]

Later on, as the company make their approach to Hobbiton and Bag End, the smokestack and surrounding landscape are revealed in even more graphic detail:

> The great chimney rose up before them; and as they drew near the old village across the Water, through rows of new mean houses along each side of the road, they saw the new mill in all its frowning and dirty ugliness: a great brick building straddling the stream, which it fouled with a steaming and stinking outflow. All along the Bywater Road every tree had been felled.
> As they crossed the bridge and looked up the Hill they gasped. Even Sam's vision in the Mirror had not prepared him for what they saw. The Old Grange on the west side had been knocked down, and its place taken by rows of tarred sheds. All the chestnuts were gone. The banks and hedgerows were broken. Great wagons were standing in disorder in a field beaten bare of grass. Bagshot Row was a yawning sand and gravel quarry.[49]

Both of the passages above speak for themselves in terms of how they relay a landscape that is suffering and yielding under the weight of an industrialised regime. What is noteworthy is that both passages are preceded or introduced by observations by the narrator that pertain to the profound emotional impact these sights have on the returning hobbits. The first passage is introduced thus: '[t]his was Frodo and Sam's own country, and they found out now that

---

46 Tolkien, *Fellowship*, p.45.
47 Andrew Light, 'Tolkien's Green Time: Environmental Themes in *The Lord of the Rings*' in Gregory Bassham & Eric Bronson (eds.), *The Lord of the Rings and Philosophy: One Book to Rule Them All*, Chicago and La Salle, Illinois: Open Court Publishing, 2003, p.151.
48 J.R.R. Tolkien, *The Return of the King*, London: HarperCollins, 1997, p.981.
49 Tolkien, *Return*, p.993.

they cared about it more than any place in the world.'⁵⁰ And as the hobbits approach the scene relayed in the second passage we are told, '[i]t was one of the saddest hours of their lives.'⁵¹ Indeed one gets a sense that even among all the great evils and misfortunes the hobbits have experienced and witnessed on their travels – the sight of their homeland in this blighted and corrupted state is the very nadir of their long struggles.

Each of the hobbits, at various times throughout the trilogy, has encountered and opposed manifestations of evil. Each has witnessed, at close hand, the environmental ruination that has inevitably accompanied such manifestations. Interestingly, the four returning hobbits, in pairs, have been immersed in and have strived to oppose the two most graphic representations of ecological devastation in *The Lord of the Rings*: Pippin and Merry at Isengard and of course Frodo and Sam in Mordor. Echoes of those same evils have now found their way to the Shire and the familiar fields of home.⁵²

The effect of this is to create a sudden point of focus, an awakening in the four hobbits (and the reader) to the true nature of what they have been resisting. They have been prime movers in, and lived through, the defining crisis of their time; they have helped to shape the great events of the Third Age: the overthrow of Sauron and Saruman and the crumbling of the powers symbolised by the two dark towers of Barad-dûr and Orthanc. But it is only when they witness how the residue of such evil can impact upon, and destroy something they know and love, something they are familiar with, that the full horror of that evil comes home to them, just as they come home to it.

A similar effect is rendered in Steven Spielberg's acclaimed film *Schindler's List*. The film, adapted from Thomas Keneally's historical novel *Schindler's Ark*, tells the story of Oskar Schindler, a member of the German Nazi party who saves the lives of a large number of Polish Jews from the death camps and the Nazi war machine. The film is shot in black and white except for very short colour sequences showing candlelight and scenes involving a little girl wearing a red dress (only the dress is shown in colour). We (and Schindler) first encounter

---

50 Tolkien, *Return*, p.981.
51 Tolkien, *Return*, p.993.
52 Matthew Dickerson & Jonathan Evans, *Ents, Elves, and Eriador: The Environmental Vision of J.R.R. Tolkien*, Lexington: Kentucky: University Press of Kentucky, 2006, p.205.

the girl moving through the war-torn streets of Krakow. Later we see the little girl again – among a mound of dead bodies. She is immediately recognisable by virtue of her red dress which draws our focus amid the surrounding black and white. David M. Crowe in *Oskar Schindler: The Untold Account of His Life, Wartime Activities, and the True Story Behind 'The List'* referring to Spielberg and his scriptwriter Steven Zaillian's idea to use colour on the little girl's dress as a point of focus states: 'The little girl in the red dress would serve as [...] the emotional prism through which Oskar Schindler would truly awaken to the horrors of the Holocaust all around him.'[53] Even though manifestations of great evil surround Schindler it is only through the 'prism' or lens of the little girl's death that the full magnitude of the evil comes home to him.[54]

Likewise for the hobbits, it takes the destruction of something familiar, something recognisable and fondly remembered – a point of focus amid the swirl of Sauron and Saruman's devastation of Middle-earth, a gaze through an 'emotional prism' – for them to fully comprehend the great evil they have been fighting.

The once far off and indistinct troubles of the wider world, the problems of wizards, elves and the counsels of the wise, have, throughout the unfolding narrative of *The Lord of the Rings*, become more and more the concern of hobbits. Since Gandalf first tells Frodo at Bag End that Sauron 'has at last heard [...] of *hobbits* and the *Shire*'[55] (emphasis in original) and the Black Riders first cross their borders, these four hobbits: Frodo, Sam, Pippin and Merry, have been gradually drawn in and embroiled in the War of the Ring, but somehow, it was never really their war – they have been caught up in it rather than truly emotionally tied to it. 'The Scouring of the Shire' changes all that and is thus arguably the most important chapter in the work. The sight of their ruined homeland causes a 'sharpening effect' in the hobbits' emotive reactions to the

---

53 David M. Crowe, *Oskar Schindler: The Untold Account of His Life, Wartime Activities, and the True Story Behind 'The List'*, Cambridge, MA: Westview Press, 2004, p.202.
54 Jeremy Roberts comments also on how the 'sharpening' effect of the little girl's red dress draws us into the film: 'The little girl runs through the crowd, her red dress sparkling with life in the dull cloud of greys on the city street. A few minutes later, we see the girl again, tossed on a heap of the dead, her dress red as blood. The young child has joined the millions killed in the Holocaust. This famous scene from the movie *Schindler's List* touches us with the horror of the Holocaust. The girl could have been any one of us. The man who sees the dress in the movie could also be any one of us.' (Jeremy Roberts, *Oskar Schindler: Righteous Gentile*, New York: Rosen Publishing, 2000, p.5).
55 Tolkien, *Fellowship*, p.58.

evil they have encountered. An exchange between Frodo and Sam at the now dishevelled and dirt-ridden Bag End goes to the heart of it:

> 'This is worse than Mordor!' said Sam 'Much worse in a way. It comes home to you, as they say; because it is home, and you remember it before it was all ruined.'
> 'Yes, this is Mordor,' said Frodo. 'Just one of its works.'[56]

Importantly with 'The Scouring of the Shire' Tolkien attains this 'sharpening effect', this elucidation of the nature of evil for the reader as well as for the hobbits because as Dickerson and Evans note that it is hobbits that 'Tolkien leads us to identify with most [...] Hobbits are presented as normal people suddenly placed in situations that require them to be heroic. More than any other people in Middle-earth, they are like us.'[57] Dickerson and Evans go on to cite Tom Shippey's observation that hobbits are 'essentially modern in attitudes and sentiment' and that they have been created so by Tolkien[58] 'to guide the reader's reactions, to help the reader feel 'what it would be like' to be there.'[59] Given the reader's sympathy then with the hobbit perspective, and given that the reader has also previously viewed the Shire in all its natural glory, and has travelled with the hobbits on their adventures – the shock and emotive reaction of the hobbits upon seeing the devastation that has been wreaked upon their homeland is replicated (to a lesser degree) in the reader's sensibilities. In a sense the reader is drawn into the hobbits' fictional world, and like the hobbits experiences a form of shock upon witnessing the unfolding ruination of the Shire. Dickerson and Evans further suggest that when '[w]e catch a glimpse of this form of evil penetrating the Shire [we] immediately think of our own homes.'[60] I accept the basic premise of the point being made here but would offer that the immediate response of the reader (due in no small part to Tolkien's skill as a writer[61]) is perhaps more likely to be one that remains within

---

56 Tolkien, *Return*, p.994.
57 Dickerson & Evans, *Ents, Elves, and Eriador*, p.204.
58 Tolkien wrote about hobbits on a number of occasions concerning what he called 'the ennoblement of the ignoble' and the 'value of Hobbits, in putting earth under the feet of 'romance'' (Tolkien, *Letters*, p.220 & p.215 respectively).
59 Dickerson & Evans, *Ents, Elves, and Eriador*, pp.204-205 and Tom Shippey, *J.R.R. Tolkien: Author of the Century*, London: HarperCollins, 2001, pp.6-7.
60 Dickerson & Evans, *Ents, Elves, and Eriador*, p.205.
61 Speaking of the 'startling sensation of primary reality' which characterises Tolkien's created world of Middle-earth, Patrick Curry declares that it 'is more real to me than many 'actual' places' (Curry, *Defending Middle-earth*, p.60).

the boundaries of Tolkien's secondary world – that is to say, in the first instance, one of empathy rather than one of self-reflection. Thereafter the implication and relevance the emotionally charged narrative holds for our own lives begins to come into view.

Certainly from an environmental perspective the portrayal offered in 'The Scouring of the Shire', of once far off and indistinct threats arriving with an all too real force and ferocity at one's own doorstep has many implications for our world. Many, even today, consider the environmental crisis to be someone else's problem, something that could never really manifest itself with any serious consequence in the 'Shires' of their own homeland. Meanwhile the Sharkeys of big business capitalism pedal their wares all the time assuaging us that Mordor will never find its way to our homes.

Some, however, are not so easily convinced by the capitalist and often political rhetoric that seeks to either downplay environmental issues or cover them up altogether. One such figure during 'The Scouring of the Shire' episode is Farmer Cotton who remains wholly opposed to the industrialisation of the Shire under Sharkey, and who could be said to share certain values with Tolkien himself. Indeed when Merry asks Cotton 'Who is this Sharkey?' Cotton's reply is not only a herald of the unmasking of Saruman as the ruffian leader Sharkey, but it also resurfaces a childhood memory of Tolkien's we noted earlier:

> He's the real Chief now, I guess. All the ruffians do what he says; and what he says is mostly: hack, burn, and ruin; and now it's come to killing. There's no longer even any bad sense in it. They cut down trees and let 'em lie.[62]

There is little doubt, given Tolkien's own love of trees, that for him their needless felling was not so much a mindless deed but an evil deed. Destroying trees for a purpose characterised by 'bad sense' was deplorable enough for Tolkien, but their gratuitous destruction was quite another, and Farmer Cotton's remark '[t]hey cut down trees and let 'em lie' certainly recalls the felling of the butcher's tree which 'they didn't do anything with'[63] from Tolkien's own childhood recollection. Moreover it is Farmer Cotton, more than any other who has lived through the industrialisation of the Shire, who voices his disapproval and distrust of Sharkey's

---

62 Tolkien, *Return*, p.989.
63 Carpenter, *Biography*, p.22.

regime. It is he who relates how Ted Sandyman's Old Mill has been levelled under the new order – only to be replaced by a more imposing and industrialised version 'full o' wheels and outlandish contraptions', and he adds that there are 'other mills like it.' The 'idea' Cotton tells the returning hobbits (for so he has been informed by Pimple) 'was to grind more and faster.' Whilst relating the events surrounding the establishment of the new industrialised mill processes in Hobbiton, Cotton comments with a tone of disdain, '[o]nly that fool Ted [Sandyman] was pleased by that, and he works there cleaning wheels for the Men, where his dad was the Miller and his own master.'[64] Although Farmer Cotton's (and thus Tolkien's) pejorative judgement on the emergence of a more progressive and efficient type of mill would appear to leave both open for criticism centred on an anti-modernist bias, there are very sound reasons for questions to be raised regarding the worth of this new technology – both in the imagined world of Middle-earth and in the primary world context of the twentieth-century (and beyond).

Firstly, within a generation, Ted Sandyman's family mill has been taken over and transformed by what amounts to an industrial corporation run by a figure whose identity and real agenda are kept hidden. Sandyman is no longer 'his own master', as Farmer Cotton puts it; his skill as a miller has been made redundant and instead he uses his energies 'cleaning wheels' within the very device that has replaced him. In other words the machine has become *his* master. Moreover the regime of Sharkey promises, at first, more convenient and efficient grinding of corn, but as Farmer Cotton reports 'since Sharkey came they don't grind no more corn at all.' Despite the termination of corn produce, the new mills still proceed to undertake some unspecified production – night and day. Cotton continues in his idiomatic manner: '[t]hey're always a-hammering and a-letting out a smoke and a stench, and there isn't no peace even at night in Hobbiton.'[65] Tolkien's portrayal of the new manufacturing processes seems to point to a regime of expansion and production without purpose. In this sense (I expand on this idea below) the mill at Hobbiton becomes an emblematic representation of technological advancement for its own sake. James G. Davis in 'Showing Saruman as Faber: Tolkien and Peter Jackson' addresses the question of Sandyman's mill as it appears in 'The Scouring of the Shire':

---

64 Tolkien, *Return*, p.990.
65 Tolkien, *Return*, p.990.

All we know is that it makes something that requires gravel and wood and produces smoke and water pollution. It is almost a phoney mock-up of a factory, full of smoke and chaos, producing nothing. Perhaps [...] the realm of Sharkey should not be seen as an accurate depiction of the contemporary world, but rather as another generally symbolic evocation of modernity.[66]

Given that the new mill seems to have no clear purpose other than the vague promise of greater efficiency, we may view Ted Sandyman, who has abandoned the trade of his forefathers and surrendered to the allure of convenience and expediency, as a representation of (what Tolkien would have viewed as) humanity's hasty and ill-considered embrace of the machine age. Sandyman both literally and metaphorically polishes the wheels of progress seemingly unconcerned (or unaware) that they have made him obsolete.[67]

All of this recalls Treebeard's prophetic assertion that Saruman 'has a mind of metal and wheels.'[68] Indeed Saruman is undoubtedly Tolkien's clearest representation of a modern industrialised mindset that remains indifferent to the damage inflicted upon the environment by destructive industry. I examine the character of Saruman in more detail in the next chapter, but, in the discussion of an episode which sees him adopt a pseudonym, I wish to focus for a moment on the question of his name(s). Tom Shippey in *The Road to Middle-earth* offers that there are indications in Tolkien's naming of the White Wizard which point to a character who is defined by his association with machines and technology: 'Saruman shows many signs of being equitable with industrialism, or technology [...] *Searu* in Old English (the West Saxon form of Mercian *saru*) means 'device, design, contrivance, art' [and] 'cunning and mechanical.'[69] In 'The Scouring of the Shire' Saruman, of course, reappears as Sharkey – Shippey proposes that this name originates from the Arabic '*shaikh* (cp. Orkish *sharkû*)' adding that

---

66 James G. Davis, 'Showing Saruman as Faber: Tolkien and Peter Jackson' in *Tolkien Studies* 5 (2008), pp.58-59.
67 In his celebrated work *Earth in the Balance: Ecology and the Human Spirit* former American Vice President Al Gore comments upon humanity's present day fascination with the trappings and promises of industry and technology: '[w]e have been so seduced by the industrialised world's promise to make our lives comfortable that we allow the synthetic routines of modern life to soothe us in an inauthentic world of our own making.' Indeed Gore could almost be talking about Sandyman – inside the industrialised mill among the wheels and workings – when he warns that with an over zealous integration and adaptation of technology into our everyday lives 'we ourselves (may begin to) behave like machines, lost in the levers and cogs.' (Al Gore, *Earth in the Balance: Ecology and the Human Spirit*, New York: Houghton Mifflin, 2000, pp.240-42).
68 Tolkien, *Two Towers*, p.462.
69 Tom Shippey, *The Road to Middle-earth*, London: HarperCollins, 2005, p.194.

'[t]o a medievalist the name might well suggest the 'Old Man of the Mountain' or leader of the Assassins as described in *Mandeville's Travels*' who 'ruled [...] by feeding his followers *hashish* and deluding them with dreams of paradise.' When we consider how Saruman/Sharkey both leads his band of followers and ensnares the Shire in the promises of his industrialised regime, the etymology Shippey provides for this nomenclature seems entirely appropriate.

Taking the origins of both names (Saruman and Sharkey) into account, and applying them to the symbolic significance of the White Wizard and his establishment of power in the Shire, Shippey contends, '[s]o we might think 'cunning man', or 'machine man', or 'technological man', keeps a Utopian carrot dangling in front of our noses, of a world of leisure and convenience where each new mill grinds faster than the one before.'[70] Referring to Ted Sandyman's ill-advised embrace of the new mechanised mill established under Sharkey's control Shippey adds '[Sandyman] ought to have realised [...] machine masters end up machine minders, and all for nothing, or rather for an insidious logic of expansion.'[71]

Having examined what I believe to be Tolkien's critique of the futility and dangers of technologies and machines that ignore the best interests of humanity (as represented in the purposelessness of the mechanised mills of Hobbiton, Bywater and elsewhere), we should remember that these industrialised mills do actually execute some things very efficiently indeed: they relentlessly pollute the waters of the surrounding area and belch toxins into the once clean air of the Shire, they cover the land in a film of grime and filth, and they risk all forms of natural life in the process. As Farmer Cotton tells Sam 'they pour out filth a purpose; they've fouled all the Water, and it's getting down into Brandywine.' And in perhaps the most damning commentary of the environmentally corrosive potential of Sharkey's new industrial regime the worldly-wise farmer adds: 'If they want to make the Shire into a desert, they're going the right way about it.'[72]

---

70 Shippey, *Road*, p.194.
71 Shippey, *Road*, pp.194-195.
72 Tolkien, *Return*, p.990.

As I have argued above, Tolkien's depiction of the relentless, yet seemingly pointless turning and grinding of Sharkey's engines, the incessant combustion of his furnace fires, and the enslavement of his followers (and those caught up in his machinations) to meaningless machines, offers us a picture of a kind of mass-production programme for its own sake – and the only discernable result of the expenditure of all this technological energy is the environmental devastation caused as a consequence of the process. And of course Farmer Cotton is correct in his inference: eventually the natural resources of the Shire that feed Sharkey's industrial regime will run out, eventually the pollution caused by the process will take its terrible final toll, and the Shire will become like Mordor – a wasteland and a desert.[73]

I have said also, as has James G. Davis, that Sharkey's regime may be read as a 'symbolic evocation of modernity.'[74] Indeed it would seem reasonable to argue that Tolkien's portrayal of Sharkey's pointless industry has no direct relevance for the real world (beyond that framed by symbolist allusion) since all industries in the primary world have a purpose (even if they are ecologically unsound), and that real life Sharkey figures would not pour time and resources into a meaningless and aimless venture. Before consigning Tolkien's depiction of Sharkey's regime to the drawer of general emblematic allusion, however, we should note that Sharkey's agenda is not pointless, even if his factory operations appear to be so. Tolkien's White Wizard, and all his deeds, are driven by ambitious tendencies that are characterised by a thirst for knowledge and self-aggrandisement, and ultimately a desire for supremacy over other things. His mill factories help him achieve this to one degree or another. His goal may not explicitly have been the

---

[73] Another environmentally telling moment of 'The Scouring of the Shire' episode in this light comes as the returning hobbits arrive at the Brandywine Bridge, touching feet again upon the hinterland of the Shire. The narrator remarks: 'The land looked rather sad and forlorn.' Although the narrator attempts to explain the perceptible sadness framing the landscape by conceding 'it was after all the first of November', this scientific and seasonal rationalization is quickly qualified by attention to a more sinister and synthetic presence in the immediate environment: '[s]till there seemed an unusual amount of burning going on, and smoke rose from many points round about' (Tolkien, *Return*, p.977). Indeed this rather elegiac portrayal of a landscape that somehow exudes sadness not only echoes a description of the region surrounding Isengard ('It was a sad country' (Tolkien, *Two Towers*, p.540)), but it also suggests that the Shire, like the lands surrounding the White Wizard's former stronghold, is undergoing a transformation; that its ecology is under siege. It is becoming visually 'a sad country' to a perception (like ours, the narrator's and the returning hobbits') which has been acquainted with its former natural beauty, and symbolically 'forlorn' under the assault of a relentless industrialised regime. The Shire, where once '[e]verything looked fresh' (Tolkien, *Fellowship*, p.45) is, it seems, losing the sustaining vitality of natural forces.

[74] Davis, 'Showing Saruman as Faber', pp.58-59.

destruction of natural phenomena, but such devastation occurs both as a result of his consuming fascination with machines and engines, and his indifference to the damage he inflicts upon the environment in the continued pursuit of knowledge and dominion. Shippey takes up the point: 'Saruman has been led from ethically neutral researches into the kind of wanton pollution and love of dirt we see in 'The Scouring of the Shire' by something corrupting in the love of machines or in the very desire for control over the natural world.'[75]

Furthermore, far from being an unrealistic portrayal of big business practices, for many modern ecologists and social philosophers, the conditions Tolkien creates in 'The Scouring of the Shire' are an accurate rendering of the kind of corporate mindset that seeks expansion upon expansion, that demands ever faster and ever more efficient processes, that outmodes its workers to accommodate new technology and that continually 'upgrades' or repackages its produce in order to justify more and greater production – all the while creating nothing of any real worth or benefit for the human race. Ecologist Murray Bookchin in his essay 'Toward an Ecological Society' declares that the modern world is a place 'where society is ruled by production for the sake of production and [where] growth is the only antidote to death' as a consequence, Bookchin adds, 'the natural world is reduced to natural resources – the domain of wanton exploitation *par excellence* [...] [o]ne might more easily persuade a green plant to desist from photosynthesis than to ask the bourgeois economy to desist from capital accumulation.'[76] Bookchin goes on to underscore the intrinsic interconnection between processes and mindsets that facilitate production for its own sake and the ecologically destructive results of such production:

> A society based on production for the sake of production is inherently anti-ecological and its consequences are a devoured natural world, one whose organic complexity has been degraded by technology into the inorganic stuff that flows from the end of the assembly line.[77]

Certainly the conditions and ecologically destructive consequences relayed in Bookchin's analysis of what he calls the 'repressive reason' of 'irrational [...]

---

75 Shippey, *Road*, p.194.
76 Murray Bookchin, 'Toward an Ecological Society' in David Pepper, Frank Webster & George Revill (eds.), *Environmentalism: Critical Concepts*, New York: Routledge, 2003, p.38.
77 Bookchin, 'Toward an Ecological Society', p.39.

institutions and modes of consciousnesses'[78] have strong parallels with Sharkey's industrialisation of the Shire. Tolkien's rendering of Sharkey's regime and the environmental devastation that accompanies it is perhaps tainted a little by the emergence of the author's own distrust of industrialisation and the characterisation of those who wield industrial power as 'ruffians', but nonetheless the episode has traceable modern connotations. In the words of Tom Shippey: '[The Scouring of the Shire] may not be a totally convincing critique of modern society, but it has clear modern relevance and is more than dislike.'[79]

(IV) Tolkien among the Machines

The central drive of *The Lord of the Rings* in particular, (as asserted in the introduction of this study and observable in the analysis of episodes such as 'The Scouring of the Shire') is a narrative in which the principal conditions of the twentieth-century are re-created, and as the unfolding story of *The Lord of the Rings* begins, Tolkien's created world of Middle-earth is, as Curry puts it:

> under severe threat from those who worship pure power, and are its slaves: the technological and instrumental power embodied in Sauron [...] and the epitome of modernism gone mad. We thus find ourselves reading a story about ourselves, about our own world.[80]

Although Curry is referring not only to the environmental corrosion which accompanied the rise of modernity in the twentieth-century, but also to the two World Wars, the common factor that exacerbated and intensified the effect of both of these realities was the rise of the machine. Tolkien had (what he no doubt would have termed as) a healthy distrust of modernity and the machine. He once referred to Sauron as 'the Lord of magic and machines' adding 'this frightful evil can and does arise from an apparently good root, the desire to benefit the world and others.'[81] This would appear to be a direct critique of technological advancements in our world that have proven to be of more harm than good, but which are developed and supported initially because they promise to aid humanity in some way. Tolkien unequivocally connects

---

78 Bookchin, 'Toward an Ecological Society', p.39.
79 Shippey, *Road*, p.195.
80 Curry, *Defending Middle-earth*, p.24.
81 Tolkien, *Letters*, p.146.

the dawn of the machine age with a desire 'to create power in this World'. The inevitable conclusion of the interweaving of the advancement of machines and the pursuit of power became manifest in Tolkien's fiction primarily in the form of Morgoth, Sauron, Saruman and the One Ring. In the primary world, also, the result for Tolkien was all too evident:

> So we come inevitably from Daedalus and Icarus to the Giant Bomber. It is not an advance in wisdom! This terrible truth, glimpsed long ago by Sam Butler, sticks out so plainly and is so horrifyingly exhibited in our own time, with it's even worse menace for the future, that it seems almost a world wide mental disease that only a tiny minority perceive it.[82]

In citing Sam Butler, Tolkien is referring to a letter penned by Butler entitled 'Darwin among the Machines' in which Butler, under the pseudonym of Cellarius, sets the evolution of man against the evolution of machines. The letter goes on to propose a 'doomsday' scenario in which humanity has been usurped by the machine.

C. W. Sullivan writes of Tolkien-related criticism, 'conventional criticism can make little of [Tolkien's works] other than reduce them to World War II allegories or mere escapist yearnings for a passing rural England.'[83] I agree with the sentiment expressed in Sullivan's words but note the clear division offered by the word 'or'. And of course Sullivan is right. Traditionally those critics who have even deemed Tolkien's work worthy of their attention, either read it as a rejection of modernity and a lament for the old world, or cast it as a symbolic response to the second great war in Europe.

I contend, however, that for Tolkien, the anxieties he felt with the onset of the industrial age and his reaction to the war were inextricably connected – united by his apprehension for the rise of the machine age. Tolkien, in what Joseph Pearce refers to as his 'rage against the machine',[84] was equally wary and fearful of machines that brought death and war, and those that quickened the industrial devastation of rural landscapes. In his fiction these twin evils were often united in Tolkien's presentation of landscapes ravaged by the march of machine-wielding

---

82 Tolkien, *Letters*, p.88.
83 C.W. Sullivan, 'Tolkien the Bard: His Tale Grew in the Telling' in George Clark & Daniel Timmons (eds.), *Tolkien and his Literary Resonances: Views of Middle-earth*, Westport: Greenwood Press, 2000, p.44.
84 Joseph Pearce, *Tolkien: Man and Myth*, London: HarperCollins, 1999, p.158.

warmongers. Rosebury takes up the point: 'the ineradicable memory of a land pulverised by 'total war' is evident (though combined with images suggestive of industrial pollution, and fully absorbed into the wider imaginative geography) in the most hauntingly repellent landscapes of [Tolkien's] work.'[85]

Tolkien, like T.S Eliot or Wilfred Owen, was of a generation that bore witness to, arguably more so than any other, the terrible destructive power of machines. Tolkien had served in the trenches in World War One, had witnessed death on a massive, production-line-scale, and had seen for the first time machines bring death from the skies. We see this reflected in *The Silmarillion* when Morgoth's sorcerers create dragons out of 'iron and flame' and unleash them upon the enemy: 'Morgoth loosened upon his foes the last desperate assault [...] out of the pits of Angband there issued the winged dragons that had not been seen before.'[86] After his own experience with war had passed, as an older man Tolkien watched as his children were sent to fight in a war in which machines were the real soulless killers. In a letter to his son Christopher (then in active war service) dated January 1945 Tolkien writes:

> There seems to be no bowels of mercy or compassion, no imagination left in this dark diabolic hour [...] the first war of the Machines seems to be drawing to its final inconclusive chapter – leaving alas, everyone the poorer, many bereaved or maimed and millions dead, and only one thing triumphant: The Machines [...] the Machines are going to be enormously more powerful. What's their next move?[87]

By which of course Tolkien means what will be their next target? It is clear from his fiction, from his portrayal of the landscapes of Middle-earth threatened by machines, engines and their destructive power that Tolkien believed the next victim was the natural world itself. Moreover he foresaw just how much danger the natural world was in when set against machines wielded by minds bereft of an environmental conscience. Although Tolkien was deeply distrustful of the development of more and more powerful machines, for him the machines (and thus new technologies) were not inherently ill-fated or evil. Indeed speaking of the ability of an aeroplane to get his 'airletter' more quickly to his son Christopher, Tolkien concedes the usefulness of some aspects of machines,

---

85 Rosebury, *Tolkien*, p.126.
86 J.R.R.Tolkien, *The Silmarillion*, edited by Christopher Tolkien, London: Unwin, 1977, p.36.
87 Tolkien, *Letters*, p.111.

although he is quicker to connect such devices with the evils of Mordor: 'I have got over 2 thousand words onto this little flimsy airletter; and I will forgive the Mordor-gadgets some of their sins, if they will bring it quickly to you.'[88] For Tolkien the evil lay in those who used technology in a destructive manner, and in the purpose for which machines and technology were being developed.[89] In a letter dated 1945, alluding to the development of the atomic bomb, Tolkien questions the sanity of those who would seek to develop technology for purposes that were clearly destructive. He exclaims: '[t]he utter folly of these lunatic physicists to consent to do such work for war-purposes; calmly plotting the destruction of the world.'[90]

Tolkien, as we have said, has been much criticised as an anti-modernist romantic who arbitrarily condemns technology, industry and machines.[91] Indeed some critics have dismissed Tolkien's presentation of the hobbits' land before Sharkey as an anti-modernist 'nirvana' constructed purely from a romanticised reworking of Sarehole and the Warwickshire countryside of his youth. I offer a more detailed analysis of Tolkien's portrayal of the pastorally themed hobbit lands in chapter five, but in terms of the current focus on machines and industry, and the previous focus on Ted Sandyman's mill, I wish to take a moment to examine Tolkien's presentation of the Old Mill as a symbolic centrepiece before and after the industrialisation of the Shire.

The Old Mill which features in many of Tolkien's own illustrations of Hobbiton is no doubt an addition to the Shire which owes much to Tolkien's memory of Sarehole Mill (cited here from an interview with Tolkien for *The Oxford Mail* dated 1966): '[t]here was an old mill that really did grind corn with two millers, a great big pond with swans on it, a sandpit, a wonderful dell with flowers, a

---

88 Tolkien, *Letters*, p.88.
89 There is, of course, evidence of technology and progress, albeit at a low level, in the Shire. In the prologue to the second edition of *The Fellowship of the Ring* we are told of changes to building techniques: 'The craft of building may have come from the Elves or Men [but] hobbit-building had long since altered, improved by devices, learned from Dwarves, or discovered by themselves' (Tolkien, *Fellowship*, p.7). Earlier in the same section, however, the hobbits are offered as creatures whose technology is more associated with ecologically friendly devices: '[t]hey do not and did not understand or like machines more complicated than a forge-bellows, a water mill, or a hand-loom' (Tolkien, *Fellowship*, p.1).
90 Tolkien, *Letters*, p.116.
91 Rosebury, *Tolkien*, p.58.

few old-fashioned village houses and, further away, another mill.'[92] Yet even though the construction, as it appears in Hobbiton, would seem to be fairly representative of Tolkien's memories of Sarehole Mill, Tolkien has been accused of offering a romanticised version. Dimitra Fimi in *Tolkien, Race and Cultural History: From Fairies to Hobbits*, offers the opinion that Tolkien's interpretation of Sarehole Mill in his fiction is one based on an unrealistically anti-modernist presentation: 'if one accepts that Sarehole Mill is indeed the model for the Old Mill of the Shire, then one cannot but recognise that the mill had been idealised in Tolkien's imagination.' Fimi traces the mill's roots from the Biddle's corn-grinding mill of 1542, through a period when it was rented by Matthew Boulton, a partner of James Watt (both prime movers in the development of the steam engine). 'Subsequently' Fimi explains, it was 'enlarged and a supplementary steam engine was added [...] but by the early twentieth century it had been outrun by factories [and] reverted to corn milling.' As such Fimi contests, Sarehole Mill 'lay at the heart of the Industrial Revolution.' She further adds that the mill, along with 'more than fifty watermills working on [Birmingham's] rivers [...] were vital as a source of power for its growing metal industries.' 'In this light' Fimi declares 'we should question Tolkien's idealised image of the mill, despite its chimney and red bricks.'[93] Fimi's implied accusation suggests that Tolkien should have researched the history of Sarehole Mill before using it as the model for a mill (portrayed as being in harmony with its environment) in a fictional land which offers a critique of industrialisation – in the midst of a very insightful and rigorous study on Tolkien, Fimi is, at best, unreasonably demanding of her subject and his employment of real world models for his fiction. Moreover this view not only negates the reality of the Sarehole Mill in Tolkien's time and memory as a corn grinding mill that worked in harmony with the natural landscape around it, but it also suggests that a given object, machine, building or device should be judged on its history and not how it is used. Tolkien, as we noted previously, was certainly wary of modernity but only in terms of how the trappings and devices of modernity were being employed. I see it as crucial to note that Tolkien did not simply label machines and new technologies as destructive or evil in and of themselves, but rather he placed

---

92 From an interview with Tolkien for *The Oxford Mail* dated 1966. Quoted in Dimitra Fimi, *Tolkien, Race and Cultural History: From Fairies to Hobbits*, Basingstoke: Palgrave Macmillan, 2009, p.182.
93 Fimi, *Tolkien, Race and Cultural History*, pp.182-83.

great emphasis on the misuse of such things. The evil, for Tolkien, lay not in the machine but in the machine-wielder.

Speaking of Sharkey's attempt to industrialise the Shire, and in particular his indoctrination of Lotho to build larger and more efficient mills Tolkien states, '[i]t would no doubt be possible to defend poor Lotho's introduction of more efficient mills; but not of Sharkey and Sandyman's use of them.'[94] Tolkien acknowledges the perceived merit of 'more efficient mills', but once the initial prospect of a possible benefit for the community has been transformed into misuse and thus something destructive, it becomes, in Tolkien's view, indefensible. Ralph C. Wood, writing from a Christian perspective in *The Gospel According to Tolkien: Visions of the Kingdom in Middle-earth*, takes up the question of Tolkien's attitude to industry and technology: 'it is important to discredit the common view that Tolkien was a Luddite who dismissed modern technology as evil and godless [...] Tolkien was careful to point out that the use of a thing – whether for good or for ill – determines its worth, not the thing itself.'[95]

Fimi's assertion that 'Tolkien mainly recalled the [Sarehole] mill as a watermill: a form of industry that utilised a more natural source of power than steam that would not be associated with the industrial revolution. The red brick and chimney recollections were attributed to the invasion of modernity into the Shire'[96] is perhaps an accurate summation of Tolkien's recollections and assignment of symbolist imagery. But, crucially, when the hobbits return to the Shire after it has been devastated by Sharkey's industrialised regime, we recall that the 'tall chimney of brick' they encounter is described as 'pouring out smoke into the evening air'[97] and 'foul[ing] [the water] with a steaming and stinking outflow.'[98] In other words the fictional mill is being used to negatively impact upon the natural world around it, and it is this use rather than the mill's association with bricks and a chimney that fashions its symbolic role.

---

94 Tolkien, *Letters*, p.200.
95 Ralph C. Wood, *The Gospel According to Tolkien: Visions of the Kingdom in Middle-earth*, Louisville: Westminster John Knox Press, 2003, p.31.
96 Fimi, *Tolkien, Race and Cultural History*, p.184.
97 Tolkien, *Return*, p.981.
98 Tolkien, *Return*, p.993.

(V) Keeping the Faith

For Tolkien, decisions to employ technology for purposes of good or ill came down to a moral choice. I examine the elusive nature of the theological climate of Tolkien's fiction at various junctures throughout this book, but in order to begin to examine the religious aspects of Tolkien's environmental worldview, it is necessary for us to return for a time to Tolkien's childhood days in Sarehole.

Mabel Tolkien had attended an Anglican service every Sunday and since the premature death of her husband, her faith had become increasingly important to her. She had begun thinking in more profound terms about her religion and, although brought up in a household fiercely opposed to Catholicism, more and more her mind was turning towards the Church of Rome.[99] She knew that any conversion to Catholicism would evoke the wrath and subsequent financial isolation of her family. Such was her devotion, however, that she converted to the Church of Rome, ignoring the threats of hardship delivered upon her by her outraged father John Suffield, and began to teach her boys the ways of the Catholic religion. The threats of her family proved to be promises that were fulfilled, and in a very real sense she suffered for her faith both financially and in terms of her health.

Around this time Tolkien was beginning to attend King Edward's School[100] in Birmingham. Unable to afford the daily train fare, and driven by a desire to give the obviously bright Tolkien the best possible start in life, Mabel Tolkien was forced to move away from what had been their serene country existence and into the smoke-filled congestion and clamour of central Birmingham. The sense of upheaval and disruption was so great for Tolkien that he fell ill and had to stay at home, missing school for long periods. After a while, however, he was forced to accept city life and reluctantly he resigned his days at Sarehole to the past. The family got on with the business of scraping by (a situation very much

---

99 Perhaps one of the triggers for Mabel's conversion to Catholicism, apart from reasons related to her sense of spiritual direction, was that she decided to do so in a kind of pact with her sister May Incledon, although the exact circumstances of her conversion (and her decision to convert) are somewhat vague.
100 Tolkien first attended King Edward's School (his father's old school) after passing the entrance exam at the second attempt. A benevolent uncle on the Tolkien side paid the fees. Later Tolkien was moved to St. Philip's because the fees were more manageable. After a great deal of home tuition by his mother, however, he won a scholarship and was able to return to King Edward's.

perpetuated by the refusal of Mabel's outraged family to assist her financially) and tried as much as possible to integrate themselves into an urban existence.

One positive factor in the lives of Mabel, Tolkien and his brother Hilary at this time was the induction of Father Francis Xavier Morgan[101] as their local parish priest. Father Morgan was to prove not only an admirable religious advisor to Mabel and the boys, but also a trustworthy and dependable friend whose light would shine brightly at the time of their greatest need.

On November 14th 1904, just four years after moving from the country hamlet of Sarehole, Mabel Tolkien died. She had fallen ill earlier in the year through a combination of diabetes and the pressure of bringing up her boys in hardship by herself. And, despite a summer convalescence for her and the boys in the countryside retreat of Rednal (arranged by Father Morgan), her health continued to deteriorate. Too ill to return to the city, she remained in the country cottage where she slipped into a diabetic coma, never to recover.

That last summer spent with their mother at Rednal was a wondrous time for the boys, and for a moment at least, the Tolkien family was able to recapture the magic of its Sarehole days. This fleeting echo of happier times, however, made what the boys saw as their mother's sudden death much harder to bear. For Tolkien, the parting was especially sorrowful. His mother had been his teacher, his mentor and his solace in a weary world. She had been his guiding light; everything that he loved he had learned from her: fairy tales, strange languages, a passion for the natural world and now the Catholic faith. Although still young (only twelve) when his mother died, and shielded by her from hardship, Tolkien began to see her death as a type of martyrdom. He was aware of the sacrifices his mother had made for him and how she had suffered so that he and his brother should have their faith. Throughout the course of his life, Tolkien was to forever associate his faith with the death of his mother, believing one to be inseparable from the other. Aged just twenty-one, Tolkien wrote: 'My own dear mother was a martyr indeed, and it is not to everybody that God grants so easy a way to his great gifts as he did to Hilary and myself,

---

101 Tolkien viewed Father Morgan as his second father, so much so that he obeyed Father Morgan's strict guidelines regarding his relationship with Edith Bratt.

giving us a mother who killed herself with labour and trouble to ensure us keeping the faith.'[102]

Writing to his own son Michael many years after, Tolkien was also to say: 'I witnessed (half-comprehending) the heroic sufferings and early death in extreme poverty of my mother who brought me into the Church.'[103] For a young boy, suddenly bereft of his mother, the faith she had fought for became her legacy to him, and her death very much 'galvanised' his devotion to the Church of Rome.

Indeed his mother's passing had a profound effect on not only Tolkien's faith, but also on everything he held dear. All that was good, all that he cherished was to become intrinsically bound up with his mother's memory. In particular, his love for growing things, so fostered in him by his mother, and his love of the countryside and of nature itself became as one with his memory of her. Those idyllic days in Sarehole and the more recent time spent in Rednal became magical, enchanted and almost sacred.

Now, his mother's death had forced him back again into the cold severity of city life. Father Morgan, named as legal guardian of the boys in Mabel's will, had found them lodgings with their aunt Beatrice Suffield[104] in Birmingham. Still suffering from deep shock – his mother's death still fresh in his mind – Tolkien now also found himself removed from the countryside. Her death had delivered him into not only the isolation experienced by any motherless child, but also into the bleak arms of the city where dark narrow streets weaved a path through endless noise and smoky factory buildings cut off the green hills from view. Just as his devotion to the Catholic faith found new meaning with the death of his mother, so now his love of nature became elevated to almost spiritual proportions.

His love and adoration for his mother and his deep sorrow at her passing transformed itself, entangled itself and renewed itself into his love for the natural world. His love for nature was in a sense reflective of his love for her, as if to

---

102 Carpenter, *Biography*, p.31.
103 Tolkien, *Letters*, p.321.
104 Father Morgan had decided upon Beatrice Suffield because she did not object to the Tolkien boys being educated in the Catholic faith. Other relatives were attempting to oppose Father Morgan's authority and have the boys transferred to a Protestant boarding school.

cherish the garden of nature was to cherish his memory of her. Carpenter also identifies this binding of mother and nature in Tolkien's affections:

> His mother's death had severed him from the open air, from Lickey Hill where he had gathered bilberries, and from the Rednal cottage where they had been so happy. And because it was the loss of his mother that had taken him away from all these things, he came to associate them with her. His feelings towards the rural landscape, already sharp from the earlier severance that had taken him from Sarehole, now became emotionally charged with personal bereavement. This love for the memory of the countryside of his youth was later to become a central part of his writing, and was intimately bound up with his love for the memory of his mother.[105]

The sense of apprehension for the natural world we see reflected in Tolkien's books in the words of those such as Treebeard who warns 'the withering of all woods may be drawing near'[106] (a prime example of the ecological warning that I contend underscores the environmental dimension of Tolkien's work) seems implicitly connected to how those happy days with his mother in the countryside (with her sudden death) came to an end. Carpenter tells us 'closely related to his mother's death [...] [Tolkien] had a deep sense of impending loss. Nothing was safe. Nothing would last. No battle would be won forever.'[107]

As I have suggested, Tolkien came to see his mother as a martyr, and as a gift from God who Tolkien believed had shown love for him and his brother by 'giving us a mother who killed herself with labour and trouble to ensure us keeping the faith.' In providing him with the stimulus for all he cherished, in becoming not only his mother, but also his mentor and his spiritual guide, this gift from God – his mother – had died so that he could follow the right path. Tolkien, therefore, would have viewed her gifts to him: her unfailing love, her sacrifices, her religious teachings, her connection with and elevation of the natural world also as gifts from God. It is true, of course, that, as a deeply religious man, Tolkien would have viewed his immediate family and all that they meant to him as 'blessings' (as a consequence of his faith), but we recall that Tolkien

---

105 Carpenter, *Biography*, pp.32-33.
106 Tolkien, *Two Towers*, p.461.
107 Carpenter, *Biography*, p.31. Although Carpenter's sentiments above perhaps miss the positive outlook which frames much of Tolkien's work, his opinion that '[n]o battle would be won forever' is played out across Tolkien's secondary world: Sauron follows Morgoth etc. Even after he had finished *The Lord of the Rings*, Tolkien was contemplating a follow up in which the Shadow of Evil returns to Middle-earth, but it was an idea he was never to realise.

said of his mother, 'it is not to everybody that God grants so easy a way to his *great gifts*' (emphasis added) thus placing her above the notion of a 'blessing' in the conventional sense, giving her almost angelic status. Rosebury believes that the quasi-blessed adoration Tolkien had for his mother manifest itself in the virtuous and angelic female characters that appeared in his fiction:

> Tolkien invested [his mother's memory] with something of the numinous intensity which radiates from the adored, benevolent intimately present or achingly distant, feminine figures of his work: Galadriel, Arwen, Goldberry, and, the most remote of all, Varda (or Elbereth Gilthoniel), the Queen of Heaven worshipped by the Elves.[108]

Indeed one could say that Tolkien's faith and his abiding love of nature meet somewhere in the profound love he had for his mother. Tolkien, as we have seen, identified the presence of God in the martyrdom and heroic suffering of his mother and also implicitly connected his mother with the wonder of the natural world – and thus his love of God, nature and his mother would have to have become intertwined – bleeding, as it were, into each other.

Wood also draws attention to what he describes as Tolkien's 'veritably religious reverence for the natural world.'[109] And, in terms of his environmental ethics (exemplified most clearly by his defence of trees) Tolkien, as a devoted Christian, viewed the natural world as one of God's creations and evidence of a divine design. In a letter specifically addressing theological matters raised by Rayner Unwin's daughter (I examine the letter in more detail in chapter four), Tolkien writes: 'our ideas of God and ways of expressing them will be largely derived from contemplating the world about us.'[110] Tolkien's love for nature is, as much as it is anything, a celebration of the natural world as of itself, yet it is grounded in an understanding that humanity shares a bond with the living world that is both physical and spiritual.

What I am really speaking of here is the coming together of Tolkien's ecological ethics and his theology. Much modern ecological thinking, of course, proposes a link between theology and nature in the sense that we, as God's children, are charged with the protection and stewardship of God's 'garden' (a concept dis-

---

108 Rosebury, *Tolkien*, p.124.
109 Wood, *The Gospel According to Tolkien*, p.27.
110 Tolkien, *Letters*, p.400.

cussed in chapter three in relation to Gandalf's role in Middle-earth). Tolkien's attitude to the natural world, however, involved a more profound embrace, and an understanding that humanity was part of the interconnected wonder of creation. Indeed it would be no wild claim, given the sentiments expressed in the letter to Unwin's daughter above, to suggest that he viewed the natural world as a waking[111] spiritual presence on Earth (and not just an example of God's work that we honour Him by caring for). This is not to suggest that Tolkien believed, in a pantheistic sense, that nature was God, but more that the natural world was 'of God' in the same way that an angel or saint is.

(VI) The Harmony of Angels

Michael N. Stanton says of Tolkien in *Hobbits, Elves and Wizards* 'he surely did not check his faith and belief at the door when he sat down to write.'[112] And, if we look for a moment at *The Silmarillion*, we can see how Tolkien's own great mythic tale of creation presents this understanding of nature as spiritual in essence but not, as a pantheist would suggest, representative of an all-encompassing immanent God.

The theological design of Tolkien's mythology is, like the Old Testament, monotheistic. And as the book opens, we are introduced first to Eru or Ilúvatar who is 'the One' (or God), and then the Ainur described as being 'the offspring of his thought.' These 'Holy Ones', who are each a type of angel, are asked by Ilúvatar to come together in harmony to make a 'Great Music'. Though Tolkien describes the music of the Ainur as being a theme with 'no flaws', as it progresses, Melkor or Morgoth (to give him his elvish name), who of all the Ainur possesses 'the greatest gifts of power and knowledge'[113] becomes discontent with the will of Ilúvatar. Seeking still greater independence and power, Morgoth introduces a discordant melody into the theme. And thus through envy and misshapen ambition, strife, turmoil and the first whispers of evil are introduced into Tolkien's mythopoetic account of creation.

---

111 In *The Lord of the Rings* the narrator describes the elven landscape of Lorien as a 'waking world'.
112 Michael N. Stanton, *Hobbits, Elves and Wizards: Exploring the Wonders and Worlds of J.R.R. Tolkien's The Lord of the Rings*, New York: Palgrave Macmillan, 2002, p.162.
113 Tolkien, *Silmarillion*, p.15.

Morgoth's disharmony with Ilúvatar bears a striking resemblance to Lucifer's dissonance with God in the biblical tradition. Indeed this and other biblical allusions illuminate Tolkien's mythology with a decidedly Christian light. We should acknowledge from the outset, however, that this is Tolkien's creation *myth* and whilst elements of Christianity inform and perhaps even shape it, they do not define it – nor should it be read as Christianity in another guise. As Trevor Hart in 'Tolkien, Creation, and Creativity' states 'Tolkien's creation myth is not an allegorical rendering of its Christian counterpart, and attempts to read it as such are likely to mislead.'[114] Hart, offering a recapitulation of Tolkien's views on the unavoidable correspondence between real life and 'the meaningful order' which emerges from 'patterns of created reality', goes on to sound a warning (as did Tolkien himself) against drawing direct lines of parallel between primary and secondary realities based on discernable universalities: '[i]n stories, as in life, things are primarily what they are, and they should be judged as such.' Indeed Hart, returning to Tolkien's mythic account of creation, asserts that whilst Christian resemblances undoubtedly come into view, the frame of reference should be broadened to allow for other theologies, legends, and 'sources [of] inspiration.' Moreover, as Hart points out 'in certain respects the detail of [Tolkien's] own story has more in common with the 'theologies' of Nordic and classical myth.'[115] The influence of Christianity on Tolkien's *legendarium* is a question I return to in my discussions of both Gandalf and the elves (chapters three and four respectively), let us therefore first focus on the matter of how the *legendarium* offers a binding of natural and spiritual elements.

In every sense Tolkien's creation myth promotes the concept of 'harmony'. The mythological design offers the World (Eä), meaning the universe containing the Earth (Arda) in which the history of Middle-earth occurs, as envisioned through the music of the Ainur. Ilúvatar upon showing them the World says, 'Behold your Music! This is your minstrelsy.'[116] This vision is then brought into being as 'the World that Is' by Ilúvatar. In depicting the mythic origin of the World in this way, Tolkien is offering us a universe and an Earth that are spiritual (fashioned in part through the harmony of angels) and therefore 'of

---

114 Trevor Hart, 'Tolkien, Creation, and Creativity' in Trevor Hart & Ivan Khovacs (eds.), *Tree of Tales: Tolkien, Literature, and Theology*, Waco: Baylor University Press, 2007, p.41.
115 Hart, 'Tolkien, Creation, and Creativity', p.42.
116 Tolkien, *Silmarillion*, p.17.

God' (because the Ainur themselves were 'the offspring of his thought') and yet which are distinctly *not* manifestations of God (Ilúvatar). Furthermore, once the World has come into being, some of the Ainur, leaving Ilúvatar, forever tie their power and destiny to that of the World:

> Thus it came to pass that of the Ainur some abode still with Ilúvatar beyond the confines of the World; but others, and among them many of the greatest and most fair, took leave of Ilúvatar and descended into it. But the condition Ilúvatar made, or it is the necessity of their love, that their power should thenceforth be contained and bounded in the World, to be within it for ever, until it is complete, so that they are its life and it theirs. And therefore they are named the Valar, the Powers of the World.[117]

There are two points of note here:

1. The Valar must take their 'leave' of Ilúvatar to descend into the World. Thus Ilúvatar (God) is not embodied or manifest in the World.
2. The Valar are intimately bound to the life of the World – 'they are its life and it theirs.'

The combination of these facts points to a World (universe and Earth) which is spiritual in nature, tied to the power of angelic spirits and derived from divinity, but which is not a manifestation of Ilúvatar (or an immanent God).

Moreover the Valar, we are told, through 'great labours in wastes unmeasured and unexplored'[118] make the Earth ready for the coming of the Children of Ilúvatar (elves and men). In other words through the Valar, Earth is transformed from a lifeless rock into a living planet. They create the natural world. Indeed the various Lords and Queens[119] of the Valar are associated with differing aspects of nature: Ulmo with the life giving power of water, Manwë (foremost and King of the Valar) with the winds and the air, Aulë with the body of matter of which the Earth is made (rock, stone etc.), and Yavanna (Queen of the Earth) with all things that grow.[120]

---

117 Tolkien, *Silmarillion*, p.20.
118 Tolkien, *Silmarillion*, p.21.
119 As with many world mythologies, Tolkien assigns gender to the various spiritual beings that parade the pages of his mythological account of creation.
120 Of the other Valar, worthy of note is Varda (Elbereth) associated with the stars – she is the one to whom Frodo and Sam cry out in times of great need.

The significance of Yavanna is of particular interest because, in ecological terms, she represents the living and green face of Earth. Through her, the spiritual essence of the living Earth is said to become manifest (not surprisingly given Tolkien's deep affection for them) in the form of a tree: 'some there are who have seen her standing like a tree under heaven, crowned with the Sun; and from all its branches there spilled a golden dew upon the barren earth, and it grew green with corn.' Tolkien, however, alluding perhaps to an interrelationship between all aspects of nature, indicates that it is the interconnectivity of all things which sustains life: 'but the roots of the tree were in the waters of Ulmo, and the winds of Manwë spoke in its leaves.'[121] Despite her power to fill the Earth with natural wonder, Yavanna also needs the tears of Nienna 'the Weeper'[122] to bring forth the Two Trees of Valinor. And, perhaps more than anywhere else in Tolkien's fiction, the account of the creation of these trees seems to present nature (the emergence of the natural world) as sacred and possessed of angelic energy:

> There was a green mound [...] and Yavanna hallowed it, and she sat there long upon the green grass and sang a song of power, in which was set all her thought of things that grow in the earth [...] In that time the Valar were gathered together to hear the song of Yavanna [...] And as they watched, upon the mound there came forth two slender shoots; and silence was all over the world in that hour.[123]

Note the reverence displayed by the gathering of the mighty Valar for the emergence of 'two slender shoots' from a 'green mound'. The 'birth' of these 'saplings' is held to be a holy and 'hallowed' event (despite the absence of Ilúvatar). Tolkien tells us also that the trees 'awoke in the world', and as such represent the waking force of nature in all Middle-earth – a waking force we later see reflected in Fangorn Forest, Old Man Willow, Treebeard and Lothlórien.

The Two Trees, however, are no ordinary trees – a light radiated from within them and we are told 'about their fate all the tales of the Elder days are woven.'[124] Indeed even after the Trees have been destroyed by Morgoth

---

121 Tolkien, *Silmarillion*, pp.27-28.
122 Nienna of all the Valar is the one who mourns for those taken by the Shadow of Morgoth. Her tears have restorative and healing powers and can instil hope and courage to those in need.
123 Tolkien, *Silmarillion*, p.38.
124 Tolkien, *Silmarillion*, p.38.

and the great spider Ungoliant who 'sucked up all light that she could find, and spun it forth again in dark nets of strangling gloom',[125] the light of the Trees endured in the Silmarils – the three jewels fashioned by Fëanor. The last surviving of these jewels became the Evening Star, guiding light of Eärendil – a symbol of undying hope in Middle-earth. The light of the Two Trees also shone in the Phial of Galadriel, given to Frodo during the War of the Ring by the elven-queen herself. It is noteworthy that Sam used the light from this phial to blind Shelob 'the last child of Ungoliant to trouble the unhappy world'[126] thus saving not only Frodo's life but also the quest to destroy the One Ring.

All through Tolkien's tales of Middle-earth the ancient and abiding spirit-light of the Two Trees of Valinor appear representative of the benevolent and sustaining power of nature itself. Indeed Dickerson and Evans refer to the Two Trees as 'powerful images of nature' which are 'closely associated with all life.'[127] Of course as well as being 'images of nature' these Trees are also characterised by their sacred 'birth' and the sense of spirituality that seems such an inherent part of their make-up. 'Arguably' conclude Dickerson and Evans 'the Two Trees are the most mythically significant symbols in all of Tolkien's writings about Middle-earth.'[128]

Throughout Tolkien's mythopoetic account of Creation, the interrelationship between theology (Ilúvatar and the Valar) and the natural wonders of the Earth (Arda) seems to take centre stage. And, as a writer and creator of a fictional universe, Tolkien appears to characterise the relationship of God, nature and the Earth thus:

1. God is distant from the Earth but remains 'the One', the Creator from whom all other creations emanate.
2. The wonders of the natural world are fashioned, sustained, and propelled by the 'sub-creative' powers of spiritual energies (the Valar), largely independent of God (although it is only by way of divine will that this 'sub-creation' may occur).

---

125 Tolkien, *Silmarillion*, p.73.
126 Tolkien, *Two Towers*, p.707.
127 Dickerson & Evans, *Ents, Elves, and Eriador*, p.11.
128 Dickerson & Evans, *Ents, Elves, and Eriador*, p.7.

3. Spiritual energy may be malevolent as well as benign and all of creation (in the absence of God) is threatened by it.[129]

These three primary principles could be said to shape the entire structural framework of *The Silmarillion*. And the struggle for supremacy between good and evil is presented, in the main, as a battle for the Earth itself.

Indeed Middle-earth would surely have to be portrayed as an 'Edenesque' place of perfect wonder (where all things lived together in flawless harmony), if sustained and fashioned only by benevolent angelic energy. But, as Tolkien once wrote 'there cannot be any 'story' without a fall – all stories are ultimately about the fall'[130] and Middle-earth, echoing but not re-creating the Christian view of our Earth, is depicted as a world stalked by sin, a world in which the choices of free will can save or condemn, a world that is, as Tolkien says, 'concerned with Fall, Mortality and the Machine.'[131]

Morgoth, present 'from the first', is the embodiment of sin in Tolkien's mythology. He pours his discordant energy into the 'harmony' of the Earth: 'meddling',[132] disrupting and twisting all that is fashioned in the name of 'the One'. The ever-present shadow of Morgoth, who says to the other Ainur '[Earth] shall be my own kingdom; and I name it unto myself' hangs over all creation. He pollutes

---

129 Although Ilúvatar could be said to be 'distant' from the creation (and subsequent unfolding) of the World in a manner in which the Valar are not, we should note that Ilúvatar (aside from being the source from which all creation springs) does, on occasion, directly and profoundly shape events. Of course we have the prime example of how he brings forth 'the Children of Ilúvatar': elves and men to first people the World. Also he admonishes Aulë for creating dwarves before elves and men have arisen on the Earth. Rather than remove dwarves from existence, however, he is merciful and causes them to 'sleep [...] in the darkness under stone' (Tolkien, *Silmarillion*, p.44) only to later awaken them and take them as among his own Children. Ilúvatar also plays a prime role in the drowning of the island kingdom of Númenor. We are told in the Akallabêth that he is called by Manwë, as the Valar set aside 'their government of Arda', and that 'he changed the fashion of the world' opening 'a great chasm [...] in the sea' (Tolkien, *Silmarillion*, p.278) into which the Númenórean kingdom was lost. Indeed, although all of these events take place before the Third Age, as the narrative of the War of the Ring plays out, there is a suggestion that some manner of divine providence is orchestrating or at least influencing certain aspects of unfolding events. We hear Gandalf (speaking to Frodo of the providential passing of the One Ring into the hands of Bilbo then Frodo himself) declare: 'There was more than one power at work'; he then underlines 'there was something else at work [...] Bilbo was meant to find the ring and not by its maker. In which case you also were meant to have it', to which Gandalf adds, hinting that a force for good (or Ilúvatar) may be behind such providence, '[a]nd that may be an encouraging thought' (Tolkien, *Fellowship*, pp.54-55). There are many other instances in *The Lord of the Rings* which hint that a great power is binding the threads of story together and all seem to point to an all-knowing, beneficent force.
130 Tolkien, *Letters*, p.147.
131 Tolkien, *Letters*, p.145.
132 Tolkien, *Silmarillion*, pp.20-21.

and opposes the work of the Valar; his envious power-lust, his indifference to nature, his corrupting malignancy seeps into the very fabric of the Earth and calls to all who are possessed of free will to join with him. In his depiction of Morgoth and those such as Ungoliant, Sauron and Saruman who also devastate the natural wonder of Middle-earth in their unyielding pursuit of power and mastery, Tolkien sets up a framework for humanity's moral choices in which the struggle between good and evil is indissolubly connected to the struggle to sustain the wonders of the natural world – this is the coming together of theology and ecology in a profound sense. The path, which leads from this understanding of the relationship between God and nature, delivers us to a perception of environmental ethics, which is driven by an explicit moral imperative.

The Valar, architects of the natural world, are evident in the splendour of their work: 'the Valar walked on Earth as powers visible, clad in the raiment of the World, and were lovely and glorious to see.'[133] The implication of Morgoth's opposition to the Valar is that he is evident in creations which are unnatural and which are characterised by an absence of an environmental conscience. We are told that he 'often walked abroad, in many shapes of power and fear.'[134] We recall Tolkien's words that the world of Middle-earth is 'concerned with Fall, Mortality and the *Machine*' (emphasis added), and one cannot help but envisage Morgoth's 'shapes of power and fear' as being representative of the ecologically unsound technology of our world or the industries that threaten to twist, ravage and meddle with the natural world in the pursuit of yet more power. Indeed Tolkien is unequivocal in connecting the devastation of the environment of Middle-earth to the activities of the malevolent will of Morgoth. The narrator of *The Silmarillion* tells us: 'Green things fell sick and rotted, and rivers were choked with weeds and slime, and fens were made, rank and poisonous [...] Then the Valar knew indeed that Morgoth was at work again.'[135]

Even in the 2007 released *The Children of Húrin* (a tale constructed under the editorial of Tolkien's son Christopher from a gathering of his father's writings on the First Age), one of the Valar, Ulmo (Lord of Waters) speaking of Morgoth's assault on the ecology of Middle-earth says, 'The Evil of the North has defiled

---

133 Tolkien, *Silmarillion*, pp.27-28.
134 Tolkien, *Silmarillion*, p.31.
135 Tolkien, *Silmarillion*, p.36.

the springs of Sirion, and my power withdraws from the fingers of the flowing waters.'[136] Ulmo seems to be warning that Morgoth's 'shapes of power' have the capacity to 'defile' or pollute the natural world to such an extent that the spiritual energy that sustains it is forced to withdraw. The ecological augury for our own times here is patent: it is our choice to either oppose such ecologically destructive manifestations of power or risk our canopy of natural wonder.

(VII) Closing Thoughts: Advance of the Machine

Morgoth is presented as the embodiment of harmful technologies and machines in the First Age. Those such as Sauron and Saruman who follow his path in the Third Age are likewise portrayed as machine-wielding technocrats, and each is presented unfailingly as being the enemies of nature as revealed in the desolate landscapes they inhabit and bring about.

The natural energy that sustains the landscapes of places such as Rivendell and Lothlórien is also under threat as the enemy and the machine advance together. Arguably, however, the most vivid (and contemporary) portrayal of environmental devastation in any of Tolkien's works comes in the penultimate chapter of *The Lord of the Rings*, 'The Scouring of the Shire'. The positioning of this episode in Tolkien's narrative leaves the reader with a powerful reiteration of some of the themes that have driven the work. Or as James Davis puts it: 'Tolkien apparently wanted to end *The Lord of the Rings* with his strongest depiction yet of the evils of modernity [...] The factory that is using up all the Shire's resources and polluting the stream is the clearest visual image in all of *The Lord of the Rings* of a modern industrial edifice.'[137]

Tolkien's creation myth, echoing his own deep embrace of nature, offers a framework for his secondary world that allows nature to be illuminated by a spiritual light. There is no overriding emphasis on Christianity or pre-Christian religion in Middle-earth and the Undying Lands – though these and other theologies come into view – rather the world (and nature) is offered as the domain of angels. These angels, pertaining to no specific doctrine, create, sustain and

---

136 J.R.R. Tolkien, *The Children of Húrin*, edited by Christopher Tolkien, London: HarperCollins, 2007, p.173.
137 Davis, 'Showing Saruman as Faber', p.58.

immerse themselves in nature. They are both absent and discernable in the waking world of the Third Age. As the agents of the machine bring chaos and destruction to the lands, Tolkien offers us a world in which nature, and thus the power of angels is under siege, binding theological and ecological themes in one mythic sweep.

There is no doubt that Tolkien's fiction reflects, to some degree at least, his worry that the modern world was too easily falling 'under the spell' of the machine, and that a gradual increase in the systematic destruction of natural phenomena would follow. In this he was right. For Tolkien, however, the injudicious machine-wielder and not the machine was the real enemy of nature and humanity. Yet this was always tempered by an underlying unease that machines or 'Mordor-gadgets'[138] had the potential, like the One Ring, to eventually devour and bring about the downfall of the machine-makers and wielders – and all of creation besides. I close this chapter by offering the philosophical words of Paul B. Sears, historically one of the world's most pre-eminent and enduring environmental champions, who in *Where There is Life* seems to recall passages in both 'On Fairy-stories' in which Tolkien railed against 'mass-production robot factories',[139] and his remark that the dangerous potential of the machine was a truth, as Tolkien states, 'glimpsed long ago by Sam Butler':[140]

> That truly beautiful mechanism, the automobile, now engages a substantial part of our labour force in its production and serving its various needs. Whether or not it is made to last, fashion dictates that we must be ready to discard it as a child does a plastic toy. In use, it alternates between clogging the lines of transport and acting as a deadly missile. Who is master, man or machine? Was Samuel Butler prescient in suggesting how easily man might become the slave of his own creations.[141]

In the two chapters that follow I offer a comparative analysis of some of Tolkien's most memorable and, from an environmental perspective, important characters. Focusing on his major work, I offer that there are clearly discernable cultures of opposition represented not only in the battle lines drawn up between the agents of evil and those who resist but also, and perhaps more vitally, in his individual character portrayals. We recall that Tolkien, speaking of the ambi-

---

138 Tolkien, *Letters*, p.88.
139 Tolkien, *Tolkien Reader*, pp.80-81.
140 Tolkien, *Letters*, p.88.
141 Paul B. Sears, *Where There Is Life*, New York: Dell Publishing, 1972, p.182.

ence of war and turmoil that seemed to mark the passing years of the Third Age of Middle-earth, declared that this sense of menace was 'mainly 'a setting' for characters to show themselves.'[142]

---

142 Tolkien, *Letters*, p.246.

Chapter Two

Contrasting Environmental Personas in *The Lord of the Rings*: Tom Bombadil and Saruman

Aspects of Tolkien's fiction which present pastoral landscapes threatened by mechanised and industrialised powers or struggles between conflicting power bases are for the most part played out against the huge vista and history of Middle-earth: great forces are mobilised, counterforces resist and somewhere in the struggle we see our own reality reflected. Below the panoramic sweep of such epic battles Tolkien allows similar force and counterforce to exist in the presentation of his individual characters. In terms of the portrayal of the struggle between the ecologically sustained landscapes of Middle-earth and the mechanised powers which threaten them, I believe Tolkien, in *The Lord of the Rings*, creates cultures of opposition in his character portrayals which mirror this struggle for the land itself. Of these perhaps the most striking contrasting portrayal is the opposition set up between Tom Bombadil and Saruman, White Wizard of Isengard. In the chapter that follows I intend to offer that Bombadil and Saruman may most vitally be understood in terms of how they represent positive and negative environmental models and moreover how these representations may be viewed as inverted mirror reflections of each other.

(I.1) The Enduring Enigma of Tom Bombadil

There is a general consensus among Tolkien commentators, even those very firmly in the pro-Tolkien camp, that Tom Bombadil is a somewhat incongruous element in *The Lord of the Rings*: an anomaly who, as Dickerson and Evans suggest, 'exists, in a sense, apart from or alongside the mainstream of the narrative.'[1] Thomas J. Gasque refers to the character of Tom Bombadil

---

1 Matthew Dickerson & Jonathan Evans, *Ents, Elves, and Eriador: The Environmental Vision of J.R.R. Tolkien*, Lexington, Kentucky: University Press of Kentucky, 2006, p.18.

simply as 'a technical failure'.² Indeed there is no doubt that Tom is a curious character who seems almost to stumble across the central plot of *The Lord of the Rings* for a time and then disappear from the 'stage'. However in terms of plot we should note that Tom does in fact save the lives of the four hobbits (Frodo, Sam, Pippin and Merry) on two occasions – once from Old Man Willow in the Old Forest and once from the Barrow-wights. He thus averts disaster for the 'Ringbearer' and company (and by extension Middle-earth itself) before their quest has even properly begun. And yet, in both early and modern adaptations of the book, Tom Bombadil has been (in many cases) the first cut: the unnecessary 'digression' in the story that may be easily cast aside.³ Indeed the majority of adaptations choose to sidestep the Bombadil sections and move the action (after Frodo, Sam, Merry and Pippin's early encounter with the Black Riders) speedily along to Bree. This is true of the two arguably most notable adaptations to date: Ralph Bakshi's (unfinished) animated version and Peter Jackson's phenomenally successful film version.⁴

Jackson, defending his decision to cut Tom, asks, 'what does Tom Bombadil ultimately really have to do with the Ring? I know there's Ring stuff in the Bombadil episode, but it's not really advancing our story.'⁵ This has been the recurrent bugbear of critics and scriptwriters alike when dealing with Bombadil. What does he contribute to the plot? What function does he serve? And, of course, who or what is he? Indeed the whole question of Tom Bombadil's role and function in *The Lord of the Rings* is integrally bound up with who or what he is – a riddle that has fascinated and engaged Tolkien critics for as long as his works have been in print.

---

2 Thomas J. Gasque, 'Tolkien: The Monsters and the Critters' in Neil D. Isaacs & Rose A. Zimbardo (eds.), *Tolkien and the Critics: Essays on J.R.R. Tolkien's The Lord of the Rings*, London and Notre Dame: University of Notre Dame Press, 1968, p.154.
3 Even when Tom Bombadil was left in, as was the case with Morton Grady Zimmerman's proposed first film adaptation, the sections involving Tom and Goldberry proved to be particularly fraught with difficulty. Indeed Tolkien believed Zimmerman's handling of the Bombadil passages to be wholly unrepresentative of his book and a prime example of how Zimmerman had, in Tolkien's words, 'lower[ed] the tone towards that of a more childish fairy-tale' (J.R.R. Tolkien, *The Letters of J.R.R. Tolkien*, edited by Humphrey Carpenter, London: HarperCollins, 2006, p.272).
4 Another very notable adaptation was the BBC's second attempt at dramatising *The Lord of the Rings* for radio in 1980. The remit for production was to closely follow Tolkien's original narrative, but although a valiant attempt was made to stay faithful to the book, the Bombadil passages were nonetheless bypassed.
5 Peter Jackson, 'Appendices Part 1: From Book to Script' in *The Lord of the Rings: The Fellowship of the Ring*, Dir. Peter Jackson, DVD Extended Version: New Line Cinema, 2002.

Many theories have arisen regarding Tom's origins and place in Tolkien's cosmology (some of which I will discuss in greater detail later). Tom has by turn been unmasked as one of the Istari, a Maia, a Vala or even as Ilúvatar (God in Tolkien's *legendarium*) and much more besides. Although, as we shall see, Tolkien was at times somewhat vague in his remarks relating to Tom, we recall that he did once famously and unequivocally comment that Tom Bombadil was 'the spirit of the (vanishing) Oxford and Berkshire countryside',[6] and in keeping with this understanding of Bombadil, the majority of Tolkien critics have concluded, in more general terms, that he is a manifestation of nature or a nature spirit of some kind. Edmund Fuller describes Tom as 'an individual figure, unclassifiable other than as some primal nature spirit.'[7] Ruth S. Noel places Tom's character in a category akin to Shakespeare's Puck, and the Greek god Pan, referring to him as 'a nature god in diminished form.'[8] Dickerson and Evans suggest that 'he may be the most explicit, concrete embodiment of the natural world – an incarnation, we might say, of environment itself.'[9] Both Tom Shippey and Patrick Curry refer to him as being 'a *genius loci*'[10] or the pervading spirit of the lands he inhabits. Shippey goes on to offer that Tom is derived 'from the land', and not just from the mythical or fictional lands of Middle-earth but, as Shippey points out, from 'the river and willow of the English midlands.'[11] Moreover, Shippey reminds us that Tolkien most likely constructed the landscape and characters of Tom's habitat, even the Barrow-wights, from lands he knew well: 'fifteen miles from Oxford begins the greatest concentration of barrows[12] in the country, where the green Berkshire downs rise from the plain.'[13] Indeed in a letter to Forrest J. Ackerman, 'would be' producer of Morton Grady Zimmerman's early planned film adaptation of *The Lord of the Rings*, Tolkien insists that Bombadil, contrary to Zimmerman's

---

6 Tolkien, *Letters*, p.26.
7 Edmund Fuller, 'The Lord of the Hobbits: J.R.R. Tolkien' in Rose A. Zimbardo & Neil D. Isaacs (eds.), *Understanding The Lord of the Rings: The Best of Tolkien Criticism*, Boston and New York: Houghton Mifflin, 2004, p.18.
8 Ruth S. Noel, *The Mythology of Middle-earth*, Boston and New York: Houghton Mifflin, 1977, p.127.
9 Dickerson & Evans, *Ents, Elves, and Eriador*, p.18.
10 Tom Shippey, *The Road to Middle-Earth*, London: HarperCollins, 2005, p.123 and Patrick Curry, *Defending Middle-earth. Tolkien: Myth and Modernity*, London: HarperCollins, 1997, p.76.
11 Shippey, *Road*, p.123.
12 A barrow or tumulus is, in general terms, a burial mound – a heap of earth or mound of stones marking a prehistoric tomb. Tolkien's creation of the Barrow-wights would certainly have drawn on old tales that warned of malevolent ghosts stalking such tombs.
13 Shippey, *Road*, pp.123-24.

portrayal, 'is not the owner of the woods' and that the wild country surrounding Bombadil's house should exude an evocation of the real world: 'We are not in 'fairy-land', but in real river lands in autumn.' Tolkien goes on in the letter to say that Goldberry, 'daughter of the river' and the female aspect of Tom's embodiment of nature, 'represents the actual seasonal changes in such lands.'[14] When we read Tolkien's description of Goldberry, we can see to what extent she (like Tom) is a spirit of nature and derived 'from the land':

> Her long yellow hair rippled down her shoulders; and her gown was green, green as young reeds, shot with silver like beads of dew; and her belt was of gold, shaped like a chain of flag-lilies set with the pale-blue eyes of forget-me-nots. About her feet in wide vessels of green and brown earthenware, white water-lilies were floating, so that she seemed to be enthroned in the midst of a pool.[15]

I am concerned in this chapter to emphasise how certain Tolkien characters, rather than settings, may be read as being representative of positive or negative environmental models. And there is no question that, distilled purely from his portrayal as a character (as opposed to the wider significance of what he may embody or represent), Tom Bombadil's harmonious relationship and kinship with the natural world around him, his understanding of the existence of things other than himself (either good or ill) casts him as a model of ecological ethics and environmental harmony. Indeed as Tom speaks to the hobbits (whose lives he has saved) about the lands and living things around him, his voice becomes melody as if reflecting the harmony of nature itself:

> Often his voice would turn to song, and he would get out of his chair and dance about. He told them tales of bees and flowers, the ways of trees, and the strange creatures of the Forest, about the evil things and good things, things friendly and unfriendly, cruel things and kind things, and secrets hidden under the brambles.
> As they listened, they began to understand the lives of the Forest, apart from themselves, indeed to feel themselves as the strangers where all other things were at home.[16]

Just in attending to Tom's words the hobbits begin to take account of other living things, to develop, one might say, their environmental conscience.[17] Yet

---

14 Tolkien, *Letters*, p.272.
15 J.R.R. Tolkien, *The Fellowship of the Ring*, London: HarperCollins, 1997, p.121.
16 Tolkien, *Fellowship*, p.127.
17 Despite the general view that hobbits live in perfect harmony with the natural world around them, there is evidence to suggest that hobbits are quick to become aggressors against the land in order to pursue their own ends – and have, no doubt in Tom's view, much to learn in terms of what we would

Tom offers no idealised portrayal of nature – the 'evil', 'unfriendly' and 'cruel things' he sings of do not exclusively refer to dark lords or orcs, but also to the harsh reality of nature as it is – '[n]ature, red in tooth and claw'[18] as Tennyson once proverbially put it.

As Tom continues to speak and sing he offers the hobbits the perspective of ancient things – the deeper and wider view of the old trees and the green hills. Speaking of the history of the Barrow-wights, Tom alludes to the transient nature of empires and he diminishes the importance of the rising and falling fortunes of war: 'Kings of little kingdoms fought together, and the young Sun shone like fire on the red metal of their new and greedy swords. There was victory and defeat; and towers fell […] but soon the hills were empty again.'[19] Tom here is taking account of a different time scale: not that of hobbits or men, but that of an ancient, elemental life-force: the forest, the land and the earth. The implication is that nature itself is possessed of a waking consciousness and Tom gives it its voice. Andrew Light in his essay 'Tolkien's Green Time' makes a similar point:

> Tom Bombadil and other primordial inhabitants of Middle-earth either implicitly or explicitly acknowledge a different time scale than the other peoples and characters in the story […] it is a time scale more attuned to the rhythms of the natural world.[20]

Indeed Tom's melodious speech takes the hobbits 'beyond their memory' and leaves them 'enchanted; and it seemed as if under the spell of his words.' Bombadil's voice has power – great power; his words have resonance and his songs carry authority and authenticity. The power inherent in Tom's voice is evident from the first moment we meet him: he begins to free the hobbits from Old Man Willow by a simple declaration to the great tree: 'Eat earth! Dig deep! Drink water! Go to Sleep! Bombadil is talking!' It is apparent also from the warning he issues that his voice contains the power to stir the elements,

---

now call their environmentalism. See chapter five and the Afterword section of this book for a more detailed discussion of hobbits and their environmental ethics.
18 Alfred Tennyson, 'In Memoriam' in *Selected Poems: Tennyson*, edited by Christopher Ricks, London: Penguin, 2007, p.135.
19 Tolkien, *Fellowship*, p.128.
20 Andrew Light, 'Tolkien's Green Time: Environmental Themes in *The Lord of the Rings*' in Gregory Bassham & Eric Bronson (eds.), *The Lord of the Rings and Philosophy: One Book to Rule Them All*, Chicago and La Salle, Illinois: Open Court Publishing, 2003, p.151.

'I know the tune for him. Old grey Willow-man! I'll freeze his marrow cold, if he don't behave himself. I'll sing his roots off. I'll sing a wind up and blow leaf and branch away.'[21] The force of nature itself lies in the melodious tones of Tom's voice, an allusion which echoes the power inherent in the Ainur, who (as Tolkien describes in *The Silmarillion*) create the Earth and Middle-earth (Arda) through the harmony of music. Indeed we recall that Ilúvatar reveals Arda to the Ainur and declares 'Behold your Music! This is your minstrelsy.'[22]

Despite Tom's obvious charm and potency as a character, Tolkien was very much aware that he did not sit as easily as other characters in the unfolding plot of *The Lord of the Rings*. As early as 1954 Tolkien writes, 'many have found him an odd or indeed discordant ingredient.'[23] But as Michael Treschow and Mark Duckworth point out in their essay 'Bombadil's Role in *The Lord of the Rings*', '[i]f we look for Bombadil to serve the story's plot we have missed the point.'[24] Although acknowledging Tom as 'a nature spirit' and a force for moral good, Treschow and Duckworth suggest that Tom's primary purpose in the work is that he is (like Beorn in *The Hobbit*) 'an adventure on the way'; a sidetracking of the main narrative in which the naïve and (up to this point in the tale) largely bungling hobbits are awakened to the real dangers which lie on the path before them.[25] In this sense, according to Treschow and Duckworth, the Bombadil episode acts as a kind of gateway through which the hobbits must pass: they are saved by Bombadil from the dangers to which they are exposed, but nonetheless they are exposed to them, and thus they become hardier, more resilient and more aware of what they must face as a result.

Although Tolkien would certainly agree with this account of Bombadil's role: 'I put [Tom Bombadil] in because I had already 'invented' him independently (he first appeared in the Oxford magazine) and wanted an 'adventure' on the way', Tolkien also is at pains to point out that Tom survives his ruthless editorial

---

21 Tolkien, *Fellowship*, p.117.
22 J.R.R. Tolkien, *The Silmarillion*, edited by Christopher Tolkien, London: Allen & Unwin, 1977, p.17.
23 Tolkien, *Letters*, p.192.
24 Michael Treschow & Mark Duckworth, 'Bombadil's Role in *The Lord of the Rings*', *Mythlore* 25:1-2 [95-96] (Fall/Winter 2006), p.180.
25 Of course, contrary to Treschow and Duckworth, one could argue that Bombadil, in preparing the hobbits for the harsh realities on the long quest ahead, is actually very much 'serv[ing] the story's plot.'

process for very different reasons. 'But I *kept* him in, and as he was, because he represents certain things otherwise left out'[26] (emphasis added). This seems to me to be a very critical distinction. Tolkien was very aware of narrative techniques such as this idea of 'an adventure on the way' (especially in a quest saga) but he wanted Tom in the book not because of his value to the narrative but because of 'something he represents'. Was Tolkien simply referring to the evocation of nature made animate in Bombadil's character?[27] Perhaps not, because we could easily attribute similar characteristics to Treebeard, whereas Tolkien specifically says that Tom embodies 'things otherwise left out'. In a letter to Naomi Mitchison, original proofreader of the first two volumes of *The Lord of the Rings*, Tolkien tackles the question of Tom's inclusion in the story:

> Tom Bombadil is not an important person – to the narrative. I suppose he has some importance as a 'comment' [...] he represents something that I feel important, though I would not be prepared to analyze the feeling precisely. I would not, however, have left him in, if he did not have some kind of function.[28]

Although unwilling to 'analyze the feeling precisely', Tolkien, in the letter, reveals that it was his objective to shroud Tom in mystery, 'even in a mythical Age there must be some enigmas, as there always are. Tom Bombadil is one (intentionally).'[29] Speaking specifically about Tom's character traits, Tolkien goes on to throw a little light on his literary worth and function, and so effectively begins to answer the question of what Bombadil's presence in *The Lord of the Rings* might represent:

> The story is cast in terms of a good side, and a bad side, beauty against ruthless ugliness, tyranny against kingship, moderated freedom with consent against compulsion that has long lost any object save mere power, and so on; but both sides in some degree, conservative or destructive, want a measure of control. But if you have, as it were taken 'a vow of poverty', renounced control, and take delight in things for themselves without reference to yourself, watching, observing, and to some extent knowing, then the question of the rights and wrongs of power and control might become utterly meaningless to you, and the means of power quite valueless. It is a natural pacifist view.[30]

---

26 Tolkien, *Letters*, p.192.
27 Tolkien declares that Bombadil appears in *The Lord of the Rings* 'as he was'. This suggests that the character of Tom Bombadil remained unchanged from that which appeared in the poem 'The Adventures of Tom Bombadil' years before.
28 Tolkien, *Letters*, p.178.
29 Tolkien, *Letters*, p.178.
30 Tolkien, *Letters*, pp.178-79.

Despite the obvious power and ability Tom possesses to control the world about him, he has no wish to rule, exploit or master. Although, as we have seen, his voice has emphatic and conspicuous influence over nature itself, Tom has nevertheless 'renounced control', relinquished his command and he seeks no advantage over other things. He has, in Tolkien's words, submitted to 'a vow of poverty' – the 'poverty' of discarded power. He takes 'delight in things for themselves', he places value not on power but on understanding – he is 'a natural pacifist' and as such is, as Tolkien says:

> an 'allegory', or an exemplar, a particular embodying of pure (real) science: the spirit that desires knowledge of other things, their history and nature, because they are 'other', and wholly independent of the enquiring mind, a spirit coeval with the rational mind, and entirely unconcerned with 'doing' anything with the knowledge.[31]

In this sense Bombadil, in part, represents the harmony of nature itself – the spirit of humanity as it was meant to be: in complicit union with the natural world,[32] seeking understanding without control. Indeed his refusal to exploit or rule the world about him casts him as 'an exemplar' of environmental ethics. Perhaps more than any other character in Tolkien's fiction, Tom Bombadil is an ideal – a 'pacifist' expression of environmental harmony.

In a drama in which all other characters to one degree or another concern themselves with the ability to control their own destiny, Tom's indifference towards the struggle for power and control of Middle-earth, his refusal to harness the might at his command and his willingness to take 'others' as they are, is found nowhere else in *The Lord of the Rings*. And whilst at first this would appear to diminish Tom's strength as a character, it is precisely in his renunciation of power that Tom manages to effectively oppose what the others cannot. Let us consider the passage in which Tom encounters the One Ring:

> Tom put the Ring around the end of his little finger and held it up to the candle-light. For a moment the hobbits noticed nothing strange about this. Then they gasped. There was no sign of Tom disappearing!

---

31 Tolkien, *Letters*, p.192.
32 We recall that listening to Tom speak of the natural world, Frodo, Sam, Pippin and Merry 'began to understand the lives of the Forest, apart from themselves […] to feel themselves as the strangers where all other things were at home' and in a sense the hobbits' view of themselves as 'strangers', set against Tom's evident harmony and union with nature represents, what Tolkien would have viewed as, humanity's gradual disconnection with nature in our world. Tom enlivens the hobbits' senses to the living force of nature but ultimately only they can release their desire to control or master it, and thus reconnect with it.

> Tom laughed again, and then he spun the Ring in the air – and it vanished with a flash. Frodo gave a cry – and Tom leaned forward and handed it back with a smile.[33]

Given what we come to know of the Ring, in terms of how it is portrayed in the story, this incident is hugely significant: Bombadil cares nothing for it, yet the Ring wields a seductive influence powerful enough to corrupt the mighty Maiar (Saruman is utterly corrupted by the Ring and Gandalf fears to use it). The wise and powerful among the elves such as Elrond and Galadriel know also that catastrophe awaits anyone who becomes ensnared by the Ring's allure. We are shown too how the hobbits (who show a remarkable ability to resist or at least hold off the effects of the Ring) eventually fall foul of its destructive power. The definitive example of this is the transformation of Smeagol (once a creature much like Frodo or Sam) into the snivelling, broken, craven half-life that is Gollum.

Indeed Tolkien devotes a lot of *The Fellowship of the Ring* to emphasising just how potent and dangerous the One Ring is to all who encounter it – yet he allows Tom to 'toy' with this perilous and treacherous object and remain unaffected or unimpressed by it. Given Tolkien's painstaking attention to detail, this decision to undermine the power of the Ring so early in the trilogy is curious – one might even say reckless. Indeed Treschow and Duckworth believe that with the inclusion of this scene, the entire credibility of Tolkien's tale is at stake: '[this] is a dangerous moment for Tolkien's story. It veers suddenly close to smashing into a wreck on Tom's unassailable virtue. The whole rationale of the quest is poised to overbalance and fall down at this moment. For Bombadil is greater than the Ring.'[34]

Of course Tolkien would have been acutely aware of the dangers of undermining the Ring in Tom's hands so early in the tale – that he decided to keep these passages intact, therefore, reveals how much importance he placed on keeping Tom (and what he represents) in the story.[35] And it turns out that a clear un-

---

33 Tolkien, *Fellowship*, p.130.
34 Treschow & Duckworth, 'Bombadil's Role in *The Lord of the Rings*', p.185.
35 In a letter to his publisher Stanley Unwin responding to Unwin's request for a follow up to *The Hobbit* Tolkien writes '[d]o you think Tom Bombadil […] could be made into the hero of a story?' (Tolkien, *Letters*, p.26). This perhaps is an indication as to how much importance and credibility Tolkien placed on Tom Bombadil as a character.

derstanding of what Tom symbolises reveals that the Ring's power has not been diminished, nor is Tom, as Treschow and Duckworth suggest, 'greater than the Ring' but rather as Gandalf explains at the Council of Elrond, 'the Ring has no power over him.'[36] For as a result of Tom's 'vow of poverty' and his renunciation of control, the Ring holds no appeal for him, he can oppose its addictive pull and it is thus powerless in his hands. In a sense this is a coming together of two wills: one that seeks domination and control and one that sets the desire for ascendancy and dominion aside in the pursuit of understanding.

More than anything else the Ring is suggestive and emblematic of a will to power. Many of the themes revealed in Tolkien's depiction of the Ring's controlling and destructive nature, and his recalling of its blood-soaked and perfidious past, are themes mirrored in the central threads which weave through the heart of the book: power-lust, tyranny, domination, corruption, exploitation, addiction, and more often than not these 'themes of vice' are played out at the expense of the environmental well-being of the landscapes of Middle-earth, and they are tied to Tolkien's understanding of evil.

Moreover, in placing the One Ring at the centre of his story, in fashioning his epic tale around it and the struggle by all to either destroy it, harness it, resist it or find it, Tolkien, whether he wished to or not, has created a single symbol for all of these themes and motifs – and more besides. In effect the One Ring becomes a gauge: an object which when dealt with, considered or handled by a given character, betrays that character's true nature and his or her susceptibility to the seduction of power (either corrupt or well-meaning). When considered from this point of view Tom's dismissal of the Ring, his obvious control over it and the fact that it has utterly no control over him (even to the point that it doesn't make him disappear) is testimony to Tom's incorruptibility, his 'unassailable virtue' and perhaps more vitally (when considering the environmental significance of his character) his lack of desire to command, control or conquer anything in Middle-earth from the smallest plant to the deadliest beast.[37] Tom

---

36 Tolkien, *Fellowship*, p.259.
37 In a sense Tom's willingness to relinquish control, to take everything from harmless plants to deadly beasts as they are, and to seek no transformation in the natural order is an antidote to imperialist and colonial ideals which seek to impose one set of beliefs upon another, and which often identify and classify less advanced civilizations (in the opinion of the colonisers) as savages or 'beasts' – whereupon moves are made to change, 'civilise' or even neutralise them.

can easily resist the One Ring because what it offers him, he simply does not want – to him it is just a trinket.

(I.2) Bombadil under Threat

In considering Tom Bombadil's significance as an environmental model I share Shippey's understanding that he is, at least in part, representative of real pastoral lands that Tolkien knew well (and his sentiment that such lands should not be exploited or controlled but valued as they are). I see it as crucial to note, however, that Tolkien did not merely state that Bombadil was 'the spirit of the [...] Oxford and Berkshire countryside' but rather 'the spirit of the (vanishing) Oxford and Berkshire countryside.'[38] The inclusion of the word 'vanishing' in Tolkien's statement, regardless of his cautionary parenthesis, transforms Tom Bombadil, in my mind at least, from some generalised nature spirit (as many have defined him) into something else entirely: a manifestation of nature under threat.

Indeed there are many instances in *The Lord of the Rings* where the mention of Tom Bombadil and the lands he inhabits is coloured by a sense of impending peril. When Frodo puts on the Ring for example to convince himself it is indeed the One Ring (in the wake of Tom's playful dismissal of it), Tom, because the power of the Ring has no influence over him, can see Frodo – and as Frodo moves towards the door Tom shouts after him, 'Hey! Come Frodo, there! Where be you a-going? Old Tom Bombadil's not as blind as that yet.'[39] The textual inclusion of the word 'yet' (although this could be read as a frivolous comment) suggests that Tom is alluding to the notion that sometime in the future he may not be able to resist the dark forces symbolised by the Ring's power.

Of course, we are told also that the Old Forest itself is merely 'a survivor of vast forgotten woods'[40] and as Frodo and company travel through the Forest and Tom's lands (before becoming ensnared by Old Man Willow) we hear Frodo sing (as much in bravado in the midst of a hostile atmosphere as anything else):

---

38 Tolkien, *Letters*, p.26.
39 Tolkien, *Fellowship*, p.131.
40 Tolkien, *Fellowship*, p.127.

> *all woods there be must end at last,*
> *and see the open sun go past:*
> *the setting sun, the rising sun,*
> *the day's end, or the day begun.*
> *For east and west all woods must fail…*[41]

The forewarning embedded in Frodo's song that, in time, 'east and west all woods must fail' indicates that the woods are, at the time of the story, in retreat and very much under threat on all sides.[42]

This theme is further recalled and revisited in the descriptions of the vista surrounding Tom's home: the main room in Tom's house is described as having windows at each end: 'one looking east and the other looking west.' On the first morning when the hobbits (now saved from Old Man Willow) awake in Tom's house 'Frodo [runs] to the eastern window' and as he gazes out we are told of his view, '[i]t was a pale morning: in the East, behind long clouds like lines of soiled wool stained red at the edges, lay glimmering deeps of yellow. The sky spoke of rain to come.' Pippin at the same time looks out of the west window and of his view we are informed, 'the Forest was hidden under a fog' and 'the stream ran down the hill [...] and vanished into the white shadows.'[43] Taken together these views, echoing the east/west motif of Frodo's song, suggest that Tom's land is under threat: 'clouds' which are 'stained red' holding 'rain to come', 'the Forest [...] hidden under a fog', and streams which vanish into 'white shadows' (despite the possible scientific accuracy of such observations) are surely ill-omens of a detrimental force which is gathering beyond Tom's borders.

Furthermore despite the portrait of Tom as a happy-go-lucky character who seems indifferent to the crisis that threatens the free peoples of Middle-earth, Gandalf tells us in Rivendell, 'he is withdrawn into a little land, within boundaries he has set, though none can see them, waiting perhaps for a change of days.'[44] The idea that a character who at some level represents such carefree natural energy should withdraw and set up protective borders whilst awaiting 'change' is surely representative of a retreating and diminishing force under threat. Indeed this sense that something is at stake, that something is to be lost, is further suggested

---

41 Tolkien, *Fellowship*, p.110.
42 The Shire and the hobbits' sometimes hostile relationship with the Old Forest plays into this sense of threat – but it is the wider regime of the Dark Lord and his assault on nature that represents the more deadly threat.
43 Tolkien, *Fellowship*, p.126.
44 Tolkien, *Fellowship*, p.259.

on the morning the four hobbits leave behind the reassurance and comfort they had experienced in Tom's house. As the hobbits say their farewells, the narrator tells us '[a] deep loneliness and sense of loss was on them. They stood silent, reluctant to make the final parting.'[45]

Of all the various pieces of evidence that Bombadil represents not just nature but nature under threat, the Council of Elrond remains, to my mind, the most compelling. The delegates are debating whether Tom, given his power over the Ring, should be entrusted with the Ring's safekeeping. Gandalf explains that 'if he were given the Ring' he would 'most likely throw it away.'[46] Glorfindel adds that even if Bombadil were to take the Ring he could not defend against the oncoming might of Sauron:

> The Lord of the Rings would learn of its hiding place and would bend all his power towards it. Could that power be defied by Bombadil alone? I think not. I think that in the end, if all else is conquered, Bombadil will fall, Last as he was First; and then Night will come.[47]

The implication is that nature itself as embodied in Bombadil would be the last bastion of resistance when all others have failed, but even *that* natural energy as it appears in the ecologically sustained landscapes of Middle-earth would pass from existence, and the lifelessness and desolation we witness in the tortured landscape of Mordor will come to dominate the entire panorama of Arda (Earth) and thus in the end to Bombadil's lands. The suggestion that Sauron has the power to not only defeat Bombadil, but also to actually purge Middle-earth of the natural forces he represents, casts Bombadil, despite his withdrawal behind borders, as being in just as much danger as the rest of Middle-earth (should Sauron prevail).

To further underscore the premise that the character of Tom Bombadil symbolises nature in retreat we hear Galdor proclaim '[p]ower to defy our Enemy is not in him, unless such power is in the earth itself.'[48] Bombadil's power to resist Sauron (and Saruman) is presented, by inclusion of the word 'unless', as measurable against the ability of the land itself to resist such onslaught. The

---

45 Tolkien, *Fellowship*, p.144.
46 Tolkien, *Fellowship*, p.259.
47 Tolkien, *Fellowship*, p.259.
48 Tolkien, *Fellowship*, p.259.

only hypothesis that fully satisfies this assertion is that, in one sense or another, Bombadil *is* the land or draws his strength from it. Therefore when the land (or nature) is wounded: every time trees and forests diminish and rivers are polluted, Tom loses a little more strength, and if the cycle of devastation continues, finally he 'will fall'.

At the time we meet him in the story it is clear, because he has withdrawn from the wider world, that the natural force Bombadil represents is already in decline. In other words the war against the land, against Middle-earth itself is at an advanced stage. This notion that, should the threat of Sauron and Saruman not be defeated, eventually 'Bombadil will fall' is borne out by Tolkien himself who writes, '[u]ltimately only the victory of the West will allow Bombadil to continue, or even to survive. Nothing would be left for him in the world of Sauron.'[49] Put plainly, just as the landscape surrounding Isengard suffers under Saruman's regime of power and the natural habitats surrounding Mordor have all but perished, so too Tom, hemmed, 'by borders he has set', into his naturally sustained enclave, faces what amounts to death.

Since I have offered that Tom Bombadil represents nature, but more specifically nature under threat, and the discussion of Tom at the Council of Elrond would seem not only to support such a claim, but also to suggest that the peril facing Tom could lead to his death – doesn't the extension of such an understanding mean that Tolkien was implying that (given an extreme set of circumstances) nature can actually die? And isn't that just a little far-fetched? Well, for a new generation of environmentalists, responding to present-day ecological concerns, perhaps not. One such environmentalist is Bill McKibben who in 2006 led the largest ever demonstration and awareness campaign warning of the dangers of (amongst other things) global warming. I had the pleasure of listening to McKibben speak (whilst I attended a conference to give a paper on Tolkien's 'green' credentials) and I was greatly moved by the passion and commitment of the man. In his book *The End of Nature*, McKibben specifically addresses the matter of nature in retreat when set against the progressive march of ecologically unsound human activity:

---

49 Tolkien, *Letters*, p.179.

> An idea, a relationship, can go extinct, just like an animal or a plant. The idea in this case is 'nature,' the separate and wild province, the world apart from man to which he adapted, under whose rules he was born and died. In the past, we spoiled and polluted parts of that nature, inflicted environmental 'damage'. But that was like stabbing a man with toothpicks: though it hurt, annoyed, degraded, it did not touch vital organs, block the path of lymph or blood. We never thought that we had wrecked nature. Deep down, we never really thought we could: it was too big and too old; its forces – the wind, the rain, the sun – were too strong, too elemental. But, quite by accident, it turned out that the carbon dioxide and other gases we were producing in our pursuit of a better life [...] could alter the power of the sun, could increase its heat. And that increase could change the patterns of moisture and dryness, breed storms in new places, breed deserts. [...] We have produced the carbon dioxide – we are ending nature.[50]

McKibben declares unambiguously that nature can 'end': nature as we understand it, as we have experienced it, as we have lived it: 'the wild province' – and although it encapsulates, like Bombadil, great strength, the power of the elements themselves, it seems that it can pass into memory. If this were the case, as McKibben suggests, what would our understanding of nature be replaced with? A distortion of what it once was? A world of deserts? Mordor perhaps? Although of course Tolkien could not have been addressing issues such as global warming, the themes he touches upon nonetheless have resonance with modern environmental theories on how the widespread progressive assault on natural resources can impact nature on a global scale.

(I.3) A Riddle of Sorts

To widen and amplify our understanding of Tom Bombadil's ecological significance in *The Lord of the Rings*, I will draw attention to what appears to be a textual anomaly related to the particular histories of Bombadil and Treebeard. Of course the two characters are similarly constructed and each is presented as (in effect) the (or a) voice of nature in Tolkien's fiction. But when we analyse what is said of their respective backgrounds, we stumble onto a riddle. When responding to Frodo's rather pointed question, 'Who are you, Master?' Bombadil replies:

---

50 Bill McKibben, *The End of Nature*, New York: Random House, 1989, p.41.

> Eldest, that's what I am [...] Tom was here before the river and the trees; Tom remembers the first raindrop and the first acorn. He made paths before the Big People [...] before the seas were bent. He knew the dark under the stars when it was fearless – before the Dark Lord came from Outside.[51]

And, as we have seen, Glorfindel at the Council of Elrond also refers to Bombadil as 'First'. Later in the story, however, Gandalf tells Legolas that Treebeard 'is the oldest living thing that still walks beneath the Sun upon this Middle-earth.'[52] Celeborn much later in the story again refers to Treebeard as simply 'Eldest'.[53] Upon first reflection this appears to be an inconsistency, and it is hard to imagine that characters such as Bombadil, Gandalf or Celeborn would be wrong or have a motive to lie. Did Tolkien then simply fail to notice the contradiction? Or is the apparent irregularity reconcilable?

In point of fact the two claims differ a little: whilst Bombadil claims to be simply 'Eldest', and Celeborn makes an equal claim for Treebeard, Gandalf is more detailed about the ent's origin, stating that he 'is the oldest *living* thing' (emphasis added). Tom Shippey suggests that this could imply that Tom is not alive in a similar way as the Nazgûl or Ringwraiths are undead – but that Bombadil's character exists nonetheless in a category of one.[54] In his essay 'Who is Tom Bombadil?' Gene Hargrove, believing that 'Tom is not a nature spirit', infers that the insinuation offered by Shippey – that Tom may not have life in a biological earthly sense – is suggestive of a possibility that Bombadil is actually a member of the Valar:

> The word 'living' probably means minimally that [Treebeard] is biotic, that is, an element belonging to the living system of the earth, the biosphere. There were in fact two classes of beings 'living' in Middle-earth, who, as beings from outside of Ea, were not part of this system: the Valar and their servants, the Maiar [...] Instead, of placing Tom in an anomalous category of one, or associating him with the undead, Shippey's 'inconsistency' may simply be a hint that Tom has extraterrestrial status as a Vala or Maia.[55]

Hargrove goes on to conclude that Tom is the Vala Aulë citing, amongst other factors, Bombadil's reluctance to seek possession or control over anything: 'since

---

51 Tolkien, *Fellowship*, p.129.
52 J.R.R.Tolkien, *The Two Towers*, London: HarperCollins, 1993, p.488.
53 J.R.R.Tolkien, *The Return of the King*, London: HarperCollins, 1993, p.959.
54 Shippey, *Road*, pp.120-22.
55 Gene Hargrove, 'Who is Tom Bombadil?', *Mythlore* 47:4 (1986), p.22.

the lack of desire to possess or own was extremely rare among the Valar and the beings of Middle-earth, [and since] no other Vala is said to exhibit this moral trait, it seems reasonable to assume that Tom and Aulë are the same person.'[56] Whilst Hargrove makes a determined case, it seems to me unwise to ignore Tolkien's own declaration that Bombadil is the 'spirit' of a dwindling pastoral landscape. Indeed in this context Tolkien's use of the word 'spirit' to describe Tom's being is interesting – as a philologist Tolkien would have been aware of the ambiguous nature of the word.

For me the possibility of differentiating between the statements that Tom is 'Eldest' and Treebeard 'is the oldest living' being in Middle-earth is indeed testament to the fact that Tom is a 'spirit' and not alive in the same sense that Treebeard is. Tom certainly has will, and power to execute that will, but as Galdor suggests, all his power lies 'in the earth itself.' He therefore is a manifestation of that natural power; waking and animate, but bound indelibly to the elemental power and fate of nature.

There is one other creation in *The Lord of the Rings* which seems alive, but yet is possessed of a similar emblematic quality to that which marks Tom's character, and understanding the nature of one may help to throw light on the nature of the other. I refer to the One Ring itself. The One Ring could not be said to be a living being in the same sense as Treebeard. The Ring, however, appears to have will and power of its own. Gandalf, recounting the history of how Gollum was parted from the Ring, tells Frodo, 'It was not Gollum, Frodo, but the Ring itself that decided things. The Ring left him.' We are also told that 'the Ring was trying to get back to its master' and that it 'betrayed'[57] Isildur.

The Ring then like Tom has influence and power over other living things but is nonetheless not alive in the truest sense. And, just as Tom is bound to the power and fate of the earth, so too the One Ring is tied to the malignant force and the destiny of Sauron, who in forging the One Ring poured much of himself and his malice into it. It is perhaps conceivable to suggest that Sauron too is not alive; we should remember, however, that although Sauron is not corporeal, he is a being: a corrupted Maia and an independent power and therefore not a

---

56 Hargrove, 'Who is Tom Bombadil?', p.23.
57 Tolkien, *The Fellowship of the Ring*, p.154.

representation or a 'spirit' of a force in the manner of Tom. In Tom Bombadil and the One Ring, however, there lies the emblematic enshrinement of conflicting forces: nature and the will to power.

(I.4) Tom as the Green Man

In closing this discussion of the character of Tom Bombadil and his ecological significance I would like to add a further thought to the raging debate of 'Who is Tom Bombadil?' Or perhaps more accurately, ask anew – what are his origins? I submit that given the following three factors:

1. Tolkien's own comments on Bombadil;
2. How Tom is portrayed and described as a character;
3. What Tom says, and what is said of him by other characters;

it is reasonable to feel comfortable with the premise that Tom is the embodiment of nature itself or, as I have argued, the spirit of nature under threat. But whether this premise is accepted or rejected, many like Gene Hargrove and Jared Lobdell have tried to account for Tom among the beings created within the spectrum of Tolkien's cosmology.

I disagree with Hargrove's conclusion that Bombadil is Aulë walking the earth in disguise (for one thing Aulë could not die whilst Arda or the World continues, as is suggested of Tom – by Tolkien) but I concur with the sentiment that underscores Hargrove's study:

> I personally find it inconceivable that there is no answer within the framework of the story to Frodo's question: "Who is Tom Bombadil?" Although Tolkien didn't want to tell his readers directly, it seems to me certain that he himself knew very well [...] although he might not have wanted to tell his readers the correct answer, feeling that enigmas are important, he would nevertheless have left some clues for those who wanted to pursue the matter.[58]

In so pursuing it, I have come to believe that the 'clues' related to Tom Bombadil's origin actually lead us outside of Tolkien's cosmology, and that the origin of 'the spirit' Tolkien refers to when he speaks of Tom is that of the

---

58 Hargrove, 'Who is Tom Bombadil?', p.21.

Green Man – an archetypal representation of the spirit of nature that dates back into prehistory.

Often the image of the Green Man, usually a bearded face wreathed in leaves, is seen adorning the architecture of old cathedrals or ancient buildings,[59] but he has found his way into every aspect of culture and art. Tolkien, as a scholar of myth and mythology would have been very familiar with the enduring legend of the Green Man, particularly as regards his studies of (and for) *Sir Gawain and the Green Knight*. In the introduction to that work Tolkien, in association with his co-editor E.V. Gordon, comments 'the greenness of the Knight, and his holly bob, are no doubt drawn from popular belief in a 'green man.''[60] Indeed some commentators such as Bob Curran in *Walking with the Green Man: Father of the Forest, Spirit of Nature* go a lot further and openly identify the Green Knight of the tale with the Green Man.

Tolkien and Gordon's edition of the great medieval poem was published in 1925 and Tom Bombadil as a literary character first appears in the *Oxford Magazine* in 1933, time enough perhaps for the Green Man to find his way into Tolkien's creative muse. John Matthews in *The Quest for the Green Man* suggests that once encountered or studied, legends related to the Green Man tend to take on 'personal meaning' for the researcher:

> They have been studied at length by an increasing number of researchers, each of whom records his or her first encounter with the Green Man in terms of wonder which soon turns to passionate curiosity. They have found within the lore surrounding this figure a huge spectrum of personal meaning, ranging from feelings of nostalgia for a past long dead to the inspired recognition of the Green Man as the spirit of nature.[61]

Certainly Matthews' articulation that 'the lore' connected or bound up with the Green Man resonates with 'feelings of nostalgia' and that he has to many become 'the spirit of nature' would ring true of Tolkien's remarks concerning Tom Bombadil. Curran offers that the appearance of the Green Man in modern culture often signifies 'a longing look backwards to a simplified, less mechanical

---

[59] Buildings which contain Green Man carvings include Canterbury, Chester and Rochester Cathedrals in England, the Abbey of Saint Denis in France, and Maria Laach Abbey in Germany.
[60] J.R.R. Tolkien & E.V. Gordon (eds.), *Sir Gawain and the Green Knight*, 2ⁿd edition revised by N. Davies, Oxford: Oxford University Press, 1967, p.xx.
[61] Matthews, *The Quest for the Green Man*, p.21.

time'[62] and again we are reminded of Tolkien's comment that Tom represented the 'vanishing' lands he knew well – 'vanishing' as Tolkien would no doubt have concluded under the industrialised regime of the machine. Moreover, further study into commonly understood 'lore' of the Green Man reveals a nature figure whose character traits (and mannerisms) are remarkably similar to those made evident in Tom Bombadil. Matthews for example tells us that across many incarnations throughout world culture the Green Man has been portrayed as a happy-go-lucky and convivial character who embraces life and the 'art' of living with an unsuppressed delight. Furthermore as Matthews explains: '[h]e is a trickster too laughing both with us and at us – with us through the sheer joy of being and at us in our inability to comprehend and so embody his aliveness in our own lives.'[63] There is little question that Tom Bombadil possesses this 'sheer joy of being' but perhaps what is most noteworthy in this description of the Green Man is how the notion that he is a 'laughing trickster' has obvious parity with the scene in which Tom takes the Ring from Frodo and mischievously causes it to disappear, laughing all the while: 'Tom laughed again, and then he spun the Ring in the air – and it vanished with a flash.'[64]

Matthews goes on to offer reflections upon the Green Man throughout history that depict him as a laughing 'spirit of the wood' and 'messenger of nature' that is 'dancing a curious springtime dance.'[65] The parallels with Tolkien's portrayal of Bombadil are striking – when we first encounter Tom in *The Lord of the Rings* he is described as 'singing carelessly and happily' whilst 'hopping and dancing along the path.'[66] Later we are told '[o]ften his voice would turn to song, and he would get out of his chair and dance about.'[67] Tom's character, wherever he appears, is decidedly marked (as are many representations of the Green Man) by this tendency to laugh, sing and dance a merry dance whatever the situation – even when faced with great danger. Tolkien instilled Bombadil with a kind of irresistible, natural life-force, and yet (as we have seen) Tolkien also cast him as a primordial, almost timeless figure. These distinguishing aspects of

---

62 Bob Curran & Ian Daniels, *Walking with the Green Man: Father of the Forest, Spirit of Nature*, New Jersey: Career Press, 2007, p.61.
63 Matthews, *The Quest for the Green Man*, p.12.
64 Tolkien, *Fellowship*, p.130.
65 Matthews, *The Quest for the Green Man*, p.12.
66 Tolkien, *Fellowship*, pp.116-17.
67 Tolkien, *Fellowship*, p.127.

Bombadil's persona are highly reminiscent of William Anderson's suggestions in *Green Man: The Archetype of Our Oneness with the Earth* that '[t]he Green Man signifies irrepressible life' and that as a character he comes to us 'from the depths of prehistory.' Anderson also points out that many cultural understandings of the Green Man present him as not only a physical representation but also as a spirit manifest in dance, verse or song:

> We think of the Green Man as a visual image [...] but the emotions he expresses transcends the form and their vitality is equally powerful when transmitted through the dance or the dramatic rituals of folk custom and in the rhythms and melodies of poetry and song.[68]

Perhaps the fact that Tom first appears, from Tolkien's imagination, in verse form in 'The Adventures of Tom Bombadil' is the clearest signifier that he is one such 'transmission' of the Green Man legacy. And the Tom Bombadil we meet in *The Lord of the Rings* was placed into the story, as Tolkien himself stated 'as he was'; in other words with the persona presented previously in verse form – intact. Indeed in *The Lord of the Rings* Tom exactly mirrors his preceding poetic outing and is possessed of a prevailing inclination for song, dance, melody and verse. Even when Tom speaks (as opposed to when he actually bursts into song) he speaks in verse form. We see this exemplified when Tom first speaks to the hobbits in the Old Forest: 'Now, my little fellows, where be you a going to, puffing like a bellows?'[69]

Many other characteristics associated with the Green Man appear reflected in Tolkien's portrayal of Tom Bombadil. Matthews for example offers that studies of the lore of the Green Man more often than not reveal an aspect of his persona to be that of a teacher or a giver of knowledge. 'From the Green Man' Matthews explains 'our ancestors learned the secrets of life [...] the mystery of the seasons and the agricultural year, the lore of medicinal herbs and plants; the companionship of the natural world.'[70] Likewise Bombadil shares such knowledge with the hobbits, explaining to them (amongst other things) 'the ways of trees' and laying bare 'secrets hidden under the brambles.'[71]

---

68 Anderson, *Green Man*, p.18.
69 Tolkien, *Fellowship*, p.117.
70 Matthews, *The Quest for the Green Man*, p.12.
71 Tolkien, *Fellowship*, p.127.

Of course as we noted earlier, Tom Bombadil has a lady by his side – Goldberry – and she is marked by many of the same characteristics that define Tom: a oneness with the natural world around her, a proclivity for song and dance, a welcoming and pleasant disposition. And as Matthews explains '[m]any aspects of the Green Man are partnered by a female aspect who bears identical or similar attributes.'[72] We see this recurrence of 'a female aspect' to the Green Man again and again throughout various interpretive 'versions' of the Green Man: Maid Marian to Robin Hood,[73] Isis to Osiris[74] and, as Tolkien would have been very aware, Lady Bercilak to the Green Knight.

Perhaps more than any other characteristic, however, it is Tom Bombadil's 'vow of poverty', his renunciation of power and his desire not to exploit but to live in harmony with the world around him that most aligns him with the legend of the Green Man. Matthews tells us, '[t]he presence of the Green Man expresses an ancient ability to interact with our environment, to take only what we need to survive, and to preserve the rest.'[75] This is precisely what Tom Bombadil exemplifies in *The Lord of the Rings*: the desire to 'interact' and understand rather than gain mastery, and in merely speaking to Frodo and the company of hobbits, Tom opens out their minds to the community of nature. We recall the narrator's words: 'As they listened, they began to understand the lives of the Forest, apart from themselves.'[76] Likewise Matthews describes the Green Man as a 'prophet' who 'reminds us that we are not the lords of creation, but partners in the vast, living ecosystem that is our planet.'[77]

---

72 Matthews, *The Quest for the Green Man*, p.110.
73 The understanding of Robin Hood as the Green Man is a much older and perhaps more accurate myth than that which casts him as Robin of Loxley or Robin of Sherwood. In the elder myth he was known as 'King of the Wood' and was an abiding symbol of fertility. Maid Marian, as his female counterpart, also was often portrayed as the mother or maid of the forest and a symbol of nature's life-giving qualities.
74 Osiris was an Egyptian god and one of the oldest known deities in civilisation, dating back to 2500BC. He was associated with the power of fertile nature and rebirth and was often depicted as being green or green-skinned. Many students of the Green Man have celebrated him as among the first manifestations of the form. Isis may best be categorised as his sister-wife. She too had many associations with nature and natural forces. For more on Osiris (and Robin Hood – see above) in this context see Gary R. Varner, *The Mythic Forest. The Green Man and the Spirit of Nature*, New York: Algora Publishing, 2006.
75 Matthews, *The Quest for the Green Man*, p.12.
76 Tolkien, *Fellowship*, p.127.
77 Matthews, *The Quest for the Green Man*, p.12.

I have argued for much of the above that Tom Bombadil is not just 'the spirit of nature' but rather the embodiment of nature under threat and I believe that is how he best may be understood. The 'clues' to his origin mentioned by Gene Hargrove do not, I contend, lead us to the halls of the Valar or the gathering of the Maiar but rather more directly to the leafy doorstep of the Green Man. Indeed prominent among the Green Man's many character traits, and emerging from many cultural understandings of his spirit, is this notion that he represents natural forces that are beginning to yield under the progressive assault of human activity. Matthews concludes 'if anything, [the Green Man] could be said to represent the spirit of nature and wildness that has been so steadily and completely encroached upon.'[78]

In fact Matthews mentions *The Lord of the Rings* in his study of the Green Man stating 'the character of Treebeard in J.R.R. Tolkien's *Lord of the Rings*, [has] brought the presence of the Green Man back into our midst.'[79] There is no doubt that Treebeard displays many of the characteristics discovered in studies of the Green Man and that visually he would more resemble traditional manifestations of the appearance, but in terms of closely mirroring those attributes that most define popular understandings of the Green Man he falls far short of Tom Bombadil's portrayal. It would be a stretching of the facts for instance to view Treebeard as a singing and dancing prankster who continually laughs whilst renouncing the power at his command. I can only suggest, therefore, that Matthews (whilst catching the spirit of Tom in Treebeard) opted for the more visually arresting of Tolkien's characters or simply that, as many have done before him, he wrongly dismissed Tom as a dispensable anomaly in the tale. The reality of course is that Tolkien may have imbued more than one of his characters with the spirit of the Green Man, offering, as it were, differing aspects of that spirit. Indeed it is interesting to note that Philippa Boyens, scriptwriter for Jackson's movie adaptation of *The Lord of the Rings*, decided, as Bombadil was cut from the script, to keep Tom's 'spirit' alive by giving some of his 'lines' to Treebeard:

---

78 Matthews, *The Quest for the Green Man*, p.39.
79 Matthews, *The Quest for the Green Man*, p.39.

[Tom Bombadil] is like a guardian of living things, and he is not in the movie, so of course we wanted to honour that spirit [...] some people may recognise some of Tom's lines as spoken by Treebeard. We figured that Tom wouldn't mind us giving his lines to Treebeard of any character in the book.[80]

(II.1) Saruman and the Machine in the Garden

I argued at the start of this chapter that, as characters, Tom Bombadil and Saruman may be most vitally understood in terms of how they represent positive and negative environmental models, and that Tolkien in his presentation of these two characters creates cultures of opposition, so that one inversely mirrors the other. In what follows I contend that Bombadil exhibits characteristics that sit in detailed and direct opposition to those displayed and played out by Saruman.

As explored earlier, one of Bombadil's defining characteristics is his renunciation of power: his lack of desire to control, order or master anything. Moreover Tom does not use the power at his command to raise his stature or enhance his position. Saruman, on the other hand, like Sauron, craves power and seeks to gain mastery over others – he desires the One Ring. Both he and Sauron are consumed by this will to power. But, as Sauron is the maker of the Ring and the Ring itself has been forged and invested with Sauron's malevolent will, one cannot really say that Sauron may be corrupted by it, since to a large degree, it *is* he – or more accurately the power he once was. Sauron wishes to regain the Ring so that he may be renewed in his former 'glory' and, as Gandalf tells Frodo, 'cover all the lands in a second darkness.'[81] Sauron's corruption as a Maiar occurs much earlier in the history of Middle-earth and the Undying Lands when he abandons his servitude to Aulë and becomes a lieutenant to the iniquity of Morgoth. In *The Lord of the Rings*, however, we witness Saruman succumbing to precisely what Bombadil resists.

I suggested earlier that the One Ring may be understood as a type of gauge that when consulted may measure the true virtue and corruptibility of a given

---

80 Philippa Boyens, 'The Appendices Part 3: From Book to Script: Finding the Story' in *The Lord of the Rings: The Two Towers*, Dir. Peter Jackson, DVD Extended Version: New Line Cinema, 2003.
81 Tolkien, *Fellowship*, p.50.

character, and it is perhaps Saruman more than any other who is most seduced by the allure of what the One Ring can offer. In this sense he is the inverse mirror image of Bombadil's 'unassailable virtue'.

Saruman, however, in the beginning (as head of the five Maiar sent to Middle-earth to help contest the will of Sauron), believes he can actually achieve good through the pursuit of such power. Gandalf recalls at the Council of Elrond how Saruman attempted to rationalise his strategy in what appeared to Gandalf to be 'a speech long prepared'. Saruman's bodily posture shifts as he pronounces 'our time is at hand: the world of Men, which We must rule. But we must have power, power to order all things as we will, for that good which only the Wise can see.'[82] His words seem more directed to himself than Gandalf, as if trying to convince himself that any means to achieve his goal are justified. David Day in *Tolkien's Ring* concludes that Saruman 'demonstrated the classic moral error of believing the 'end justifies the means.'' Thus he abandons the 'moral code' held so highly by Gandalf and embarks upon his own destructive path. Day continues:

> In his attempt to overthrow the forces of the evil Sauron, Saruman gathers forces that in themselves are just as evil, and is himself corrupted by this desire for power. Unwittingly, Saruman becomes a mirror image and ally of the evil being he initially wished to overcome.[83]

Saruman's initial will to power is wrapped in self-deceiving words. He is perhaps unaware that he is gradually becoming what he set out to oppose. But still key phrases in Saruman's 'speech' such as 'we must rule' and 'we must have power' begin to betray the corruption that has stolen in upon him. The 'we' he refers to insinuatingly includes Gandalf, and he further tries to convince Gandalf that in joining with Sauron's power they may eventually overthrow it, 'the Wise such as you and I, may with patience come at last to direct its courses, to control it.'[84] The more he tries to reason his intentions to Gandalf, however, the more he cannot help but reveal that it is the desire for power for its own sake which consumes him. Eventually in his entreaty to Gandalf, Saruman's thoughts turn to the One Ring and what may be achieved by gaining possession of it.

---

82 Tolkien, *Fellowship*, p.252.
83 David Day, *Tolkien's Ring*, London: Pavilion Books, 2001, p.38.
84 Tolkien, *Fellowship*, p.253.

'The Ruling Ring? If we could command that, then the power would pass to us.' As he speaks of the One Ring and his suspicion that Gandalf may know of its whereabouts, we are told that his eyes shone with 'a lust he could not conceal.' Indeed if we compress some of the phrases used by Saruman in this short passage, omitting the entreaties made to Gandalf, we can see Saruman's true nature appear:

> We must rule [...] we must have power, power to order all things [...] Victory is at hand; and there will be rich reward [...] the high and ultimate purpose: Knowledge, Rule, Order [...] The Ruling Ring? If we could command that, then the Power would pass to us.[85]

Read in contrast to what Tolkien described as Bombadil's 'vow of poverty' and 'delight in things for themselves',[86] Saruman's words betray him as an emergent autocrat whose desire for power is insular, small-minded and utterly unconcerned with the inherent value of 'things for themselves'. As we shall see in greater detail later, Saruman's rise to and pursuit of power takes on a pronounced industrialised and mechanised form. And this, coupled with his insularity of purpose, casts Saruman, in environmental terms, as representative of technologies, powers and industries in our world that have eyes fixed firmly on the 'prize' of a desired outcome whilst ignoring the damage caused to the natural world that is served up as a by-product of their endeavours.

Gandalf of course cuts through the subterfuge of Saruman's words and reads between the lines of his stated intent. For Gandalf is aware that no good may come of strength gathered in the name of the Ring and he knows that Saruman's offer of a union in power is hollow because, as he points out, 'only one hand at a time can wield the One.'[87] Indeed, although to all intents and purposes Saruman seems to be using the word 'we' to petition Gandalf, the shadow of Gollum also lurks somewhere in Saruman's recurrent use of 'we', suggesting that, like Gollum, the moral side of the White Wizard has fallen and he is utterly consumed by his desire for the kind of power possession of the One Ring would deliver upon him. In this sense despite what he may tell himself or Gandalf, Saruman has utterly

---

85 Tolkien, *Fellowship*, pp.252-53.
86 Tolkien, *Letters*, p.179.
87 Tolkien, *Fellowship*, p.253.

changed: he has become a little Sauron, a dark lord in waiting. Marjorie Burns in her essay 'Gandalf and Odin' concurs: 'Saruman is, after all, a would-be Sauron, a Sauron in-training, a wizard who desires the Ring and who is attempting, by his Orthanc and his White Hand orcs, to imitate Sauron's Barad-dûr and his band of Red-Eye orcs.'[88]

Saruman may well be 'a would-be Sauron', but whatever power he has (as the mightiest of the Istari Wizards and as a Maiar) he now employs to mercilessly pursue yet greater power and the One Ring – with all other concerns or purposes cast aside. And as Saruman gathers his forces and his strengths about him, it is predominately at the expense of the land itself – for Saruman's treachery against Middle-earth, as we noted in the previous glimpse of Isengard, takes on a mechanised form. Indeed Tolkien's description of Isengard reveals Saruman's seat of power to be nothing less than an industrialised factory of war:

> [T]he ground trembled. The shafts ran down by many slopes and spiral stairs to caverns far under; there Saruman had treasuries, store-houses, armouries, smithies, and great furnaces. Iron wheels revolved there endlessly, and hammers thudded.[89]

The phrase 'the ground trembled' contains a wonderful duality of meaning: firstly it tells us that the ground literally trembled as the earth shook under the mechanised might of Isengard with the relentless grinding of its '[i]ron wheels' and 'hammers'. The phrase 'the ground trembled' also suggests, however, that the land or even nature itself 'trembled' with fear as the sheer destructive force of the industrial 'enemy' made itself known. Indeed with this second understanding of the phrase we are reminded of the motif of nature under threat that I suggest is made manifest in the character of Bombadil. Given this understanding it is perhaps no surprise to find that Tom (whose power and persona are bound up with that of the Earth) has 'withdrawn into a little land' where no mechanised 'enemy' has yet appeared. Indeed as we are shown the environmental damage inflicted upon the lands surrounding the industrialised stronghold of Isengard, it is clear that Bombadil has much to fear:

---

88 Marjorie Burns, 'Gandalf and Odin' in Verlyn Flieger & Carl F. Hostetter (eds.), *Tolkien's Legendarium: Essays on the History of Middle-earth*, Westport CT: Greenwood Press, 2000, pp.222-23.
89 Tolkien, *Two Towers*, p.541.

> [M]ost of the valley had become a wilderness of weeds and thorns [...] No trees grew there; but among the rank grasses could still be seen the burned and axe-hewn stumps of ancient groves. It was a sad country.
> [...] Once it had been fair and green [...] all about it there had lain a pleasant, fertile land.[90]

Saruman's pursuit of power has done nothing but yield a bitter harvest, and like many industrialised power agendas in our world, his regime has crippled the very landscape that sustains it. Machines and new technologies have taken root in the land as the trees have become uprooted – one usurping the other in a feeding frenzy of environmental devastation. But, callously and coldly, Saruman orders that the regime continue – for him power is the only objective, the only concern. Rutledge Fleming in *The Battle for Middle-earth: Tolkien's Divine Design in The Lord of the Rings* comments upon Saruman's unremitting mechanistic assault on the land, '[Saruman] has become a soulless technocrat, besotted with machinery and technology, indifferent to the precious vulnerable variety of 'growing things'.'[91]

(II.2) Plotting to Become a Power

Tom Bombadil desires to understand such 'growing things' on their own terms, and to gain knowledge of things other than himself, but to remain, as Tolkien writes, 'entirely unconcerned with 'doing' anything with the knowledge'[92] and as such he exemplifies a desire to interconnect with rather than to gain mastery of his environment. This is the implementation of green politics in its purest form. Indeed it is no doubt a desire to understand the folk of the Shire that drives Tom to occasionally visit and talk with Farmer Maggot of whom he says fondly '[t]here's earth under his old feet and clay on his fingers.'[93] Saruman also seeks knowledge and understanding, but in direct contrast to Bombadil, Saruman desires knowledge of other things in order that he may aggrandise his position and gain wisdom that may aid in his rise to power. Treebeard, talking with Merry and Pippin about how the industrialised hand of the White

---

90 Tolkien, *Two Towers*, p.540.
91 Rutledge Fleming, *The Battle for Middle-earth: Tolkien's Divine Design in The Lord of the Rings*, Michigan: Eerdman's Publishing, 2004, p.153.
92 Tolkien, *Letters*, p.192.
93 Tolkien, *Fellowship*, p.130.

Wizard had brought devastation to Fangorn Forest, ponders upon Saruman's desire for knowledge:

> I used to talk to him. There was a time when he was always walking about my woods. He was polite in those days [...] always eager to listen. I told him many things that he would never have found out by himself; but he never repaid me in like kind. I cannot remember that he ever told me anything [...] I think that I now understand what he is up to. He is plotting to become a Power.[94]

Note how Treebeard remarks 'I cannot remember that [Saruman] ever told me anything.' Saruman it seems is a one-way information channel – this is because his only focus of interest is himself and his will to power. Bombadil on the other hand is more than forthcoming with his knowledge and wisdom. As we have noted, he selflessly furnishes Frodo and the other hobbits with all manner of secrets, truths, histories, songs and tales.

Because we know that Saruman has walked in Fangorn Forest and learned much from Treebeard it seems all the more treacherous that he should begin to ravage the ent's home and annihilate his trees and groves so brutally. Given Saruman's tendency to persistently gather knowledge and his standing as White Wizard of the Istari, he would of course have been aware of the far-reaching damage he was inflicting upon both Fangorn and Middle-earth in general, and as such he represents the ecologically unsound technologies of our world that remain 'selectively' indifferent to the devastation they cause. Rutledge Fleming takes up this point:

> The wanton destruction of trees by Saruman therefore signifies a more than ordinary recklessness and savagery; the very foundations of the earth's intricate network of living things is being attacked. This has clear implications for our time, when so much of the natural environment is being destroyed or irreparably altered.[95]

Treebeard's indication (through the phrasings '[t]here was a time' and 'in those days') that he had spoken with Saruman before the wizard had yet come to great power suggests that Saruman had for a long time harboured a longing to set himself up as a ruler and tyrant. J.E.A. Tyler in the encyclopaedic *The Complete Tolkien Companion* remarks 'Saruman had long desired to become

---

94 Tolkien, *Two Towers*, p.462.
95 Fleming, *The Battle for Middle-earth*, p.152.

a power in himself [...] it was this weakness which was the beginning of his slow downfall.' Tyler adds:

> For many years he dwelt in peace with his neighbours; but all the time the Wizard was secretly searching the tower of Orthanc for a long lost treasure of the Dúnedain, the possession of which would immeasurably strengthen the power he craved. This was the Palantír of Orthanc, one of the fabled Seeing-stones of Gondor.[96]

Indeed it is this motif of possession that most characterises Saruman: he seeks possession of secret knowledge, the Palantír, the One Ring and ultimately Middle-earth itself, and he holds possession of a secret purpose. He uses the ents, the birds, beasts and minions at his command to attain degrees of power and then he exploits the environment around him to literally feed the fires of his ambition. To Saruman these things are mere commodities, a means to an end, and his exploitation of his environment puts him under the sign of a ruthless capitalist investor who values things, even living beings, only in terms of how they may advance his 'cause'. Alison Milbank in *Chesterton and Tolkien as Theologians* draws a similar parallel with respect to Saruman's command of his foot soldiers: 'capitalism turns objects into commodities, workers into 'hands' and instrumentalises both. (A clear example of this in *The Lord of the Rings* is Saruman's dehumanising treatment of his workers, who march under his 'hand' emblem).'[97]

In this sense Saruman represents everything that Tom Bombadil is not. Every fibre of Saruman's being craves what Bombadil would cheerfully exchange for the sight of a flowing river through a fertile land. In ecological terms, Saruman embodies humanity's desire to master the environment to which it is bound, to see itself as not only set apart from the ecosystems which sustain and drive the natural world, but also as rightful possessor of them and thus entitled to use or exploit them at will. Colin Duriez tells us that '[p]ossession is a unifying theme in [Tolkien's] stories, from the desire of Morgoth to have God's power of creation to the temptation of wielding the One Ring.'[98] Indeed, as I shall examine more fully in chapter five, Tolkien in 'On Fairy-stories' warns us that once we gain possession or 'appropriation' of things 'we [lay] hands on them,

---

96 J.E.A. Tyler, *The Complete Tolkien Companion*, 3rd edition, London: Pan Books, 2002, p.563.
97 Alison Milbank, *Chesterton and Tolkien as Theologians*, London and New York: T&T Clark, 2007, p.120.
98 Colin Duriez, *J.R.R. Tolkien and C.S. Lewis: The Story of Their Friendship*, Stroud, Gloucestershire: The History Press, 2005, p.149.

and then [lock] them in our hoard [and cease] to look at them.'[99] In our reality the environmental implication of Tolkien's view of 'appropriation' warns that we must wake up to, and place greater value upon, the natural wonder all around us rather than view it as a commodity or a familiar given. For Saruman, in Tolkien's epic tale, the implication is that even in his desire to gain possession of Middle-earth, he has lost sight of what Bombadil can clearly see. Bombadil has no desire to possess or gain 'appropriation' of Middle-earth. He values it and its natural wonders for their own sake. Saruman values these things only in terms of the power they may afford him. His eyes are on what he would take to be a bigger prize: the power to rule – and this is only attainable through possession of the Ruling Ring, the 'trinket' that Bombadil casually casts aside.

Saruman, like many of the dark forces that have threatened Middle-earth, has abused and misused the power at his command. Unlike Tom Bombadil's 'vow of poverty', Saruman has turned his power, his sorcery, ingenuity and understanding towards creating unnatural engines and beings that may propel him forward in his purpose, or aid in his assault on Middle-earth. In a very real sense he is a meddler in natural things. Duriez points out that '[t]he wrong use of power is often expressed by Tolkien in magic, the mechanical and the technological',[100] and there is no doubt that Saruman's employment of power to create new engines and machines, his experiments with breeding and genetic engineering, places him in direct opposition to the kind of environmentalist and pacifist outlook embodied in Tom Bombadil.

In Tolkien's portrayal of Saruman's misuse of power and technology we are shown reflections of our own reality – indeed as Tom Shippey observes, '[Saruman's] orcs used a kind of gunpowder at Helm's Deep, and later on he uses against the Ents a kind of napalm.'[101] Shippey goes on to discuss the 'strong applicability' to modern environmentalism of Tolkien's depiction of Saruman's meddling and mechanistic nature:

> the Sarumans of the real world rule by deluding their followers with images of a technological Paradise in the future, a modernist Utopia; but what one often gets […] are the blasted landscapes of Eastern Europe, strip-mined, polluted, and even

---

99 J.R.R. Tolkien, *The Tolkien Reader*, New York: Ballantine Books, 1966, p.77.
100 Duriez, *J.R.R. Tolkien and C.S. Lewis*, p.149.
101 Tom Shippey, *J.R.R. Tolkien: Author of the Century*, London: HarperCollins, 2001, p.170.

radioactive. One may disagree with Tolkien's diagnosis of the situation [...] but there can be no doubt that he has at least addressed a serious issue, and tried to give it both a historical and a psychological dimension nearly always missing elsewhere.[102]

(II.3) The Voice of Saruman

Shippey's observation that 'the Sarumans of the real world rule by deluding their followers' leads us to the question of Saruman's voice and his ability to delude, deceive and beguile merely by the power of his voice. Saruman wraps his true purpose in seductive rhetoric. We recall how he attempted to deceive Gandalf and perhaps even himself with placatory words and phrases. In Shippey's words he 'talks like a politician.'[103] Even at the doorstep of defeat, from the tower of Orthanc, Saruman comes to address the company gathered below not with hostile words but first with the tone 'of a kindly heart aggrieved' and then with a welcoming and courteous greeting. The narrator describes the effects of Saruman's address:

> Those who listened unwarily to that voice could seldom report words that they heard; and if they did, they wondered, for little power remained in them. Mostly they remembered only that it was a delight to hear the voice speaking, all that it said seemed wise and reasonable, and desire awoke in them by swift agreement to seem wise themselves. When others spoke they seemed harsh and uncouth by contrast.[104]

Saruman's voice is spellbinding; he speaks with, as David Day puts it, 'the honeyed tongue of poets and orators',[105] he appeals to the sensibilities of his listeners and appears to offer wisdom and rationality. Representing, as he does, an industrialised force that lays waste the land, in environmental terms the beguiling nature of Saruman's voice is evocative of 'big business' market-leading industries and political institutions who produce well polished reports and offer well rehearsed speeches to attempt to justify their ecologically damaging activities and allay the concerns of the public.

There is a suggestion of course that Saruman's power as a speaker is the result of sorcery. If it is, then there are some who, without magic of their own, can resist the spell. Éomer for example cuts over Saruman's rhetoric

---

102 Shippey, *Author of the Century*, p.171.
103 Shippey, *Road*, p.135.
104 Tolkien, *Two Towers*, p.564.
105 Day, *Tolkien's Ring*, p.38.

calling him 'an old liar with honey on his forked tongue.'[106] Even when his power as a wizard has diminished and his staff is symbolically broken, the power of Saruman's (now Sharkey's) voice, his political machinations, and rhetoric, manages, as we noted in the previous chapter, to embroil the community of hobbits in his plans to industrialise the Shire. Robert Plank believes this magic-free version of Saruman paints the account of the 'Scouring of the Shire' with a more realistic hue: '[w]hatever headway [Saruman] makes [in the Shire] he makes as a politician rather than as a sorcerer. In other words the Scouring of the Shire is not a fantasy. It is a realistic story.'[107]

Whether Saruman's 'honeyed tongue' is the result of sorcery or not, his voice is a weapon in his armoury; his seductive rhetoric and deceptively reasoned phrases are designed to conceal a purpose. Set against this, the natural power portrayed in Tom Bombadil's voice appears in stark contrast. Bombadil's uncomplicated and down-to-earth phrases convey a weight of power but they do so effortlessly and without subterfuge. We recall his words to Old Man Willow. 'Eat earth! Dig deep! Drink Water! Go to Sleep! Bombadil is talking!'[108] Indeed when the hobbits first encounter Tom in the Old Forest the narrator describes how they are compelled to stand still by the mere sound of his voice, "Whoa! Whoa! Steady there!' cried [Tom Bombadil], holding up one hand, and they stopped short, as if they had been struck stiff.'[109]

(III) Closing Thoughts: Counterpoints

Of all the characterisations portrayed in Tolkien's fiction, Saruman could be said most closely to resemble the real threat which Tolkien perceived was looming over the natural landscapes of the primary world: the emergence and seemingly unstoppable rise of industrialised power and the ever-growing potency of the machine. In *The Lord of the Rings* Saruman

---

106 Tolkien, *Two Towers*, p.565.
107 Robert Plank, 'The Scouring of the Shire: Tolkien's view of Fascism' in Jared Lobdell (ed.), *A Tolkien Compass*, Chicago and La Salle, Illinois: Open Court Publishing, 2003, p.107.
108 Tolkien, *Fellowship*, p.118.
109 Tolkien, *Fellowship*, p.117.

could be said to represent (more than Sauron) modern civilisation, and humanity's (as Tolkien would have viewed it) injudicious embrace of the machine age. Tom Shippey describes Saruman as 'the most contemporary figure in Middle-earth, both politically and linguistically',[110] and although Sauron perhaps posed a greater threat to Middle-earth, the overtly mechanistic portrayal of Saruman's threat to, not only the free peoples of Middle-earth, but also to the landscape itself seems all the more recognisable and thus all the more suggestive of reality. Indeed Saruman's assault on the ecology of Middle-earth becomes a vivid evocation of everything Tolkien feared could threaten the pastoral lands he knew well. Tolkien's casting of the character of Tom Bombadil as the 'spirit of the (vanishing) […] countryside',[111] therefore, sets the two portrayals as contrasting yet parallel elements within *The Lord of the Rings*. Set out in table form one character appears as the inverted mirror image of the other:

---

110 Shippey, *Author of the Century*, p.76.
111 Tolkien, *Letters*, p.26.

Ecologically Positive Presentation	Ecologically Negative Presentation
Tom Bombadil	Saruman
1. Seeks to understand nature and other things on their own terms.	1. Seeks to twist, ravage and exploit nature and other things for his own gain.
2. Renounces mastery of his environment – discards his power.	2. Pursues mastery of his environment in the pursuit of power.
3. Is in complicit union with the natural world around him.	3. Is an aggressor against the natural landscape surrounding Isengard.
4. Is presented as a representation of nature or nature under threat.	4. Is presented as a representation of environmentally destructive technology and industry that threatens the natural world.
5. Remains unaffected by the allure of the One Ring.	5. Is utterly corrupted by the allure of the One Ring.
6. Uses his voice to sing, share knowledge and evoke simple natural power.	6. Uses his voice to beguile, deceive and conceal his purpose. Does not share knowledge.

The two characters are at odds, at counterpoint, but they are united by the environmentally themed thread which runs through both creations; each can be understood most vitally in terms of how they represent positive or negative environmental models, each defined by how they positively or negatively mirror the other.

Chapter Three

Contrasting Environmental Personas in *The Lord of the Rings*: Gandalf and Sauron

Leading on from the previous chapter in which I discussed how Tom Bombadil and Saruman may most vitally be understood in terms of how they represent positive and negative environmental models, and how these portrayals may be read as inverted mirror reflections of each other, in the chapter that follows I will discuss the characterisations of Gandalf and Sauron. The chapter will further consider how Tolkien's main themes and the environmental dimension of his work are revealed in the analysis of his major characters, and offers a comparative examination of Gandalf and Sauron. The discussion will also include a consideration of the nature of evil as represented by Sauron, and how this may feed into a mindset that engages in environmentally corrosive activity. Interweaved with these considerations I address the question of Gandalf's role in Middle-earth as steward, guide and teacher of those who unite to resist the threat before them – and consider to what degree Tolkien's Christian faith could be said to define the ecological wisdom and moral judgements of the Grey Wizard.

(I.1) Gandalf: Emissary of the Valar

Of all of Tolkien's characters, arguably the most famous and most loved is Gandalf. His origins in Tolkien's cosmology are those of a Maia, an angelic being of lesser stature than the Valar. As the Dark Lord Sauron begins to return to prominence, Gandalf is sent to Middle-earth by the Valar to oppose his power as one of the five Istari or wizards, and is incarnated in mortal form. This transition from absolute spiritual being into flesh and blood casts Gandalf as a kind of strange half-man/half-angel. Indeed Tolkien himself found it difficult to explain (in conventional terms) the exact nature of Gandalf's character as he appears in the Third Age: '[t]here are naturally no precise modern terms to say what he was. I [would] venture to say that he was an *incarnate* 'angel."[1] Tolkien goes on to explain that by 'incarnate' he means to allude to the fact that Gandalf, in his physical manifestation, is subject to all of the temptations, trials and weaknesses that afflict mortal beings.

Gandalf the Grey Wanderer, the wizard, the 'mortal angel', arrives, then, among the peoples of Middle-earth with a clear purpose and by virtue of a pre-determined design. Tolkien in one letter tells us that Gandalf 'was an emissary of the Valar, and virtually their plenipotentiary in accomplishing the plan against Sauron.'[2] From Tolkien's categorization of Gandalf as plenipotentiary of the Valar, we may gather that Gandalf (although in a weakened state of corporeal being in comparison to his former manifestation as a Maia) has been invested by the Valar with the full power of authority and governance to act at his own discretion – to do what he believes is necessary for them to succeed in their plan against Sauron. Gandalf thus carries with him a defined purpose and an explicit goal. As such he is on, what one may loosely term, a mission from the gods (or perhaps more specifically in terms of the cosmology of Tolkien's *legendarium* – a mission from the demi-gods). The manner in which Gandalf achieves success for his task, however, is entirely down to him. But, of course, we must ask: what would Gandalf and thus the Valar (and by extension Ilúvatar) consider success against Sauron to be? Or put another way: what exactly is Gandalf's mission? And is bringing about the downfall of Sauron at any cost his sole aim? In answering these questions I will begin to establish Gandalf's credentials as a powerful pro-environmental force whose promotion of the interrelationship and worth of all living things may be viewed as representative of a more holistic understanding of what it means to be a steward of the green face of the world.

The nature of Gandalf's mission has been defined by many Tolkien commentators quite correctly as representing a direct opposition to the rise and the machinations of Sauron. Robert S. Ellwood states that 'Gandalf's work in [Middle-earth] is a particular task, contesting the power of Sauron.'[3] J.E.A. Tyler records Gandalf as being '[t]he greatest opponent of the Dark Lord in the Third

---

1 J.R.R. Tolkien, *The Letters of J.R.R. Tolkien*, edited by Humphrey Carpenter, London: HarperCollins, 2006, p.202.
2 Tolkien, *Letters*, p.327.
3 Robert S. Ellwood, *Frodo's Quest*, Wheaton: Theosophical Publishing, 2002, p.39.

Age.' 'Gandalf', Tyler adds, 'passed through fire, earth, water and death – and was afterwards reborn – in fulfilment of the destiny long appointed for him: to be the chief architect of Sauron's Downfall.'[4] But of course if Gandalf's sole and only purpose was to defeat Sauron, shouldn't he just have taken the Ring from Frodo and together with the combined power of the other Istari, and the united peoples of Middle-earth, marched on Mordor, calling upon all his power and trusting in his own beneficence? Saruman, a wizard of arguably greater stature than Gandalf, falls foul of such temptation. In attempting to understand how and why Gandalf resists what Saruman (and others) cannot, we may begin to draw closer to the true nature of Gandalf's purpose and explore how Gandalf's wider view of the misuse of power and the worth of powerless and defenceless things exemplifies and represents a wholly positive environmental worldview.

(I.2) Gandalf: Steward of Middle-earth

For Gandalf, Sauron's rise to power and his assault on Middle-earth is more than an assault on the free peoples of the Third Age – it is also a sustained attack on the land itself. Gandalf knows that Sauron and his forces 'torture and destroy the very hills'[5] as Galdor puts it at the Council of Elrond. He knows that Sauron and his servants, in pursuit of absolute power, lay waste the green places of the world. He knows that if Sauron's evil succeeds the result would be a Middle-earth that resembles Mordor where nature itself has lost the power to heal the broken landscape. He knows too that in opposing Sauron with the Ring one must become a Dark Lord, and as such the evil is not removed but altered. Yet although the machinations of Sauron threaten every aspect of Middle-earth, for Gandalf the success of his purpose is not wholly dependent on the absolute destruction of Sauron or indeed the preservation of mighty kingdoms or great lineages, but rather on his ability to protect even the most insignificant representations of life. The defeat of Sauron at any cost, in other words, is not an option for Gandalf. The land must prevail; the soil and all things that grow must be protected, as Gandalf tells Denethor in Gondor:

---

4 J.E.A. Tyler, *The Complete Tolkien Companion*, 3rd edition, London: Pan Books, 2002, p.265.
5 J.R.R. Tolkien, *The Fellowship of the Ring*, London: HarperCollins, 1997, p.259.

all worthy things that are in peril as the world now stands, those are my care.
And for my part, I shall not wholly fail of my task, though Gondor should perish,
if anything passes through this night that can still grow fair or bear fruit and
flower in the days to come. For I also am a steward. Did you not know?[6]

Gandalf's words to Denethor signify a deep embrace of the environment of Middle-earth, and carry with them a real anxiety for the passing of the green face of the land (Gandalf clearly believes that the ecology of their world is 'in peril'). As such these words to Denethor are reflective of Tolkien's own anxieties for the vanishing green face of the primary world and represent a key example of the ecological augury I contend characterises the green dimension of his work.

What is also of note here is that Gandalf refers to himself as 'a steward'. Even from an ecologically positive standpoint, the word steward brings with it religious connotations derived predominately from the Christian faith – namely that humanity has a moral responsibility, as trustee, to tend to the 'garden' of God's Earth. Robin Attfield in his study on *Environmental Ethics* comments:

> Since at least the seventeenth century, it has been explicitly maintained that human beings hold the Earth as a trust, and are not only responsible for its care, but also responsible for the delivery of their role as stewards or trustees. Not surprisingly, these beliefs have religious origins, particularly among Christians.[7]

This is a principally positive interpretation of Christian stewardship and one that some Tolkien commentators such as Dickerson and Evans argue underpins Tolkien's environmental worldview. Whilst, as I suggested in the introduction of this book and elsewhere, I accept that Tolkien's Christianity informed much of what constituted his embrace of nature, I do *not* accept that it governed it absolutely – nor do I recognise that Christianity is the blueprint from which Tolkien's fiction has taken its design. Indeed understandings of stewardship in a Christian context, however environmentally aware, espouse the view that humanity, as the centre of God's design, has some manner of pre-eminence over nature. Set against this central idea there is a spectrum of Christian interpretations and understandings of stewardship. The most environmentally sympathetic of

---

6 J.R.R. Tolkien, *The Return of the King*, London: HarperCollins, 1997, p.742.
7 Robin Attfield, *Environmental Ethics*, Cambridge: Polity Press, 2003, p.21.

these understandings (akin to Attfield's above) asserts that humanity, as steward, must care for God's other living creations and the 'garden' of the world – as a servant is charged to look after a master's interests and possessions. The other extreme is put forth in Lynn White Jr.'s famous 1967 essay, 'Historical Roots of Our Ecological Crisis', where he goes as far as to say that Christianity and the Bible may be sourced as one of the root causes of modern environmental problems precisely because they advance the express notion that humanity is separate from, and holds lordship over nature – thereby providing justification for unsound ecological practice. I return to the focus of White Jr.'s essay in relation to Tolkien's myth in more detail in the next chapter. What I wish to address here is the supposition that Gandalf, in declaring that he is a steward of Middle-earth, provides us with evidence that both he as a character, and the entire green dimension of Tolkien's work are fundamentally Christian in essence. Dickerson and Evans, in particular, in *Ents, Elves, and Eriador: The Environmental Vision of J.R.R. Tolkien* propose that Tolkien, throughout his *legendarium*, presents a purely Christian understanding of stewardship of the natural world. In their introduction the authors assert: 'Tolkien's environmental ethic was firmly rooted in a deeply Christian, Catholic understanding of the world and its creator.'[8] Later, they suggest that one of Tolkien's key strategies in the promotion of his Christian ecology is the fact that 'he gives us Gandalf – both the wizard's *words* about stewardship and his explicit *model* of stewardship.'[9]

Taking the question of 'the world and its creator' in relation to Tolkien's fiction, we are drawn back to his creation myth. We have already noted that viewing Tolkien's 'Ainulindalë' (the story of creation) as Genesis in disguise is a critical strategy that is, as Trevor Hart puts it, 'likely only to mislead.'[10] Moreover the theological framework of the 'Ainulindalë' and the events relayed in *The Silmarillion* are the foundation[11] from which all of Tolkien's Middle-earth writings proceed.[12] In attempting to place (or offer) the character of Gandalf within

---

8 Matthew Dickerson & Jonathan Evans, *Ents, Elves, and Eriador: The Environmental Vision of J.R.R. Tolkien*, Lexington, Kentucky: University Press of Kentucky, 2006, p.xxii.
9 Dickerson & Evans, *Ents, Elves, and Eriador*, p.39. Emphasis in the original.
10 Trevor Hart, 'Tolkien, Creation, and Creativity' in Trevor Hart & Ivan Khovacs (eds.), *Tree of Tales: Tolkien, Literature, and Theology*, Waco: Baylor University Press, 2007, p.41.
11 Ralph C. Wood also refers to Tolkien's creation myth as 'the foundation for everything else.' Ralph C. Wood, *The Gospel According to Tolkien: Visions of the Kingdom in Middle-earth*, Louisville: Westminster John Knox Press, 2003, p.41.
12 We should note, of course, that although the writings and tales that make up *The Silmarillion* were

a religious context, therefore, one must look to the spiritual climate that brought him forth. Indeed Hart is pronounced in his views regarding the importance of Tolkien's founding myth: 'in a profound sense [the Ainulindalë] provides the clue for understanding all that follows.'[13] Those who view the theological landscape of Middle-earth (and thus Gandalf) as essentially Christian cite the hierarchical ordering of Tolkien's creation myth as clear evidence that such a proposition is valid. In the attempt to counter contentions, made by Dickerson, Evans (and others) that Gandalf's ecological ethics are rooted in Christianity, perhaps this question of hierarchy and 'divine sovereignty' should be addressed.

Tolkien's creation myth undoubtedly resembles Christianity in terms of structure. The 'chain of command', which descends from an all powerful god figure, through degrees of 'holy' angels down to earthly life, is indeed suggestive of Christian doctrine. The rationale behind Tolkien's employment of a hierarchical structure and the existence of a sovereign deity in his fiction, however, owes more to his views on sub-creation than any desire to replicate Christianity in his secondary world. I return to the question of sub-creation in chapter five but will outline the key points, such as Tolkien understood them, here: Tolkien viewed *all* secondary imagination and creation – i.e. the work of the Valar and the elves in his secondary world, and works of literature, art and wider imagination in the primary world (such as *his* imaginative creation of the Valar in the first place) – as creation under God or sub-creation. The configuration of one God over all – or the evocation of 'divine sovereignty' in his cosmological design is thus an intentional compliance to the core principle which he understood governed the relationship between Creator and sub-creator. With regards to this core understanding, Tolkien, as Hart asserts, 'applied a brake to his sense of imagination' – not a sentiment to be connected unduly to Tolkien's fiction, but the suggestion is entirely apt in attempting to account for the significance of his mythic design. Hart further explains:

---

begun and developed before either *The Hobbit* or *The Lord of the Rings*, the work was published last – edited and put together from his father's collected tales of and writings on the First Age by Christopher Tolkien.

13 Hart, 'Tolkien, Creation, and Creativity', p.41.

> [Tolkien] was conscious of a deep sense of artistic responsibility [...] not so much to his church and its creeds as to the basic nature of reality as he believed it to be, and as the artist, therefore, was obliged to attend to it.[14]

Whilst feeling duty-bound to stay artistically faithful to his views on the nature of creativity, the spiritual climate that is in evidence in Tolkien's fiction cannot be said to be Christian in essence. As Hart and others have pointed out, within Tolkien's creation myth, and the spiritual ambience it promotes, there are distinct traces of ancient pre- and non-Christian mythologies. The light of Christianity certainly falls over Middle-earth and the Undying Lands, but Tolkien's world of elves, men, dragons and demi-gods is not an allegorical reproduction of it, and should not be 'decoded' as such – even if the hierarchical positioning of creation under angels under one God tempts us to.

Tolkien's myth offers a coming together of disparate faiths and religious understandings and is not governed by, or delivered from any fixed creed. As Brian Rosebury puts it 'Tolkien constructs a vision informed by what can only be called religious intuitions, yet does not begin from any foundation of assumed dogma.'[15] Within the same secondary world parameters, we find Christian virtue, biblical structure and spirits of the wood, wind and water. Indeed certain aspects of Tolkien's fiction hint very plainly at animism where, as White Jr. says, '[i]n Antiquity every tree, every stream, every hill had its own *genius loci*, its guardian spirit.'[16] Certainly, as discussed in the previous chapter, Tom Bombadil (and Goldberry) could be described in this fashion. We recall that *genius loci* is the exact term both Shippey and Curry use to describe Bombadil. Moreover we find sentience all across Tolkien's fiction: in every aspect of the natural world but also in objects such as swords and magic rings. In chapter one I discussed the Valar – angelic demi-gods, each sourced in and associated with an aspect of nature: Ulmo with the waters of the Earth, Yavanna with things that grow and so on. Each of these 'characters' could be said to be the guardian spirit or the 'steward' that watches over and tends the natural element in which they are

---

14 Hart, 'Tolkien, Creation, and Creativity', p.43.
15 Brian Rosebury, *Tolkien: A Critical Assessment*, New York: St. Martin's Press, 1992, p.138.
16 Lynn White Jr., 'Historical Roots of Our Ecological Crisis' in Cheryll Glotfelty & Harold Fromm (eds.), *The Ecocriticism Reader: Landmarks in Literary Ecology*, Athens and London: University of Georgia Press, 1996, p.10.

sourced. Indeed Yavanna appears on occasion in the form of a tree, and Ulmo may be perceived in the sights and sounds of flowing water.

And what of Gandalf and his stewardship of Middle-earth? Well, Gandalf is strictly a Maia, a spirit, or in Tolkien's own words, 'an *incarnate* 'angel".[17] As a Maia or lesser Vala, Gandalf is not strictly human but rather one of many angelic powers or spirits who have, throughout the history of creation in Tolkien's cosmology, been tasked with the stewardship of Middle-earth. Colin Duriez takes up the point:

> The Valar, or angelic powers, first take on the role of preparing the world for the arrival of elves, and later, humankind. They steward the world and provide its light [...] In the Third Age, when the events of *The Lord of the Rings* take place, several lesser Valar, or Maiar – most famously Gandalf – take on human form in order to serve as guardians against the reviving power of Sauron.[18]

Gandalf and the Valar are indeed 'angelic powers', but to hijack the Christian understanding of 'angel' in order to account for those such as the Valar, Bombadil or Gandalf is not in keeping with Tolkien's portrayal of these literary creations. To view them as some re-designed cult of saints is equally misguided. They are more precisely spiritual beings in a moral universe. Indeed, as noted in the early part of this chapter, Tolkien preceded his indistinct categorisation of Gandalf as a kind of angel by saying '[t]here are naturally no precise modern terms to say what he was.'[19] Furthermore in *The Book of Lost Tales Part One*, in 'The Coming of the Valar' there is a clear parallel drawn between lesser Vali and non-Christian primary world myth:

> With [Manwë and Varda] came many of those lesser Vali [...] these are the Mánir and the Súruli, the sylphs of the airs and of the winds [...] About them [Aulë and Palúrien] fared a great host who are the sprites of trees and woods, of dale and forest and mountain-side, or those that sing amid the grass at morning and chant among the standing corn at eve.[20]

If one strain of lesser Valar is painted with such an animistic hue, perhaps it follows that the Maiar (likewise lesser Valar – of which Gandalf is one) also are

---

17 Tolkien, *Letters*, p.202, emphasis in the original.
18 Colin Duriez, *J.R.R. Tolkien and C.S. Lewis: The Story of their Friendship*, Stroud, Gloucestershire: Sutton Publishing, 2005, pp.99-100.
19 Tolkien, *Letters*, p.202.
20 J.R.R. Tolkien, *The Book of Lost Tales Part One*, edited by Christopher Tolkien, London: George Allen & Unwin, 1983, p.66.

constructed without recourse to a strictly Christian frame of reference. Similarly, in terms of the Christian doctrine that declares humanity as 'chosen' and the centrepoint of God's design; this key aspect of Christianity is not played out in the words which Tolkien allows Gandalf to use concerning the world around him. It is clear from Gandalf's words that his ideas regarding stewardship pertain to a more holistic[21] view that considers the peoples of Middle-earth as part of the interconnected wonder of nature.

Indeed Gandalf's remark 'I also am a steward' coming after, as it does, his declaration that his concerns lie with 'that [which] can still grow fair or bear fruit and flower'[22] is an overtly ecocentric[23] and environmentalist allusion. In the midst of the War of the Ring, Gandalf is declaring that the landscapes and ecology of Middle-earth are as of much worth to him as the peoples and races who inhabit the land – and *more* important than the great empires, kingdoms and seats of power that those such as Sauron, Saruman and even Théoden and Denethor value so highly. But rather than conclude that Gandalf prioritises the environment over the people, I believe his outlook may best be understood by asserting that he places no priority on one aspect of creation over another. Gandalf thus becomes recast as a positive environmental model who views the biodiversity of living things: the people, the land, the wildlife, the trees and

---

21 Viewing Gandalf as representing a holistic interpretation of stewardship is perhaps the best way of reconciling his use of the term and his outlook. Ecologists J.L. Chapman and M.J. Reiss whilst acknowledging that 'the notion of stewardship' is 'a significant theme in [...] writings on Christianity', offer an understanding of the term that seems more in alignment with the ideology promoted by Gandalf: 'Narrowly understood, stewardship still implies something of a 'them' (rest of the world) versus 'us' (humans) situation. However, there is a more holistic view of our relationship to the rest of creation which can be described as one of 'mutuality'. This reflects the ecological understanding that a relationship is mutual if it benefits both partners. The word 'mutuality' is therefore intended to avoid overtones of hierarchy and superiority [...] humanity can be viewed as having a depth of inter-relatedness with the rest of the natural order that transcends an understanding which has humanity as somehow set apart from, or above, the rest of creation.' (J.L. Chapman & M.J. Reiss, *Ecology: Principles and Applications*, 2nd edition, Cambridge: Cambridge University Press, 1999, p.271).
22 Tolkien, *Return*, p.742.
23 Early in *The Fellowship of the Ring* we are provided with another interesting insight into how Gandalf represents a more eco-centric understanding of stewardship, and how he may most vitally perceive the threat of Sauron. When speaking to Frodo at Bag End concerning the re-emergence of the Dark Lord's destructive force, he describes the peril they face as a force that will 'cover all the lands in a second darkness' (Tolkien, *Fellowship*, p.50). The phrase he uses, for all its wider metaphorical connotations, is nonetheless nature-themed in essence, referring as it does specifically to 'the lands'. Given Galdor's characterisation of Sauron's power as a threat against the physical landscape, and Gandalf's declaration that success for his defence of Middle-earth may be measurable, in part, against his ability to protect life forces that 'still grow fair or bear fruit and flower', Gandalf's choice of words reveals a worldview that consistently places focus on the natural world.

flowers as part of the same ecosystem of 'worthy things' in his care. In this light, Gandalf's employment of the word 'steward' to describe himself needs to be re-evaluated beyond its Christian allusions.

Although I disagree with Dickerson and Evans' Christian framing of Gandalf's (and Tolkien's) ecological worldview, we do share environmentally themed common ground. One aspect in particular is the importance of the opposing versions of stewardship offered by Gandalf and Denethor – and it is to this that I now turn.

Gandalf, in claiming that he is '*also* a steward' (emphasis added) to Denethor matches his own notion of stewardship against that demonstrated and declared by Denethor, who is himself a steward – Steward of Minas Tirith and Gondor. Denethor's understanding of his role as Steward of Gondor, however, is defined in terms of rule and dominion. Whenever he refers to himself and his role, Denethor seems always to emphasise his position as 'lord' of Gondor. He has lost sight of his need to serve the good of Gondor and instead has become preoccupied with the thirst for power and rule.

Speaking to Pippin about Sauron, Denethor seems to marvel at, and even aspire to how the Dark Lord maintains his power: '[Sauron] uses others as his weapons […] so do all great lords if they are wise, master Halfling. Or why do I sit here in my tower and think, and watch, and wait, spending even my sons?'[24] It is clear from this thinly veiled acclamation of Sauron that Denethor views both himself and Sauron as great and wise lords[25] – his judgement is based *not* on the rights and wrongs of rule, *not* on the destruction visited on the world as a result of rule, but on the worth of rule itself. He promotes the need to use others or 'spend' other things, 'even [his] sons', in order to maintain power and hold on to control. Environmentally speaking, Denethor's version of stewardship would be one based on an exploitation of the natural world that is governed by

---

24 Tolkien, *Return*, p.744.
25 Interestingly although Denethor carries the deportment of a great and powerful lord and presents himself as such, when he comes to face the humbly dressed and understated Gandalf, we are told through the filter of Pippin's perception that, despite appearances to the contrary, it is Gandalf who exudes a greater wisdom and power. The narrator of *The Lord of the Rings* describes the scene: 'Denethor looked indeed much more like a great wizard than Gandalf did, more kingly, beautiful, and powerful; and older. Yet by a sense other than sight Pippin perceived that Gandalf had the greater power and the deeper wisdom, and a majesty that was veiled. And he was older, far older.' (Tolkien, *Return*, p.740).

an understanding that humanity is lord over all creation. Denethor sees himself as a ruler who must exploit or 'spend' all that is at hand in order to sustain his grip on power and it is made clear that he would not have hesitated to use the One Ring if it had come into his hands.

When he asks Pippin to repeat an oath of allegiance to Gondor, the oath Pippin is duty-bound to recite includes a clear reference to Denethor's status as ruler – and a requirement for Pippin to not only pledge allegiance to Gondor, but also to Denethor himself: '[h]ere do I swear fealty and service to Gondor, and to the Lord and Steward of the realm.'[26] Furthermore directly subsequent to Pippin offering his service, Denethor, rather than making a request of Pippin, issues a command to his new servant: 'my first command to you: speak and be not silent! Tell me your full tale, and see that you recall all that you can of Boromir, my son.'[27] Although the command is perhaps tinged with a conversational nuance, it nonetheless immediately underscores Denethor's lordship over the hobbit.

In an exchange with Gandalf related to the peril which threatens all of Middle-earth, Denethor again displays his insularity and narrow-minded attitude: 'there is no purpose higher in the world as it stands now' Denethor declares 'than the good of Gondor; and the rule of Gondor, my lord, is mine and no other's, unless the king should come again.'[28] Denethor, of course, does not want the king to return, he is concerned primarily with his continuing status as ruler of Gondor and dismisses the troubles of the wider world. Denethor's take on his stewardship of Gondor is marked by his wish to continue to rule and master. In response to Denethor's declaration Gandalf states humbly 'the rule of no realm is mine, neither of Gondor, nor any other, great or small.'[29] Gandalf's understanding of stewardship is not one based on the desire to rule, but one that seeks to preserve the wonder of the living world around him. He understands that all of creation is interconnected, and in preserving one tiny part of creation he helps to preserve it all. His model of ecological stewardship places humanity as part of rather than as 'lord' of the natural system of

---

26 Tolkien, *Return*, p.740.
27 Tolkien, *Return*, p.740.
28 Tolkien, *Return*, p.741.
29 Tolkien, *Return*, pp.741-42.

living things. And, as modern ecology now tells us, in caring for the natural world, humanity cares for itself. Gandalf seems to know this implicitly. This non-anthropocentric understanding of environmental stewardship has only, in recent years, begun to take centre stage in the studies and writings of forward thinking ecologists like Robin Attfield[30] whose simple yet profound assertion that 'trees had needs before people existed and cannot be supposed to have lost them'[31] perfectly frames the case for an ecocentric point of view.

It is clear that *part* of Gandalf's purpose in Middle-earth is not only to oppose evil (specifically that represented by Sauron) but also to act as steward over the entire interconnectedness of living things. This aspect of Gandalf's character alone reveals him to have been created with an environmentally positive dimension that profoundly reflects Tolkien's own understanding of humanity's need to view all living things and the canopy of nature as precious and worthy of protection, not just as commodities to meet the needs of the human race but as wonders in their own right – to delight as Tom Bombadil would in their 'otherness'. Gandalf's recognition of the value of all life across creation, and his affirmation that he seeks to protect 'things that are in peril' underlines the environmental significance of his worldview for our reality where countless non-human life forms remain very much 'in peril' or have already passed into extinction. Indeed Gandalf's willingness to extend his aid and protection even to plant life in the midst of the crisis of the Third Age, presents him as an environmental maverick and liberal thinker. As such Gandalf could be said to be a kind of Middle-earth version of someone like Albert Schweitzer, the liberal Christian missionary and contemporary of Tolkien who won the Nobel Peace Prize in 1952 for his *Reverence for Life*. Schweitzer, whose ideas espoused a moral imperative that humanity must view all life as precious, is widely regarded as one who helped ignite the modern green movement.[32] Schweitzer's thoughts on the value of living things closely

---

30 See Attfield's chapter 'Taking the Future Seriously' in *Environmental Ethics*, Cambridge: Polity Press, 2003, in which he discusses the need to adopt a non-anthropocentric understanding of stewardship which does not promote the superiority of humankind.
31 Attfield, *Environmental Ethics*, p.54.
32 See Ara Paul Barsam, *Reverence for Life: Albert Schweitzer's Great Contribution to Ethical Thought*, Oxford: Oxford University Press, 2008, in which Barsam discusses the importance and influence of Schweitzer for a developing green movement. Indeed Rachel Carson's *Silent Spring* (1962), a work which has been widely acclaimed by ecocritics such as Greg Garrard as the 'founding text of modern environmentalism' (Greg Garrard, *Ecocriticism*, London and New York: Routledge, 2004, p.2), is

mirror those advocated by Gandalf (and thus Tolkien).³³ Schweitzer defines what he calls his 'fundamental principle of morality' within the tenet: '[i]t is *good* to maintain and cherish life; it is *evil* to destroy and check life' and goes on to expound on this basic principle:

> A man is only ethical really when he obeys the constraint laid on him to help all life which he is able to succour [...] he does not ask how far this or that life deserves sympathy as valuable in itself, nor how far it is capable of feeling. To him life as such is sacred. He shatters no ice crystal that sparkles in the sun, tears no leaf from its tree, breaks off no flower, and is careful not to crush any insect as he walks.³⁴

The thoughts, words and deeds of Gandalf certainly echo this ecocentric ethic. Although Gandalf takes part in battles against the armies of Sauron and Saruman, he does so out of necessity and out of a wish to pursue the greater good. As we shall examine more fully later Gandalf is decidedly reticent to use his powers in anger, and in response to Frodo's declaration that he wished Bilbo had killed Gollum, Gandalf remarks 'do not be too eager to deal out death in judgement.'³⁵ In other words Gandalf understands on a very fundamental level the connection between evil and the desire 'to destroy and check life' without justifiable cause. Moreover, echoing the pronounced ecocentric focus of Schweitzer's 'principle of morality' Gandalf (as we have noted) is acutely aware that Sauron threatens *all* life in Middle-earth and that the need to survive and prevail against Sauron's assault is not the preserve of the free peoples that inhabit the land, but also a necessity shared by all representations of life across Middle-earth: from the forests to the grasslands of Rohan to the woodland creatures and the manifold beasts who exist under the sun (even those that have been exploited under Sauron's hand). This ideology and sense of union among living things is a predominant theme in Schweitzer's

---

actually dedicated to Schweitzer. See chapter five of this discourse for my comparative study of *The Lord of the Rings* and Carson's *Silent Spring*.

33 See chapter four, in which, under a wider discussion of Lynn White Jr.'s criticisms of the anti-ecological rhetoric observable in traditional Christian doctrine, I also draw parallels between Gandalf and St. Francis of Assisi, due, in part, to the Grey Wizard's affinity with the birds and beasts of Middle-earth. His friendship with (rather his than lordship over) Shadowfax the horse and Gwaihir the eagle are cases in point. Radagast the Brown, of course, comes to mind also in this regard, and is similarly discussed – although the common traits observable between Gandalf, St. Francis and indeed Schweitzer are, I contend, the more compelling.

34 Quoted in Richard L. Fern, *Nature, God and Humanity: Envisioning an Ethics of Nature*, Cambridge: Cambridge University Press, 2002, p.40.

35 Tolkien, *Fellowship*, p.58.

Reverence for Life. James Brabazon, author of *Albert Schweitzer: A Biography*, offers the following understanding of Schweitzer's philosophy:

> *Reverence for Life* says that the only thing we are really sure of is that we live and want to go on living. This is something that we share with everything else that lives, from elephants to blades of grass – and, of course, every human being. So we are brothers and sisters to all living things, and owe to all of them the same care and respect, that we wish for ourselves.[36]

This is a uniting principle and a philosophy that Tolkien (evidenced in his fiction and private papers) no doubt would have shared. Later in this chapter I discuss the premise that Gandalf, perhaps more than any other character in his fiction, carries the worldview of Tolkien himself. But first, in order to fully understand the environmental significance of Gandalf, I shall explore the exact nature of Gandalf's role and place in Middle-earth in its time of need – a role that Gandalf, as plenipotentiary of the Valar, decided upon and carved out for himself.

(II.1) Gandalf's Role in Middle-earth

When we (and Bilbo) first meet Gandalf in *The Hobbit*, he appears simply as 'an old man with a staff.' The narrator tells us, however, that '[t]ales and adventures sprouted up all over the place wherever he went, in the most extraordinary fashion.'[37] The inference of the narrator's words is that Gandalf himself stirs adventure out of a still world. Indeed Gandalf seems to admit as much in his conversation with the unsuspecting Bilbo: 'I am looking for someone to share in an adventure that I am arranging.'[38] One's first perception of the old wizard, dressed in his blue hat and long grey cloak, is that of a 'disturber of the peace'. This view of Gandalf persists through time and among many of the peoples who populate Middle-earth – Gandalf's reputation as a rabble-rouser precedes him. Tyler takes up the question of his sometime ill-favoured reputation:

> To many western folk, including the hobbits, Gandalf was 'just a wizard' – a vain, fussy old conjuror with a long beard and bushy eyebrows, whose chief asset was his uncommon skill with fireworks – while many men of the South

---

36 James Brabazon, *Albert Schweitzer: A Biography*, 2nd revised edition, Syracuse: Syracuse University Press, 2000, p.44.
37 J.R.R. Tolkien, *The Hobbit*, London: HarperCollins, 1997, p.5.
38 Tolkien, *The Hobbit*, p.6.

regarded him as little better than a pest, a homeless vagabond, a meddler in affairs of state and a herald of ill-news.[39]

Indeed Bilbo, upon realising that the old man with whom he speaks as *The Hobbit* begins is the much famed (or ill-famed) Gandalf, proclaims with some unease, '[n]ot the Gandalf who was responsible for so many quiet lads and lasses going off into the blue for mad adventures?'[40] Even midway through *The Lord of the Rings*, as Gandalf and company arrive upon the borders of Rohan to offer assistance in a time of need, we hear King Théoden declare: 'your welcome is doubtful here, Master Gandalf. You have ever been a herald of woe.'[41] Although Théoden's thoughts have been, in part, corrupted by the aptly named Gríma Wormtongue, who pejoratively labels Gandalf 'Stormcrow' and '*Láthspell*'[42] (the later translated as 'ill-news'), no doubt Gandalf's reputation and the king's own experience of how, as he puts it '[t]roubles follow [Gandalf] like crows'[43] have made Wormtongue's sneering words seem all the more reasonable.

In responding to the charges made specifically by Théoden and Wormtongue, Gandalf, although quickly losing patience with Wormtongue's contemptuous tone, offers an insightful defence of his character: 'in two ways may a man come with evil tidings. He may be a worker of evil; or he may be such as leaves well alone, and comes only to bring aid in a time of need.'[44] Gandalf's riposte is intended, of course, to reverse the charge against him and relay that it is he who chases on the tails of trouble in order to aid those things it threatens, rather than being 'a worker of evil' who brings trouble and evil with him as a consequence of his arrival. Gandalf's 'either-or' remark relates expressly to one who brings 'evil tidings', but if we break his statement down into three possibilities rather than two, we create three categories which account for the position of every life force in Middle-earth at any given moment as the crisis of the Third Age unfolds:

---

39 Tyler, *The Complete Tolkien Companion*, p.265.
40 Tolkien, *The Hobbit*, p.7.
41 Tolkien, *The Two Towers*, London: HarperCollins, 1997, p.501.
42 Tolkien, *Two Towers*, p.502.
43 Tolkien, *Two Towers*, p.501.
44 Tolkien, *Two Towers*, p.502.

1. A worker of evil (intentional or not, corrupted or enslaved).
2. One who leaves well alone (oblivious to, unconcerned with or dismissive of that which threatens the world).
3. One who brings aid in a time of need (intentional or not).

Of course there are many of Tolkien's creations that move from one category to another as events and incidents come to pass. Treebeard and the ents for example are rooted very much in category 2 until Treebeard encounters Merry and Pippin in Fangorn Forest after which they move to category 3. Saruman, by express purpose, begins in category 3 but is utterly corrupted by the allure of power and slips to category 1. Even Gollum moves from 1 to 3 when the quest to destroy the Ring arrives at its most perilous moment. Gandalf, of course, begins and remains in category 3. Indeed the true function and purpose served by Gandalf as Sauron returns to power is not to wield his power in opposition to Sauron, but rather to stir up, guide, teach, prepare, empower, and bring together native forces that will. Moreover Gandalf helps these pockets of resistance to find the strength and will to oppose that which at first seems invincible. More precisely, in terms of the categories laid out above, Gandalf's purpose is to do everything within his power to persuade, cajole and recruit those who are in category 1 and 2 to find it within themselves to move to category 3.

He is not the embodiment, therefore, of the struggle against evil, but more as Tyler suggests 'the chief architect' of that struggle. In a letter to his proof reader Naomi Mitchison, Tolkien offers a little insight into the nature of the Istari, to which Gandalf belongs: 'their proper function, maintained by Gandalf, and perverted by Saruman, was to encourage and bring out the native powers of the Enemies of Sauron.'[45] It is interesting to note that Tolkien uses the phrase 'native powers', because it suggests that the true resistance against the evil of Sauron must come primarily from within – that is to say from those who are part of Middle-earth and not from spiritual powers beyond the world. In another letter Tolkien becomes a little more specific with regards the Istari's purpose saying 'what they were primarily sent [to Middle-earth] for' in the Third Age 'as the great crisis of Sauron loomed on the horizon' was to:

---

45 Tolkien, *Letters*, p.180.

train, advise, instruct, arouse the hearts and minds of those threatened by Sauron to a resistance with their own strengths; not just to do the job for them. Thus they appeared as 'old' sage figures. But in this 'mythology' all the 'angelic' powers concerned with the world were capable of many degrees of error [...] the 'wizards' were not exempt, indeed being incarnate were more likely to stray, or err. Gandalf alone fully passes the tests, on a moral plane anyway (he makes mistakes in judgement).[46]

The 'wizards' must allow and empower the world to save itself, to aid and advise certainly, but to not become beguiled by their own innate power. For as Gandalf knew, such temptation could only deliver them away from their true purpose and bring them under the spell of the power in Mordor. This is of course what happens to Saruman, who certainly proved himself to be 'capable of [...] error'. His purpose becomes perverted by the will to power and all his deeds become tainted by that perversion. As mentioned in the previous chapter, Saruman becomes 'a would-be Sauron', and just as the evil of Sauron devastates the lands around Mordor, so too the landscape around Isengard, suffering under the industrialised hand of the White Wizard, becomes a reflection of, or more accurately a foreshadowing of Mordor, or a Mordor in the making. The environmental devastation that Saruman visits upon the landscape surrounding Isengard in his pursuit of power demonstrates how far he has fallen from his intended purpose – namely to muster 'native powers' and 'arouse the hearts and minds' of the peoples of Middle-earth to resist an evil force which would destroy, enslave and pervert Middle-earth itself – not just the people but the land also. Tolkien tells us that 'Gandalf alone fully passes the tests, on a moral plane', and alludes not only to Gandalf's ability to resist the temptation to which Saruman falls, but also to Gandalf's understanding that all living things must come under his care, for it is these things too that Sauron's regime threatens. To truly oppose Sauron is to protect the naturally sustained environments of Middle-earth. Gandalf not only understands this instinctively but in his role as guide and teacher, he also instils it in others, and as Jared Lobdell points out in *A Tolkien Compass* '[i]nstinctive reactions are crucially important in a world in which birds, plants, trees and even the weather (as on Caradhras) may be part of the moral struggle between Good and Evil.'[47]

---

46 Tolkien, *Letters*, p.202.
47 Jared Lobdell, *A Tolkien Compass*, Chicago and La Salle, Illinois: Open Court Publishing, 2003, p.46.

(II.2) The Istari

Amid his treachery and his fall from grace Saruman declares that he still seeks to oppose Sauron (and thus hold true to his purpose) and that there is not 'any real change in [his] designs, only in [his] means';[48] but in laying waste the land and trees around his stronghold Saruman has already lost sight of his true purpose and failed the test that Gandalf passes. Indeed as Gandalf, early in the sequence of events of *The Lord of the Rings*, is held prisoner by Saruman on the high reaches of Orthanc, he surveys the lands beneath him and later recalls the view of the surrounding valley, there is a perceptive sadness in his tone: 'I looked on [the landscape] and saw that, whereas it had once been green and fair, it was now filled with pits and forges.'[49] Saruman too strays from his intended roles as teacher, advisor and guide to those of lesser stature or power. Seeing his ultimate purpose as 'Knowledge, Rule, Order' he dismisses the need to bring out the native powers of those who would also oppose Sauron believing himself to have been 'hindered rather than helped by [these] weak and idle friends.'[50] Indeed as we have seen, Saruman exploits rather than assists those around him. When he can gain no assistance from Gandalf or the peoples and races that follow Gandalf's (and Elrond's) model of opposition against Sauron, he turns to the orcs, and creates a great army, and eventually becomes an extension of Sauron's evil. In petitioning Gandalf's aid to pursue his goals, Saruman even attempts to exploit another of the Istari, to drag another of the emissaries of the Valar astray. Gandalf of course is too wise, and morally too resistant, to fall foul of Saruman's attempts. Saruman, we are told, however, does succeed in exploiting another wizard of the Istari – Radagast. When Gandalf tells Saruman that Radagast has brought him a message concerning the coming forth of the 'Nine Black Riders', the narrator tells us that Saruman 'no longer concealed his scorn' for the other Istari wizard, and instead boasted of how he had used Radagast in his machinations. 'Radagast the Bird-tamer! Radagast the simple! Radagast the Fool! Yet he had just the wit to play the part that I had set him. For you have come, and that was all the purpose of my message.'[51] It is clear both in word and deed that Saruman, unlike Gandalf (and Radagast), has no time or energy to expend on lesser life forces.

---

48 Tolkien, *Fellowship*, p.253.
49 Tolkien, *Fellowship*, p.251.
50 Tolkien, *Fellowship*, p.253.
51 Tolkien, *Fellowship*, p.252.

It is perhaps worth mentioning in this consideration of the role of the Istari, and the positive environmental model that Gandalf represents, that Radagast, and even more so the other two remaining Istari wizards, 'the Blue Wizards', most likely named Alatar and Pallando,[52] played little or no part in the events of the Third Age; but we know they all came with one united purpose, 'to contest the power of Sauron.'[53] That Radagast and 'the Blue Wizards' therefore play no significant role in the struggle against Sauron is perhaps testimony to Tolkien's comment that the Istari messengers 'were capable of many degrees of error.' Indeed in the chapter on the Istari in *Unfinished Tales*, we are told that 'the Istari being clad in bodies of Middle-earth, might even as men and elves fall away from their purposes.' We are further told that Radagast 'became enamoured of the many beasts and birds that dwelt in Middle-earth, and forsook elves and men, and spent his days among the wild creatures.' Of the other two Istari known as *Ithryn Luin*, 'the Blue Wizards', the reason for their apparent inactivity or at least ineffectiveness against the regime of Sauron is less clear, but perhaps rather sinisterly we are told that 'they passed into the East with Curunír [Saruman], but they never returned.' The narrator makes no further suggestion that Saruman may have had something to do with their disappearance but simply adds 'whether they remained in the East, pursuing there the purposes for which they were sent; or perished; or as some hold were ensnared by Sauron and became his servants is not known.'[54] Of the fate of the two 'Blue Wizards' Tolkien, in a letter dated 1958, writes 'they went as emissaries to distant regions, East and South, far out of Númenórean range: missionaries to 'enemy-occupied' lands as it were. What success they had I do not know; but I fear they failed, as Saruman did, though doubtless in different ways.'[55]

Four out of the five Istari wizards, then, effectively fail in the task set for them; only Gandalf stays true to his purpose. It is interesting to note that Radagast is generally viewed to have failed in his task to oppose the threat of Sauron because he concerned himself *too much* with only one aspect of the natural

---

52 There is a little uncertainty as to the names of the two remaining Istari called 'Blue Wizards' but it is generally accepted among Tolkien scholars that Alatar and Pallando are they. See Tyler, *The Complete Tolkien Companion*, under the entry 'Wizards' p.705.
53 Tolkien, 'Appendix B' in *The Return of the King*, p.1059.
54 J.R.R. Tolkien, *Unfinished Tales*, edited by Christopher Tolkien, London: HarperCollins, 1998, p.504.
55 Tolkien, *Unfinished Tales*, p.518.

world – the welfare of birds and beasts (called *kelvar* in Tolkien's cosmology), or as Tyler puts it 'it was later felt, by some of those who had sent him, that [Radagast] had become too enamoured of these *kelvar* and thereby neglected his real mission.'[56] Only Gandalf displays a view of the natural order that places all things together as worthy of concern.

(II.3) Gandalf: Guide and Activist

As we have seen, in environmental terms, Gandalf, like Tom Bombadil, takes account of the worth of things on their own terms. His concerns (unlike those of Radagast) lie equally with the fate of both the races and the ecology of Middle-earth, and his wish to protect the green face of the world is indelibly bound up with his desire to elicit resistance against Sauron, precisely because the threat that Sauron represents is directed toward both the Free Peoples and the landscapes of Middle-earth. Gandalf's environmental positioning then resembles that made explicit in Tom Bombadil – both take delight in the natural world, both value the living world on its own terms, without seeking to control or shape it in any way. But whereas Bombadil represents a pacifist expression of nature under threat, Gandalf, in seeking to stir opposition against forces that would destroy the ecology of Middle-earth, represents environmental activism in our world. His words of advice, his insights into the nature of Sauron's evil, his discovery and making public of the corruptions of others, his gathering together of disparate peoples and races under one banner of resistance, his empowerment of hitherto untouched resources (like the hobbits) portray him as a prevailing activist influence in the struggle against the crisis which faces the Third Age – one which, in many respects, reflects the environmental crisis of Tolkien's own time and the ongoing ecological problems facing our world today.

The notion of environmental activism in our world, however, has, on occasion, been somewhat tainted with the emergence of radical factions (or individuals) who pursue their agenda in the absence of a prevailing sense of right and wrong. Like Saruman, these radical elements use one form of wrongdoing to counter another. In general, however, the promotion of environmental good

---

56 Tyler, *The Complete Tolkien Companion*, p.529.

sense, and activism which seeks to address (or redress) specific environmental problems has produced many positive results. Greg Garrard in *Ecocriticism* tells us that, 'the mainstream environmental movement [...] has significant successes on specific issues such as Ozone-depleting CFC emissions to its credit.' These far-reaching advancements in the global response to environmental problems, however, are but one aspect of the effects and activities that constitute environmental activism. Garrard explains: '[a]ctivism may range from recycling bottles and buying organic food to major commitment to conservation activity.'[57] Moreover, environmental activism, which begins on a small scale, with perhaps one individual decision to recycle or monitor electricity consumption may (and often does) lead to greater and greater environmentally positive decisions and outcomes. In environmental terms then, Gandalf, as one who stirs others to action and in many cases awakens them to the crisis in their midst, may be read as an environmental activist who seeks to empower others to rise to the defining challenge of his and their time.

Indeed as Gandalf in Bag End awakens Frodo to the threat posed by Sauron, and tells him that the ring left to him by Bilbo is the One Ring that Sauron is employing all his power to find 'to give him strength and knowledge to beat down all resistance,' Frodo at first grumbles that the developing crisis has come so squarely upon his shoulders; that his lifetime should be so disrupted by the emergence of the evil now in his midst. As such he shirks a little at the responsibility he must soon face as Ringbearer:

> 'I wish it had not happened in my time,' said Frodo.
> 'So do I,' said Gandalf, 'and so do all who live to see such times. But that is not for them to decide. All we have to decide is what to do with the time that is given us. And already, Frodo, our time is beginning to look black.'[58]

Gandalf's reaction to Frodo's words is to make him aware that he is not alone in such thoughts, and that 'all who live to see such times' feel the heavy burden of responsibility. But more importantly Gandalf emphasises that although the burden will be heavy, and the responsibility great, there is still a free choice, and thus an opportunity to affect 'the time that is given'. This is an ennobling and empowering ideology that offers a direct choice: either turn away and of-

---

57 Garrard, *Ecocriticism*, p.19.
58 Tolkien, *Fellowship*, p.50.

fer no resistance to the defining crisis of the age or stand up and be counted among those who struggle against it. Considered in relation to the environmental crisis that looms over our world today, Gandalf's simple yet profoundly moral ideology represents a call to individual ecological activism. The phrase 'all we have to decide is what to do with the time that is given us' speaks to all of humanity across the ages, implying an obligation to do all we can with our time and strength to preserve the natural wonder around us, to heal that which has been damaged, to reject those technologies and powers which unnecessarily impact negatively upon nature, in short to make the world a better place for those who will follow. Ecologically speaking this ideology runs to the very heart of green politics. Dickerson and Evans also allude to the universality of applicability evoked by the 'moral imperative' suggested in this exchange between Frodo and Gandalf:

> Taken at face value, Gandalf does not speak merely of *Frodo's* time and responsibilities; he speaks of *all* people's. Of course according to the internal logic of the novel, this means Frodo, Gandalf, and all the other characters alive in Middle-earth at the end of the Third Age. But in one of the many instances when the implications of the narrative slide imperceptibly from the inner world of fantasy to the outer world of reality, Tolkien advances a point that is applicable to both. He articulates a moral imperative that he implies is a universal principle applicable to all people, including *us*.[59]

Of course Gandalf warns Frodo that there is no escaping or ignoring the crisis or peril that is before them: the rise of the Dark Lord, and that even towards the hitherto safe environment of the Shire, the threat of Sauron now turns, 'he has at last heard, I think, of *hobbits* and the *Shire*.'[60] Apart from simply telling Frodo that, due to Gollum's capture in Mordor, Sauron has become aware of the Shire and its possible connection with the One Ring, the wider implication of Gandalf's words is that, in reality, Frodo may choose to reject the burden of responsibility and turn away from the distant spectre of Mordor, but in the end the threat of Sauron will come to the Shire, and even those innocent hobbits who know nothing of the peril which hangs over them will become enslaved under the shadow of his evil. Indeed as we find out, an extension of Sauron's malevolence eventually reaches the Shire in the form of Sharkey and becomes manifest in the industrialised devastation visited upon the once green and fair

---

59 Dickerson & Evans, *Ents, Elves, and Eriador*, p.46.
60 Tolkien, *Fellowship*, p.88. Emphasis in the original.

landscape of the hobbits' home. Again there is a powerful ecological message reflected in Gandalf's warning to Frodo which becomes Tolkien's warning to us: we may choose to ignore the environmental problems which afflict the world today, we may view them as indistinct and too far removed from the familiarity and comfort of our everyday lives, but eventually the gathering effects of a global environmental crisis will come to our doorstep. Richard Kerridge, introducing *Writing the Environment: Ecocriticism and Literature*, attempts to explain why apathy towards green issues persists: 'Environmental questions are large scale and long-term. They are usually rumours, things scientists disagree over; things happening elsewhere.'[61] The sentiment suggested by Kerridge's statement could accurately sum up the attitude of many of the peoples of Middle-earth as Sauron returns to prominence – this is a vague threat, a rumour that great warriors and lords discuss, and therefore nothing that should cause any immediate alarm. The central purpose of Gandalf's presence in Middle-earth at the end of the Third Age is to shake whoever and whatever he can from such indifference, apathy and lethargy, to guide and teach them in order that they may find the strength and courage to resist the very real threat that Sauron represents.

Wherever Gandalf's presence is felt in Middle-earth, one can see that he is constantly guiding and stirring those around him, teaching and empowering them to stand on their own. He alone is responsible for catapulting the hobbits into the epicentre of the events that shape the resistance against Sauron. Others like Elrond, Aragorn and Thorin Oakenshield's company of dwarves play their part in this process but ultimately it is Gandalf who is the catalyst and the prime mover in these affairs. From the moment he manipulates Bilbo into leaving Bag End and going off on an adventure we see the hand of Gandalf at work in shaping the rise in standing of the hobbits in the Third Age. Without even being aware of it Bilbo finds courage, determination and understanding as a result of his adventures. Gandalf for a time travels with him, and occasionally intercedes to offer assistance, but in crucial moments in *The Hobbit*, he withdraws to attend to 'pressing business' thus leaving Bilbo and the company of dwarves to survive on 'luck' and their 'courage and sense'.[62]

---

61 Richard Kerridge, 'Introduction' in Richard Kerridge & Neil Sammells (eds.), *Writing the Environment: Ecocriticism and Literature*, London and New York: Zed Books, 1998, p.2.
62 Tolkien, *The Hobbit*, p.125.

Jane Chance suggests that aside from acting as 'guide and teacher to Bilbo', Gandalf almost takes on the role of a parent in this regard:

> In *The Hobbit* Gandalf acts as a guide and teacher to Bilbo […] and encourages Bilbo by sparking the hobbit's enthusiasm for the adventure with a few tales. Like any good parent though, Gandalf realizes he must depart (in chapter 7) in order for Bilbo to develop his own physical, intellectual and spiritual qualities […] in the process his initial physical bumbling turns to real dexterity, then skill, and is finally aided by the courage of the newly confident hobbit.[63]

For Gandalf to have remained with Bilbo throughout his adventure would have been to cause Bilbo to lean on him like a crutch in difficult times, but even here in *The Hobbit* we see Gandalf begin to attend to his purpose, for Sauron, lurks in the shadows of the story of *The Hobbit*. In a letter dated 1951, three years before the publication of *The Lord of the Rings*, Tolkien takes up the question of Gandalf's 'abandonment' of Bilbo in times of need – alluding to the fact that at such times Gandalf had the 'problem' of Sauron (the Necromancer) in mind: 'Gandalf the wizard is called away on high business, an attempt to deal with the Necromancer, and so leaves the hobbit without help or advice in the midst of his 'adventure' forcing him to stand on his own two legs, and become in his mode heroic.'[64]

The same pattern emerges in *The Lord of the Rings*, with Gandalf encouraging, advising and assisting Frodo, Sam, Pippin and Merry, and indeed the many races who make up the Fellowship, but it is Frodo more than any other about whom Gandalf is most concerned as the story begins. Chance remarks that 'in part Gandalf constitutes a spiritual guide for Frodo.'[65] Gandalf puts Frodo on the right path, counsels him in moral choice and the nature of pity, but like Bilbo, in order to survive his trials, Frodo must find an inner strength, understand things for himself, and rather than meekly follow the path or the philosophy shown to him by Gandalf, Frodo must see the reasons why he must shoulder his responsibilities and struggle against the might of Sauron.[66] In environmental

---

63 Jane Chance, *Tolkien's Art: A Mythology For England*, Lexington, Kentucky: University Press of Kentucky, 2001, p.66.
64 Tolkien, *Letters*, p.159.
65 Chance, *Tolkien's Art*, p.152.
66 Of course, Frodo does rise to meet his personal challenge and the crisis of the age. As all the other delegates in attendance at the Council of Elrond fall silent 'with downcast eyes' when a decision needs to be made concerning who will undertake the almost impossible task of taking the Ring, the deadliest object (and the symbol of all sin) in Middle-earth, to Mordor – it is Frodo, the once hesitant and

terms, this need for an awakening to individual responsibility and understanding is paramount for any mass response to ecological problems in the real world to succeed. Crucial environmental research and evidence may reach our ears; green activists may lead the way in the struggle to get the facts about the state of nature to us and stir us into response, but it is up to us as individuals to take responsibility for our own 'carbon footprint', to stir and face the real emergency that is all around us, and to develop our own green conscience.

(III) Circles of Light, Fire & Alter-egos

Gandalf, like Tom Bombadil, despite harbouring an innate desire to preserve the ecology as well as the freedom of the peoples of Middle-earth could not have resisted Sauron's might, or averted environmental catastrophe in the Third Age alone, nor could he have found such resistance among one race. Gandalf had to reach the wider world and unite strength against the evil before him. His true worth as an agent of resistance and an exemplar of environmental activism is that he systematically enlists forces from across the entire stage of the drama to aid in the defence of Middle-earth. The concept of 'the Fellowship' exemplifies this, and although Elrond is instrumental in casting the 'Nine Walkers', it is Gandalf in his dealings with elves, dwarves, humans and hobbits who is the true catalyst for this alliance of resistance. Faramir says of Gandalf, believing that he has fallen in Moria, that he was 'a great mover of the deeds that are done in our time.'[67] Directly or indirectly Gandalf's influence may be felt in the stirring of all those who come to oppose Sauron.

---

fearful hobbit, who speaks as the portentous 'noon-bell' rings: 'I will take the Ring [...] though I do not know the way.' This phrase, which is clearly evocative of Christian virtue, marks the true coming of age, and the ennoblement of the hobbits. Indeed as Frodo speaks, the narrator tells us that 'Elrond raised his eyes and looked at him.' The elf-lord then pronounces in admiration, '[t]his is the hour of the Shire-folk, when they arise from their quiet fields to shake the towers and counsels of the Great. Who of all the Wise could have foreseen it?' (Tolkien, *Fellowship*, pp. 263-64). Although, as Elrond suggests, Gandalf may not have 'foreseen' the magnitude of Frodo's selflessness and rise to valour in Middle-earth's darkest hour, nonetheless the Grey Wizard, 'of all the Wise' has, from the first, foreseen the potential of hobbits. He, above all others, has been responsible for kindling the flame of hobbit-heroism and guiding the Shire-folk so that they may, as Tolkien puts it, 'become in [their] mode heroic' (Tolkien, *Letters*, p.159.)

67 Tolkien, *Two Towers*, p.655.

Maria Raffaella Benvenuto in her essay 'From *Beowulf* to the Balrogs: The Roots of Fantastic Horror in *The Lord of the Rings*' alludes to Tolkien's employment of the recurrent motifs of 'darkness and light' in his most famous work. These motifs, inherited as Benvenuto suggests from folk and gothic tales, North European myths such as the *Völuspá* and writers such as the Brothers Grimm, tap into archetypal fears related to what Tolkien terms in *The Monsters and the Critics* as the 'offspring of darkness'[68] – or more precisely the monsters which we imagined (or imagine still) under our beds. Many of Tolkien's most vivid 'monsters' are created thus: the Ringwraiths (who later become the winged Nazgûl) appear as faceless manifestations of the night or Black Riders. The Balrog arrives to assail the Fellowship from the darkest abyss of Moria, and, of course, Sauron, the Dark Lord, remains veiled behind the Black Gate of Mordor and is only made manifest as an eye wreathed in flame – distant and withdrawn into the dark but ever-watchful. The agents of evil and the places from which they originate in *The Lord of the Rings* (and elsewhere in Tolkien's fiction) are, in many cases, portrayed as associated with the motif of darkness. Tolkien refers to the places that act as shielding havens against the 'offspring of darkness' as 'circles of light'.[69] 'Out of these' Benvenuto states 'the main characters [of *The Lord of the Rings*] must venture to face the 'offspring of darkness' [...] After a while, even the protection of the 'circle of light' of places like the Shire, Tom Bombadil's house, or the elvish realms, will not be enough to stem the tide of darkness threatening to engulf Middle-earth.'[70]

One of Gandalf's primary goals, and perhaps his most effective strategy as the crisis of the Third Age of Middle-earth unfolds, is to bring together and empower these 'circles of light' so that a unified resistance may brightly and boldly stand against the darkness of Sauron's regime. Although Benvenuto categorises these 'circles of light' exclusively as places or havens amid the dark, in terms of Gandalf's purpose, these 'circles of light' are also evident in the rising courage and resolve of the hobbits, the coming together of elves, dwarves and men, the

---

68 J.R.R.Tolkien, *The Monsters and the Critics*, edited by Christopher Tolkien, London: HarperCollins, 1997, p.33.
69 Tolkien, *The Monsters and the Critics*, p.33.
70 Maria Raffaella Benvenuto, 'From *Beowulf* to the Balrogs: The Roots of Fantastic Horror in *The Lord of the Rings*' in Lynn Forest-Hill (ed.), *The Mirror Crack'd: Fear and Horror in JRR Tolkien's Major Works*, Newcastle: Cambridge Scholars Publishing, 2008, p.8.

putting aside of old grudges and long held suspicions, and the awakening of the ents to the crisis before them.[71]

Related to this theme of light and flame we should note that Gandalf carries with him Narya, the Ring of Fire, given to him by Círdan. And we see the theme of fire manifest in every aspect of his character: his ability to metaphorically and actually light the path ahead (in the Mines of Moria he brings light forth from his staff), his penchant for fireworks and his sometimes fiery nature, but most of all his ability to fire up or kindle the resolve of those around him. Tolkien refers to Gandalf in one letter as being the 'bearer of the Ring of Fire, the Kindler: the most childlike aspect shown to the Hobbits being fireworks.'[72] And Gandalf is indeed a 'kindler' of hearts and minds, but crucially his 'fire', unlike that unleashed by the Balrog of Moria, is tempered by a great wisdom and kinship with all living things. Indeed he is acutely aware of the disastrous results of fighting 'fire with fire' – more precisely attempting to overthrow Sauron with the Ring. It is a wisdom that is utterly lost on those such as Saruman, Denethor and Boromir.

Gandalf's purpose in Middle-earth, as we have said, was to gather opposition against Sauron and in *Unfinished Tales* we are told of Gandalf: 'warm and eager was his spirit (and it was enhanced by the ring Narya), for he was the Enemy of Sauron opposing the fire that devours and wastes with the fire that kindles.'[73] In point of fact we seldom see Gandalf use his powers in anger – notably on the rare occasions he does call on his 'magic' it is almost always set against other 'supernatural' beings like the Balrog or Saruman. As Tolkien puts it, Gandalf tends to use such powers 'sparingly' and 'for specific beneficent purposes'. Tolkien describes Sauron's use of power, on the other hand, as being a means to

---

71 From an ecological perspective, and relating the gathering together of 'circles of light' to the environmental crisis threatening our world, Gandalf's endeavours to gather enclaves of resistance together, and his catalytic role in the formation of the Fellowship of the Ring may be read as the coming together of disparate factions and threads of modern environmentalism: Friends of the Earth, Greenpeace, Conservationism, Deep Ecology, Ecocriticism etc. under one banner: 'The Green Movement'. The beacons of environmentalist concern that flickered with a fragile flame in the early part of the twentieth century now burn so brightly that almost every major political party on the planet has drawn up a 'green policy'. In other words the politics of environmentalism united has become a central rather than a peripheral force.
72 Tolkien, *Letters*, p.390.
73 Tolkien, *Unfinished Tales*, p.519.

'bulldoze both people and things.'[74] Indeed the struggle for Middle-earth itself is characterised by the contrast in the representation of the benign and compassionate will of Gandalf and the destructive will of Sauron. Sauron lays assault on the people and the land and Gandalf endeavours to defend each equally. Tolkien states unequivocally that 'Gandalf's opposite was, strictly, Sauron.'[75] And, in direct opposition to the wisdoms and environmentally sound ideologies of Gandalf, Sauron gathers forces around him who are quick to wreak havoc on the environment of Middle-earth, powers that see only the pursuit of rule in the here and now, and take no account of those who may follow. Sauron does not always specifically target the naturally sustained landscapes of Middle-earth, but they are destroyed as a consequence of his indifference to such things – we see the same indifference to the land manifest in those who fall under his power.

In the chapter 'The Last Debate' in book five of *The Lord of the Rings*, poised upon the moment of battle before the Black Gate opens, Gandalf, in addressing the gathering of captains, offers them a context for the battle ahead which draws very heavily on natural imagery, and takes account of the future generations of Middle-earth:

> Other evils there are that may come; for Sauron is himself but a servant or emissary. Yet it is not our part to master all the tides of the world, but to do what is in us for the succour of those years wherein we are set, uprooting the evils in the fields that we know, so that those who may live after may have clean earth to till. What weather they shall have is not ours to rule.[76]

Although he has been tasked with opposing the evil of Sauron, Gandalf knows that Sauron is but one representation of 'evils […] that may come.' In other words Gandalf is telling the captains that Sauron represents the defining crisis of their time but that what lies before them is not the final battle against all manifestations of evil, and all they can do is rise to that challenge before them and uproot 'the evils in the fields that [they] know.' Gandalf here is reiterating or redefining the conversation he had with Frodo in Bag End previously, and calling on the captains and the forces now gathered to stand and be counted as Frodo has done, as those who would take responsibility for opposing the evil in their own time in whatever form it may take. As before, Gandalf's words seem to break free from

---

74 Tolkien, *Letters*, p.200.
75 Tolkien, *Letters*, p.180.
76 Tolkien, *Return*, p.861.

the confines of the story and speak universally to humankind. That Gandalf's words are laden with natural imagery is perhaps suggestive of Tolkien's own concerns that soon the defining crisis facing the real world, the new evil, would be the progressive destruction of the natural world and the devotion to machines, technologies and powers which bring such devastation. In alluding to the need to leave future generations 'clean earth to till' and hinting at future 'weather' Gandalf (and thus Tolkien) is touching upon environmental issues that trouble the real world today: the irreversible damage inflicted upon once bio-diversely rich and bountiful landscapes, and (as we have seen in recent years) the impact of environmentally negative human affairs on systems of weather. And although this passage may be read metaphorically, the ecological augury that emerges from the words and the choice of imagery is nonetheless striking.

On many occasions Gandalf's words to those around him are sounded as warnings that reach out from the pages of Tolkien's fiction and become *his* warnings to us. Indeed there are many similarities between the ideologies of Gandalf and those of Tolkien himself. Tolkien's own view regarding the worth of natural things, his willingness to go to war for a righteous cause (tempered by a compassion for the other side), is made evident in Gandalf. George Clark in his essay 'J.R.R. Tolkien and the True Hero' suggests that Gandalf is Tolkien's 'alter ego', adding that in his works of fiction he, like Gandalf, searched to find (or create) a hero who could further reflect and uphold his (and Gandalf's) principles:

> Tolkien sought a true hero motivated by a heroic ideal consistent with his own religious and moral ideals, but he could not rid himself of his desire for the glorious heroes of old. In *Hobbit* he shares the search for the new hero with the wizard Gandalf, an alter ego, and they find Bilbo Baggins of Bag End.

Clark goes on to say that '[i]n response to World War II, Tolkien renewed his and Gandalf's search, now an urgent quest for moral meaning in a world of horrors.'[77] Certainly Tolkien's own sense of religious and moral right and wrong and his environmental sympathies would have led him to share Gandalf's desire to oppose every facet of Sauron's regime, both against the people and the land. Also in 1944 in a letter to his son Christopher (who was in the army) Tolkien, speaking of the nature of good and evil writes:

---

77 George Clark, 'J.R.R. Tolkien and the True Hero' in George Clark & Daniel Timmons (eds.), *J.R.R. Tolkien and his Literary Resonances: Views of Middle-earth*, Westport: Greenwood Press, 2000, p.39.

there was a solemn article in the local paper seriously advocating systematic extermination of the entire German nation as the only proper course after military victory: because, if you please, they are rattlesnakes, and don't know the difference between good and evil! (What of the writer?) The Germans have just as much right to declare the Poles and Jews exterminable vermin, subhuman, as we have to select the Germans: in other words no right, whatever they have done.[78]

Tolkien's sentiments here (no doubt a little controversial at the time) not only evoke Albert Schweitzer's 'fundamental principle of morality': '[i]t is *good* to maintain and cherish life; it is *evil* to destroy and check life'[79] but his attitude is also highly reminiscent of that espoused by Gandalf as Frodo expresses a wish that Bilbo had killed Gollum when he had the chance. Frodo refers to Gollum as 'just an enemy and deserv[ing of] death' to which Gandalf responds '[m]any that live deserve death. And some that die deserve life. Can you give it to them?' We recall that he further adds '[t]hen do not be too eager to deal out death in judgement.'[80] Clearly Tolkien and Gandalf's sense of right and wrong are in alignment. Indeed it would be no wild claim to suggest that, given Gandalf's highly developed environmental anxieties and sympathies, his code of morality (which closely mirrors that of Tolkien), and the spiritual field of reference against which Gandalf's character is sourced, Gandalf carries with him across the trials, landscapes and battles of Middle-earth, the worldview of Tolkien himself. However, in aspects other than a philosophical perspective Tolkien, by virtue of his love of bright waistcoats, pipe and ale, has perhaps more in common with the hobbits of Middle-earth than any of the other races.[81]

Michael White in his biography of Tolkien states that Tolkien 'poured his own personality into his work' and created fiction 'infused with his own personality' including themes that addressed 'the superiority of Nature over technology' and 'the struggle between good and evil.' These things, according to White, were 'reflections of Tolkien's deep-rooted beliefs.'[82] And of course in creating fiction that offers a reflection of his own anxieties, in fashioning his tales with

---

78 Tolkien, *Letters*, p.90.
79 Quoted in Richard L. Fern, *Nature, God and Humanity: Envisioning an Ethics of Nature*, Cambridge: Cambridge University Press, 2002, p.40.
80 Tolkien, *Fellowship*, p.58.
81 See Tolkien, *Letters*, p.227, p.265, pp.288-89, and Joseph Pearce, *Tolkien: Man and Myth*, London: HarperCollins, 1999, pp.160-78.
82 Michael White, *Tolkien*, London: Abacus, 2004, p.215.

such vivid and unmistakable environmental themes which unite to become an ecological warning for the real world, Tolkien, intuitively or not, like Gandalf, may be read as one who gathered resistance against the evils he perceived to be threatening the world of his time. Tolkien, particularly with regard to *The Lord of the Rings* (given its popularity and the success of Peter Jackson's films which preserve the environmental dimension) has undoubtedly raised some awareness of ecological issues pertaining to the primary world. In a very real sense, the struggle for the land and the green face of Middle-earth threatened by industrialised, power-hungry technocrats has resonated with many readers (and filmgoers) who make implicit connections between Tolkien's secondary world crisis and the environmental crisis facing the real world. Patrick Curry relays the profound effect Tolkien's fiction had on one of the founding members of Greenpeace:

> In 1972, David Taggart sailed into a French nuclear testing area, an action which led directly to the founding of Greenpeace. His journal records that 'I had been reading *The Lord of the Rings*. I could not avoid thinking of parallels between our own little fellowship and the long journey of the Hobbits into the volcano-haunted land of Mordor' […] Nor had it escaped Taggart's notice, or that of other attentive readers, that Mordor's landscape is one of industrial desolation, polluted beyond renewal; and that such desecration is inseparable from its autocratic, unaccountable and unrestrained exercise of political power.[83]

In our reality the environmental crisis, of course, still threatens the entire planet and many have yet to wake up to the defining crisis of the age. It seems that more resistance and more 'circles of light' must be gathered. In the fictional world of Middle-earth, however, Gandalf proved equal to the task appointed for him in his time. Indeed as Tolkien points out, the Valar would, in their plan to oppose the might of Sauron, have sent to aid Middle-earth a spirit capable of defeating Sauron:

> To the overthrow of Morgoth [Manwë] sent his herald Eönwë. To the defeat of Sauron would he not then send some lesser (but mighty) spirit of the angelic people, one coëval and equal, doubtless, with Sauron in their beginnings, but not more? Olórin was his name. But of Olórin we shall never know more than he revealed in Gandalf.[84]

---

83 Patrick Curry, *Defending Middle-earth. Tolkien: Myth and Modernity*, London: HarperCollins, 1997, p.55.
84 Tolkien, *Unfinished Tales*, p.395.

(IV) Sauron and the Nature of Evil

As we have seen, although Gandalf possesses great power, he is reticent to wield it primarily because he has a clear understanding of the dangers of power. Gandalf is acutely aware of the destructive allure of power (most vitally symbolised in the One Ring). He knows how it can corrupt and lead good intentions astray. We do see Gandalf on occasion calling upon his power – the breaking of Saruman's staff for example, but one of the most prevalent aspects of his wise orchestration of the struggle against Sauron is his consistent refusal to wield power unnecessarily – indeed Tolkien, certainly throughout *The Lord of the Rings*, but also in both *The Silmarillion* and *The Hobbit*, draws continual parallels between the misuse of power and the nature of evil. Time and time again we are shown the consequences of misused power, not only in terms of how the characters in his stories fall from grace but also in terms of how the abuse of power impacts upon the landscape. In this sense there is a perceptible connection between the will to power, evil and environmental devastation. One could almost say that the greater the evil the more extreme the environmental havoc visited upon the surrounding landscape. Perhaps the clearest example of this is Sauron whose negative influence upon the ravaged land of Mordor is dramatic in the extreme. Extreme as this vision of environmental evil may be, still the symbolic nature of Mordor resonates with instances and regimes of ecological ruin, which are beginning to dominate the landscapes of our world. We recall that Tolkien referred to Sauron's use of power and magic in terms of it 'bulldoz[ing] people and things.'[85] Tolkien's employment of 'bulldozing' imagery to describe Sauron's regime of power is, of course, no accident. It calls to mind the systematic demolition and levelling of pastoral landscapes, woods and groves, green-belts and wild regions in the primary world in order that they may accommodate industry or big business corporations.

Sauron's desire for control over Middle-earth, characterised by his wanton misuse of power, is unambiguously called 'an incarnation of Evil'[86] by Tolkien. This 'Evil' brings with it, by ever gathering degrees of devastation, the wilful destruction of the ecologically sustained landscapes of Middle-earth. In terms of Tolkien's

---

85 Tolkien, *Letters*, p.200.
86 Tolkien, *Letters*, p.160.

anxieties for the rural landscapes he knew well in the primary world – the green places that he perceived were gradually diminishing against the rise of industry and machine-driven technologies – it is no surprise to find that in Middle-earth Tolkien infuses the forces of 'the Enemy' and those who have fallen under the will of Sauron with a predilection for unnatural things: machines, engines and new-fangled weapons of war. 'The Enemy' Tolkien writes in a letter to Naomi Mitchison 'or those who have become like him, go in for 'machinery' – with destructive and evil effects.'[87] We see these 'evil effects' in Isengard and later in the Shire under Sharkey, but they have their origins somewhere behind the Black Gate of Mordor. Indeed we recall that Sauron is described by Tolkien, in a letter to Milton Waldman, as the 'Lord of magic and machines.'[88] And, just as Gandalf is the architect of resistance against the evil that threatens to cover the world in a 'second darkness',[89] Sauron is the architect of the regime which leads to the creation of devices, machines and engines which threaten both the land and the peoples of Middle-earth. Similarly whilst Gandalf attempts to bring together his 'circles of light', Sauron by one method or another has lured, gathered and mustered forces of darkness and destruction around him. Of these 'followers' and servants of his will, almost all are corrupted creatures that have become distorted, perverted versions of a once natural life force. A prime example is the Ringwraiths or the Nine Riders who were once mortal men. Sauron ensnares them, giving them each a Ring of Power, thus tempting them with the allure of great power and long life. The narrator of *The Silmarillion* explains the fate of those tempted by the Nine Rings:

> Those [Men] who used the Nine Rings became mighty in their day, kings, sorcerers, and warriors of old. They obtained glory and great wealth, yet it turned to their undoing. They had, as it seemed, unending life, yet life became unendurable to them. They could walk, if they would, unseen by all eyes in this world beneath the sun, and they could see things in worlds invisible to mortal men; but too often they beheld only the phantoms and delusions of Sauron. And one by one, sooner or later, according to their native strength and to the good or evil of their wills in the beginning, they fell under the thraldom of the ring that they bore and of the domination of the One which was Sauron's. And they became forever invisible save to him that wore the Ruling Ring, and they entered into the realm of shadows.[90]

---

87 Tolkien, *Letters*, p.200.
88 Tolkien, *Letters*, p.146.
89 Tolkien, *Fellowship*, p.50.
90 J.R.R. Tolkien, *The Silmarillion*, edited by Chr. Tolkien, London: Allen & Unwin, 1977, p.289.

Sauron uses his Rings of Power, held under the control of the One Ring, to dominate, twist and corrupt other life forms. He seeks primacy over all of creation: not only the kingdoms and peoples of Middle-earth but over every manifestation of life. In other words Sauron has no intention of sharing power with any other force – and that includes nature itself.

Although growing ever more powerful, Sauron is nonetheless in diminished form in the Third Age of Middle-earth. He gathers *his* strength from the strength of that which he enslaves. The forces and life forms he corrupts do his bidding; he turns them to his purpose and takes away their will. Tolkien, as we have said, drew on many sources in the creation of his fiction including old myths, dark legends, and gothic tales. Certainly given the manner in which Sauron draws his victims into his shadowy world and dominates their wills so that they succumb, in mind and body, to his purposes (such as those he enslaves, and transforms into the undead Ringwraiths), we may say that he is vampire-like.

Gwyneth Hood in her 1987 essay 'Sauron and Dracula' believes that the similarities and parallels between the two literary creations run much deeper than the mere superficial comparison of their more obvious traits. Referring to their shared ability to secure 'psychological domination' over those they prey upon, Hood points out '[b]oth tyrants use hypnotic eyes to feed their visions into the minds of their victims' (I discuss the question of Sauron's portrayal as a single eye below). Describing their mutual corruption of the natural order, Hood also casts Sauron and Dracula together as 'counter-creators of a mode of existence' whose regimes for control are 'parasitical on the natural life of creation and at active war with it.' This war on creation, in the case of Sauron particularly (who ultimately will let no other force exist unless it is under his control), manifests itself in Mordor as a war against the elemental powers of nature. Under Sauron's regime there are only two choices: servitude or death – even for nature itself. Hood takes up the question of Sauron's assault on natural phenomena:

> Sauron must weaken nature before it will serve him. He has no elements for allies except the ones he artificially tampers with, such as the smoggy wind which puts Minas Tirith and Mordor into darkness during the crisis of the war, only to be blown aside at significant moments by the true elemental

> wind [...] A good deal of nature must die in this 'taming' process, even when Sauron does not destroy deliberately. Mordor is choked with what resembles industrial pollution.[91]

Hood, of course, is quite right to foreground the environmentally corrosive effects of Sauron's evil in a discussion concerning his resemblance to a vampire because Sauron is draining the life force from the land, he is twisting and distorting nature so that the landscape resembles a shadow of what it once was. The land of Mordor, has fallen completely, has become like Sauron – it exists yet is bereft of life, it is undead. Other landscapes in Middle-earth too are undergoing change. Sauron in this sense symbolises the power that humanity has collectively attained to change the face of the planet. Writing in the mid-twentieth century, ecologist Paul B. Sears, recalling Tolkien's 'bulldozing' imagery, states:

> Every bite of a great power scoop, every snorting push of a bulldozer, every pipe pouring wastes into once clear streams, every stack belching fumes into the mushroom cap of unclear air that hovers over our great cities is testimony of man's growing power to change his environment.[92]

When Gandalf tells Frodo that Sauron wishes to cover the world in a 'second darkness' this is not simply a symbolic reference to the dark fate which will inevitably accompany Sauron's success, but rather Gandalf is alluding to Sauron's ability to subvert and disrupt the natural order, where the laws of nature may be made to yield and bend under the assault of the Dark Lord. Kristine Larsen in 'Shadow and Flame: Myth, Monsters and Mother Nature in Middle-earth' discusses Tolkien's recurrent use of eclipse-like events to signify disturbances in the natural order brought about by the agents of darkness: '[i]n the etiological mythology of Middle-earth' Larsen notes 'eclipses of both the sun and moon appear, explained as the result of chaos in Arda [the Earth] and of the intentional attacks Morgoth waged against the sun and moon.'[93] Eclipse-like phenomena thus may be brought about in Tolkien's fictional world as a result of the kind of attacks upon natural forces that Sauron has already undertaken as the story of *The Lord of the Rings* unfolds. When Gandalf speaks of the world being

---

91 Gwenyth Hood, 'Sauron and Dracula' in *Mythlore* 52:11-17 (1987), p.15.
92 Paul B. Sears, *Where There Is Life*, New York: Dell Publishing, 1972, p.181.
93 Kristine Larsen, 'Shadow and Flame: Myth, Monsters and Mother Nature in Middle-earth' in Lynn Forest-Hill (ed.), *The Mirror Crack'd: Fear and Horror in JRR Tolkien's Major Works*, Newcastle: Cambridge Scholars Publishing, 2008, p.177.

covered in a 'second darkness' therefore he is most likely speaking literally and not metaphorically. The implication that the environmentally destructive force represented by Sauron can, if allowed to assail the ecology of Middle-earth unimpeded, eventually affect and disrupt the most elemental of natural phenomena (sunlight and darkness) is an allusion with which twenty-first century humanity can surely identify as the ecological crisis we face threatens to reach apocalyptic proportions.

The desolation of Mordor is the first 'phase' of Sauron's assault on Middle-earth, yet Tolkien, in his depiction of Mordor, leaves us in no doubt that the natural environment of Sauron's lands has been exposed to an ecological devastation that will have a lasting effect. Many of the passages describing this land speak of a dense smoke-filled sky which even sunlight cannot break through: 'It was already day, a windless and sullen morning [...] No sun pierced the low clouded sky.'[94] The very air, it seems, is polluted around Mordor and we are told that 'it grew altogether dark: the air itself seemed black and heavy to breathe.'[95] Elsewhere Tolkien describes the light as 'reluctant', as if to offer us a scene where even the light of day is loath to fall on the lifeless and broken land – perhaps because the life-giving and revitalizing power of daylight has lost its purpose there. The water too, we are told, has been polluted: 'one vast fen was really an endless network of pools, and soft mires, and winding half-strangled water-courses.'[96] The entire panorama of Mordor is one huge environmental wasteland and each new descriptive passage offers us yet another view of what Tolkien ultimately calls 'this forsaken country':

> It was dreary and wearisome. Cold clammy winter still held sway in this forsaken country. The only green was the scum of livid weed on the dark greasy surfaces of the sullen waters. Dead grasses and rotting reeds loomed up in the mists like ragged shadows of long forgotten summers.[97]

The culmination of these descriptions 'greasy surfaces of the sullen waters', 'the air [...] black and heavy', '[d]ead grasses and rotting reeds' is highly suggestive of a contaminated and perhaps irreversibly damaged landscape in our reality

---

94 Tolkien, *Two Towers*, p.612.
95 Tolkien, *Two Towers*, p.613.
96 Tolkien, *Two Towers*, p.612.
97 Tolkien, *Two Towers*, p.612.

where the activities of industrialisation or pollution have turned a once green region into a 'forsaken country'.

The science fiction writer Isaac Asimov describes below how such a sight had an arresting effect on both him and his wife, consequently informing their understanding of Tolkien's work:

> One day, [my wife] Janet and I were driving along the New Jersey Turnpike, and we passed a section given over to oil refineries. It was a blasted region in which nothing was growing and was filled with ugly pipelike structures, which refineries must have. Waste oil was leaking at the top of tall chimneys and the smell of petroleum products filled the air. Janet looked at the prospect with troubled eyes and said, 'There's Mordor.' And of course it was and that was what had to be in Tolkien's mind. The Ring was industrial technology, which uprooted the green land and replaced it with ugly structures under a pall of chemical pollution.[98]

This account, much like Greenpeace founder David Taggart's journal entry above (there are many more examples), demonstrates how Tolkien's portrayal of Mordor is more than an imaginary landscape – it is a concept rendered in fictional form and a warning for the primary world.

Tolkien, throughout his fiction, consistently and vividly makes direct connections between the misuse of power, evil and environmental catastrophe. Yet although Tolkien depicts Sauron as predominantly evil and morally corrupt, he qualifies this depiction of Sauron as evil incarnate by telling us that in fact Sauron was once an angelic being who became corrupted by Morgoth. In a letter responding to Peter Hastings, manager of a Catholic bookshop in Oxford, Tolkien addresses the idea of evil in relation to Sauron and alludes to the fact that he was not always iniquitous: 'Sauron was of course not 'evil' in origin. He was a 'spirit' corrupted by the Prime Dark Lord.'[99] Corruption is a recurrent theme in Tolkien's work and although Sauron, like Gandalf, was once numbered among the benign Maiar, through a process of corruption characterised by an unhealthy desire to pursue knowledge at any cost, Sauron eventually becomes what Tolkien describes as 'a thing lusting for Complete Power.'[100] Interestingly from an environmental perspective,

---

98 Isaac Asimov, 'Concerning Tolkien' in *Magic: The Final Fantasy Collection*, New York: HarperPrism, 1996, p.155.
99 Tolkien, *Letters*, p.151.
100 Tolkien, *Letters*, p.151.

those characters like Gandalf, Sam Gamgee, Galadriel and Tom Bombadil who are possessed of an inner strength and a resolve to resist temptations of power are portrayed as having an affinity for nature or the natural wonders of Middle-earth – those such as Sauron and Saruman who fall from grace, are likewise clearly associated with a desire for the knowledge to create unnatural things.

Acts of environmental devastation occur in Tolkien's works sometimes with clear predetermination. The very fact that Galdor determines that Sauron can '*torture* and destroy the very hills'[101] is evidence enough that natural phenomena sometimes become the target of his malice. Indeed it should be restated that Sauron is a primordial malevolent being who has long been in opposition to those such as the elves. He would, therefore, of course, as a hoarder of lore and knowledge, be very aware of the profound interconnections between the elves and the land (discussed in more detail in chapter four). He would thus know that by destroying and mutilating the natural world, he is, in effect, wounding and weakening the elves, causing them to withdraw from the wider world and seek solace in enchanted realms such as Rivendell and Lothlórien. In assailing nature, Sauron knows also that he strikes directly at Yavanna, Manwë, Ulmo and the other naturally sourced Valar and lesser Vali. This alone explains why he should conduct a war on nature and take the time to 'torture and destroy the very hills'. Despite a desire to strike at and cripple the sustaining power of nature, Sauron probably does not have the destruction of landscapes as a priority in his assault against Middle-earth. These things occur precisely because of his indifference to whether the land suffers or not in the execution of his dark intent. Sauron's point of focus, his objective, eclipses and occludes all other concerns both literally and metaphorically. His eye, his gaze is on expediting and imposing his vision (of absolute control) upon all of Middle-earth.

Tolkien on one occasion associated Sauron's pursuit of the control of Middle-earth with 'reformers' or those who wish to bring major and widespread change, '[Sauron] was not indeed wholly evil, not unless all 'reformers' who want to hurry up with 'reconstruction' and 'reorganization' are wholly evil.'[102] Although Sauron's regime against Middle-earth is primarily a quest for dominion, there is a sug-

---

101 Tolkien, *Fellowship*, p.259, emphasis added.
102 Tolkien, *Letters*, p.190.

gestion here that Tolkien cast part of Sauron's character not only from a tyrant's mould but also from that of a big business, capitalist industrialist who ruthlessly pursues power, profits and ambition whilst intentionally turning a 'blind eye' to the effects his environmentally unsound activities have upon the world about him. This of course is a depiction of someone who lives in a kind of egocentric isolation, divorced from or unconcerned with the welfare of others and apathetic to the consequences of his actions. This 'blinkered', limited and tunnelled lack of vision is perhaps reflected in Tolkien's presentation of Sauron as a single eye unable or unwilling to take in a wider view. Indeed Sauron's ego-driven and maniacal worldview could not be more removed from that of Gandalf who we recall urges the peoples of Middle-earth 'to do what is in us for the succour of those years wherein we are set, uprooting the evils in the fields that we know, so that those who may live after may have clean earth to till.'[103]

Furthermore, in associating the characterisation of Sauron and his servants with machines and environmentally unsound technologies, Tolkien depicts a crisis in the Third Age of Middle-earth that inevitably reflects one of the defining crises of the modern age. In the following passage taken from the previously quoted letter to Peter Hastings, Tolkien offers an insight into how Sauron's knowledge of technology and machines (inherited from Morgoth and desired by the high-elves) and his misuse of power has parallels for the primary world (Tolkien mentions Catholics specifically because Hastings asked for his view on Catholic ideologies related to the concept of evil):

> The particular branch of the High-Elves concerned, the Noldor or Loremasters, were always on the side of 'science and technology', as we should call it: they wanted to have the knowledge that Sauron genuinely had [...] I should regard them as no more wicked or foolish (but in much the same peril) as Catholics engaged in certain kinds of physical research (e.g. those producing, if only as by-products, poisonous gases and explosives): things not necessarily evil, but which, things being as they are, and the nature and motives of the economic masters who provide all the means for their work being as they are, are pretty certain to serve evil ends.[104]

There is a very clear environmental allusion made here. Tolkien refers to 'economic masters' who bank-roll research in the name of progress producing

---

103 Tolkien, *Return*, p.861.
104 Tolkien, *Letters*, p.190.

'poisonous gases' and 'explosions' – and one cannot help but think of certain economically-driven power bases in our world who conduct all manner of ecologically damaging activities supposedly in the pursuit of progress. Sauron in this sense is one such 'master' who lures others with the promise of knowledge and power whilst imperiling that which is essential to life.

(V) Sauron: Machine-maker

Sauron's search for power is defined by his search for the One Ring. The Ring is the ultimate symbol for the desire to wield power, even if that power comes at the expense of the well-being of other life forms. David Day in *Tolkien's Ring* comments that Sauron's desire for yet greater power is a form of evil, '[t]he pursuit of power is in itself evil' but that this becomes absolute evil with the desire for ultimate control of all things (even nature) and that this ruthless desire for dominion is thus 'embodied in the ultimate power of the One Ring.'[105] Many commentators have associated the One Ring with the development of machines and weapons capable of mass destruction and even the unrestricted advancement of technology. Patrick Curry has described the One Ring as a 'Megamachine',[106] Colin Duriez has determined that 'The Ring itself is a machine, the result of Sauron's technological skills.'[107] The Ring is, as we have said, a symbol of the will to power but it likewise represents technology and machinery that whilst professing to offer advancement and progress for humanity also has the capacity to wreak enormous destruction on both the natural world and humanity itself. In the opening chapter, 'Rage Against the Machine', I discussed how Tolkien was mistrustful of the kind of machines and technology that the power of the One Ring calls to mind. In *The Lord of the Rings* it is Gandalf who cautions those such as Saruman, Boromir and even Frodo and Bilbo that the 'magic' and might of the One Ring is not to be trusted.

---

105 David Day, *Tolkien's Ring*, London: Pavilion Books, 2001, p.39.
106 Curry, *Defending Middle-earth*, p.76.
107 Duriez, *J.R.R. Tolkien and C.S. Lewis*, p.149.

(VI) Closing Thoughts: A Light in the Dark

In Tolkien's own words Gandalf is a spirit 'coëval and equal' with Sauron, but Gandalf's strength is not in his magic or the power of command he wields. Instead his greatest strength is his wisdom. He sees the value of all creation and he does not use his own considerable might to resist Mordor but rather he teaches and guides the free peoples of Middle-earth to find resistance within themselves. He is a clear guiding light in the darkest hour of the Third Age. Gandalf's enduring gift to Middle-earth is the wisdom he imparts to others and the strength of will he fosters in them to resist new corruptions and old evils. The unfolding tale of *The Lord of the Rings* offers, in its character portrayals and themes, opposing attitudes to the worth of power, technology and the living world. These cultures of opposition are also indelibly bound up with themes of good and evil. As Jane Chance points out:

> Tolkien intentionally contrasts the hierarchy of good characters, linked by the symbolic value of fellowship into an invisible band or chain of love, with the hierarchy of evil characters and fallen characters linked by the literal rings of enslavement [... Middle-earth] has become 'old' and decrepit, governed by the spiritually old and corrupt influence of Sauron. Symbolically [...] 'heirs', as the young, represent vitality, life, newness: Frodo is Bilbo's nephew and heir, Gimli is [Gloin's], Legolas is Thranduil's, Strider is Isildur's [...] only Gandalf as the good counterpart to Sauron is old.[108]

Gandalf's role as teacher, guide and catalyst in the resistance against Sauron enlivens a younger generation of resistance against the old Enemy. The old wars of the First and Second Ages, where Sauron and Morgoth before him were opposed by the old order of elves and men, are past. This is resistance of a different kind. It is resistance from an alliance of races from across the lands of Middle-earth. In particular we see how Gandalf has aided in the rise of the hobbits in the Third Age. By the time we reach 'The Scouring of the Shire', it is clear that Frodo has grown in wisdom and strength. In the following passage as Frodo and Sam confront the fallen Saruman, Frodo's words seem to echo the 'reverence for life' exhibited in Gandalf previously, and even Saruman (unmasked from his alias of Sharkey) is forced to acknowledge a change in Frodo:

---

108 Chance, *Tolkien's Art*, pp.151-52.

> 'No Sam!' said Frodo 'Do not kill him even now.' [...] '[Saruman] was great once, of a noble kind that we should not dare to raise our hands against. He is fallen, and his cure is beyond us; but I would still spare him, in the hope that he may find it.' Saruman rose to his feet, and stared at Frodo. There was a strange look in his eyes of mingled wonder and respect and hatred. 'You have grown, Halfling,' he said. 'Yes, you have grown very much. You are wise, and cruel. You have robbed my revenge of sweetness, and now I must go hence in bitterness, in debt to your mercy.'[109]

Frodo, it seems, has learned much from Gandalf and now the resistance against Sauron and Saruman has come from very unlikely but altogether worthy sources. Gandalf has instilled grace and mercy into this new generation of resistance, and he has been instrumental in bringing old and new alliances together. In allowing the Fellowship to be made up of once disparate races, and including trees and cleansing waters to aid in the struggle against Sauron and Saruman, Tolkien raises to a higher power both the human and the non-human to present his own ecosphere of interconnections, in which the fate of the elves and men is intrinsically tied to the fate of hobbits, dwarves, ents and Maiar (I discuss this concept in greater detail in the next chapter). This of course has parallels for the real world, where all of humanity (not just selected superpowers) must come together in order to hope to oppose large-scale environmental catastrophe.

Gandalf's express purpose is to oppose the machinations of Sauron. He does this, however, by not just mobilising strength against the Dark Lord, but by becoming an opposing force to Sauron in every sense. I have argued above that the model of stewardship Gandalf promotes transcends any specific religious doctrine. His environmental ethics are governed by a simple understanding that all life is precious – he cares for the green face of Middle-earth as much as for its peoples, and considers himself to be a steward 'of all worthy things that are in peril.'[110] He seeks to empower others rather than exercise authority over them. He remains uncorrupted by the desire to possess the One Ring and is instrumental in the decision to attempt to destroy the most powerful object in Middle-earth, something that Sauron cannot even conceive of. Gandalf uses his powers only when it is absolutely necessary and almost always in the protection of others. As in the previous chapter, set out in a table (overleaf) we can see

---

109 Tolkien, *Return*, p.966.
110 Tolkien, *Return*, p.742.

how Gandalf and Sauron exemplify worldviews in direct conflict. Whichever worldview prevails upon the panorama of the wider tale of *The Lord of the Rings* will decide the fate of all life in Middle-earth:

Ecologically Positive Presentation	Ecologically Negative Presentation
Gandalf	Sauron
1. A Maia spirit who seeks to preserve the landscape of Middle-earth and 'all worthy things that are in peril.'	1. A Maia spirit who seeks to cover the landscape of Middle-earth in the shadow of his destructive malice.
2. Considers himself a steward of Middle-earth.	2. Considers himself Lord of Middle-earth.
3. Does not seek mastery of his environment.	3. Seeks absolute mastery of his environment.
4. Is chief architect of the resistance against Sauron and the preservation of the environments of Middle-earth.	4. Is chief architect of the assault on the Free Peoples and environments of Middle-earth
5. Resists the allure of the One Ring and hides its whereabouts from Sauron.	5. Is obsessed with regaining the One Ring, searches endlessly for its hiding place.
6. Sets his power aside, guides, teaches and empowers others.	6. Deceives and tricks others. Does not share power.

Although as I have said, Gandalf is created with many of Tolkien's own values, and as the table above shows, the purpose he serves in the epic tale of the Third Age is to oppose the malevolence represented by Sauron, nonetheless, as teacher and guide, Gandalf's role is one that resonates with many of the world's oldest legends. Joseph Campbell's magnificent cross-cultural study of myth and hero, *The Hero with a Thousand Faces* (a work I will return to in considering Tolkien's theories on the creative process in chapter five) suggests that many of the world's most enduring myths display similarities in structure, or stages that, as Campbell argues, are distilled from an archetype or monomyth. Among these stages Campbell lists 'Supernatural Aid'. This stage, according to Campbell, is marked by the appearance of a guide and guardian who leads the hero onward to adventure: 'the first encounter of the hero-journey is with a protective figure (often a little old crone or old man).'[111] Campbell goes on to offer that '[n]ot infrequently, the supernatural helper is masculine in form. In fairy lore it may be some little fellow of the wood, some wizard, hermit, shepherd, or smith, who appears to supply the amulets and advice that the hero will require.'[112]

In *The Hobbit*, but perhaps more fittingly as regards Campbell's theory, *The Lord of the Rings*, Gandalf would appear to fill this role – he is the watchful guide who directs the journey of those who would be heroes of their time and although he is heroic and leads the action on occasion, Gandalf is primarily a teacher and an advisor who guides others to find their own inner strength, their own heroism to face the trials before them.

In closing, and before moving on to the next chapter in which, among other concerns, I examine the role of elves in Tolkien's works, let me offer a final thought regarding all of the above. When I first began to examine the ecological dimension of Tolkien's fiction, and set out a plan for its study, I always knew that Tolkien's green themes and even his worldview on such matters would only fully come into view in the close analysis of his major characters. I knew also that Gandalf, arguably Tolkien's most famous and most loved character, would feature prominently in such a strategy and that he would be set against the malevolent and environmentally destructive force of Sauron. In the execution of this comparative analysis I have found that the multifaceted nature of Gandalf: the wizard, the spirit, the steward, the guide, the teacher, the kindler of hearts, and the old man with a fiery temper and gentle heart has dominated the frame. The reason for this is simple: the narrow-minded, unrelenting desire for power and control symbolised by Sauron and his single eye, has nothing much of worth to say to humanity – no similar regime ever has – and Sauron has lost the battle for words here, just as he lost the battle for Middle-earth when matched against Olórin, Stormcrow, Mithrandir, most commonly known as Gandalf the Grey.

---

111 Joseph Campbell, *The Hero With a Thousand Faces*, Princeton: Princeton University Press, 2004, p.63.
112 Campbell, *The Hero With a Thousand Faces*, p.66.

Chapter Four

Seeing the World through Elvish Eyes: An Examination of the Human & Non-Human in Tolkien's Fiction

Tolkien works are alive with beings and races that are by definition non-human. Humanity (when understood as the race of men) in Tolkien's cosmology is but one component part in the sphere of creation, and is forced to take its place alongside (as opposed to being considered superior to) the non-human. What follows is an examination of the foregrounding of the non-human in Tolkien's fiction. In accordance with their centrality in Tolkien's writings, particular focus will fall on the race of elves and their portrayal as beings that are inherently bound up with nature, not just as protectors and stewards of natural phenomena, but also as literary creations whose power and life force are intimately bound up with the life of the land and the green face of the world. The elves, despite their central role in Tolkien's major works, are but one example of how Tolkien elevates the non-human to present his own ecosphere of interconnections in which the fate of races such as elves, men and hobbits is intrinsically tied to the fate of all other life forms in Middle-earth and the Undying Lands. With this in mind, I consider the theme of a non-human perspective in Tolkien's prominent works. Alongside the centrality of the elves in this regard, other non-human perspectives are also considered and I further discuss how the presentation and promotion of the non-human in Tolkien's fiction may offer insights into the reconciliation of his Christian and environmental ideologies. As part of the examination of Tolkien's predilection to foreground the non-human, I also consider the premise that Middle-earth itself may be considered as a major character in Tolkien's *legendarium* – as important and vital to his unfolding myth as Gandalf, Fëanor, Elrond or Saruman. The questions I seek to raise here are also concerned with how the mortality and comparatively ephemeral lifespan of men (or humanity), when considered alongside beings such as the elves, feeds into each race's understanding and attitude towards the natural world.

(I) Elves and Men: Firstborn and Followers

Tolkien's elves, like many of the creations that inhabit his fiction, do not come directly to us from his imagination but rather are forged and re-interpreted from previous manifestations. They arrive on the pages of Tolkien's works from old fairy stories and older mythologies. As Tom Shippey tells us: '[t]here are many references to elves in Old English and Old Norse and Middle English, and indeed in modern English.'[1] Tolkien's elves may inherit many of the same motifs as their mythic predecessors, but the elves of Middle-earth and the Undying Lands are nonetheless unique. They are a complicated, flawed and at times contradictory race whose beauty, selflessness and transcendent grace are contaminated by occasional lapses into pride, covetousness and conceit. They are both welcoming and hostile, both immortal and in danger of death. They possess great power and yet they are powerless to prevent their own doom. And perhaps most pertinent to this discourse, their power and very existence are presented as interconnected with natural forces. They are driven by a desire to preserve and protect natural beauty, and yet the folly of a key branch of their race, the high-elves, has given rise to the appearance of the Rings of Power and thus the technology that threatens the very land they seek to protect. All of the above considered, Tolkien does not give us the two-dimensional elves of the Brothers Grimm tales who mend shoes in the night, or the mischievous sprites of Shakespeare, but rather a fully-fashioned race of beings complete with their own history, language(s), culture and lore.

The first recorded appearance of elves in Tolkien's writings is in the poem 'Kortirion among the Trees'.[2] Like many of Tolkien's other early works, themes,

---

1 Tom Shippey, *J.R.R. Tolkien: Author of the Century*, London: HarperCollins, 2003, p.89.
2 Tolkien was to work on the poem sporadically over many years (such was the significance he placed on the themes expressed) and three versions of it were published by his son Christopher in *The Book of Lost Tales Part One*. Other early poems: 'Wood-sunshine' (July, 1910) and 'Goblin Feet' (April, 1915) are also highly suggestive of what we would come to know of Tolkien's elves. In 'Wood-sunshine' (discussed in the Conclusion section of this book) Tolkien mentions 'light fairy things' and 'Sprites of the wood' that are faced with the possibility that their presence may 'fade' from the world. In 'Goblin Feet' the creatures alluded to in the poem are referred to as 'enchanted leprechauns' or 'gnomes' who live among 'the fairy lanterns', and similar to the mood expressed in 'Wood-sunshine', phrases such

ideas and even the geographical features of the poem were re-written, refashioned and became part of the foundation or 'feeder' material that went into the creation of *The Silmarillion*.³ Begun in 1915 when Tolkien was in training with the Lancashire Fusiliers prior to his deployment in the Great War, the poem encapsulates much of the nature of elves and what they would later come to represent in Tolkien's more prominent works.

> The holy fairies and immortal elves
> That dance among the trees and sing themselves
> A wistful song of things that were, and could be yet.
> They pass and vanish in a sudden breeze,
> A wave of bowing grass – and we forget
> Their tender voices like wind-shaken bells
> Of flowers, their gleaming hair like golden asphodels.⁴

The short extract above imbues the elves (Tolkien's early writings would occasionally refer to elves as fairies) with the characteristics and qualities that would come to define them in Middle-earth. Here, as in the later fully formed *legendarium*, the elves are 'immortal', and offered as being possessed of an aura of spirituality. Their 'wistful song' and the idea that they 'pass and vanish' evokes the melancholy of their passing from the world in the Third Age. The reference to 'things that were, and could be yet' singularly recalls Galadriel's words to Frodo and Sam as she invites them to look into the Mirror at Lothlórien: 'it shows things that were, and things that are, and things that yet may be', and, of course, they are clearly associated here with nature and natural imagery. Indeed the poem was inspired by and written as a dedication

---

as 'they are fading' and 'the echo of their padding feet is dying' imbues the poem with a melancholy that would later characterise the elves of Middle-earth. The word 'elves', however, is nonetheless never mentioned in these poems. As such, although Tolkien would sometimes refer to elvish creatures as 'fairies' in early works – elves, under the name elves, are first directly mentioned and first appear in 'Kortirion among the Trees'.

3 Kortirion was conceived of as a city of elves upon a green hill in the centre of the Lonely Isle (later to become Tol Eressëa). Kortirion original related to Warwick and the Lonely Isle to England. For more on Tolkien's early design to relate his mythology to the geography of the British Isles see J.R.R. Tolkien, *The Book of Lost Tales Part Two*, edited by Christopher Tolkien, London: George Allen & Unwin, 1983, pp.278-94.
4 J.R.R. Tolkien, *The Book of Lost Tales Part One*, edited by Christopher Tolkien, London: George Allen & Unwin, 1983, p.34. Asphodels are clusters of flowers which belong to the lily family. In Greek mythology they were associated with Hades, the dead and Persephone (Queen of the Underworld). This is perhaps symbolic of the fact that Tolkien's elves are presented in the poem (and elsewhere) as beings that, to the modern world in actuality and perception, have died and no longer exist.

to the natural beauty of Warwick where Tolkien spent time as a younger man and, as Carpenter states, 'found Warwick, its trees, its hill, and its castle, to be a place of remarkable beauty.'[5]

Clearly, even in his earliest writings, Tolkien had made profound conceptual connections between the race of elves and natural, or even passing natural wonder (connections and associations that built upon, but went much further than existing understandings of elves as 'nature sprites'). Before fully delving into the environmental considerations and aspects of Tolkien's portrayal of elves, however, let us take a moment to briefly outline and clarify the key facts of their metaphysical positioning in his fictional cosmology – a positioning that is essential to any understanding of the elves as literary creations. The first fact, already alluded to, is that Tolkien's elves, as they appear in his *legendarium*, are immortal. More precisely their lives are tied to the life of the world – across all the ages of its history and possible future. We are told unequivocally in *The Silmarillion* 'Elves die not until the world dies.'[6] Their immortality then is not everlasting in the strictest sense, but rather it is qualified by and measured against the life force that sustains the world in which they exist. Fact two: these elves can experience a corporeal death in the sense that their physical bodies may perish. When elves experience this physical death, however, they either perpetuate in incorporeal form or they become reincarnated and live again. In a letter replying to enquiries from Michael Straight, editor of *New Republic*, Tolkien attempts to explain the peculiar metaphysical ordering of his elves, stating explicitly that they *are* immortal, before adding:

> Not 'eternally' [immortal], but to endure with and within the created world, while its story lasts. When 'killed', by the injury or destruction of their incarnate form, they do not escape from time, but remain in the world, either discarnate, or being reborn.[7]

The race of men in Tolkien's major works are, of course, most closely aligned with and representative of the human race of the primary world, and, as the narrator of *The Silmarillion* explains, 'Men dwell only a short space in the world alive, and are not bound to it, and depart soon whither the Elves know not

---

5 Humphrey Carpenter, *J.R.R. Tolkien: A Biography*, London: Allen & Unwin, 1977, p.66.
6 J.R.R. Tolkien, *The Silmarillion*, edited by Christopher Tolkien, London: Allen &Unwin, 1977, p.42.
7 J.R.R. Tolkien, *The Letters of J.R.R. Tolkien*, edited by Humphrey Carpenter, London: HarperCollins, 2006, p.236.

[...] Death is their fate.'⁸ This central metaphysical disparity between men and elves in Tolkien's *legendarium* is what fundamentally defines them as individual races and literary creations. As I examine more fully later Tolkien conceded that, as with all his races, elves represent a specific aspect of humanity (he once stated 'my 'elves' are only a representation or an apprehension of a part of human nature'⁹), yet his elves are nonetheless, by design, distinctly non-human in their essential make-up. As noted earlier, elves did not arrive on the pages of Tolkien's fiction direct from his imagination; rather he reinterpreted them from existing myth – and although he presents them as an aspect of humanity, the circumstance of their secondary world existence separates them fundamentally from the human race. Brian Rosebury takes up the point: 'Tolkien's Elves, like Rilke's Angels in *Duino Elegies*, represent a reworking of a familiar mythical archetype: that of an order of beings close in nature to humankind, and yet sundered from it by some metaphysical fact.'¹⁰

Given that elves are 'sundered from' humanity, and thus non-human, one distinctive aspect of Tolkien's portrayal of them in his work, and one key to this discussion, is that he allows us to see 'the world' from their viewpoint, independent of a human perspective.¹¹ Offering the elvish point of view is something, as Tom Shippey notes 'which no ancient text had ever tried to penetrate.'¹² Indeed in a letter to Milton Waldman, editor of Collins publishers, Tolkien describes the then unfinished *The Silmarillion* as 'differ[ing] from all similar things' for 'not being anthropocentric' adding '[i]ts centre of view is not Men but 'Elves'.'¹³ The fact that an involved and elaborate piece of work such as *The Silmarillion* should not take an anthropocentric focus (the same could be said to a lesser

---

8 Tolkien, *Silmarillion*, p.42.
9 Tolkien, *Letters*, p.149.
10 Brian Rosebury, *Tolkien: A Critical Assessment*, New York: St. Martin's Press, 1992, p.136.
11 For a long time Tolkien considered framing his myth with a human narration. He conceived of a human sailor, Eriol, who after a storm stumbles upon the elven lands, and receives their legends and tales. Although this would have presented his myth cycle in a different, human-led frame, Tolkien always viewed his *legendarium* as elf-centered. The tales recounted by Eriol would still have amounted to an elvish myth. But, given that his early ideas regarding his *legendarium* proposed that the location of Middle-earth and the Undying Lands should correspond to the geography of the British Isles – the character of Eriol was considered by Tolkien not as a way to make humanity central to, or offer a human perspective on his mythology, but rather as a way to explain how this myth came into human hands in the first place. For an insightful analysis of Eriol see Thomas Honegger, 'Aelfwine (Old English 'Elf-Friend')' in Michael D.C. Drout (ed.), *J.R.R. Tolkien Encyclopedia: Scholarship and Critical Assessment*, New York: Routledge, 2006, pp.4-5.
12 Tolkien, *Letters*, p.90.
13 Tolkien, *Letters*, p.147.

degree of Tolkien's other main works) is, by default, testimony to Tolkien's elevation of the non-human and his prescience with regard to the significance of taking account of the non-human world as of itself – a way of viewing the world that has since become central to many green philosophies and agendas. Indeed many points of tension and narrative exposition in Tolkien's works centre on the plight of life forms that are expressly non-human. Aside from the centring of the elves in Tolkien's fiction, by turn, in the *legendarium* of Middle-earth and the Undying Lands, we are exposed to the concerns of everything from forests and talking trees to dwarves and shape-shifting bears. Humanity and the concerns of men are made to take their place amid the swirl and multiplicity of creation. But crucially in terms of Tolkien's environmentalism, these concerns and the narratives of men are interconnected and intertwined with the narratives of the non-human to deliver one unifying panorama of story where the activities and resultant fate of one impacts manifestly upon the activities and resultant fate of the other. Indeed Tolkien, in consideration of the point of view offered by his tales of Middle-earth and the Undying Lands, writes, '[a]s the high Legends of the beginning are supposed to look at things through Elvish minds. So the middle tale of the Hobbit takes a virtually human point of view – and the last tale blends them.'[14] His bringing together or blending of perspectives both promotes a coming together of created life and undermines notions of human superiority. In this sense, despite his deeply-held religious beliefs, Tolkien's work emerges as a counterpoint to ideologies that consider humanity to be the high point and the centre of creation.

We should recall also that Tolkien was unambiguous in stating that the events relayed in his *legendarium* were conceived of as part of the history of our own Earth: 'Middle-earth [...] is not a name of a never-never land without relation to the world we live in [...] imaginatively this 'history' is supposed to take place in a period of the actual Old World of this planet.'[15] Thus, this non-anthropocentric world is presented as our own imaginary past – a time before men (therefore humanity) became principal players in world history. Indeed we could say that the unfolding myth cycle of Tolkien's *legendarium* is the story of humanity's inheritance of the Earth. And, although 'men' in Tolkien's fiction may be read

---

14 Tolkien, *Letters*, p.145.
15 Tolkien, *Letters*, p.220.

as a literary manifestation of an aspect of human nature, the race of men in Tolkien's secondary world is, of course, nonetheless closest in form and nature to the human race of the primary world. Indeed given Tolkien's insistence regarding the historical placement of his legends, the unfolding story of men in Middle-earth as a race who, after the departure of the elves and the dwindling of the other non-human societies, will come to prominence, points directly to the human race of our reality. The pertinent point here is that Tolkien's secondary world, created as a mythic alternative to, or a long lost and recovered period of our own real past, presents a world where humanity is not the master of all creation but merely one component part of that creation. Moreover the narrator of *The Silmarillion* states that elves 'awake' first on the Earth and men follow: 'the Children of Ilúvatar are Elves and Men, the Firstborn and the Followers.'[16] This ordering represents a further 'dethroning' of humanity as the jewel in the crown of creation. Tolkien was persistently unambiguous in determining and asserting the centrality of elves in what he referred to as 'the Myth on which all is founded' and the tangential, albeit increasingly emergent role of men. Writing in 1958 he states: 'it must be remembered that *mythically* these tales are Elf-centred, not anthropocentric, and Men only appear in them, at what must be a point long after their Coming.'[17] Elsewhere he was explicit in pointing out that humanity's most defined representation in his fiction, men, were, to use a common term, 'also-rans' in his mythological design: 'Men came in inevitably: after all the author is a man, and if he has an audience they will be Men and Men must come in to our tales, as such, and not merely transfigured or partially represented as Elves, Dwarfs, Hobbits, etc. But they remain peripheral – late comers, and however growingly important, not principals.'[18]

In the previous chapter I discussed my understanding that Gandalf's version of stewardship is not, as some have argued, one rooted in Christian doctrine. One of the clearest indicators that Gandalf's stewardship represents a more holistic environmental worldview is his declaration that his concerns lie equally with *all* manifestations of life. This promotion of equality of esteem across creation, is evident not only in Gandalf's version of stewardship but also in Tolkien's

---

16 Tolkien, *Silmarillion*, p.18.
17 Tolkien, *Letters*, p.285, emphasis in the original.
18 Tolkien, *Letters*, p.147.

presentation of a secondary world and a fictional past that foregrounds a non-human perspective and offers humanity as, what amounts to, a supporting role in his unfolding myths and tales, Tolkien's work, whether he intended it or not, thus challenges conventional ideologies and doctrines which view humanity as being the focus of all creation.

Indeed environmentalists and eco-writers such as Christopher Manes and Lynn White Jr. have placed part of the blame for our modern ecological crisis squarely at the doorstep of such doctrines. Manes in 'Nature and Silence' discusses key moments in the development of human superiority theory such as the establishment of the *scala naturae* or 'the Great Chain of Being', a 'cosmological model' devised by the Church and aristocracy of the Middle Ages which depicted humanity's position as 'higher than beasts and a little less than angels.'[19] This, according to Manes, would eventually lead to what he describes as a 'teleological craze' that became evident in the discourse of prominent figures such as Francis Bacon: 'Man, if we look to final causes, may be regarded as the centre of the world; inasmuch that if man were taken away from the world, the rest would seem to be all astray, without aim or purpose.'[20]

This anthropocentric point of view was (and is), of course, also reflected in the vast majority of literature (I examine the tragic mode in this light as the chapter closes). Even in traditional fairy stories or epic sagas the human perspective tends to dominate the narrative frame. In *The Silmarillion*, in particular, however, the perspective and ordeals of elves govern the text. Great events and moments of turmoil in elvish history come and go without recourse to a human presence. Fëanor's impassioned speech for instance, urging the Noldor (or high-elves) to leave Valinor for Middle-earth in pursuit of Morgoth[21] after he learns that Morgoth has stolen the Silmarils and murdered his father Finwë, is delivered by an elf lord to other elves, and eloquently relays the woe of their race.

---

19 Christopher Manes, 'Nature and Silence' in Cheryll Glotfelty & Harold Fromm (eds.), *The Ecocriticism Reader: Landmarks in Literary Ecology*, Athens and London: University of Georgia Press, 1996, p.20.
20 Taken from *The Philosophical Works of Francis Bacon*, edited by Robert Leslie Ellis & James Spedding, Freeport and New York: Books for Libraries Press, 1970, and quoted by Manes, 'Nature and Silence', p.21.
21 It was Fëanor who named the dark lord of the First Age Morgoth which means 'Black Foe of the World'. His original name among the Ainur was Melkor. Fëanor curses Melkor with the name Morgoth because of his theft of the Silmarils and his murder of Fëanor's father.

Humanity is distinctly absent: '[h]ere once was light, that the Valar begrudged to Middle-earth, but now dark levels all. Shall we mourn here deedless for ever, a shadow-folk, mist-haunting, dropping vain tears in the thankless sea?'[22]

In *The Lord of the Rings* also we are shown the world through elvish eyes and on occasion we become privy to moments of elvish reflection. Galadriel's song from the swan-ship as the Fellowship departs from Lórien, for example, is not directed at another, nor is it a song of farewell; rather it is an elegy which acts as a window onto the private anguish of the elf queen:

> *O Lórien! The Winter comes, the bare and lifeless Day;*
> *The leaves are falling in the stream, the River flows away.*
> *O Lórien! Too long I have dwelt upon this Hither Shore*
> *And in a fading crown have twined the golden elanor*
> *But if of ships I now should sing, what ship would come to me,*
> *What ship would bear me ever back across so wide a Sea?*[23]

Whilst Tolkien's elves were imbued with human qualities and represented, in part, an aspect of the human race, they were nonetheless expressly non-human and indelibly connected to nature which to them was precious above all other concerns. The fact that Tolkien allocates them, therefore, particularly in *The Silmarillion*, such a central role in his fiction, and that he composed long passages in which no humans appear, shows the extent to which Tolkien's fiction resists external notions of anthropocentric superiority. Indeed there are passages in *The Silmarillion* where even the elves are absent and we are offered a narrative that describes a struggle between evil and benign spirits in which the land, where 'new-made green was yet a marvel', is both the prize and the victim. And as the battle between these spirits ensues we are told 'lands were broken and seas rose in tumult.'[24] The unfolding of the *legendarium*, then, offers us a different view: a world in which humanity is not the centre of the cosmic design, or the race that is raised above all else, but merely a component part of creation. Indeed, this displacement of the superiority of humanity in Tolkien's fiction is further underlined when we consider that, in general, the race of men we encounter in Middle-earth and the Undying Lands appears less powerful,

---

22 Tolkien, *Silmarillion*, pp.82-83.
23 J.R.R. Tolkien, *The Fellowship of the Ring*, London: HarperCollins, 1997, p.363.
24 Tolkien, *Silmarillion*, pp.36-37.

less wise and more flawed than, not only the elves, but also perhaps the ents who are, despite their ability to talk and move freely – essentially trees.

(II) A Question of Morality

Despite Tolkien's foregrounding of the non-human and relegation of the importance of humanity in his major works, it should be noted that both elves and men, in Tolkien's *legendarium* do seem to have been set apart in that they are said specifically to be 'the Children of Ilúvatar'. It could be argued, therefore, that elves and men are God's (Ilúvatar's) creation and the focus of his cosmological design in a way that dwarves,[25] ents, dragons, birds, flowers, and trees are not. Crucially in Tolkien's cosmology, however, Ilúvatar also creates the Valar who in turn sub-create the wonders of the Earth and all the natural life forces therein. Of the relationship between the Valar and the Earth we are told 'they are its life and it is theirs. And therefore they are named the Valar, the powers of the World.'[26] The Valar it seems are, and collectively become, the power and wonder of nature itself, and if 'God' created one he is responsible for creating the other. Put another way, the Valar *are* created by Ilúvatar with the capacity to both *become* and sub-create natural forces or phenomena – this is his divine will – the natural things and powers they bring about and become are thus the creations of Ilúvatar, just as elves

---

25 The dwarves are an interesting facet of Tolkien's cosmological design; they are ceated by Aulë in his desire to bring forth life and are later adopted by Ilúvatar. They were viewed as an enemy of the trees. Yavanna, from the first, remonstrates with Aulë because, in her words to him, 'thou hiddest this thought from me until its achievement, thy children will have little love for the things of my love. They will love first the things made by their own hands, as doth their father. They will delve in the earth, and the things that grow and live upon the earth they will not heed. Many a tree shall feel the bite of their iron without pity.' Thinking of how the dwarves may cause endless damage to trees Yavanna muses 'Would that the trees might speak on behalf of all things that have roots, and punish those that wrong them.' In this moment she conceives of the ents whom she refers to as the 'Shepherds of the Trees' and addressing Aulë once more she declares 'let thy children beware! For there shall walk a power in the forests whose wrath they will arouse at their peril' (Tolkien, *Silmarillion*, pp.45-46). The dwarves prove themselves, however, to be a worthy addition to the united stance by the peoples of Middle-earth against the Dark Lord. Indeed Gimli's friendship with Legolas stands as a symbolic representation of the harmony of once warring races and peoples who come together to resist the crisis before them. The dwarves' biggest adversary in Middle-earth proved not to be the ents as Yavanna had foretold but their own greed for Mithril and gold – the Balrog devastation of the dwarvish kingdom of Moria and the fall of Balin represent, in part, an externalisation of the dwarves' own self-destructive greed. For they had 'delved too greedily and too deep' in the pursuit of Mithril (Tolkien, *Fellowship*, p. 309). The dwarves' awakening of the Balrog also may be read as a representation of disturbing powerful elemental forces in nature through greed and exploitation of resources.
26 Tolkien, *Silmarillion*, p.20.

and men are. Furthermore, documenting the elves' devotion to the natural world, Tolkien tells us 'they have a devoted love of the physical world, and a desire to observe and understand it for its own sake and as 'other' [...] as a reality derived from God in the same degree as themselves – not as a material for use or as a power-platform.'[27] The key phrase here is 'in the same degree' which implies that the Earth in all its natural wonder is not considered to be a lesser creation than 'the Children of Ilúvatar'. Furthermore if the natural wonders of the world *are* the Valar in manifest form ('they are its life and it is theirs') nature itself is afforded 'angelic' status. Indeed the fact that the elves have 'a devoted love of the physical world' suggests that the elves do not in any way consider themselves to have dominion over, or be masters of the natural world. In this sense the elves, to some degree mirroring Tolkien's own environmental philosophy, practice a pure form of green politics: they view the natural world not as a storehouse to be plundered at will or as a power to be harnessed for the advancement of their race but as a thing of wonder and beauty – a thing to be cherished and cared for, as Tolkien points out, 'for its own sake.' In presenting the creation of the physical world and 'God's children' in such a way, Tolkien is offering an understanding of creation which elevates the natural world from being the mere playground and larder of humanity to being a creation of God that is equal in wonder to that of the human race. The wider implication of such a presentation points to a human relationship with nature that is not defined in terms of master and slave but one which promotes a mutual harmony of existence in which humanity takes what is needed from the bounty of nature (as does all of creation) whilst accepting that the green face of the Earth and all that lives and grows in nature are wonders in their own right.

Although aspects of Christianity are discernable in Tolkien's cosmology (the supreme sovereignty of an all powerful God for example), and given that the events of his passing Ages 'take place in a period of the actual Old World of this planet'[28] – and thus the race of men is intentioned as humanity – the fact that the strictly human component of Tolkien's fiction is afforded no dominion or pre-eminence over the non-human draws in the question of Tolkien's own faith.

---

27 Tolkien, *Letters*, p.236.
28 Tolkien, *Letters*, p.220.

Indeed given this portrayal of human and non-human in parity in his fiction, the ethos of his created secondary world would seem to fly in the face of his own devout religious beliefs. Prominent passages from the Bible and conventional Christian doctrine, particularly in relation to *The Book of Genesis* determine that humanity, made in the image of God,[29] is master of all creation:

> So God created human beings in his image. In the image of God he created them. He created them male and female. God blessed them and said, 'Have many children and grow in number. Fill the earth and be its master. Rule over the fish in the sea and over the birds in the sky and over every living thing that moves on the earth.'[30]

Although this dominion over nature is described before The Fall it still accounts for humanity in terms of its superiority over nature. Indeed there is no doubt that the Bible, whilst affirming the inherent worth of the natural world as God's creation, does on occasion underline human lordship over the natural world. Luke 12:6-7 is a case in point: 'Are not five sparrows sold for two farthings, and not one of them is forgotten before God? But even the very hairs of your head are all numbered. Fear not therefore: ye are of more value than many sparrows.'[31] This notion of superiority or mastery over nature is certainly not a premise we find reflected in the philosophies of Gandalf, Treebeard or the elves of Middle-earth. Moreover as discussed throughout this discourse and fundamental to the ecological augury which I contend suffuses his fiction, the whole question of domination and mastery is associated with evil in Tolkien's work. And as detailed in previous chapters

---

29 Dickerson and Evans have pointed to the fact that elves and men as the 'Children of Ilúvatar' (and also hobbits as a strain of men, and dwarves as Ilúvatar's adopted children) in their 'special relationship' with God, correspond directly to Christian teaching that humanity, made in the image of God, is his chosen race – in that elves, men, hobbits and dwarves all look visually human. This takes little account of the fact that elves, whilst reflective of humanity, are not human by metaphysical design. Nor does it adequately address the fact that Tolkien refers to ents in the Appendices of *The Return of the King* as 'The most ancient *people* surviving in the Third Age' (Tolkien, *Return*, 1997, p.1104, emphasis added). The word 'people' used in this context (despite Dickerson and Evans' suggestion that this was a generic term) surely affords ents, who are, of course, not at all visually human, a humanistic quality – raising them as a race of beings to the same 'humanesque' status as dwarves, hobbits or elves. There is further blurring of the human/non-human lines in Tolkien's work – the dragons or 'Great Worms' for example are certainly not human in form but they nonetheless have other human qualities, not the least of which is their clever use of sophisticated language to trick, beguile or persuade. Orcs, of course, are, to a degree, visually human, but they are best understood as corruptions of other life forms. For their framing of the visually human assertion, see Matthew Dickerson & Jonathan Evans, *Ents, Elves, and Eriador: The Environmental Vision of J.R.R. Tolkien*, Lexington, Kentucky: University Press of Kentucky, 2006, pp.49-55.
30 Genesis 1:27.
31 Luke 12:6-7.

Tolkien unequivocally connects the environmental devastation of landscapes with the desire for control, power and supremacy. In almost every instance those who damage the green face of Middle-earth wish to be its master and have primacy over other life forms, and those who care for the land harbour no such thoughts. We recall Goldberry's response to Frodo asking if the lands of the Old Forest belonged to Tom Bombadil – the River Daughter's reply clearly indicates that she considers the land to have no master: '[t]he trees and the grasses and all things growing or living in the land belong each to themselves.'[32]

All of the above considered, how do we reconcile Tolkien's Christian beliefs with the cosmic design and environmentally themed, ecocentric frame presented in his fiction? Can we perhaps say that Tolkien's fiction was just that – fiction, and as such it did not accurately reflect his theological views? Or does the cosmological structure made evident in Tolkien's secondary world and the prominence of non-human races such as the nature-loving elves reveal something more about Tolkien's privately-held views on the question of Judeo-Christian assertions related to humanity's mastery over nature? In terms of the first of these hypotheses, I would agree with Michael N. Stanton's understanding that Tolkien 'surely did not check his faith and belief at the door when he sat down to write',[33] and so an exploration of the observable parallels between Tolkien's fictional presentation of creation and his own reconciliation of his environmental and religious understandings is valid.

In the pursuit of this exploration, let us first put the contention that Judeo-Christian dogma promotes human superiority (and thus the exploitation of nature) into context. In 'Historical Roots of our Ecological Crisis' White Jr. accuses Christian doctrine of actually advancing or allowing for the exploitation of the natural world. He asks, '[w]hat did Christianity tell people about their relations with the environment?'[34] and offers his answer:

---

32 Tolkien, *Fellowship*, p.122.
33 Michael N. Stanton, *Hobbits, Elves and Wizards: Exploring the Wonders and Worlds of J.R.R. Tolkien's The Lord of the Rings*, New York: Palgrave Macmillan, 2002, p.162.
34 Lynn White Jr., 'Historical Roots of Our Ecological Crisis' in Cheryll Glotfelty & Harold Fromm (eds.), *The Ecocriticism Reader: Landmarks in Literary Ecology*, Athens and London: University of Georgia Press, 1996, p.9.

> Man shares, in great measure, God's transcendence of nature […] establish[ing] a dualism of man and nature but also insist[ing] that it is God's will that man exploit nature for his proper ends […] By destroying Pagan animism Christianity made it possible to exploit nature in a mood of indifference to the feelings of natural objects.[35]

Moreover White Jr. asserts that emergence and continued existence of environmentally harmful technology can to some degree be attributed to a Western understanding of the Christian faith which relegates nature to the status of a mere commodity:

> modern technology is at least partly to be explained as an Occidental, voluntarist realization of the Christian dogma of man's transcendence of, and rightful mastery over, nature. But, as we now recognize, somewhat over a century ago science and technology – hitherto quite separate activities – joined to give mankind powers which, to judge by many of the ecological effects, are out of control.

White Jr., who states that humanity cannot hope to escape the clutches of an ecological crisis 'until we find a new religion, or rethink our old one', goes on to lay bare the conceit of exponents of the superiority of the human race who give rise to declarations such as the one made by the then Governor of California: 'when you've seen one redwood tree, you've seen them all.' Using this rather bombastic remark as a prime example of how the West, led by the teachings of orthodox religion, has come to view nature as vastly inferior to the human race, White Jr. adds: '[t]o a Christian a tree can be no more than a physical fact. The whole concept of the sacred grove is alien to Christianity and to the ethos of the West.'[36]

Whilst White Jr.'s observation makes a valid point, it surely suffers a little from over-generalisation and takes no account of the environmental ethics of a Christian such as Tolkien whose willingness, as we noted in the first chapter, to take the part of trees and thus the non-human over a human agitator is testimony alone to his green credentials. White Jr.'s assertion that we cannot hope to remedy the current environmental crisis 'until we find a new religion, or rethink our old one', perhaps also lays a little too much blame for environmental problems at the doorstep of religion and fails to take sufficient

---

35 White Jr., 'Historical Roots of Our Ecological Crisis', p.10.
36 White Jr., 'Historical Roots of Our Ecological Crisis', p.12.

account of environmentally damaging policies and regimes that derive from purely business-driven or secular philosophies. The very fact that he envisions a remedy for environmental ills should come *from* religion is testimony to this. Moreover there are many instances in the Bible where environmental ethics are promoted and acts of pollution are denigrated. Ezekiel 34:18 reads:

> Seemeth it a small thing unto you to have eaten up the good pasture, but ye must tread down with your feet the residue of your pastures? And to have drunk of the deep waters, but ye must foul the residue with your feet?

And Revelation 11:18 sounds out a warning to those who would bring ruination to God's Earth: 'give reward unto thy servants the prophets, and to the saints, and them that fear thy name, small and great; and *shouldest destroy them which destroy the earth*' (emphasis added).

Indeed, to a certain degree, White Jr.'s 'hard-line' assessment of the culpability of Christian doctrine in advancing the ecological crisis fails to fully offer a representative context in terms of the positive associations between Christian understandings and environmentalism (and thus he fails to account for the validity of a devout Christian, like Tolkien, with a pronounced ecological worldview).

Richard Bauckham in the chapter entitled 'Human Authority in Creation' from his work *God and the Crisis of Freedom: Biblical and Contemporary Perspectives*, offering a response to White Jr.'s work, states that it is 'important to keep in view other aspects of Christian thought about creation that could be seen to qualify or moderate what is said about the human dominion.'[37] Bauckham goes on to discuss ecologically positive portrayals of Christian faith such as the hermits of Christian eremitic life, living in nature and apart from human society in order that they may find a union with God, and in doing so they, as Bauckham points out, 'learned to appreciate the beauty of wild nature and to love the natural world for its own sake as God's creation.'[38] In a particularly subtle and insightful discourse Bauckham goes on to propose that even if Christianity *does* seem to present a hierarchy in creation, it is not a simple

---

37 Richard Bauckham, *God and the Crisis of Freedom: Biblical and Contemporary Perspectives*, Louisville: John Knox Press, 2002, p.132
38 Bauckham, *God and the Crisis of Freedom*, p.144.

question of dominion and subservience, but rather, when considered across a wide spectrum of Christian tradition (rather than focusing on or 'cherry-picking' specific passages from the Bible) a more nuanced ideology that deals with freewill and a mutually beneficial order. In many Christian-framed stories and verses, 'hierarchical order', according to Bauckham, 'is understood as a state of harmony that benefits all God's creatures.' He goes on to contend that in numerous other Christian stories concerning saints, animals 'are not the saint's slaves, but are frequently portrayed as friends and companions of the saint, and as objects of the saint's care and concern'[39] and these *friends* of the saints (and indeed the hermits), rather than being subservient creatures, 'willingly serve those that serve God' – and 'the servants of God care for and protect the animals.' The hierarchy in these instances of Christian lore, therefore, is predicated on a creature's willingness to serve a righteous servant of God. Moreover, as Bauckham asserts 'the sense of hierarchy is strongly qualified by a sense of common creatureliness.'[40] Bauckham also underlines that, in these examples, the idea of exploitation is absent: 'the animals willing serve but are certainly not exploited.'[41] These ideas concerning creatures being friends with righteous individuals and willingly offering their service, certainly recall aspects of Tolkien's fiction such as Gandalf's friendship with Shadowfax, never commanding but asking favours of the horse – and he has a similar relationship with Gwaihir the eagle. Indeed the acts of service offered by Shadowfax and Gwaihir are for the benefit of all as Sauron rises to power in the Third Age. Stories such as those of the hermits or the saints which speak of a oneness with aspects of nature, as Bauckham suggests, 'step right outside of the theological and exegetical tradition'[42] or the kind of biblical analysis and interpretation that was undertaken and advanced by White Jr.

Of course, we should note that White Jr., as part of his famous essay, sets his criticisms of traditional Christian doctrine aside for a time and nominates St. Francis of Assisi as a possible patron saint for the ecology movement,[43] citing St.

---

39 Bauckham, *God and the Crisis of Freedom*, p.146.
40 Bauckham, *God and the Crisis of Freedom*, p.148.
41 Bauckham, *God and the Crisis of Freedom*, p.146.
42 Bauckham, *God and the Crisis of Freedom*, p.146.
43 Bauckham agrees entirely with White Jr.'s call that St. Francis should be patron saint of ecologists adding '[n]o other figure in Christian history so clearly, vividly and attractively embodies a sense of the world, including humanity, as a community of God's creatures, mutually interdependent

Francis's promotion of what White Jr. calls 'a democracy of all God's creatures'[44] which in itself echoes Tolkien's own commentary on the 'community of living things'.[45] And, although in the previous chapter, I have drawn associations between the environmentally-themed philosophies of Gandalf and those of Albert Schweitzer, in ecological (and spiritual) terms, there are also parallels observable between Tolkien's portrayal of the Grey Wanderer and the philosophies and activities of St. Francis. Indeed it is clear from Gandalf's words and actions that he also believes in egalitarianism across creation. Moreover, calling to mind understandings of St. Francis's friendship with nature's creatures, Gandalf's relationship with the various creatures and animals of Middle-earth, such as with Shadowfax and Gwaihir mentioned above, could be described as friendships or associations that are built on mutual respect rather than dominion. Of course the very fact that Gandalf *speaks* to these representatives of the animal kingdom (even in a secondary world setting) is evidence enough that he views them as more than 'dumb' creatures which are beneath him in some chain of command. Similarly, Roderick Nash in his essay 'The Greening of Religion', alludes to accounts of St. Francis as one who related to the natural world and its creatures in the same manner as he did to human society, in that he offered 'canticles and prayers' which 'addressed nonhuman beings', and 'preached sermons to birds.'[46] Another 'legend' concerning St. Francis, mentioned by White Jr., tells of a fearsome wolf that was terrorizing the land around Gubbio in the Apennines. The legend has it that St. Francis, as White Jr. puts it, 'talked to the wolf and persuaded him of the error of his ways.'[47] We see similar communicative powers in operation between Gandalf and the creatures of Middle-earth. As the Fellowship prepare to enter the Mines of Moria, for example, Gandalf, persuading Sam that Bill the pony should not enter with the party, sends the pony on its way with words of praise and advice. The narrator describes the

---

[…] inspir[ing] in Christians an attitude of appreciation, gratitude, respect and love for all God's creatures'; but he adds that White Jr. was wrong in trying to portray 'Francis as a completely exceptional figure in Christian history' (Bauckham, *God and the Crisis of Freedom*, p.148) who, in White Jr.'s words, 'tried to depose man from his monarchy over creation and set up a democracy of all God's creatures' (White Jr., 'Historical Roots of Our Ecological Crisis', p.12). Indeed Bauckham, referring in part to the hermits and the stories of the saints, states that historically St. Francis was 'the climax of a tradition' in Christianity (Bauckham, *God and the Crisis of Freedom*, p.148).

44 White Jr., 'Historical Roots of Our Ecological Crisis', p.12.
45 Tolkien, *Letters*, p.400.
46 Roderick Nash, 'The Greening of Religion' in Roger S. Gottlieb (ed.), *This Sacred Earth: Religion, Nature, Environment*, London and New York: Routledge, 1996, p.199.
47 White Jr., 'Historical Roots of Our Ecological Crisis', p.12.

scene: '[Gandalf] laid his hand on the pony's head, and spoke in a low voice. 'Go with words of guard and guiding on you [...] you are a wise beast, and have learned much in Rivendell. Make your ways to places where you can find grass." The narrator goes on to indicate that the pony has understood: 'seeming to understand well what was going on, [the pony] nuzzled up to [Sam], putting his nose to Sam's ear.'[48]

Drawing parallels between the character of Gandalf and St. Francis of Assisi may help us understand how Tolkien was able to reconcile his Christianity with his environmental ideals. Certainly Gandalf, as an incarnate angel, was created by Tolkien within a spiritual and religious context, and the quality of esteem the Grey Wizard affords supposedly lesser life-forms cast him in this 'Franciscan' light. It is worth noting, however, that another of the Istari – Radagast the Brown – exudes qualities and characteristics that are also highly suggestive of St. Francis (commonly depicted in a distinctive brown habit). Indeed Radagast's earlier Maia (or Quenya) name Aiwendil means 'bird-friend', a phrase that singularly recalls St. Francis's association with birds, and the Brown Wizard's pronounced concern for not only the birds but also the beasts of Middle-earth parallels St. Francis's own famed inclination to intercede for and even preach to non-human life forms. Of course, as previously noted in discussions of how aspects of the Green Man are observable in *both* Tom Bombadil *and* Treebeard, Tolkien could have imbued both Radagast and Gandalf with the spirit of St. Francis, casting each with a differing interpretation or transmission of that spirit. Tolkien, however, featured the environmentally-themed activities and philosophies of Gandalf in his major works in a way he did not with Radagast, and as we noted earlier, Radagast was generally understood to have neglected his task as an Istari because he focused *too much* on specific aspects of creation (something St. Francis and indeed Gandalf could not be accused of). In the previous chapter, as noted above, I drew associations between the ecological

---

48 Tolkien, *Fellowship*, pp. 295-96. Guglielmo Spirito, himself a friar from the Franciscan order, discusses other examples of how Tolkien foregrounds the communicative and rational qualities of animals such as the fox, in *The Lord of the Rings*, who thinks it is strange to see the company of hobbits in the woods. Father Spirito also alludes to the passage in *The Hobbit* where we are told that animals do the 'housework' in Beorn's hall, and the scenes in 'Farmer Giles of Ham' where Giles' dog Garm, as Spirito puts it, 'uses the vulgar tongue, but remains dog-like, he communicates, but is not really 'humanized'' (Guglielmo Spirito, 'Speaking With Animals: A Desire that Lies Near the Heart of Faërie' in Margaret Hiley and Frank Weinreich (eds.), *Tolkien's Shorter Works. Essays of the Jena Conference 2007*, Zurich and Jena, Walking Tree Publishers, 2008, p.24).

philosophies and practices of Gandalf and those of Albert Schweitzer, and it is interesting to note that Nash draws similar parallels between St Francis and Schweitzer: '[a]nticipating Albert Schweitzer by seven centuries, St. Francis commonly removed worms from paths where they might be crushed.'[49] The discernible common ground that exists between St. Francis, Schweitzer and Tolkien's Grey Wizard is common ground that advances the notion of a parity of esteem across creation, or promotes, as Tolkien himself put it, the 'community of living things'.

As already mentioned in this discourse, for Tolkien the heart of the problem and the blame for (as he saw it) the ever-gathering environmental crisis lay not with religious teachings or secular technologies but with the use and misuse of power – in other words with personal choice and morality – and it is primarily within the arena of morality where Tolkien's Christian beliefs and his ecological conscience are reconciled. In a letter I referred to in the 'Keeping the Faith' section of the first chapter, Tolkien, responding to the rather profound question '[w]hat is the purpose of life?', raised by Rayner Unwin's daughter Camilla for a school project, offers that such an enquiry inevitably begs the question 'Is there a God, a Creator-Designer'? It is here where Tolkien specifically refers to creation as 'the community of living things', and he goes on to address the theological question of morality within a decidedly environmental frame of reference:

> With that we come to religion and the moral ideas that proceed from it. Of these things I will only say that 'morals' have two sides, derived from the fact that we are individuals (as in some degree are all living things) but do not, cannot, live in isolation, and have a bond with all other things, ever closer up to the absolute bond with our own human kind.
> So morals should be a guide to our human purposes, the conduct of our lives: (a) the ways in which our individual talents can be developed without waste or misuse; and (b) without injuring our kindred or interfering with their development.[50]

Tolkien here is clearly advocating a human relationship with the natural world that is governed by a moral imperative and an understanding that all creation shares a bond and a kinship not only with God but also with each other.

---

49 Nash, 'The Greening of Religion', p.93.
50 Tolkien, *Letters*, pp.399-400.

Indeed the whole question of 'human purposes' and 'individual talents' being 'developed without waste or misuse' expresses more than the sentiment that we should not waste the gifts God has given us as individuals, it also promotes the premise that humanity, as a race, should not misuse the power of its imagination – imagination that has been used not only to create art and beauty, but also to develop ever more powerful technology and machines. As mentioned previously Tolkien was not a Luddite who dismissed technology as inherently evil, but he did believe that humanity had a moral responsibility to develop and use technology, as he states above, 'without injuring our kindred' – 'our kindred' being the other life-forms with which we share our planet.

As part of the same letter, Tolkien, alluding to the distinction between revering all that is about us (pantheism) and finding divinity in the wonders of nature, implies that an understanding of God may be discovered in the contemplation of the non-human, and again he presents his thoughts on religious matters within a green context:

> Those who believe in a personal God, Creator, do not think the Universe is in itself worshipful, though devoted study of it may be one of the ways of honouring Him. And while as living creatures we are (in part) within it and part of it, our ideas of God and ways of expressing them will be largely derived from contemplating the world about us.[51]

Although the phrase 'a personal God' is suggestive of a close and private relationship with one's God, as opposed to an embrace of the abstract notion of divinity, the phrase also implies a personal engagement with and understanding of religious doctrine and the word of God. Given his unapologetically ecocentric worldview, Tolkien clearly derived his ideas about God, in part, by 'contemplating the world about' him, and for Tolkien this was no abandonment of his Christian beliefs. Indeed Tolkien closes his letter to Unwin's daughter by referencing 'Psalm 148' and 'The Song of the Three Children in Daniel II' where humanity and the non-human stand together as creations of God in praise: 'in moments of exaltation we may call on all created things to join in our chorus [...] all mountains and hills, all orchards and forests, all things that creep and birds on the wing.'[52]

---

51 Tolkien, *Letters*, p.400.
52 Tolkien, *Letters*, p.400.

All of the above are certainly not the thoughts or words of a man who considers nature to be a commodity or a tree to be 'no more than a physical fact'. Indeed it is apparent not only from such writings but also from his fiction that, to some degree at least, Tolkien must have attempted to, and perhaps in his own mind succeeded in, reconciling his religious beliefs with his 'green' ethics. Certainly Tolkien's fiction presents a world that is not defined by conventional religious understandings of human superiority, and in a very real sense works such as *The Lord of the Rings* and *The Silmarillion* are ecocentric texts. Patrick Curry suggests that through the presentation of ecocentric narratives Tolkien rises 'above the dogmas of his own religious upbringing [and] made it possible for his readers to unselfconsciously combine Christian ethics and a neo-pagan reverence for nature.'[53] Perhaps to say that Tolkien was rising above his religious creed is putting the case a little too strongly, but rather I would suggest that he incorporated his green philosophy into his Catholic faith and promoted, through the culture of his elves and others, an environmental ethos which can legitimately consider the natural world to be a valued creation of God in its own right, valued for its beauty as well as its sustaining worth.

From this perspective White Jr.'s rather uncompromising assertion, '[t]o a Christian a tree can be no more than a physical fact'[54] falls short of accounting for the Christian led but environmentally predisposed thought processes of one such as Tolkien. Indeed much like the spiritual climate evident in his fiction, Tolkien's environmental worldview complimented[55] rather than compromised his own faith. Perhaps Tolkien's individual position is more accurately mirrored in the proverbial words of William Blake written over two hundred years ago: '[t]he tree which moves some to tears of joy is in the eyes of others only a green thing that stands in the way [...] But to the eyes of the man of imagination, nature is imagination itself.'[56] Blake's words not only cut to the heart of the divide between

---

53 Patrick Curry, *Defending Middle-Earth, Tolkien: Myth and Modernity*, London: HarperCollins, 1997, p.29.
54 White Jr., 'Historical Roots of Our Ecological Crisis', p.12.
55 Those such as Carpenter, Caldecott and Hart have also described the spiritual atmosphere and the creation myth in Tolkien's fiction in terms of it being 'complimentary' to Christianity. See Humphrey Carpenter, *J.R.R. Tolkien: A Biography*, London: George Allen & Unwin, 1977, p.93; Stratford Caldecott, *Secret Fire: The Spiritual Vision of J.R.R. Tolkien*, London: Dartman, Longman & Todd, 2003, p.74; and Trevor Hart, 'Tolkien, Creation, and Creativity' in Trevor Hart & Ivan Khovacs (eds.), *Tree of Tales: Tolkien, Literature, and Theology*, Waco: Baylor University Press, 2007, p.43.
56 William Blake, from a letter to Rev. Dr. Trusler, dated 23rd August 1799, in *The Complete Writings of William Blake*, edited by Geoffrey Keynes, London: Oxford University Press, 1925, p.793.

environmentalism and industries (validated by presumptions on the superiority of humanity) that place the needs of the human race and profit margins above all else, but by invoking the realm of imagination they also reflect the divide in attitude which exists between many of the opposing forces in Tolkien's fiction. For we not only see Tolkien himself as one who may conceivably be 'move[d] to tears of joy' by the beauty of a tree or celebrate the wonder of nature but also the elves, the ents, the Valar, Gandalf, Tom Bombadil, Sam Gamgee, Niggle and Smith of Wootton Major (discussed below). And emerging from those who consider trees and natural phenomena to be 'thing[s] that stand [...] in the way' we find Morgoth, Ungoliant, Sauron, Saruman and the orcs.

Indeed we should emphasise the fact that Tolkien was creating his fiction in a time when the damaging effects of industrialisation, and humanity's focus upon itself and its reliance on technology was beginning to take its toll on the environment. His fiction, therefore, elevating as it does the sphere of the non-human (whilst reflecting and warning of the ecological crisis of the primary world) really must be placed alongside Blake's as among the most significant green texts ever written – a contention I make more resolutely in the chapter to come. Certainly it would be no unfounded claim, considering the many letters and papers that reflect his concerns for the plight of nature in the primary world, to suggest that Tolkien, through the unfolding of an extrapolated universe, anticipated the scale of the modern environmental crisis to come – this is central to the question of ecological augury. Tolkien's fiction takes the environmental crisis of the real world, magnifies it and expands it to a possible outcome (Mordor), and thus his fiction becomes a warning, an augury for the real world.

(III) Whose Myth is it Anyway?

The mere fact that Tolkien's fiction is one of the very few that takes account of and promotes perspectives other than those of humanity (whilst including the human viewpoint) casts it as a paragon of eco-literature. Indeed the shifting from non-human to human perspective in Tolkien's work has led scholars such as Verlyn Flieger to ask, in relation to the presentation of his most famous work as a myth, fundamental questions such as 'whose myth is it? Whose perspective, understanding, and worldview is the story carrying?'[57] The fact that Tolkien's *legendarium* begins chronologically in the First Age with the coming of elves in *The Silmarillion* of which Tolkien states categorically 'the point of view is Elvish'[58] and concludes with the coming of men and the blended perspective to be found in *The Lord of the Rings* in the Third Age begs Flieger's question[s]: 'Whose myth is it? Does it belong equally to both [elves and men] and relate equally to both?' Such enquiry, as Flieger rightly points out, concerns the question of death and the fact that 'Men die and leave the world; Elves do not; Men are mortal; Elves are immortal.'[59] I address the question of the respective mortality and immortality of men and elves later in this chapter, but for now let us attend to the question of divided perspective, considering Tolkien's writings on Middle-earth and the Undying Lands as a unified myth.

In terms of addressing the focus of the entire spectrum of his *legendarium*, Tolkien could be somewhat unclear. Flieger points to two seemingly unequivocal but nonetheless contrasting statements: 'The point of view of the whole cycle is Elvish',[60] Tolkien wrote in a letter to Waldman probably late 1951, and, according to Christopher Tolkien around 1958 his father also wrote '[t]he mythology must actually be a 'Mannish' affair [...] what we have in the *Silmarillion* etc. are traditions [...] handed on by 'Men' in Númenor and later in Middle-earth (Arnor and Gondor).'[61] So, as Flieger asks '[i]s the mythology Elvish? Is it Mannish?'[62] Flieger's concluding thoughts, after a considered analysis of the differing worldviews presented in Tolkien's work, and the metaphysical differences between elves and mortals (revealed in microcosm in the 'Athrabeth' – a cosmological discussion between the elven king Finrod Felagund and Andreth, a mortal woman) further underscore the polycentric nature of his narratives. 'The whole point of the 'Athrabeth'', concludes Flieger, 'was to show that myth does not, cannot speak with one voice.'[63] Similarly

---

57 Verlyn Flieger, *Interrupted Music: The Making of Tolkien's Mythology*, London and Kent, Ohio: Kent State University Press, 2005, p.45.
58 Tolkien, *Letters*, p.147.
59 Flieger, *Interrupted Music*, p.46.
60 Tolkien, *Letters*, p.147.
61 J.R.R. Tolkien, *Morgoth's Ring: The Later Silmarillion*, (The History of Middle-earth vol. 10), edited by Christopher Tolkien, London: HarperCollins, 2002, p.370.
62 Flieger, *Interrupted Music*, p.47.
63 Flieger, *Interrupted Music*, p.54.

she states earlier in the study that Tolkien's mythology 'belongs to whoever is speaking whenever they are speaking [...] the whole *legendarium* has been presented as tales told by a variety of tellers. We have heard multiple voices both Elven and human coming from different times and different Middle-earth cultures.'[64] From an ecocritical point of view we could expand Flieger's 'variety of tellers', 'multiple voices' and 'Middle-earth cultures' beyond those of elven and human origin. Treebeard and Tom Bombadil, for example, each to some degree representing the voice of nature in Tolkien's work, give us 'the long perspective' of the land itself, of Middle-earth and the deeper rhythms of creation. For although the elves are immortal, the land, the forests and woods, the soil, the mountains and the hills were created long before the arrival of elves.[65] Andrew Light referring to this 'long perspective' as 'green time' comments:

> through the characters of Tom Bombadil and the ents, *The Lord of the Rings* makes comprehensible a sense of the past through which 'nature' sets the context for events in the present [...] Tolkien helps us understand the importance of nature as the foreground and background of all events of any significance to us, while at the same time encouraging our responsibility for it.[66]

Speaking specifically of the narrative worth of the ents Light adds, '[b]ut what [Treebeard] and the other ents do is not simply care for the forest as much as they serve as a narrative device that allows part of nature to speak for itself.'[67] Reconsidering Flieger's assertion that 'the whole *legendarium* has been presented as tales told by a variety of tellers', we may also include the voice of nature as one of the 'tellers'. In a very real sense Tolkien's created myth offers an ecosphere of perspective that rejects the dominance of humanity over other life forms. Yet despite the fact that a representation of humanity in parity with the non-human and his ecocentric narrative would appear at odds with his Catholic faith, as we noted earlier, Tolkien somehow manages to navigate around the trap doors of religious dogma. He offers a secondary world in which humanity becomes unseated from the throne of

---

64 Flieger, *Interrupted Music*, p.49.
65 Tolkien, *The Silmarillion*, p.37.
66 Andrew Light, 'Tolkien's Green Time: Environmental Themes in *The Lord of the Rings*' in Gregory Bassham & Eric Bronson (eds.), *The Lord of the Rings and Philosophy: One Book to Rule Them All*, Chicago and La Salle, Illinois: Open Court Publishing, 2003, p.152.
67 Light, 'Tolkien's Green Time', p.154.

creation and in which the natural world and the non-human find central roles – a world in which the elves' devotion to nature paints the narrative with a decidedly non- or pre-Christian hue. At the same time Tolkien, whilst making or including no overt reference to Christianity, manages to invoke powerful and unmistakable Christian themes and motifs. In this regard, however, Tolkien's *legendarium* was not unique. Tolkien had a blueprint for the presentation of a 'pagan', ecocentric secondary world that could reflect Christian belief – Celtic mythology.

(IV) Elves and the Celtic 'Otherworld'

Tolkien was, of course, well-acquainted and conversant with the legends of Celtic mythology. He was drawn to it in the first instance through his interest in Celtic languages, particularly the Welsh language,[68] which first caught his attention as a boy. Humphrey Carpenter describes how Tolkien's early fascination with the Welsh language was ignited by the 'curious names' he saw written on coal trucks. These according to Carpenter were,

> odd names which he did not know how to pronounce but which had a strange appeal to him. So it came about that by pondering over *Nantyglo, Senghenydd, Blaen-Rhondda, Penrhiwceiber,* and *Tredegar,* he discovered the existence of the Welsh language. Later in childhood he went on a railway journey to Wales, and as the station names flashed past him he knew that here were words more appealing to him than any he had yet encountered, a language that was old and yet alive [...] however brief and tantalising the glimpse, he had caught sight of another linguistic world.[69]

Although Tolkien was an avid student of Celtic mythology (as he was with many other mythological traditions), his attitude towards it seemed to fluctuate. In a letter to Stanley Unwin dated 1937 Tolkien rejected the Celtic 'tag' placed on his work by Edward Crankshaw, an outside reader for Unwin. Crankshaw, having read Tolkien's 'Quenta Silmarillion' (an early version of writings that were later to form part of *The Silmarillion*) broadly classified the work as Celtic. He expressed a dislike of what he called its 'eye-splitting Celtic names' before

---

68 Despite his declared love of the Welsh language, Tolkien had no great fondness for the Irish language, which he referred to as 'wholly unattractive'. He did however declare a fondness for Ireland (Southern Ireland in particular) and would take trips there as often as he could. See Tolkien, *Letters*, p.289.
69 Carpenter, *Biography*, p.28.

concluding of the work, '[i]t has something of that mad, bright-eyed beauty that perplexes all Anglo-Saxons in face of Celtic art.'[70] Tolkien's response was to deny that his work was classifiable as Celtic, adding 'I do know Celtic things (many in their original languages Irish and Welsh), and feel for them a certain distaste: largely for their fundamental unreason. They have bright colour, but are like a broken stained glass window reassembled without design.'[71] Some fourteen years later, however, Tolkien, speaking of his long-held desire to construct a mythology for England, confesses a wish that such work should posses 'the fair elusive beauty that some call Celtic' although he added in parenthesis 'it is rarely found in genuine ancient Celtic things.'[72] And, in a letter written to Naomi Mitchison in 1954, Tolkien comments on the construction of his invented elvish language, *Síndarin*: 'The living language of the Western Elves' Tolkien writes, is 'deliberately devised to give it a linguistic character very like (though not identical with) British-Welsh.' He goes on to state that he based the elvish *Síndarin* on aspects of the Welsh language 'because it seems to fit the rather 'Celtic' type of legends and stories told of its speakers.'[73] Here, despite his earlier rejection of such a comparison, Tolkien seems to be admitting that his own 'legends and stories', specifically those concerning elves, have strong parallels with Celtic myth or at least that they exude Celtic characteristics.

Of course Tolkien drew influences from many diverse mythologies. The central role of nature and landscape in Tolkien's work and the association he fashioned between aspects of nature and sentient beings reflected the characteristics of older mythology. Alfred K. Siewers in 'Tolkien's Cosmic-Christian Ecology' suggests that Tolkien's elves, ents and even Tom Bombadil, portrayed in Middle-earth as closely related to their respective environments, had 'precedents in indigenous narratives of northern Europe.' Celtic myth in particular, however, presented Tolkien with an example of how Christian ideologies could be 'written in' and radiate from a non-Christian setting in which the natural world takes centre stage. Siewers continues:

> Early Celtic (really Welsh and Irish) Otherworld texts helped provide Tolkien with a pattern for an ecocentric Middle-earth – that is, for portraying the natural

---

70 Tolkien, *Letters*, p.25.
71 Tolkien, *Letters*, p.26.
72 Tolkien, *Letters*, p.144.
73 Tolkien, *Letters*, p.176.

world as a central character beyond human control or even human concerns, integrated rather than separated from the divine [...] Tolkien's fantasy could stretch beyond his own Augustinian Catholicism to embrace the imaginations of a wide range of religious and secular beliefs. The mingling of his Catholic faith with an interest in Celtic languages was responsible.[74]

Like many Celtic 'Otherworlds', Tolkien's Middle-earth comes alive – it is a world where the natural landscape is animate and not merely a backdrop against which the action occurs. The land is possessed of a waking consciousness. Moreover natural features such as the forests, woods, rivers and mountains of Middle-earth are characterised by differing 'personalities' – Fangorn Forest for example is described as 'a brooding presence, full of secret purpose.'[75] The mountains also are given a life force and, as a mighty storm prevents the Fellowship from passing over Mount Caradhras, we hear Gimli say 'it is no ordinary storm. It is the ill will of Caradhras. He does not love Elves and Dwarves.'[76] In a letter to the editor of the *Daily Telegraph* concerning the representation of trees in Middle-earth, Tolkien refers to forests in his work as having 'memory' and harbouring antagonism towards an 'enemy': 'forests [in Middle-earth]' he writes 'are represented as awakening to consciousness of themselves. The Old Forest was hostile to two legged creatures because of the memory of many injuries. Fangorn Forest was old and beautiful, but at the time of the story tense with hostility because it was threatened by a machine-loving enemy.'[77] The landscape of Tolkien's story thus becomes more than a setting, it becomes a presence – not in the same way as the landscape of a work such as Emily Brontë's *Wuthering Heights* looms and broods over the action, reflecting and feeding the dark personas of the characters, but actually a living entity. Indeed Middle-earth itself could justifiably be classified as one of the major players in Tolkien's *legendarium*. Curry takes up the point:

> It wouldn't be stretching a point to say that Middle-earth itself appears as a character in its own right. And the living personality and agency of this character are none the less for being non-human; in fact that is just what allows for a sense of ancient myth, with its feeling of a time when the Earth itself was alive.

---

74 Alfred K. Siewers, 'Tolkien's Cosmic-Christian Ecology' in Jane Chance & Alfred K. Siewers (eds.), *Tolkien's Modern Middle Ages*, New York: Palgrave Macmillan, 2005, p.140.
75 Tolkien, *Fellowship*, p.431.
76 Tolkien, *Fellowship*, p.285.
77 Tolkien, *Letters*, pp. 419-20.

Curry goes on to suggest that the 'character' of Middle-earth is capable of evoking 'a sense of relief' in a reader, 'relief' and solace that in this non-human character one may discover an antithesis to what Curry calls the 'bloated solipsism' of humanity which in the primary world 'has swollen to become everything.'[78] Indeed Tolkien's foregrounding of nature as a character rather than a backdrop is what, perhaps more than any other aspect of his work, promotes the environmental dimension of his fiction. Cheryll Glotfelty in *The Ecocriticism Reader: Landmarks in Literary Ecology* considers the foregrounding of the natural world across differing disciplines of the humanities to be a crucial strategy in the promotion of 'environmental restoration', believing that discourses that take serious account of the natural world should consider 'nature not just as the stage upon which the human story is acted out, but as an actor in the drama.'[79]

Considering Middle-earth as 'a character in its own right' in Tolkien's work, we may ask what role does this character play? How does it serve the plot? Could we describe this character as easily as we could describe the character of Gandalf or Frodo or Galadriel (a task not easy in itself)? Of course given the diverse nature of the differing natural landscapes in Middle-earth and the associated 'personalities' thereof it becomes difficult in the extreme to pinpoint specific defining characteristics for our major player – the brooding hostilities of Fangorn Forest, Mirkwood and Mount Caradhras are not representative of the welcoming meadows of the Shire or the sweeping, green plains of Rohan. In general, however, taking the lands of Middle-earth collectively, we can offer one characteristic description that may help answer, in part, all of the questions above. Middle-earth may be best described as a character that is slowly dying, dying at the hands of other characters who attack it relentlessly – both wilfully and as a consequence of other goals, but always without justifiable cause. The collective agents of destruction view the character of Middle-earth as a slave to be mastered, mocked and tormented. This in itself is a deeply Christian motif; we see this character in progressive states of decay from the vibrancy of the Shire before Sharkey to the death-like desolation of Mordor where no green thing grows. Many Tolkien commentators have spoken of viewing the sacrifices and trials of characters such

---

78 Curry, *Defending Middle-Earth*, p.61.
79 Glotfelty, 'Introduction' in *The Ecocriticism Reader: Landmarks in Literary Ecology*, p.12.

as Gandalf (who died and was resurrected) and Frodo (who carried the symbol of the world's sins) from a Christian perspective (both Gandalf and Frodo carry the wounds of their sacrifice as does the landscapes of Middle-earth), surely the 'character' of Middle-earth may also be viewed as an innocent, like Christ, that faces torture and even death at the hands of a political regime. The narrative of the gradual decay of this character both informs and influences the main plot line(s) of the myth cycle, indeed the struggle to save and free this enslaved and slowly dying character lies behind all of the action which propels the narrative of *The Lord of the Rings* forward. In this sense, at a very fundamental level, Tolkien's work is both ecocentric and Christian in form. Furthermore, the slow decay of the vibrant landscapes of Middle-earth is mirrored in the culture of the elves. The elves in the Third Age are leaving Middle-earth and the natural energy and vitality they represent is passing also from the land.

Of course aside from the Christian themes that come into view when Middle-earth is considered as a character, Tolkien's secondary world exudes spirituality, not in an exaggerated or overt way, not in a way that openly identifies religions of the primary world, but in an understated and almost withdrawn fashion. Indeed Tolkien, referring specifically to Arthurian legend, stated that its explicit association with Christian religion was 'fatal' in terms of the presentation of legends, adding '[m]yth and fairy-story must, as all art, reflect and contain in solution elements of moral and religious truth (or error), but not explicit, not in the known form of the primary 'real' world.'[80] Indeed although the Middle-earth of the Third Age is the same land and the same story as that depicted in *The Silmarillion*, the God figure of Ilúvatar and other overt manifestations of spirituality are withdrawn. Very occasionally a suggestion of religious practice comes into view like the Gondorian convention of facing west before a meal, in remembrance of the old Númenorian Temple. Aside from a few faint religious allusions, however, on the surface, religion and religious practices in Tolkien's major work are almost completely absent. Despite this absence of explicit religious allusion, Tolkien manages to create a secondary world that radiates with a sense of an all pervading spirituality; upon reading *The Lord of the Rings* one is instantly struck by its spiritual dimension. In part this comes from the inclusion of characters such as Tom Bombadil, Gandalf and the race

---

80 Tolkien, *Letters*, p.144.

of elves. In the main, however, this sense of a perceptible spiritual ambience is seemingly without source. Perhaps the best description of this comes in a letter Tolkien wrote as late as 1971. In that letter Tolkien mentions receiving a communication from an atheist of sorts, who whilst reading *The Lord of the Rings* perceives a spiritual climate which seems to have no origin:

> I had [a letter] from a man, who classified himself as 'an unbeliever', or at best a man of belatedly and dimly dawning religious feeling [...] 'but you' he says, 'create a world in which some sort of faith seems to be everywhere without a visible source, like 'light from an invisible lamp'.'[81]

This 'light from an invisible lamp' is woven deep into the fabric of Tolkien's portrayal of the world of Middle-earth, and although, like the Celtic legends of old, Christianity seems to materialise from the text, it is nowhere specifically referred to. Tolkien of course purposely wished his work to reflect Christian virtue but only in this withdrawn fashion. He writes in 1953:

> *The Lord of the Rings* is of course a fundamentally religious and Catholic work; unconsciously so at first, but consciously in the revision. That is why I have not put in, or have cut out, practically all references to anything like religion, to cults or practices, in the imaginary world. For the religious element is absorbed into the story and the symbolism.[82]

Indeed although Christian/Catholic sensibilities are discernable in *The Lord of the Rings* they share, as we noted in the first chapter, the narrative frame and the spiritual ambience of the work with non-Christian understandings of spirituality (like the elves' reverence of nature). In terms of his own faith, however, crucially, in setting his *legendarium* in our world's own distant past, in a time before our familiar religions found form, Tolkien allows for the emergence of Christianity and the coming of Christ (long after the Third Age – when elves have passed and men inherit Middle-earth). Trevor Hart asserts that this strategy affords Tolkien the freedom to avoid real world religious parallels being drawn:

> [Tolkien] deliberately casts his own imaginary world [...] in a remote pre-Christian and pre-Jewish stage of earth's past, a move which frees him conveniently from expectations of finding any close correlations between the religious outlooks of the two stages, while yet leaving the truth (as he certainly saw it) of the Christian 'myth' – as yet (i.e., in Middle-earth) to be revealed – unscathed.[83]

---

81 Tolkien, *Letters*, p.413.
82 Tolkien, *Letters*, p.172.
83 Hart, 'Tolkien, Creation, and Creativity', p.42.

Chapter IV

This understanding further promotes the idea that Tolkien's *legendarium* is more the story of the elves, carrying their worldview and their spiritual climate, than it is a tale of men, whose time in the narrative, is yet to come.

More than anything else, however, it is the assimilation of the spiritual and physical realms that characterises the religious tone of Tolkien's work. The landscapes of Middle-earth are portrayed as precious, even sacred to those such as the elves. The elven lands in particular are depicted as 'edenesque' paradises where healing and restoration of body and mind await the weary or injured traveller. As the narrator explains of Frodo's revitalised awakening in Rivendell, 'the last Homely House east of the sea', after his near fatal encounter with the Ringwraiths, '[m]erely to be there was a cure for weariness, fear, and sadness.'[84] Even one's mood it seems may be lifted and lightened in the elven realms. Pippin speaking to Frodo in Rivendell remarks 'it seems impossible, somehow, to feel gloomy or depressed in this place.'[85] The elven kingdoms, despite the fact that they are part of the physical topography of Middle-earth, are possessed of an 'otherworldly' quality, as if in entering these physical places a visitor steps through a portal or gateway to another reality. When Frodo and the Fellowship first see the elven wood of Lothlórien, to Frodo's perception, it seems as if he is looking into a place that is not the Middle-earth he knows: '[t]he others cast themselves down upon the fragrant grass, but Frodo stood awhile still lost in wonder. It seemed to him that he had stepped through a high window that looked on a vanished world.'[86] Later we are told that '[t]hough he walked and breathed, and about him living leaves and flowers were stirred by the same cool wind as fanned his face, Frodo felt that he was in a timeless land that did not fade or change or fall into forgetfulness.'[87] There is an implied suggestion here that although the elven lands are physical, tangible places which are blown by the same earthly winds and subject to the same material make-up as the other landscapes of Middle-earth, they are also lands which are in some sense 'timeless' and somehow removed from their worldly setting, existing almost in another dimension of time and place. In this sense the elven kingdoms of Middle-earth echo the fairy and otherworldly kingdoms of Celtic mythology which exist in

---

84 Tolkien, *Fellowship*, p.219.
85 Tolkien, *Fellowship*, p.220.
86 Tolkien, *Fellowship*, p.341.
87 Tolkien, *Fellowship*, p.342.

a kind of parallel reality with the physical world – removed from and yet part of the landscape. Indeed it is this focus on the non-human, otherworldly and worldly landscapes, and natural and supernatural realms in both Tolkien's work and Celtic myth that casts them as ecocentric narratives. Siewers suggests that this aspect of Tolkien's fiction, the co-existence of seemingly supernatural elven lands with natural topography, or 'overlay landscape' as he terms it, is the most recognisably Celtic aspect of Tolkien's *legendarium*:

> The overlay landscape of the Elven realms in Tolkien's fantasy is its most distinctive Celtic element, echoing the Otherworld common to both early Welsh and Irish literatures. In Tolkien's fantasy we see immortal realms interlaced with the everyday world of physical experience and natural topography, as in the early medieval Welsh *Mabinogi* and the Irish *Táin Bó Cualinge*, the effect is a deeper dimensionality to landscape and ultimately nature that undergrids the ecocentricity of Tolkien's work.[88]

Aside from the fantastical and otherworldly nature of their lands, Tolkien's elves have other characteristics in common with Celtic myth. Marjorie Burns in *Perilous Realms: Celtic and Norse in Tolkien's Middle-earth* remarks upon the metaphysical similarities between elves and characters in Celtic myth particularly in relation to reincarnation (an aspect of elvish existence I discuss below): '[Tolkien's] immortal elves (who in fact can die) are born again, like privileged figures in Celtic belief.'[89] One of the 'privileged figures' Burns alludes to is Edain of the Tuatha Dé Danann, a race of god-like beings who dabble in enchantment and magic. Edain is described in Celtic myth as being a beautiful blonde queen who is considered to be the personification of reincarnation. The Tuatha Dé Danann, in popular Irish legend are associated with the fairies who watch over the supernatural kingdoms and enchanted realms of mythic Ireland. The elves too are presented in Tolkien's fantasy as similar 'in nature' to the god-like Ainur 'though' as the narrator of *The Silmarillion* adds, they are 'less in might and stature.'[90] Indeed Tolkien, in early drafts of his writings on elves, referred to them as fairies. Christopher Tolkien unearthed the following passage from his father's notes for *The Book of Lost Tales Part Two*: '[n]ow

---

88 Siewers, 'Tolkien's Cosmic-Christian Ecology', p.143.
89 Marjorie Burns, *Perilous Realms: Celtic and Norse in Tolkien's Middle-earth*, Toronto: University of Toronto Press, 2005, p.21.
90 Tolkien, *Silmarillion*, p.41.

on a time the fairies dwelt in the Lonely Isle after the great wars with Melko[91] and the ruin of Gondolin and they builded a fair city amidmost of that island, and it was girt with trees.' Burns suggests that the fact that Tolkien once cast his elves as fairies reveals that they were derived in part from Celtic origins: '[m]ost telling of all (for the Celtic argument), Tolkien's Elves are fairies under an alternate name.'[92]

Tolkien's elves, like the Celtic fairies, exist mainly in otherworldly realms sourced in natural landscapes. These landscapes, like Rivendell and Lórien, are representations of a land ethic, a view of how society and nature may live in harmony, each providing for, sustaining and protecting the other.[93] Tolkien wrote of the relationship between the Golden Wood of Lothlórien and the elves who dwelt there: 'Lothlórien is beautiful because there the trees were loved.'[94] Presumably part of the beauty of Lothlórien is that it flowers and blooms and brings forth all that the elves need to sustain their society. And although Tolkien never really allows us to see how the elves engage in producing or farming their food, there is nonetheless an implied suggestion that the havens of natural wonder in which they exist provide them with a rich and plentiful harvest.[95]

Elven kingdoms, however, offer us more than a glimpse of a natural paradise in which land and dweller exist in mutual dependency and harmony. Depicted as they are amid the desolation we witness in the landscapes surrounding Mordor and Isengard and the industrial devastation that comes to the Shire, the elven realms in a very real sense show us a world that is passing. The natural beauty we

---

91 Melko was an early variant of Melkor. Tolkien would often, after large sections of writing were produced, decide to change the names of characters or places, and begin to rewrite. One famous example is the name of Strider which was originally to be Trotter.
92 Burns, *Perilous Realms*, p.22.
93 On the interrelationship between people and their land, see also Thomas Honegger, 'From Bag End to Lórien: the Creation of a Literary World' in Peter Buchs & Thomas Honegger (eds.), *News from the Shire and Beyond – Studies on Tolkien*, Cormarë Series 1, second edition, Zurich and Berne: Walking Tree Publishers, 2004, pp.59-81.
94 Tolkien, *Letters*, p.419.
95 Those who stay or rest in the elven lands are often given sumptuous meals that appear well prepared and cultivated – there is no *clear* suggestion in Tolkien's descriptions of the elves, however, that they attempt to 'organise' or order the natural lands they inhabit to facilitate food production. Dickerson and Evans state that although the *lembas* or way-bread of Lothlórien may 'hint at an entire invisible industry in which grain is cultivated and harvested, ground, refined, and baked', and the golden elven brew that is offered to the Fellowship as they rest is suggestive of a 'viniculture', in the main, from the portrayal Tolkien affords us of elves, we can conclude that 'Elves do not engage in any sort of organised farming or even gardening but simply partake of the earth's bounty as it occurs naturally' (Dickerson & Evans, *Ents, Elves, and Eriador*, p.97).

see in these places is but a haven of natural wonder, hemmed in on all sides by an advancing machine-armed enemy. There is an implicit warning in Tolkien's portrayal of these wonderlands as places which soon, like the elves themselves, may leave the physical world and pass into legend and memory. Indeed when Aragorn, on the doorstep of Lothlórien, expresses a hope to the Fellowship that elves may offer them assistance, Gimli replies '[i]f Elves indeed still dwell here in the darkening world.'[96] Gimli's remark and the usage of the word 'here' could, of course, simply refer to a thought that the elves may have gone from Lothlórien. The phrase 'here in the darkening world', however, could be read as a more general statement, indeed it seems to imply that Gimli is referring to all of Middle-earth and a contemplation that the elves as a race have gone from the world. If this is what Gimli is implying (or wondering), his remark is curious to say the least considering that Legolas, an elf, is standing next to him – unless the intimation is that he believes that since leaving Rivendell, all the other elves *except* Legolas (thus the plurality of his comment) may have already departed Middle-earth and passed over the sea. Either way 'the darkening of the world' is connected with the passing of the elves, as if the diminishment of one increases the other. And as the elves leave Middle-earth, so too does the rich, natural wonder and beauty of their lands, for there is no doubt, given Tolkien's descriptions of the elves and their connection to their environments, that the elves in passing from the shores of Middle-earth will take with them much of the beauty and vibrancy of their natural habitats.

(V) Elves as Humanity and Natural Magic

We recall that Tolkien once stated 'my 'elves' are only a representation or an apprehension of a part of human nature.'[97] And given their pre-occupation with the preservation of natural beauty (as opposed to simply engaging in the preservation of nature as a resource) the elves, by virtue of their love for the aesthetic beauty of the world about them, come to stand for the artistry, nobility and grace of the human race: they are artisans and protectors of beauty whose society and underlying principles are directed by their environmentalism and

---

96 Tolkien, *Fellowship*, p.329.
97 Tolkien, *Letters*, p.149.

their devotion to the natural world. As we shall examine, they have their weaknesses and are by no means an idealised version of humanity but, as Michael N. Stanton puts it, '[t]he Elves are the height of what humans might be, and their relationship to the world of nature and of society is one of harmony and wisdom.'[98]

Like Tom Bombadil, the elves seek knowledge of the multiplicity of natural things, of 'the other', but like Tom they pursue such knowledge in order to better understand the world about them. They wish to secure no dominion over nature or over Middle-earth. Instead they celebrate and eulogise both the beauty of the natural world and their own interconnected place within it. They are also, of course, connected to men in the panorama of nature. Tolkien once wrote that 'Elves and Men are evidently in biological terms one race'[99] and although, as Verlyn Flieger states, 'Tolkien clearly thought of Elves and Men as two quite distinct kinds of beings, almost different species', as literary creations they each symbolise particular characteristics of humanity or in Flieger's words, 'different aspects of the human race.'[100] The inherent artistic capability of the elves is much more highly developed than is seen in men and is one of their defining characteristics. Tolkien comments: 'I should say that [Elves] represent Men with greatly enhanced aesthetic and creative faculties, greater beauty and longer life.'[101] This elvish predilection for aesthetic pursuits, however, is no idle pastime and it is ineradicably linked to their love of nature. Furthermore, all of the characteristics and qualities made evident in the elves: their devotion to natural beauty, their desire to understand the 'other', and their dedication to safeguarding the natural world from harm are influenced and informed by their 'longer life' and 'the problem of Death' such as it is from their perspective. Writing in 1956, in a letter responding to queries put to him by Michael Straight, Tolkien, whilst highlighting both the kinship and the differing representative traits of elves and men, also draws in the question of their respective mortality:

> Of course, in fact exterior to my story, Elves and Men are just different aspects of the Humane, and represent the problem of Death as seen by a finite but

---

98 Stanton, *Hobbits, Elves and Wizards*, p.35.
99 Tolkien, *Letters*, p.189.
100 Verlyn Flieger, *Splintered Light: Logos and Language in Tolkien's World*, 2nd revised edition, Kent and London: Kent State University Press, 2002, p.51.
101 Tolkien, *Letters*, p.176.

> willing and self-conscious person. In this mythological world the Elves and Men are in their incarnate forms kindred, but in the relation of their 'spirits' to the world in time represent different 'experiments', each of which has its own natural trend, and weakness. The Elves represent, as it were, the artistic, aesthetic, and purely scientific aspects of the Humane nature raised to a higher level than is actually seen in Men. That is: they have a devoted love of the physical world, and a desire to observe and understand it for its own sake and as 'other'.[102]

As we have noted, the elves are immortal but their immortality is one that connects the span of their life with the life of the world rather than affording them unending existence. The life force of elves is therefore connected to the life force of nature – they do not age to the eyes of men because the time scale they exist within seems ageless to human perception. But they do become older and weaker, as the world itself does. Tolkien explains:

> [t]he Elves were sufficiently longeval to be called by man 'immortal'. But they were not unageing or unwearying. Their own tradition was that they were confined to the limits of this world (in space and time), even if they died, and would continue to exist in it until 'the end of the world'.[103]

The very fact that elves are bound to the life of the world means that their power is deeply intertwined with the power of nature or Arda (the Earth), unlike men who, after a relatively ephemeral life, pass on to the mysteries of an afterlife (which Tolkien refers to as the 'Second Music'). The elves, however, know nothing of what awaits them when all time has passed – they know only that they must share the unfolding fate of the world. Tolkien writes, 'in this mythical 'prehistory' *immortality*, strictly longevity co-extensive with the life of Arda, was part of the nature of the Elves; beyond the End nothing was revealed. *Mortality*, that is a short life-span having no relation to the life of Arda, is spoken of as the given nature of Men; the Elves called it *the Gift of Ilúvatar*.'[104]

The elves view the mortality of men as a 'gift' because they, as a race grow weary of time and because they must remain earthbound until all the troubles and evils of earthly history have run their course. We hear Elrond declare, even as the council at Rivendell gather to face the peril of the Third Age, that he was present when Isildúr cut the One Ring from the hand of Sauron in the

---

102 Tolkien, *Letters*, p.236.
103 Tolkien, *Letters*, p.325.
104 Tolkien, *Letters*, p.285, emphasis in the original.

First Age of Middle-earth. Elrond (and the elves as a race) never really see an end to the evils that afflict Middle-earth. They find resistance to a great evil of one era only to see it return in another era renewed. The elves thus have a long-term view of how the actions (good or ill) of one generation may impact another. Considered from an ecological viewpoint, the green ethics that the elves practice in the natural landscapes of Middle-earth, and their wisdom with regards the crisis of the Third Age, is thus reflective of environmentally-centred strategies in our world that seek to override the immediate needs of an industrialised world in favour of preserving the green face of the planet for future generations.

As referred to above, as a consequence of living through all the wars and struggles of Middle-earth's history, particularly those that inflict devastation on the natural world, the immortality of the elves becomes not a blessing to be cherished but rather a burden that they must carry. This notion of immortality as a burden is further emphasised in a passage from *The Silmarillion* which alludes both to the sorrow of the 'immortal' elves and the enviable mortality of men:

> The children of Men dwell only a short space in the world alive, and are not bound to it, and depart whither the Elves know not. Whereas the Elves remain until the end of days, and their love of the Earth and all the world is more simple and more poignant therefore, and as the years lengthen ever more sorrowful. For the Elves die not until the world dies, unless they are slain or waste in grief [...] But the sons of Men die indeed, and leave the world; wherefore they are called Guests, or the Strangers. Death is their fate, the gift of Ilúvatar, which as Time wears even the Powers shall envy.[105]

There is a clear interconnection here between the elves' position as creatures bound to the Earth in an immortal state and their devotion for and love of the Earth. Because of their bond with nature and the Earth, the elves are consumed by a deep sense of loss when part of the world's natural beauty is lost. As immortals they witness (and feel) all the environmental damage, throughout all of time that is visited upon the natural landscapes of the world at the hands of the many manifestations of evil. They are forced to confront not only the death of other races but also the reality of a changing world where nature is in decline. Miranda Wilcox in her essay 'Exilic Imagining in *The Seafarer* and *The Lord of the Rings*' comments: '[a]lthough immortal, the Elves must come to

---

105 Tolkien, *Silmarillion*, p.42.

terms with mortality since they interact with mortal beings and are inhabitants of a world in constant flux.'[106]

That the elves are not immortal in the strictest sense but rather endure in alignment with the life of the world, and that fact that we are told in *The Silmarillion* 'Elves die not until the world dies, unless they are slain or waste in grief' raises the question of what happens to elves if they die as described (before the world has ended). What emerges and what Tolkien allows for is the premise that elves may be reincarnated. Michael Devaux in 'Elves: Reincarnation' comments:

> The very existence of elves, who are immortal, raises the issue of the death of the other races. If it already seems to be a scandal when all creatures naturally die, it appears to be a crucial problem when one race does not die. Yet are the Elves completely immortal? [...] The immortality of Elves, which entails a passage through death, is tantamount to reincarnation. This theological possibility separates them from men.[107]

The appearance of reincarnation in Tolkien's secondary world (albeit attributable to non-human beings) was challenged by Peter Hastings, manager of a Catholic Bookshop in Oxford, who suggested that with the inclusion of episodes of reincarnation, Tolkien had 'over-stepped the mark in metaphysical matters.' Tolkien's response, given his devout Catholic faith, again displays the extent to which his theological ideas extended beyond those of traditional Christian creed: "[r]eincarnation' may be bad *theology*' he writes 'as applied to Humanity [...] but I do not see how even in the Primary World any theologian or philosopher, unless very much better informed about the relation of spirit and body than I believe anyone to be, could deny the possibility of re-incarnation as a mode of existence.'[108] The fact that Tolkien makes reference to the primary world in his response is worthy of note and reveals that in matters divine or metaphysical Tolkien displayed some degree of open-mindedness. Furthermore, Tolkien's allusion to 'spirit and body' in terms of the reincarnation of elves suggests that, if they cannot escape the Earth, even in death, but are reborn in 'spirit and body' within the natural cycle of the earthly sphere, in one sense or another it is the

---

106 Miranda Wilcox, 'Exilic Imagining in *The Seafarer* and *The Lord of the Rings*' in Jane Chance (ed.), *Tolkien the Medievalist*, London and New York: Routledge, 2003, p.141.
107 Michael Devaux 'Elves: Reincarnation' in Michael D.C. Drout (ed.), *J.R.R. Tolkien Encyclopedia: Scholarship and Critical Assessment*, New York: Routledge, 2006, p.154.
108 Tolkien, *Letters*, p.189.

sub-creative power of nature which remakes or recreates them, just as they in turn create natural wonders of their own.

Indeed the question of 'who made who?' in terms of the elves and their natural environment, comes to the fore as Frodo and Sam walk together in Lothlórien. Frodo asks Sam for his opinion on elves, particularly in the light of those he has encountered in the Golden Wood. Sam's reply suggests that he, a man of the soil, a man who has worked the land and tilled the earth, recognises an interconnection between the elves and the landscape they inhabit, '[w]hether they've made the land, or the land's made them, it's hard to say.'[109] Sam's perceptive remark casts the elves as somehow interchangeable with their environment. But perhaps more importantly his uncertainty regarding the question of power or more precisely the question of creation reveals that the elves, to Sam's perception at least (a viewpoint that many readers of *The Lord of the Rings* have come to trust as clear-seeing), exude or exercise no dominion over the land, rather they appear as a race whose strength and power is tied up with natural forces in some kind of harmonious mutual bond. Of course the extreme beauty and vibrancy of Lothlórien is sustained by one of the elven Rings – Nenya, 'the Ring of Adamant', worn by Galadriel. A further remark made by Sam, however, '[i]f there's any magic about, it's right down deep, where I can't lay my hands on it'[110] suggests that this sustaining 'magic', such as it is, is entwined with the natural strength of the trees and the soil, enhancing and drawing on what already exists in nature. In 'On Fairy-stories' Tolkien makes a clear distinction between the 'magic' of the elves, which he terms 'enchantment' and the kind of 'magic'[111] used by Saruman and Sauron to gain dominion over other wills through the creation and abuse of technologies such as The One Ring, or the engines which drive the industrial regime of

---

109 Tolkien, *Fellowship*, p.351.
110 Tolkien, *Fellowship*, p.351.
111 On 'enchantment' and 'magic' see Patrick Curry, 'Magic vs. Enchantment' in *Journal of Contemporary Religion* 14.3 (1999), pp. 401-12, Patrick Curry, 'Iron Crown, Iron Cage: Tolkien and Weber on Modernity and Enchantment' in Eduardo Segura & Thomas Honegger (eds.), *Myth and Magic. Art according to the Inklings*, Cormarë Series 14, Zurich and Berne: Walking Tree Publishers, 2007, pp.99-108, Tom Shippey, 'New Learning and New Ignorance: Magia, Goeteia, and the Inklings' in Eduardo Segura & Thomas Honegger (eds.), *Myth and Magic. Art according to the Inklings*, Cormarë Series 14, Zurich and Berne: Walking Tree Publishers, 2007, pp.21-46, and Dieter Bachmann, 'Words for Magic: *goetia*, *gúl* and *lúth*' in Eduardo Segura & Thomas Honegger (eds.), *Myth and Magic. Art according to the Inklings*, Cormarë Series 14, Zurich and Berne: Walking Tree Publishers, 2007, pp.47-55.

Isengard. 'Enchantment' however, as Tolkien explains, is 'Art, delivered from many of its human limitations: more effortless, more quick, more complete.' The purpose of the elves' use of 'enchantment' in Middle-earth, Tolkien tells us, is 'the old motive of their kind, the adornment of earth, and healing of its hurts.'[112] The elves then do not use 'magic' as such, at least in the way that Tolkien interprets magic in his fantasy. Instead the elves call on their artistic abilities to adorn or enhance the inherent powers of nature. Curry remarks: '[i]n the context of *The Lord of the Rings*, enchantment is the art of the elves; and as such, it has a special affinity with nature both as its principal inspiration and as the object of its enchantment.'[113]

This notion of 'enchantment' drawing on natural phenomena is further exemplified as the Fellowship prepares to depart from Lothlórien. As morning breaks on the day of departure each member of the company is given an elven cloak and hood which seem able to change colour to fit in with a given landscape. Pippin asks rather bluntly if the cloaks are 'magic'. The leader of the elves seems a little confused by Pippin's question and his reply is as follows:

> I do not know what you mean by that [...] They are fair garments, and the web is good, for it was made in this land. They are elvish robes certainly, if that is what you mean. Leaf and branch, water and stone: they have the hue and beauty of all these things under the twilight of Lórien that we love; for we put the thought of all that we love into all that we make.[114]

The leader of the elves, dismissing the overt notion of 'magic', declares that whatever worthy qualities are inherent in these cloaks come from a natural source and that they are weaved with 'the thought of all that [the elves] love', in other words the beauty and potency of nature itself. As the leader continues his response, however, he references characteristics for the cloaks that one could denote as magical: 'they are light to wear, and warm enough or cool enough at need. And you will find them a great aid in keeping out the sight of unfriendly eyes, whether you walk among the stones or the trees.'[115] Clearly, the idea that a cloak, without any adjustment from the wearer, could offer such shifting attributes would seem to indicate that it is possessed of magi-

---

112 J.R.R.Tolkien, *The Tolkien Reader*, New York: Ballantine Books, 1966, p.73.
113 Curry, *Defending Middle-earth*, p.73.
114 Tolkien, *Fellowship*, p.361.
115 Tolkien, *Fellowship*, p.361.

cal qualities, and yet we have come to know that similar attributes occur in our own natural world. The chameleon adapts the hue of its skin to blend in with its environment, and the same thick fur that keeps a camel warm in the chill wind of a desert night also reflects the intense sunlight of the desert sun causing the skin under not to sweat, retaining fluid and thereby keeping the camel's temperature sufficiently low. Making a similar point, Michael N. Stanton, categorises the enchantments of the elves as having 'a deep affinity with and understanding of the natural world.'[116]

Unlike the enslaving and 'bulldozing' technologically-themed magic used by Sauron and others, the enchantments created by the elves within their lands are used to hold off the evil and the environmental devastation which afflicts other landscapes in Middle-earth. As the Fellowship prepares to enter the 'enchanted' realm of Lórien we hear Legolas remark to Gimli, 'Lórien is not yet deserted, for there is a secret power here that holds evil from the land.'[117] The elves use a magic of sorts then in order to protect, heal and restore the land or the Earth. Indeed it was this desire to heal that led to Sauron learning the craft of 'Ringmaking'. He deceived the high-elves into believing that his intention in desiring knowledge of magic was to protect and repair the world. Tolkien writes, 'many of the Elves listened to Sauron [...] his motives and those of the Elves seemed to go partly together: the healing of the desolate lands.' But from this deception the Rings of Power came into existence and working alongside Sauron, the elves of Eregion forged three Rings of Power that were 'directed to the preservation of beauty' but Sauron made the One Ring that could rule and pervert all that was made by the elven rings. When the elves learned of the deception, they waged war against the emergent Dark Lord, and, as Tolkien points out, '[i]n the resulting war between Sauron and the elves, Middle-earth, especially in the west, was further ruined [and] the elves came their nearest to falling to 'magic' and machinery.'[118]

---

116 Stanton, *Hobbits, Elves and Wizards*, p.47.
117 Tolkien, *Fellowship*, p.329.
118 Tolkien, *Letters*, p.152.

(VI) Elves in Tolkien's Shorter Works

When we think of Tolkien's elves, we, as readers (or perhaps even as filmgoers), are arguably most likely to think of the imposing, yet noble and graceful elves of Tolkien's *legendarium*. Elves, however, are very much a recurring feature of Tolkien's wider fiction, appearing not only across the vistas and ages of all his Middle-earth-centred writings, but also in his lesser known poetry, and prose works such as *Roverandom*, *Smith of Wootton Major* and even *The Father Christmas Letters*.

In *Roverandom*, a children's story concerning a dog that is transformed by a wizard into a toy (the transformation from natural to mechanical portrayed as a curse), which also includes sea-fairies, serpents and dragons, we are told that, 'Roverandom thought he caught a glimpse of the city of the Elves on the green hill.'[119] The view, seen as Roverandom is carried by the whale Uin across the ocean by the borders of 'Faeryland', is glimpsed amid the 'Mountains of Elvenhome', a setting mentioned in the earliest writings of *The Silmarillion*. 'The city of Elves', associated with the naturally themed 'green hill', is a reference to Kortirion.

The elves that appear in *The Father Christmas Letters*, whilst small in stature and more akin to the traditional Victorian understanding of elves,[120] do have some aspects in common with their Middle-earth equivalents in that they are friendly and seek to protect the essential goodness of the world (represented by the benevolent Christmas ethos of giving and caring for others) against a troublesome

---

119 J. R.R. Tolkien, *Roverandom*, London: HarperCollins, 2005, p.73.
120 Tolkien had a dislike for traditional literary representations of diminutive elves. In this context, however, it should be noted that these letters were written from a father to his children at Christmas, and as such they borrow a little from traditional Christmas motifs: the home of Tolkien's Father Christmas is the North Pole, he is attended by a snowman and a polar bear, he receives letters from children, makes and delivers presents with helpers and so on. Indeed Tolkien didn't intend or anticipate that these letters would ever become published. Nonetheless Tolkien's innate gift as a teller of tales invades even this whimsical family tradition, and the letters become more like little stories as time passes with each contributing to a longer narrative reaching across the letters. New characters and themes are introduced and Tolkien maintains the age-old battle between good and evil throughout. The appearance of the Man in the Moon in his Christmas letters is an example of how Tolkien, even in a private family and fatherly context, allows one shard of myth and story to bleed into another. Another point of interest is the manner in which Tolkien details problems and mishaps in his letters from Father Christmas which account for why more expensive presents desired by the Tolkien children could not be delivered during real times of hardship for the Tolkien parents. This is yet another example of Tolkien colliding and blurring the lines between the spheres of reality and fiction.

goblin threat. In later letters one particular elf, Ilbereth, whose name is highly suggestive of Elbereth (elven 'Star-queen' and spouse of the Valar Manwë) as secretary to Father Christmas, narrates the North Pole yearly events, composes narrative poems and even writes in a form of elvish. In environmental terms, however, it is interesting to note that Tolkien's version of Father Christmas, although mirroring many conventional aspects of Santa Claus in appearance and circumstance, nonetheless hints at not only the religiously themed St. Nicholas (Nicholas is given as his first name), but also at the older English myth that portrayed Father Christmas as a representation of winter and seasonal festivities. In one letter, written in 1930, we hear Tolkien's Father Christmas speak of his 'Green Brother' an allusion which Deborah and Ivor Rogers suggest may refer to summer, and in particular, the summer solstice.[121] In this light the 'Christmas Elves', although diminutive and quite 'un-Middle-earth-like' in form, still exude an important characteristic of the elves of Tolkien's prominent works in that they strive to defend aspects or representations of nature against hostile enemies.

In *Smith of Wootton Major* recently reissued in a new expanded form under Verlyn Flieger's editorial and containing, amongst other things, Tolkien's essay on the nature of Faery, is a work which not only includes elves (removed from their *legendarium* setting and context) but also features them prominently. The story itself, the last to be published while Tolkien was still alive, brings together the realms of imagination and reality: the everyday village of Wootton Major where the central character Smith lives and works as man and boy, and the 'perilous realm of Faery' into which he is granted entry by virtue of his swallowing a magical 'fay-star' hidden in a slice of cake. Smith's journeys into the realm of imagination are set against the elf-king Alf's journey back into the 'mundane' world of Wootton Major where he adopts the guise of cook's apprentice. The Master Cook, Nokes, however, enveloped by his attention to the humdrum of duty, lacks the imagination to discover the true nature of Alf or the land of Faery. The story is tinged with regret and sorrow, as Smith is eventually made to surrender his 'fay-star' and thus his passage into the perilous realm. As such the tale is read by some commentators as 'an expression of

---

121 Deborah & Ivor A. Rogers, *J.R.R. Tolkien*, Boston: G.K. Hall, 1980, p.64.

grief and renunciation of powers at the approach of old age'[122] as Flieger puts it, or a literary testimony of acceptance by Tolkien that he was coming to the end of his career as a writer. Elsewhere it has been read as a symbolic presentation of the interconnection of the primary world of reality and the secondary world of imagination – or a playing out of theories related to sub-creation offered by Tolkien in 'On Fairy-stories' (discussed in the next chapter). Of more significant interest here, however, is the prominent role that elves and natural phenomena play in the four recounted 'Otherworld' adventures of Smith. The elves, much like their Middle-earth counterparts, are presented as guardians of nature and agents in the story who seek to oppose the destructive tendencies of men – and even as advisors who warn against such destructive tendencies in the primary world. Their main role, however, is to protect and shelter the wild provinces of the perilous realm, which include 'Dark Marches of which men knew nothing' from human invasion, even from those such as Smith who possess the 'fay-star' passport to the realm. The natural scenery of the Faery lands is so alluring that we are told Smith, on occasion, spent his shorter visits 'looking only at one tree or one flower.'[123] Indeed the elf-king's (and thus the elves') connection with nature is symbolised by an extraordinary 'royal' tree that 'bore at once leaves and flowers and fruits uncounted, and not one was the same as any other that grew on the Tree.'[124] Tolkien himself acknowledges the importance of natural imagery in the work: 'in this tale Forest and Tree remain dominant symbols. They occur in three of the four 'remembered' and recorded experiences of the Smith.' Indeed referring specifically to the role of 'Elvenfolk', Tolkien underlines that one of their prime objectives is 'to assist in the protection of our world, especially in the attempt to re-direct Men when their development tends to the defacing or destruction of their world.'[125]

Given that the tale *Smith of Wootton Major*, in part, deals with the interaction of primary and secondary worlds, reality and imagination, the depiction of elves as voices and forces from a secondary world which seek to warn the human race of the primary world against the wanton destruction of its home in the name of

---

122 Verlyn Flieger, '*Smith of Wootton Major*' in Michael D.C. Drout (ed.), *J.RR.Tolkien Encyclopedia: Scholarship and Critical Assessment*, New York: Routledge, 2006, p.619.
123 J.R.R.Tolkien, *Smith of Wootton Major*, edited by Verlyn Flieger, London: HarperCollins, 2005, p.26.
124 Tolkien, *Smith of Wootton Major*, p.28.
125 Tolkien, *Smith of Wootton Major*, pp.93-94.

'development' or progress, is perhaps an emblematic allusion which epitomises and illuminates the environmental augury which I contend characterises the green element of much of Tolkien's fiction. Certainly Tolkien, by virtue of his presentation of a secondary world that seeks to impact upon and influence the primary world, is saying something quite profound about the power of art and literature to warn us against our own folly, specifically in this case the folly of needless environmental damage which may provide us with a short term advantage but which ultimately usurps and destroys the green face of our home.

(VII) Closing Thoughts: Comedy as Fantasy

Despite the anthropological significance we can take from Tolkien's imagined races, the portrayal of elves in Tolkien's fiction offers us a centring of the non-human in his work, a non-anthropocentric perspective and a race that is presented as fundamentally connected to the natural world. The elves have what Tolkien calls 'a devoted love of the physical world, and a desire to observe and understand it for its own sake',[126] and yet they display very human failings in weaker moments. Their folly and desire for knowledge leads to the creation of the Rings of Power – technology which eventually gives rise to the defining crisis of the Third Age and brings devastation to the very lands the elves would seek to preserve. Due to their particular metaphysical make-up, the elves, as immortals, are tied to the life of the world and as such their life force and power is bound up with natural things. As a consequence of this, they suffer environmental damage and assaults on the natural world more profoundly than any other race. Tolkien's foregrounding of, not just the elves, but other non-human aspects of his work is perhaps indicative of how prominent environmental issues were in his mind.

Despite his profound Christian faith, Tolkien's fiction resists notions of human lordship over nature. Indeed he offers a blended perspective of the human and non-human. Even Middle-earth with its beautiful and desolate landscapes may be read as a character in the unfolding narratives of the mythology. I have contended that Middle-earth, viewed as a character, may best be understood as a character that is under threat and slowly dying, besieged by agents of destruc-

---

126 Tolkien, *Letters*, p.236.

tion whose ultimate goal is control and domination. This, of course, recalls my commentary on Tom Bombadil – but since I have contended that Tom's power is bound up with nature and the land, it follows that if Bombadil is under threat, then Middle-earth itself would also be.

In considering Tolkien's narratives as fiction that elevates the non-human and offers non-anthropocentric perspectives, we draw in a wider theological debate regarding humanity's perceived superiority over nature. Indeed, as we have noted, those such as Lynn White Jr. have accused religious doctrine of contributing to notions of human supremacy over creation, thus justifying exploitation of the natural resources of the planet.

In *The Comedy of Survival: Studies in Literary Ecology*, a work described by Jonathan Bate as '[t]he first book of explicitly ecological criticism'[127] Joseph Meeker also addresses humanity's tendency to view itself above the rest of creation. Meeker suggests that the history of literature, through its constructs of humanity, and humanity's relationship to the rest of creation, has also perpetuated and contributed to such understandings. Meeker's study concerns the contrasting depiction of the human race and the individual through the literary traditions of Tragedy and Comedy. Tragedy depicting its heroes as noble beings struggling with abstract issues of morality, grace and hopelessness was a flattering picture of humanity. The tragic mode had little time for its heroes and dominant characters to take account of the rest of creation.

Comedy, however, offered a very different picture of the human condition. 'Its only concern' states Meeker 'is to affirm man's capacity for survival and to celebrate the continuity of life itself, despite all moralities.'[128] The comic mode thus offered unflattering depictions of characters that were too busy trying to avoid death to be concerned with any lofty matters of spirituality or grace. Not surprisingly, as Meeker suggests, the tragic mode, offering characters such as Hamlet, depicted as struggling with grand metaphysical questions and profound despair whilst tasked from the spiritual plane with righting a great wrong, appealed to cultural taste. Meeker concludes that the embrace of Tragedy with its promotion

---

127 Jonathan Bate, *The Song of the Earth*, London: Picador, 2000, p.180.
128 Joseph Meeker, *The Comedy of Survival: Studies in Literary Ecology*, New York: Charles Scribner's Sons, 1974, p.24.

of anthropocentric values promoted a cultural separation from nature that has contributed to the environmental crisis.

Don Elgin's *The Comedy of the Fantastic: Ecological Perspectives on the Fantasy Novel*, taking Meeker's study as starting point, suggests that the fantasy novel is an 'antidote' to the promotion of Tragedy in literature. Elgin underlines Meeker's assertions, and states that 'the adoption of the tragic mode and its promulgation through literature as the highest, noblest, and most worthwhile of human activities actually reduces all other events or ideas to a secondary role.'[129]

'The fantasy novel', however, has, as Elgin points out, 'adopted a comic conception of humanity, placing its emphasis upon humanity as part of a total environment or system and acknowledging the absolute dependence of humanity upon that system.'[130] Certainly Tolkien, in the elevation of the non-human aspects of his fiction and in the presentation of different creatures and beings alongside his most explicit rendering of humanity, men, with each equally under threat, offers a depiction of an environmental system that is the concern of all creation. Furthermore he allows us to view the crisis filtered through more than just the human perspective. We even get the perspective and the voice of nature itself in Treebeard and the ents (and indeed Tom Bombadil).

Elgin states that writers such as Tolkien, C.S. Lewis and Frank Herbert have 'offered an alternative to the tragic conception which has brought humanity and its environment to the point of imminent destruction.'[131] As such works of fantasy and authors such as Tolkien, can, according to Elgin, provide positive ecological perspectives for the primary world. Indeed in allowing us to see the world through elvish eyes, Tolkien, in elevating the non-human perspective in his work, reminds us that we are part of nature and in destroying nature we destroy ourselves.[132]

---

129 Don D. Elgin, *The Comedy of the Fantastic: Ecological Perspectives on the Fantasy Novel*, Westport and London: Greenwood Press, 1985, p.15.
130 Elgin, *The Comedy of the Fantastic*, p.23.
131 Elgin, *The Comedy of the Fantastic*, p.24.
132 Tolkien in 'On Fairy-stories' mentions drama and tragedy, and its preoccupation with human woes. In contrast, he speaks of 'eucatastrophe' which he describes as 'the consolation of the happy ending' which he believed was 'perhaps' the ultimate purpose of fairy-stories. He writes: 'Almost I would venture to assert that all complete fairy-stories must have it. At least I would say that Tragedy is the true form of Drama, its highest function; but the opposite is true of Fairy-story. Since we do not appear to possess a word that expresses this opposite, I will call it *Eucatastrophe*. The *Eucatastrophic* tale is the true form of fairy-tale, and its highest function.' (Tolkien, *Tolkien Reader*, p.85).

Chapter Five

Tales That Grew in the Telling

In the previous chapters, from differing thematic viewpoints (and under the characterisation of an ecological augury) I have undertaken (and here continue to undertake) a green reading of Tolkien's works. In modern critical parlance this discourse is thus a work of ecocriticism – a fact, one might say, that is self-evident. But rather than allow the ecocritical tag to remain pinned to this work as a matter of course, in what follows I will consider Tolkien the writer and Tolkien the literary theorist against some of the principal ideologies, tropes and works of what is now understood as ecocriticism. The chapter will begin by discussing the similarities in approach and form of Tolkien's *The Lord of the Rings* and Rachel Carson's 'A Fable for Tomorrow': a fictional account of environmental disaster many ecocritics believe is the starting point of modern ecocritical study. I will continue by considering Tolkien's depiction of the hobbits and the Shire as representations of the pastoral tradition in English literature. I will go on to discuss Tolkien's progressive views on the creative process, in the light of modern ecocritical theory that posits the possibility that there is an implicit connection between literature and nature, and attempt to reconcile this with Tolkien's deeply held religious beliefs.

(I) Ecocriticism: The Emergence of Green Studies

Publishers Routledge have been responsible for a series of (what may be described as) introductory guides to differing (and generally long accepted) aspects of literary study. These include works that discuss and foreground not only literary terms such as *Realism*, *Narrative* and *Parody*, but also more critically centred understandings of literature including *Colonialism/Postcolonialism* and *Modernism*.[1] The texts, published under the series heading *The New Critical*

---

1 I include capitalised and italicised terms here because these terms are also the titles of the works in *The New Critical Idiom* series.

Idiom, are described by Routledge as 'an indispensable approach to *key* topics in literary studies' (emphasis added). In 2004 Routledge added *Ecocriticism* to their catalogue of literary guides. This is a good indication as to just how far the once rather ill-determined or even unlikely notion of a green approach to literary studies has come.

Before proceeding, I should take a moment to offer definitions of ecocriticism from some of the more prominent ecocritics. In the introduction to the ISLE[2] reader's tenth anniversary anthology in 2003, Michael Branch and Scott Slovic acknowledge that a finite definition of ecocriticism is elusive 'except for the understanding that ecocriticism was a scholarly perspective attuned to the place of the more-than-human world in particular works of art'.[3] Cheryll Glotfelty in *The Ecocriticism Reader* offers a more expansive and unambiguous understanding:

> ecocriticism is the study of the relationship between literature and the environment. Just as feminist criticism examines language and literature from a gender-conscious perspective, and Marxist criticism brings an awareness of modes of production and economic class to its reading of texts, ecocriticism takes an earth-centred approach to literary studies.[4]

Author of Routledge's *Ecocriticism*, Greg Garrard broadly describes ecocriticism as 'the study of the relationship of the human and the non-human, throughout human cultural history.'[5] Indeed we recall that this question of 'cultural history' finds focus in Meeker's *The Comedy of Survival: Studies in Literary Ecology*, and later in Elgin's *The Comedy of the Fantastic*.

Although ecocriticism, as an area of literary enquiry, is a relatively contemporary phenomenon, there are, of course, many works that have proven to be amenable (retrospectively) to the broad scope of ecocritical analysis. As such ecocriticism has attempted to tap into or claim a heritage of literary works, both fictional and non-fictional, which place focus on representations of nature, or which may be read as offering the non-human world as more than

---

2 *ISLE: Interdisciplinary Studies in Literature and Environment* is the journal affiliated to ASLE: Association for the Study of Literature and Environment.
3 Michael P. Branch & Scott Slovic, 'Introduction' in Michael P. Branch & Scott Slovic (eds.), *The ISLE Reader: Ecocriticism, 1997-2003*, Athens and London: University of Georgia Press, 2003, pp.xiv-xv.
4 Cheryll Glotfelty, 'Introduction' in Cheryll Glotfelty & Harold Fromm (eds.), *The Ecocriticism Reader: Landmarks in Literary Ecology*, Athens and London: University of Georgia Press, 1996, p.xiv.
5 Greg Garrard, *Ecocriticism*, Abingdon and New York: Routledge, 2004, p.5.

just a backdrop against which a human drama may unfold. The claiming of this literary heritage, along with specific works of ecocriticism, amounts to a green canon. The two works mentioned above fall within the scope of this ecocritical canon, the former much more so than the latter. But, in differing degrees, diverse works such as Shakespeare's *The Tempest*, the poems of the Romantics such as Blake, Clare (although writing a little after the vogue), Coleridge, Wordsworth and Keats, Henry David Thoreau's *Walden*, John Muir's *My First Summer in the Sierra*, Thomas Hardy's *Return of the Native* and *Tess of the D'Urbervilles*, and Mary Austin's *The Land of Little Rain* (amongst many others) have also been cited as prominent green texts. As we noted in the previous chapter Elgin has argued that the fantasy mode of expression also lends itself to a promotion of the non-human and an embrace of the natural systems of life and death (and humanity's place therein). Thus works by authors such as C.S. Lewis, Charles Williams, Frank Herbert and Joy Chant may be read as offering environmentally aware perspectives and narratives. We could easily add John Wyndham (*The Day of the Triffids*), William Golding (*Lord of the Flies*) and Stephen Donaldson (*The Chronicles of Thomas Covenant*) to the list. It has been Tolkien, however, more so than any other author, who has delivered the fantasy mode to the attention of the modern psyche. Indeed Elgin writing in 1985 suggests that Tolkien's works are 'most responsible for the critical attention which has been given to the fantasy tradition within the last thirty years.'[6] With an ever-increasing interest in Tolkien's work since that time, due, in no small part, to the success of Peter Jackson's film versions of *The Lord of the Rings* trilogy,[7] we could extend Elgin's time frame to the present day. Works of fantasy, however, and Tolkien's

---

6 Don D. Elgin, *The Comedy of the Fantastic: Ecological Perspectives on the Fantasy Novel*, Westport and London: Greenwood Press, 1985, p.24.
7 As I write this, a film adaptation of *The Hobbit*, to be released in two parts, is in production. The release date for the first film was originally scheduled for 2011, but it has now been put back until the end of 2012. Guillermo Del Torro, however, who originally agreed to take on directing duties, has relinquished those duties citing the overly protracted production time for the films as his reason. Director of *The Lord of the Rings* films, Peter Jackson, initially executive producer, has since taken up the directing reins of *The Hobbit* films. Ongoing problems with the filming have included threats to take the production away from New Zealand over financial wrangling, a potential actors' boycott, and the unexpected hospitalisation of Jackson for ulcer surgery. Despite all of this, members of the original *The Lord of the Rings* cast who have been confirmed for the new films are Ian McKellen (Gandalf), Hugo Weaving (Elrond) and Andy Sirkus (Gollum). British actor Martin Freeman has been cast as Bilbo Baggins. These films one imagines, when all problems are overcome (and they finally get made), can only serve to generate further interest in Tolkien's works.

works in particular (as the most widely celebrated example of the genre), despite the fact that they tend to foreground and promote the non-human, have never quite found their way (despite some very honourable mentions) into the ecocritical mainstream or the centre ground of what is now considered to be the green canon. As stated in the previous chapter, and by virtue of the evidence I present throughout this study, I contend that Tolkien's work should be placed alongside Blake's, Thoreau's and Wordsworth's as among the most significant green texts ever committed to print. Across the chapters of this book I have argued that the environmental dimension of Tolkien's works, exemplified in the opposing characters, plots, sub-plots and narrative design of *The Lord of the Rings* in particular, not only reflects the modern ecological crisis, but also acts as a warning against the pursuit of power and progress in the absence of a responsible environmental ethic. By way of placing Tolkien in a wider ecocritical context and offering *The Lord of the Rings* as a key green text, what follows is a comparative thematic analysis of his major work and a work of fiction that, despite its brevity, many ecocritics believe is environmentalism's literary point of origin.

(II) Fables for Tomorrow

Garrard opens his literary study guide to ecocriticism thus: 'It is generally agreed that modern environmentalism begins with 'A Fable for Tomorrow', in Rachel Carson's *Silent Spring* (1962).' Garrard goes on to describe how Carson concentrates 'on images of natural beauty' to underline a representation of an idealised town in harmony with the natural world – a harmony that is, according to Garrard, 'a picture of essential changelessness, which human activity scarcely disturbs.' This wondrous, idyllic and imagined landscape, however, soon faces cataclysmic environmental devastation or, as Garrard puts it, 'pastoral peace rapidly gives way to catastrophic destruction.'[8]

'A Fable for Tomorrow' is an overtly fictional representation of Carson's environmental concerns: it is an imaginative expression of her fears for the natural world and it serves to provide the reader with a vivid and immediately accessible

---

8 Garrard, *Ecocriticism*, p.1.

reflection of those fears. The business of unearthing and analysing such literary reflections Greg Garrard calls ecocriticism.

In 1954, eight years before the publication of 'A Fable for Tomorrow' and indeed *Silent Spring*, Tolkien's *The Lord of the Rings* first entered the public domain. And although *The Lord of the Rings* is not an explicitly and scientifically environmental work in the manner of *Silent Spring*, one can nevertheless draw quite striking parallels between Tolkien's epic work and Carson's brief introductory fable. Let us look first at how Carson depicts her imagined world in 'A Fable for Tomorrow':

> There was once a town in the heart of America where all life seemed to live in harmony with its surroundings. The town lay in the midst of a checkerboard of prosperous farms, with fields of grain and hillsides of orchards where, in spring, white clouds of bloom drifted above the green fields. In autumn, oak and maple and birch set up a blaze of colour that flamed and flickered across a backdrop of pines. Then foxes barked in the hills and deer silently crossed the fields, half hidden in the mists of the autumn mornings.
> Along the roads, laurel, viburnum and alder, great ferns and wildflowers delighted the traveller's eye.[9]

Carson is describing here an agrarian society where the natural world exists in accord with 'the town' and those who inhabit it. Carson offers us evidence of this accord in the form of 'prosperous farms', 'fields of grain' and 'hillsides of orchards'. The town is depicted as a flourishing place that seems at first to be free of any contaminating agent.

If we turn our attention to the opening of Tolkien's *The Lord of the Rings* we find (predominantly) a portrayal of hobbits – inhabitants of an imagined land (the Shire) where nature and the social order also appear in harmony. And like Carson's 'checkerboard of prosperous farms' the domain of hobbits is described as 'a well-ordered and well-farmed countryside.'[10] Even as disaster looms at the very edge of its borders, we are told of the Shire, '[e]verything looked fresh, and the new green of Spring was shimmering in the fields and on the tips of the trees' fingers.'[11] Indeed as Frodo, Sam and the company of hobbits camp in a wood after fleeing Hobbiton we hear, '[t]hey were still in the heart of the

---

9 Rachel Carson, *Silent Spring*, London: Penguin, 2000, p.21.
10 J.R.R. Tolkien, 'Prologue' in *The Fellowship of the Ring*, London: HarperCollins, 1997, p.17.
11 Tolkien, *Fellowship*, p.71.

Shire. A few creatures came and looked at them [...] a fox passing through the wood on business of his own stopped several minutes and sniffed.'[12] The creatures of the Shire, just like those of Carson's fabled land seem in harmony and at ease with the world around them. Carson's depiction of this imaginary American town, like Tolkien's portrayal of the Shire, could be said to be somewhat idealised – I examine claims that the Shire represents Tolkien's nostalgic and idealised portrayal of rural England below – but any such sentimentalist depiction is soon cast aside as Carson's agrarian society falls foul of what she describes as 'some evil spell' and we are told that '[e]verywhere was the shadow of death' and 'mysterious maladies swept'[13] throughout the livestock. Suddenly Carson's world is transformed into a dark, ominous and sickly place where not even children at play are safe from this strange and all-consuming malady.

Garrard describes Carson's use of phrases such as 'evil spell' and 'mysterious maladies' as 'supernatural terminology'. He goes on to say that she employs 'the literary genres of pastoral and apocalypse' in her fable which he proposes are 'pre-existing ways of imagining the place of humans in nature.'[14] Certainly pastoral and apocalyptic imagery permeate Tolkien's work, and the rise of the shadow of evil represented by Sauron, the Ringwraiths and others could be said to be supernatural in essence. Perhaps the most arresting passage in Carson's fable, however, is that which depicts the silent spring of the book's title:

> There was a strange stillness. The birds for example – where had they gone? [...] The few birds seen anywhere where moribund; they trembled violently and could not fly. It was a spring without voices [...] only silence lay over the fields and woods and marsh [...]
> The roadsides, once so attractive, were now lined with brown and withered vegetation as though swept by fire. These, too, were silent, deserted by all living things.[15]

Carson's once idyllic and vital landscape is rendered lifeless as 'the shadow of death' casts its 'evil spell' upon it. Similarly the harmonious agrarian world of the hobbits (and indeed all of Middle-earth) is soon threatened by a shadow of great malice. And although the hobbits are largely oblivious to the peril that threatens them, nevertheless, as we have seen in 'The Scouring of the Shire', the 'shadow'

---

12 Tolkien, *Fellowship*, p.105.
13 Carson, *Silent Spring*, p.21.
14 Garrard, *Ecocriticism*, p.2.
15 Carson, *Silent Spring*, p.22.

of devastation falls over their homeland: '[t]he pleasant row of old hobbit-holes in the bank on the north side of the Pool were deserted, and their little gardens that used to run down bright to the water's edge were rank with weeds [...] an avenue of trees had stood there. They were all gone.'[16] The scene of the Shire's devastation, as we noted earlier, echoes Tolkien's descriptions of Mordor and Isengard. However of note here, is that amid Tolkien's description of the Dead Marshes and the lands that lead to the Black Gates of Mordor we are told:

> The only green was the scum of livid weed on the dark greasy surfaces of the sullen waters. Dead grasses and rotting seeds loomed up in the mists like ragged shadows of long-forgotten summers [...] There was a deep silence, only scraped on its surfaces by the faint quiver of empty seed-plumes, and broken grassblades trembling in small air-movements that they could not feel.
> 'Not a bird!' said Sam mournfully.
> 'No, no birds,' said Gollum.[17]

Again we see that there are analogous and corresponding environmental themes and motifs in Tolkien and Carson's fiction. In particular the portentous imagery of a 'birdless' silence lends each description a manifestly apocalyptic character. Indeed the same imagery was employed by Philip Larkin to help create a scene of hopelessness, doom and death in his poem 'Next Please', published in 1955:

> Only one ship is seeking us, a black-
> Sailed unfamiliar, towing at her back
> A huge and birdless silence. In her wake
> No waters breed or break.[18]

Tolkien, like Carson (and Larkin) destroys the familiar in order to sharpen the senses of the reader to the desolation he is describing. But for Tolkien and Carson it is not merely the imagined 'deep silence' (as Tolkien puts it), which creates this effect – Carson's American farmland town is also easily recognizable and identifiable, and so when such shattering ruination is visited upon it, the imagined devastation is quite literally 'brought home' to the sensibilities of the reader. Likewise Tolkien's Shire is a familiar representation of a rural community: the farms, water mills, markets, post-offices and even the local public houses such as *The Ivy Bush* and *The Green Dragon* all serve to create a

---
16 J.R.R. Tolkien, *The Return of the King*, London: HarperCollins, 1997, p.981.
17 J.R.R. Tolkien, *The Two Towers*, London: HarperCollins, 1997, p.612.
18 Philip Larkin, *Collected Poems*, edited by Anthony Waite, London: Faber & Faber, 2003, p.50.

convincing and recognizable countrified vision. So much so that, as I suggested in the first chapter, when the blighted landscape of the Shire under the 'industrialised' hand of Sharkey is revealed to us through the eyes of the returning hobbits, we cannot help but share their sense of loss.

The threat which hangs over Middle-earth and the environmental havoc that rages throughout its landscapes are directed in the main by the will of supernatural and ancient, malevolent beings who seek power at all costs. Carson closes her fable, however, by telling us that 'no witchcraft, no enemy action had silenced the rebirth of new life in this stricken world. The people had done it themselves.'[19] This would seem at first to set the two narratives at odds. And yet those who cast their shadow of doom across Middle-earth cannot so easily be collectively or abstractly dismissed as a marauding supernatural enemy that operates independently of those who oppose it.

Indeed the power of Sauron returns to torment the Third Age of Middle-earth only because Isildur, after cutting the One Ring from Sauron's hand, is beguiled by it and refuses to destroy it – a weakness to act which is not lost on Elrond, who recounts the events at the council in Rivendell: 'Isildur took [the Ring], as should not have been. It should have been cast then into Orodruin's fire [...] But Isildur would not listen to our counsel.' Elrond goes on to relate the consequences of Isildur's refusal to set aside self-interest in the cause of a greater good, 'Sauron was diminished, but not destroyed [...] The Dark Tower was broken, but its foundations were not removed; for they were made with the power of the Ring, and while it remains they will endure.'[20]

Even though Isildur is conspicuously on the side of good, he is nonetheless corrupted by the allure of the Ring (Elrond tells us '[Isildur] took it to treasure it'[21]) and his failure to act ultimately contributes to the very forces he opposes. Similarly it is the desire for power which first corrupts Sauron, once a benign Maia spirit (and Melkor/Morgoth before him). In a letter responding to W.H. Auden's review of *The Return of the King* in the *New York Times*, Tolkien comments, '[Sauron] had gone the way of all tyrants: beginning well, at least on

---

19 Carson, *Silent Spring*, p.22.
20 Tolkien, *Fellowship*, pp.237-38.
21 Tolkien, *Fellowship*, p.237.

the level that while desiring to order all things according to his own wisdom he still at first considered the (economic) well-being of other inhabitants of the Earth.'[22]

One could say that all manifestations of evil that occur and appear in *The Lord of the Rings* (and Tolkien's wider fiction) are not evil in and of themselves but rather representations of either:

1. A weakness to resist power.
2. A failure to recognise the danger inherent in one's actions or lack of action.
3. The corruption of once good intentions or benign wills.

All of the above categories have profound environmental implications for our reality and, in terms of accounting for evil in Tolkien's fiction, do not necessarily present iniquity as something arriving from some supernatural 'otherworld'.[23] Indeed Tolkien states categorically of *The Lord of the Rings*, '[i]n my story I do not deal in Absolute Evil. I do not think there is such a thing.'[24] Even the orcs, who are the foot soldiers of Middle-earth's doom and thus responsible for much of the ecological damage inflicted upon it, are let off the hook of being cast as pure evil – Tolkien, answering questions put to him by Naomi Mitchison states that orcs 'are nowhere clearly stated to be of any particular origin' adding 'since they are the servants of the Dark Power, and later of Sauron, neither of whom could, or would, produce living things, they must be 'corruptions'.'[25]

There are undoubtedly instances of 'witchcraft' and sorcery in *The Lord of the Rings*, but it is not sorcery itself necessarily that brings environmental devastation to the landscapes of Middle-earth. Almost exclusively such devastation occurs as a result of the weakness to resist the corruptive allure

---

22 Tolkien, *The Letters of J.R.R. Tolkien*, edited by Humphrey Carpenter, London: HarperCollins, 2006, p.243.
23 Perhaps Ungoliant, the Great Spider of the First Age, and her lesser offspring, of which Shelob was a descendant, could be argued to be pure evil. Tolkien leaves the origins of Ungoliant vague but *The Silmarillion* tells us that she was an evil being, before the world was made, who took on the appearance of a spider. As the prime Dark Lord Melkor/Morgoth was once a benign spirit whose corruption spread to those who followed like Sauron, one can assume that Ungoliant suffered a similar fate. Her insatiable pursuit of the gems of the Noldor (and the Silmarils in particular) marks her out as a literary creation that is consumed by personal gain at all costs.
24 Tolkien, *Letters*, p.243.
25 Tolkien, *Letters*, p.178.

of power, dominion and wealth. We recall that the dwarves of Moria for example 'delved too greedily and too deep'[26] into a rich vein of the precious and much coveted mithril silver, unleashing a Balrog upon both their own people and an unsuspecting world – an act which later causes the Fellowship to lose Gandalf, thus plummeting them into even greater depths of peril and crisis.

Indeed the crisis that faces Middle-earth may be traced back against a catalogue of frailty and error among the forces of good. Even the forging of the One Ring itself comes about as a result of the elven-smiths inability to resist the seductive pull of yet greater knowledge:

> [Elrond] told of the Elven-smiths of Eregion and their friendship with Moria, and their eagerness for knowledge, by which Sauron ensnared them [...] they received his aid and grew mighty in craft, whereas he learned all their secrets and betrayed them, and forged secretly in the Mountain of Fire the One Ring to be their master.[27]

Perhaps if Elrond, who is depicted by Tolkien as incorruptible, was to have been asked at the council in Rivendell how the shadow of evil had been able to steal back in to threaten the free people of Middle-earth, his answer may have been simple – 'The people had done it themselves.'

As this, the final phrase of 'A Fable for Tomorrow', rings out with an unambiguous and portentous environmental warning, Carson returns the reader to the real world with a jolt: 'This town does not actually exist [...] yet every one of these disasters has actually happened somewhere [...] A grim spectre has crept upon us almost unnoticed, and this imagined tragedy may easily become a stark reality we all shall know.'[28] With the act of making a direct connection between her fable and actuality Carson not only almost single-handedly kick starts a 'green' approach to literary studies, but also underlines why stories, fables and even epic myths are such an important and necessary aspect of the human condition, a sentiment echoed by Jonathan Bate in *The Song of the Earth*: '[t]elling stories is the characteristically human way of humanizing the

---

26 Tolkien, *Fellowship*, p.309.
27 Tolkien, *Fellowship*, p.236.
28 Carson, *Silent Spring*, p.22.

big questions [...] Myths are necessary imaginings, exemplary stories which help our species to make sense of its place in the world.'[29]

If, as Bate suggests, a key function of fiction is to aid in our understanding of humanity's 'place in the world' and the wider universe, then the pursuit of literary analysis is not, as some would contend, mere 'navel gazing' but more a strategy which enables humanity to better understand itself and its position in relation to all that is not human. This, of course, becomes particularly significant when we consider fiction from an environmental perspective because an analysis of the literary and cultural reflection of humanity's connection (or rather interconnection) with nature and the non-human is precisely what ecocriticism is all about.

In this light it is interesting to note that Garrard's opening to *Ecocriticism* specifies that 'modern environmentalism begins' not with the rigorous scientific data of *Silent Spring* but 'with 'A Fable for Tomorrow'.' In other words it is the story, the fiction, the 'humanizing' myth that sets the wheels of 'modern environmentalism' in motion and not the methodical study that follows.

Carson's employment of a story to introduce her, as Garrard puts it, 'impressive array of scientific evidence'[30] in *Silent Spring* demonstrates firstly that she fully expected her readership to understand the implicit reflective connection between her work of fiction and the external reality of her ecological message, and secondly that she believed fiction to be an important weapon in her struggle to raise awareness of the dangers posed by organic pesticides. In other words Carson consciously invested her energies into creating fiction that would mirror a real human and environmental crisis and as such cast her readers as ecocritics. To paraphrase another well-known fable, she left a very clear trail of breadcrumbs, leading from her fiction to the environmental peril she wished to expose. That a writer such as Tolkien does not collapse the parameters of his fictional world, but rather consistently presents them with all the verisimilitude of external reality

---

[29] Jonathan Bate, *The Song of the Earth*, London: Picador, 2000, p.25.
[30] Garrard, *Ecocriticism*, p. 2.

does not preclude us from finding the way on our own. It is, as Tolkien himself stated 'in the freedom of the reader.'[31]

Although I do not claim that Tolkien's fiction offers an explicit, overtly intentioned and singularly focused ecological warning in the manner of Carson, it is nonetheless hard to ignore the environmentally-themed parallels we may draw between the two. Indeed both, in their own way, could be said to be – upon time of publication and even today – fables for tomorrow.

As we have noted, Tolkien fervently believed in the promotion and preservation of the tale for the tale's sake, but he, like Carson, was acutely aware of the potential of fiction to provide powerful and revealing representations of reality – not in any direct, allegorical point-for-point association, but rather reality as applied through the perception of a reader, and re-discovered through the lens of a secondary world prism. Moreover, as we shall examine more fully towards the end of this chapter, he believed every story to contain some element or shard of truth. Indeed as a literary theorist and professor of English the study of literature was his 'bread and butter' pursuit. And, given the powerful reflections on reality his fiction provides, this is a fact that should not be easily cast aside.

In terms of the applicability of his own fiction to external reality, on quite a number of occasions Tolkien used facets of his own stories to reflect issues related to the outside world: in an airgraph to his son Christopher during World War II Tolkien uses the figurative notion of Sauron to philosophise on the futility of war: 'we are attempting to conquer Sauron with the Ring. And we shall (it seems) succeed. But the penalty is, as you will know, to breed new Saurons.'[32] We recall he also referred to Tom Bombadil in relation to the disappearing green face of the Oxfordshire and Berkshire countryside. In a lighter, but no less environmentally pertinent vein, whilst attending a reception organised by a bookseller of Rotterdam, Holland in 1958, Tolkien, referring to the continued growth of the industrial sector, proclaimed to rapturous applause 'I look East, West, North and South, and I do not see Sauron; but I see that Saruman has many descendants. We Hobbits have against them no

---

31 Tolkien, *Fellowship*, p.xv.
32 Tolkien, *Letters*, p.78.

magic weapons. Yet, my gentlehobbits, I give you toast: To the Hobbits. May they outlast the Sarumans and see spring again in the trees.'[33]

Silent Spring is of course no work of fiction: it is a social and scientific[34] commentary on the damaging effects of pesticides such as DDT on the environment. Yet, in Garrard's words this 'founding text of modern environmentalism [...] begins with a decidedly poetic parable.' Moreover, as we have seen, this parable, this fable, this work of fiction with which Carson introduces her momentous and pioneering environmental discourse employs language, imagery, motifs and apocalyptic versus pastoral oppositions which appear strikingly similar to those published by Tolkien eight years earlier[35] in *The Lord of the Rings*.

(III) Tolkien and the Pastoral Tradition

One of the major criticisms levelled at Tolkien's work, and one noted in the introduction to this book, is that it is fundamentally escapist – merely a portal through which, once Tolkien, and now his readership may disappear for a time and shelter from the harsh reality of modern life. Detractors of Tolkien, such as Catherine Stimpson, accuse him of not only being escapist but also of creating an idealised, utopian, pastoral society in the form of the hobbits and the Shire – which they say is nothing more than a romanticised representation of the English countryside of his youth. The escapism? Not just from reality but from a modern industrialised world he neither cared for nor really understood. Stimpson's particular accusation drew in the wider field of the pastoral tradition, 'Tolkien', she wrote, 'celebrates the English bourgeois pastoral idyll.'[36]

Even the most strident of Tolkien's defenders would have difficulty in rejecting the assertion that some kernel of truth feeds all of the above. It is certainly

---

33 Tolkien, *Letters*, pp.225-26.
34 *Silent Spring* has frequently been included among the best non-fiction works of the last century as well as having been named as one of the twenty-five greatest science books ever written by the editors of *Discover Magazine*, a subsidiary of the American giant *Time Magazine*.
35 There is no clear evidence to suggest that Carson or 'A Fable for Tomorrow' was in any way influenced by Tolkien, and that is not what I am trying to infer. Rather the point of the comparison is to demonstrate to what extent Tolkien's fiction resonates with the same environmental themes and motifs that inform and propel Carson's more 'ecocritically' famed work.
36 Quoted in Patrick Curry, *Defending Middle-Earth. Tolkien: Myth and Modernity*, London: HarperCollins, 1997, p.40.

no secret, for example, that Tolkien's suspicions regarding the onset of the industrial age, whilst based on justifiable concern related to the destructive potential of the machine (and focused on the *misuse* of technology rather than technology itself), did carry with them a measure of nostalgic longing for a simpler time and a predilection for the simpler things in life.[37] But for Tolkien (and for renowned cultural commentators such as Raymond Williams, as we shall see) this was no great revelation, but rather a very human sentiment. In a radio interview for BBC Radio 4's 'Now Read On' programme when asked if he, in real life, held 'home, fire, pipe, bed' in the same high regard as those such as the hobbits, Tolkien responded rather pointedly, 'Don't you?'[38] Some, however, like Stimpson have cast Tolkien as a writer whose work is *overtly* and *pejoratively* marked by backward-looking sentimentalist rhetoric and imagery, particularly in relation to his portrayal of the hobbits and the Shire. What immediately follows is an attempt to consider Tolkien's depiction of the society of hobbits and their homelands in the context of the dual accusation that:

1. Tolkien has created a purely idealised representation of rural life that bears little or no relevance to actuality.

2. This idealised portrayal contributes to and draws from a pastoral tradition in English literature that has always romanticised the countryside and its communities.

With the second of these accusations in mind, let us first place the notion of the pastoral tradition in context.

What we now understand as the pastoral tradition comes to us from as far back as the poet Theocritus (born around 300 BC) who delighted audiences in the

---

37 Humphrey Carpenter refers to Tolkien's anti-modernist leanings as being among his 'strongest-held opinions'. Later in life, according to Carpenter, these became 'obsessions', and often 'he would see a new road that had been driven across the corner of a field and cry, 'There goes the last of England's arable!' By this time of his life he would maintain that there was not one unspoilt wood or hillside left in the land.' (Humphrey Carpenter, *J.R.R. Tolkien: A Biography*, London: George Allen & Unwin, 1977, p.125). These recollections, along with Tolkien's letters, papers and interviews, merely confirm the premise that Tolkien was a vociferous and passionate supporter of the natural world who viewed the industrialisation of his homeland with mistrust – as he got older no doubt such deeply held beliefs became obsessive in nature. It is, I believe, unfair, however, to label his fiction as overtly nostalgic and idealised. I argue further on in the main body of this chapter that, upon closer inspection, the hobbits are not as idealised as they first would appear. Moreover, the hobbits are but one race among many, and the wider world of Middle-earth is a wild place where nature is presented as a dangerous foe to cross.
38 Taken from Tolkien's interview with Denys Geroult for BBC Radio 4's 'Now Read On' programme, 16th December 1970.

Greek city of Alexandria with his *Idylls* of a simpler, more enchanted country 'pasture' beyond their urban domain. Even then the notion of pastoral is defined, not only by its association with green pastures and scenes of nature, but also in terms of its opposition to what it is not – namely a municipal, urbanized cityscape. David Baker in 'The Pastoral: First and Last Things' makes the point that pastoral depictions of society, only fully understood by what they are not, are in danger of washing over or disregarding reality: '[f]irst, the pastoral is identified by its location – the quiet, serene pasture. But it also locates or situates itself, very knowingly, *in opposition to* a setting or situation erased or ignored. The point is that what is ignored is what is inevitable, the real world.'[39]

It was the Romantic poets, however, more than any other who employed this notion of the 'pastoral in opposition' to react to or even to rally a defence against the onset of industrialisation. This, according to Greg Garrard, has deeply influenced how we look at nature itself: '[s]ince the Romantic movement's poetic responses to the Industrial Revolution, pastoral has decisively shaped our constructions of nature.' Used as a means to *undermine* what they are not, pastoral representations can easily become romanticised and idealistic and therefore flawed. Indeed Garrard suggests that '[n]o other trope is so deeply entrenched in Western culture, or so deeply problematic for environmentalism.'[40]

It is not just the tendency for pastoral portrayals to become idealised which draws criticism; such depictions incline also to be nostalgic and sentimentalised: they often look back with fond charm towards a quainter, less complicated time and mourn its passing. This, of course, is not just true of reactions to the Industrial Revolution which yearned for a pre-mechanised world – Raymond Williams in *The Country and the City* argues that nostalgia has always been a principal feature of the pastoral tradition. Williams asserts that all down through history, writers and thinkers alike have eulogised collectively about better times that have passed into fond memory. Williams suggests that 'the initial problem is one of perspective'[41] and describes the idea of looking always toward a better yesterday as analogous with being taken by an 'escalator' that

---

39 David Baker, 'The Pastoral: First and Last Things' in *Southern Review* 42.4 (Autumn 2006), p.785.
40 Garrard, *Ecocriticism*, p.33.
41 Raymond Williams, *The Country and the City*, London: Hogarth, 1993, p.9.

is 'moving without pause' on a 'perpetual recession into history.'[42] Jonathan Bate in *The Song of the Earth* discusses Williams' insights:

> Raymond Williams reflects on exactly this problem of historical perspective in his book *The Country and the City*: the better life is always just behind us, 'over the last hill'. We imagine that there was an 'organic community' in the time of our parents (perhaps) or our grandparents (for sure), but they in turn look back to the 'good old ways' and sun-drenched idylls of their own childhood. Williams portrays rural nostalgia as an escalator reaching further and further back into the past. 'Where indeed shall we go, before the escalator stops?' he asks. To which 'One answer, of course, is Eden'.[43]

Those who view Tolkien as an author who idealises and eulogises the pastoral in his work would perhaps believe Tolkien's answer to the question posed by Williams – 'Where indeed shall we go, before the escalator stops?' – would not be 'Eden' but rather the Shire. In other words an idealised, rustic, escapist fantasy where the past has been delicately pieced together and resurrected to soothe the disquiet of its creator. Let us then, in the light of these criticisms, examine Tolkien's portrayal of the Shire and the society of hobbits who live there.

There is no doubt that Tolkien, in his descriptions of the Shire and the hobbits, is guilty of creating a somewhat romanticised portrayal of a pastoral lifestyle. The hobbits live in a picturesque, old-fashioned world full of quaint dwellings and scenic gardens where no motorcar engine ever disturbs their peace and the splendour of an unspoiled countryside surrounds them. Tolkien describes them in the 'Prologue' to the second edition of *The Lord of the Rings* as being a self-sufficient people with 'hardly any 'government'' who 'for the most part managed their own affairs.' Moreover the spectre of cut-throat capitalism seems absent from the Shire and we are told that because of the hobbits' 'contented and moderate' nature, 'estates, farms, workshops, and small trades tended to remain unchanged for generations.'[44] Crime also seems almost absent from the Shire and the hobbits' version of the police, the Shirriffs, of whom there are only twelve, are 'more concerned with the straying of beasts than of people.'[45]

---

42 Williams, *The Country and the City*, pp.11-12.
43 Bate, *The Song of the Earth*, p.25.
44 Tolkien, 'Prologue' in *Fellowship*, p.9.
45 Tolkien, 'Prologue' in *Fellowship*, p.10.

All in all this is a world of charming Englishness; it has about it a sense of nostalgia and a sense of pre-industrial allure. Tolkien's descriptions of the hobbits and the Shire: of Bywater, Hobbiton and Buckland therefore can be read almost as an elegy for a bygone age, in the manner described by Williams and Bate, and as such they run risk of being cast as a portrayal which selectively ignores the harsh reality of country life in the quest to defame the industrialised urban model. Indeed Garrard observes that pastoral representations that seek primarily to 'retreat from the city' or modernity become 'an idealisation of rural life that obscures the realities of labour and hardship.'[46]

Although Tolkien's depiction of the world of hobbits may be termed generally idyllic and romanticised, it is not exclusively so. Indeed there is evidence of a pronounced economic divide within the social stratum of hobbits and we hear that '[t]he poorest [hobbits] went on living in burrows of the most primitive kind, mere holes indeed, with only one window or none; while the well-to-do still constructed more luxurious versions.'[47] Certainly the notion of living in a 'mere hole' is not one which ignores 'hardship' and lends itself to a strictly idealised portrayal. Tolkien's description of life in the Shire also includes many references to infighting, jealousy and one-upmanship. We recall Bilbo's mistrust of the Sackville-Bagginses[48] and their envy of his comparative wealth. On numerous occasions also we hear residents of one region of the Shire denounce another – we are told also that Sam 'had a natural mistrust of the inhabitants of other parts of the Shire.'[49] Dickerson and Evans suggest that 'this attitude, endemic to the Shire farms, can be read as an implied critique of rural provincialism in our world.'[50] Indeed this ingrained suspicion of others is especially extended to outsiders. Farmer Maggot, for example, who is described as 'a terror to trespassers',[51] tells Pippin, '[i]t's lucky for you that I know you. I was going out to set my dogs on any strangers' adding 'we do get queer folk wandering

---

46 Garrard, *Ecocriticism*, p.33.
47 Tolkien, 'Prologue' in *Fellowship*, p.6.
48 The Sackville-Bagginses believed that they would inherit Bag End from Bilbo and were much put out when Bilbo unveiled Frodo as his heir. *The Lord of the Rings* opens with a discussion in *The Ivy Bush* concerning this very matter. After his birthday party and departure from the Shire, Bilbo leaves Lobelia Sackville-Baggins a case of silver spoons as an ironic parting gift believing as he did that she had stolen most of his spoons while he had been off on his adventures with the company of dwarves.
49 Tolkien, *Fellowship*, p.91.
50 Matthew Dickerson & Jonathan Evans, *Ents, Elves, and Eriador: The Environmental Vision of J.R.R. Tolkien*, Lexington, Kentucky: University Press of Kentucky, 2006, p.75.
51 Tolkien, *Fellowship*, p.89.

in these parts at times.'[52] Likewise the rather comically observed Shirriff police force may in fact call upon a more sinister auxiliary force who are 'employed to 'beat the bounds', and to see that Outsiders of any kind, great or small, did not make themselves a nuisance.'[53]

What is of note is that this narrow and provincial outlook, this desire to close off borders and shut out strangers exists in the Shire even before there is evidence that the hobbits have anything to fear. Patrick Curry observes, 'Tolkien's portrait [of hobbits] is not altogether a flattering one; it includes greed, small-minded parochialism and philistinism, at least – even if Frodo, Sam and the other hobbits of his story were able to rise above these regrettable characteristics of the English bourgeoisie.'[54] Arguably, the main reason that Frodo, Sam, Merry, Pippin and even Bilbo avoid becoming all of the above is because they travel out of the society of the Shire and embrace the wider world beyond. John C. Hunter in his essay 'The Evidence of Things not Seen: Critical Mythology in *The Lord of the Rings*' whilst describing Tolkien's portrayal of the Shire as fundamentally romanticised, also concedes that Tolkien ultimately rejects this idealised depiction:

> The hobbit life is a perfect patrician fantasy of traditional rural English contentment, with little or no crime, no resentment of economic imbalances, and a purely ceremonial political structure. As idyllic as life in the Shire seems in Book One, though, Tolkien makes it clear that this is a dream and that the whole Shire needs to awaken from it.[55]

If Tolkien set out to represent a perfect society in his portrayal of the hobbits then upon closer inspection we can say that he failed. Certainly no portrayal that concerns itself so openly with small-mindedness, xenophobia and backbiting could be considered as perfect. In point of fact Tolkien emphatically states that 'hobbits are not a Utopian vision, or recommended as an ideal in their own or any age.'[56] Indeed although there is a general propensity to associate the hobbits with an idyllic existence living in unblemished harmony with nature, hobbit characters such as Ted Sandyman and Lotho 'Pimple' Sackville-Baggins (as

---

52 Tolkien, *Fellowship*, p.90.
53 Tolkien, 'Prologue' in *Fellowship*, p.10.
54 Curry, *Defending Middle-Earth*, p. 38.
55 John C. Hunter, 'The Evidence of Things not Seen: Critical Mythology in *The Lord of the Rings*' in *Journal of Modern Literature* 29.2 (Winter 2006), p.141.
56 Tolkien, *Letters*, p.197.

we have seen) prove that hobbits may be just as quick to choose industry and ruination of the landscape over nature if it provides power or pecuniary reward. Moreover as Frodo and company first enter the Old Forest at the beginning of *The Lord of the Rings*, Merry who knows something of the history of the hobbit relationship with the forest (and more about its legends) tells his companions about an incident involving hobbits felling and burning hundreds of trees in a response to the Old Forest's attempts to cross into the Shire. This incident and its implications for the perception of hobbits as an ideal portrayal of humanity in harmony with nature is discussed in detail in the 'Afterword' section of this book – referenced here, however, it further demonstrates that hobbits are not as idealised as some have supposed.

It would be remiss to deny, however, that the society of hobbits does represent, in some aspects, a romanticising of the English countryside that Tolkien feared was disappearing before his eyes. In a letter to his publisher Rayner Unwin, Tolkien writes 'The Shire is based on rural England […] the toponymy of The Shire […] is a 'parody' of that rural England, in much the same sense as are its inhabitants.'[57] The Shire and its people, however, unlike the rural England of Tolkien's time, are an imagined pre-mechanised and pre-industrial society: there are no factories, no production lines, no mechanised tools and no motorcars. The Shire therefore represents a pastoral innocence before the age of the machine. In this sense it is romanticised and has inherited the pastoral tradition passed down from those such as William Blake, whose opposition to the 'dark Satanic mills' of the Industrial Revolution was unreserved. David Baker suggests that this expression of the pastoral, as a reaction to the forbidding presence of factories and chimney stacks was not flawed, but vital: 'at the inception of the smoky Industrial Revolution, nature – the pastoral – had never been more appropriate or necessary: as a haven, a refuge, a place to grieve, perhaps to heal […] a place to think, to meditate.'[58] Indeed as noted earlier, Tolkien's 'homely houses', places such as Rivendell, are presented as natural havens where rest and healing await a weary traveller.

---

57 Tolkien, *Letters*, p.250.
58 Baker, 'The Pastoral', p.785.

This manifestation of the 'pastoral in opposition' extends itself to Tolkien's depiction of the Shire. The dark power of Mordor and the mechanistic shadow of Isengard loom on the horizon, and the Shire (as *The Lord of the Rings* begins) is everything they are not. This opposition may be read as the expression of Tolkien's concerns that the industrial age in the real world posed a very immediate threat to the long-term survival of rural communities, landscapes and ecologies.

I specify landscapes and ecologies because when Tolkien allows us to see the damage inflicted upon Middle-earth by the masters of the dark towers, although we see how the living races suffer as a result, it is predominately damage caused to the natural landscapes and even to nature itself which occupies the foreground of his descriptions.

When considering Tolkien's portrayal of the hobbits and the Shire as pastoral tropes, it is worth bearing in mind that they are only part of the wider story. And the pastoral vision of the hobbit lands only account for a small percentage of the narrative exposition of *The Lord of the Rings* (and *The Hobbit*). Beyond the borders of the Shire lie the other lands and peoples of Middle-earth and Tolkien's portrayal of war, desolation, suffering and hardship make up the greater part of his tales of the Third Age.[59]

(IV) Tolkien and the Creative Process

In a chapter which aims to consider, not just Tolkien's literary works, but also his ideas on the relationship between literature, imagination and external reality against contemporary ecocritical theory, I turn to what is perhaps the most radical aspect of ecocritical thinking – the creative process and literature's relationship to, and place within the physical world – and offer that Tolkien's theories on such things are arguably equally as radical. Indeed in certain respects his thoughts on the creative process seem to be, if not entirely consistent with contemporary ecocritical theory, then certainly suggestive of it.

---

59 It is worthy of note that many of Tolkien's races share characteristics that have been described as pastoral when associated with hobbits: there are no factories, machines or slaves in Rohan, Gondor or Rivendell just as there are none in the Shire (before Sharkey). These races, like the hobbits, live off the land, distrust machines and engines, travel on horses (ponies in the case of hobbits) and sing songs at suppertime. Any assertion therefore that Tolkien was a creator of a purely idealised, pastoral fiction must concede that many of the characteristics of the rustic race of hobbits appear also among the warlike or sylvan peoples of Middle-earth.

Taking her lead from Barry Commoner's first law of ecology: 'everything is connected to everything else',[60] Cheryll Glotfelty says in her introduction to *The Ecocriticism Reader*, 'we must conclude that literature does not float above the material world in some aesthetic ether, but, rather, plays a part in an immensely complex global system, in which energy, matter, *and ideas* interact.'[61] The notion that literature and the creative impulse may be influenced by the interconnectivity of 'energy, matter *and ideas*' is one that is beginning to find some prominence among ecocritics. Ecologists for quite some time have been positing theories pertaining to humanity's interrelationship with the natural world, suggesting that all things are interconnected in an astonishing and elaborate ecosphere with everything impacting upon, fashioning, affecting and unsettling everything else. Indeed since humanity is utterly dependent on the life-giving systems of nature, and connected indissolubly to solar radiation, photosynthesis and the protective shelter of the sky, it is perhaps not so farfetched to propose that we cannot hope to (or are arrogant to attempt to) claim autonomy for any aspect of the human condition – literature and imagination included. So human creativity, as Glotfelty suggests, must be viewed as part of the interactive swirl of creation and held to be a factor within the repertoire of natural energies.

With this theory in mind let us turn to Tolkien's rather avant-garde comments regarding the creation of his own fiction. When speaking of his own creative process, in particular with relation to his mythical world of Middle-earth, Tolkien often said he was struck by a sense that he was not so much creating literature as relaying passages and ideas that had arisen in his mind as 'given things', that he 'had at times to wait till 'what really happened' came through',[62] and that he was aware of and surprised by a certain sense of mysterious distance between himself and the words he had written:

> Take the Ents, for instance. I did not consciously invent them at all. The chapter called 'Treebeard' [...] was written off more or less as it stands, with an effect on myself [...] almost like reading some one else's work. And I like Ents now because they don't seem to have anything to do with me. I daresay something has been going on in the 'unconscious' for some time, and that

---

60 Barry Commoner, *The Closing Circle: Confronting the Environmental Crisis*, London: Cape, 1972, p.44.
61 Glotfelty, 'Introduction' in *The Ecocriticism Reader*, p.xv, emphasis in the original.
62 Tolkien, *Letters*, p.212.

accounts for my feeling throughout, especially when stuck, that I was not inventing but reporting.[63]

Referring to periods of high productivity during the writing of *The Lord of the Rings* Tolkien was also to say 'the thing seems to write itself once I get going, as if the truth comes out then.'[64] Again and again Tolkien was to focus upon this notion that his conscious creative imagination was only part of, what I will term, a wider gathering of energies, which seemed to have the power to, if not reveal his fiction to him, then to influence the direction and substance of his tales[65] – Tolkien even insisted on occasion that his role in the creation of his *legendarium* was akin to that of a character inside the story. Indeed in the following passage, taken from the introduction to *Tree and Leaf*, Tolkien places himself alongside the hobbits, sharing their bewilderment and perhaps more interestingly their despair at what may or may not happen next:

> the LR [*Lord of the Rings*] was beginning to unroll itself and to unfold prospects of labour and exploration in yet unknown country as daunting to me as to the hobbits. At about that time we had reached Bree, and I had then no more notion than they had of what had become of Gandalf or who Strider was; and I had begun to despair of finding out.[66]

The above passage could be read as a rather fanciful way of describing 'writer's block', the suggestion that *The Lord of the Rings* was 'beginning to unroll *itself*' (emphasis added), however, is saying something very different. Indeed Charles Moseley also highlights this repeated claim by Tolkien that he felt as if he was discovering rather than writing his fiction: 'The story itself is cast as active, [Tolkien] as passive [which] implies the story as somehow independent of its redactor.' Moseley points out that this claim originates from the very first sen-

---

63 Tolkien, *Letters*, pp.211-12.
64 Tolkien, *Letters*, p.104.
65 In the series of books entitled *The History of Middle-earth* Christopher Tolkien has documented the evolution of the writing of Tolkien's major works, including references to numerous rewrites, amendments and developmental stages – all of which point to an author who was very much steering the course of his own fiction. My rationale for this portion of the chapter is not to dismiss the evolutionary stages or the painstaking detail with which Tolkien created his fiction, nor to dilute Tolkien's individual talent as a writer, but rather to explore Tolkien's own recurring claims that (in a wider sense) he was aware of more than his own conscious design in the creation of his work. Thereafter, to set this notion against Tolkien's own thoughts on the creative process and the power of literature – whilst considering all in the light of modern ecocritical theories on the creative impulse and the interaction of thought, matter and energy. I do not consider the fact that Tolkien was a writer who evolved his work in stages to be at odds with ideas related to a wider consideration of the attendance of other influencing factors in the creation of literature (clearly nor did Tolkien).
66 J.R.R. Tolkien, 'Introduction' in *Tree and Leaf*, London: Unwin, 1964, p.5.

tence of *The Hobbit*. Thus he views Tolkien's work as one continuous flow, one book which sprang from that moment: 'The stories of Middle-earth are really one book, and writing it took Tolkien all his life: and unawares [...] he seems not to have planned, so much as discovered what he has to say.'[67]

Another insight into how Tolkien viewed his fiction to be something that was possessed of a degree of autonomy, or as Moseley suggests, something that 'took [him] unawares' is revealed in the manner in which Tolkien reacted to inconsistencies he came across in his work. Carpenter describes how Tolkien, upon discovering 'an apparent contradiction in the narrative or an unsatisfactory name', would not react as one might expect of a writer of a complex fictional work by saying to himself, '[t]his is not as I wish it to be; I must change it'. 'Instead' as Carpenter explains 'he would approach the problem with the attitude: 'What does it mean? I must *find out*.''[68] A particular example of this arose when Tolkien realised that, across the history of Middle-earth, he had given two of his elven characters the same name – Glorfindel. One dies during a battle with a Balrog in the First Age, and the other rides from Rivendell to bring aid, and the loan of a horse to Frodo in the Third Age. Tolkien discovered the name repetition before the publication of *The Lord of the Rings* (his writings on the First Age, of course, were not published in his lifetime). But rather than come up with an alternative name for one of the elves, he asserted that the two elves *must* be the same person, and thus, as Gene Hargrove puts it, 'he had stumbled onto a rare case of reincarnation among the Elves.' As Hargrove goes on to add '[h]e then devoted some time to an examination of the theological implications of this special case.'[69]

Taken in isolation, any one of Tolkien's assertions that he felt as if he was receiving aspects of his own fiction, or that his fiction possessed a degree of autonomy could be read as an attempt to modestly withdraw from the creative arena of his own work. We should note, however, that Tolkien made similar claims on numerous occasions and at differing times in his life – both as he

---

67 Charles Moseley, *J.R.R. Tolkien*, Plymouth: Northcote House Publishers, 1997, p.30.
68 Humphrey Carpenter, *J.R.R. Tolkien: A Biography*, London: George Allen & Unwin, 1977, pp.94-95; emphasis in the original.
69 Gene Hargrove, 'Who is Tom Bombadil', *Mythlore* 47.4 (Autumn/Winter 1986), p.20.

wrote and retrospectively. These remarks, therefore, must be taken at face value and thus add up, not to a idiosyncrasy, but to a conviction – namely that Tolkien believed that he, as a writer, was not creating fiction as an independent or isolated artistic force, but rather there were other energies or factors at work. This in itself is curious given that Tolkien referred to *The Lord of the Rings* as having been 'written in [his] life-blood'[70] and more than once, he alluded to a heartfelt desire and *intention* that he might create a 'mythology for England'.[71]

Carpenter qualifies *his* account of Tolkien's attitude to fictional inconsistencies (mentioned above) by referring to it as a kind of 'intellectual game', nonetheless Carpenter concedes that Tolkien's distinctive reaction to such things was down, in part, to 'his belief in the ultimate *truth* of his mythology.'[72] I have already alluded to Tolkien's theories on 'true myth' and return to them in more detail below, but essentially Tolkien's belief was that, not only was history (truth) and myth made up 'ultimately of the same stuff'[73] but also that myths were not lies but tales which carried fragments of truth originating from divinity. Or in Joseph Pearce's words: 'Tolkien argued [that] inevitably the myths woven by us, although they contain error, reflect a splintered fragment of true light, the eternal truth that is with God.'[74] As we shall examine below this view that some fragment of truth prevailed in every myth was part of Tolkien's wider belief that all tales were ultimately connected, and bled into his understanding that, in the strictest sense, he was not solely responsible for his own creative output.

Given Tolkien's conviction, however, that the human capacity for artistry, the human ability to imagine and construct secondary worlds, originated from God (thus all myth contains truth), can we deduce that his allusion to an awareness of a degree of autonomy in his creative impulse was an acknowledgement that he was receiving aspects of his fiction *direct* from a divine source? If this was his belief he clearly did not say so and, at the very least, it is a peculiar omission for a deeply religious man, who wrote openly on both divinity *and* the creative process. Indeed on one occasion Tolkien seems to refute any notion that he

---

70 Tolkien, *Letters*, p.122.
71 See Tolkien, *Letters*, p.144. The term 'a mythology for England' is not used as such, though.
72 Carpenter, *Biography*, pp.94-95; emphasis in the original.
73 Tolkien, *Tree and Leaf*, p.30.
74 Joseph Pearce, *Tolkien: Man and Myth*, London: HarperCollins, 1998, p.58.

was receiving 'truth' in the sense of a religious 'message' direct from God: 'As for 'message'' he writes, 'I have none really, if by that is meant the conscious purpose in writing *The Lord of the Rings*, of preaching, or of delivering myself of a vision of truth specially delivered to me.'[75]

Perhaps Tolkien, as a student of world myth, was, in his attempts to claim that he was aware of other energies at work in the creation of his fiction, offering a coded allusion to the ancient muses. He would certainly have been aware of the goddesses, sprites and spirits of classical mythology who are said to inspire creativity in the arts.[76] However, we should note that some of Tolkien's thoughts on the apparent autonomy of aspects of his creative imagination were relayed in *private* correspondence to friends and family. Any suggestion, therefore, that these claims were part of 'an intellectual game', or part of an oblique allusion to classical myth, seems misplaced. Indeed reading Tolkien's many claims and references to such matters one is struck by the conviction and sincerity of his words.

There are, of course, other possibilities to account for Tolkien's sense that he was not solely responsible for his creative work among theories related to artistic inspiration and universal knowledge. Perhaps the most famous of these is Carl Gustav Jung's theory on the collective unconscious. This is a very complex and detailed theory which seeks to offer the human psyche in terms of layers of consciousness from the personal perceptive organisation of the conscious mind, to the personal unconscious, to the collective unconscious – a repository of humanity's universal experience of existence which takes in all religious and mythological symbols and concepts or patterns of life. Any true understanding of Jung's theory on the existence of an intuitive 'universal unconscious' can only be achieved by a detailed analysis of his study

---

75 Tolkien, *Letters*, p.267.
76 It occurred to me as I considered the possibility that Tolkien was referring to the muses when he spoke of energies other than his own conscious will at work in the creation of his fiction, that the number nine is significant in Tolkien's writing. There are nine Black Riders (later nine Nazgûl) and nine walkers of the Fellowship. Although the muses were once said to number three, more popular classical legend refers to the nine muses – the daughters of Zeus. Tolkien, of course, took inspiration from many world myths in the creation of his own mythology and if he was offering any coded allusion to the ancient muses perhaps it was in the numbering of the Fellowship set against Sauron's deadliest servants.

Archetypes and the Collective Unconscious, but his core ideas are represented, to a degree, in the following passage (taken from that work):

> in addition to our immediate consciousness, which is of a thoroughly personal nature and which we believe to be the only empirical psyche (even if we tack on the personal unconscious as an appendix), there exists a second psychic system of a collective, universal, and impersonal nature which is identical in all individuals. This collective unconscious does not develop individually but is inherited. It consists of pre-existent forms, the archetypes, which can only become conscious secondarily and which give definite form to certain psychic contents.[77]

Referring, in part, to creativity Jung also states that '[a]rchetypes [...] manifest themselves only through their ability to *organize* images and ideas, and this is always an unconscious process which cannot be detected until afterwards.'[78] Although Tolkien was often aware of 'a stir in the flux' of his creative process *as he wrote*, as opposed to being unable to detect it 'until afterwards', his assertion (cited earlier) that 'something has been going on in the 'unconscious''[79] would certainly seem to owe something to Jung's ideas – and I do not discount them completely as a means to account for Tolkien's claims. Indeed there are certain aspects of Jung's premise that would account for Tolkien's declaration that some things were being revealed to him – in that such an understanding would mean these aspects would have to have pre-existed. Jung's theory, however, made clear distinctions between the personal and the collective unconscious. He referred to the personal unconscious as an individual storehouse of a lifetime's experience that has passed from the conscious to the subconscious spheres of perception. Whereas he categorised the collective unconscious as a pre-existing repository of archetypal patterns of instinctive thinking or universal processes that are inherited and pre-date the individual mind. As we shall see below, Tolkien's description of the organic nature of an emerging story in the human mind is firmly rooted in personal experience and memory, and whilst his understanding that all stories are fundamentally connected would seem to 'buy into' Jung's theory, I contend that the coming together of Tolkien's views not only anticipate modern ecocritical theory, but are best understood in that light.

---

77 Carl Gustav Jung, *Archetypes and the Collective Unconscious*, Abingdon and New York: Routledge, 1991, p.43.
78 Carl Gustav Jung, *The Structure and Dynamics of the Psyche*, The Collected Works of C.G. Jung Volume 8, Princeton: Princeton University Press, 1981, p.231; emphasis in the original.
79 Tolkien, *Letters*, p.212.

To facilitate a better understanding of Tolkien's views on the creative process and the nature of myth and story, and as a lead in to an examination of these views in the light of ecocritical theory, I offer first a brief analysis of Tolkien's short story 'Leaf by Niggle'.

One of Tolkien's less famed works, and a quirky tale to boot, 'Leaf by Niggle' is the moving story of a peculiar painter who is obsessed with trying to complete his painting of a tree. Niggle endeavours to draw a leaf, a task for which he is especially gifted, but finds that 'it became a tree; and the tree grew, sending out innumerable branches.' Niggle tirelessly works on his tree but the more he paints the more his picture seems to expand and take a form of its own: '[A]ll around the Tree, and behind it, through the gaps in the leaves and boughs, a country began to open out.'[80] Niggle is unable to finish his work because of constant interruptions from the outside world and is forced to go on a journey, for which (despite due warning) he has not prepared, finding himself finally in a kind of purgatorial abyss. Most Tolkien commentators (many of whom see the work as autobiographical)[81] identify Niggle's journey with death.

As Niggle (by virtue of the consent of 'otherworldly' voices) is eventually allowed to leave his 'purgatory', he travels to a place where 'the curves of the land were familiar', and walking across its grasslands he finds himself facing his tree – the tree he had, as an artist, been unable to complete. Looking around, Niggle realises that his painting has become real: 'before him stood the Tree, his Tree, finished.' The tree is complete in a manner we are told, 'Niggle had so often felt and guessed, and so often failed to catch.'[82] It is worthy of note that Tolkien once referred to *The Lord of the Rings* as 'my own internal Tree' saying 'it [is] growing out of hand and, revealing endless new vistas.'[83]

Tolkien here seems to be throwing up questions regarding the creative process; blurring the lines between the conscious will of the artist and the ability of art (including literature) to take on a life of its own. Although a profoundly

---

80 J.R.R. Tolkien, *The Tolkien Reader*, New York: Ballantine Books, 1966, p.101.
81 See Tom Shippey, *J.R.R. Tolkien: Author of the Century*, London: HarperCollins, 2001, chapter 6, in which he discusses how the story of Niggle reflects Tolkien's anxiety regarding finishing his lifetime's work before death could rob him of the chance.
82 Tolkien, *Tolkien Reader*, p.105.
83 Tolkien, *Letters*, p.321.

spiritual tale 'Leaf by Niggle' seems most of all to be suggesting that the creative impulse is propelled not only by the conscious will of the artist but also by factors external to that will – a clear reflection of his own experiences when writing.

Moreover it is interesting to note that Tolkien again chooses a tree, a living organic entity, to be the representation of a partially self-propelling artistic energy. Indeed Tolkien made a habit of symbolising aspects of the creative process in the form of tree imagery. Turning to 'On Fairy-stories' we find that Tolkien describes all stories and myths that have ever been, or ever *will* be written as fundamentally connected – in order to convey this idea more vividly he suggests that what appear as differing fables, myths, or stories (told or written) are but 'branches on the Tree of Tales.'[84] Likewise Tolkien refers to the process of creating literature in terms of how it resembles a germinating seed which lies deep in the psyche – fed by experience and watered by distant memory. Here Tolkien offers his own insights concerning the creation of *The Lord of the Rings* as an example:

> One writes such a story not out of the leaves of trees still to be observed, nor by means of botany and soil-science; but it grows like a seed in the dark out of the leaf-mould of the mind: out of all that has been seen or thought or read, that has long ago been forgotten, descending into the deeps. No doubt there is much selection. As with a gardener: what one throw's on one's personal compost-heap; and my mould is evidently made largely of linguistic matter.[85]

Note again that Tolkien is referring to the story itself as active: 'it grows like a seed.' Indeed if we look a little closer at Tolkien's observation above – this notion of the creation of fiction as analogous with a seed that grows could be said to perfectly encapsulate (or anticipate) ecocritical theories which suggest that literature is, as Cheryll Glotfelty asserts, 'part [of] an immensely complex global system, in which energy, matter, *and ideas* interact.'[86]

The first thing we may say about a seed is that a seed contains the 'code' or the locked information of what it may become, and thus it has some degree of self-determination. Of course if the seed is cast on barren ground and deprived

---

84 Tolkien, *Tolkien Reader*, p.46.
85 Quoted in Carpenter, *Biography*, p.126.
86 Cheryll Glotfelty, 'Introduction' in *The Ecocriticism Reader*, p.xv.

of the elements it needs, it will never take root, unravel or fulfil its locked potential. It is only in the interrelatedness of factors such as sunlight (energy) and fertile soil (matter) that a seed may prosper and unfold its final form. In this sense Tolkien's imagery regarding literature fits Glotfelty's premise and for any disciple of ecocriticism the correlation is apt.

For a perception not filtered through an ecocritical perspective, however, Tolkien's analogy and Glotfelty's hypothesis seem to collapse together – each as inappropriate and fanciful as the other in accounting for the creative process. Indeed when we take this understanding of an interconnected process in nature and try to apply it to offer an explanation of how literature is created, the transition does not occur easily and significant questions begin to arise: what external factors act upon a writer who sits alone pouring his creative ideas onto a blank page? If we propose that there *are* external factors – aren't notions of a 'seed' with coded information best understood with recourse to Jung's ideas related to archetypes and the collective unconscious? And if not – is it not true to say that Tolkien's analogy which depicts 'a story [growing] like a seed in the dark […] out of all that has been seen or thought or read, that has long ago been forgotten' simply refers to the creative unconscious of the writer? Indeed rather than pursue far-fetched notions which speak of external forces impacting upon the creation of literature, or even more fanciful theories which suggest that thought processes and ideas may be influenced by the physical world, shouldn't we simply accept the somewhat obvious assertion that any process which takes place, occurs, as Tolkien himself determines 'out of the leaf-mould of the mind' – in other words exclusively internally?

In attempting to address these questions we must first recall Barry Commoner's first law of ecology 'everything is connected to everything else' and then apply it to the image of a writer, alone, creating fiction. Whilst Jung's ideas on the collective unconscious do come into play here, even *they* are taken account of under Commoner's ecologically framed assertion.[87] Indeed for all of humanity's collective experiences and patterns of knowledge to flow into the psyche of our 'lonely writer' we must concede that all thought, ideas and stories are connected. Commoner's premise and Glotefelty's application of that premise, however, very clearly alludes to *all* matter, energy and ideas (*everything* is connected) and thus the physical world as well as thought processes – so how are these ideas reconcilable against the image of a writer creating fiction alone, as Tolkien suggests, 'out of all that has been seen or thought or read'?

Well, for 'our' writer to have read or seen anything, we must assume that it has once existed in physical form (matter). Even the thoughts and works of other writers (ideas) exist as physical books (matter), which must be opened and engaged with (energy).[88] Indeed William Rueckert's essay 'Literature and Ecology: An Experiment in Ecocriticism' proposes that 'a poem is stored energy'[89] (I return to this idea towards the end of this chapter) and that when one engages with a poem (and by extension literature) one is unlocking the 'stored energy' within and allowing it to flow from the external world to the internal mind. The same is true of experience or trauma – physical actuality becomes thought and memory. Even words appearing *on* a computer screen (ideas *on* matter) also must be engaged with (energy) or when we hear someone speak (ideas becoming sound, and moving air – matter), we listen and process the information (energy).

---

[87] In point of fact Jung's concept of archetypes (the underlying principle of his collective unconscious theory) has parallels with ecological theories determining an interconnection of all things. Indeed Jung extended his concept of archetypes to take in the physical world as well as the mind. He suggested that archetypes existed not only in the collective unconscious of the human psyche but also as governing principles which conditioned constructs and reactions of organic matter and all manifestations of life. The concept of archetypes was one Jung used in relation to all aspects of creation and the physical world. Similar to ecological theories by those such as Commoner, Jung believed that all matter, life and energy were linked. He referred to the underlying unity of existence as the 'unus mundus' or the 'one world' principle. How differing aspects of the unus mundus 'behaved' or unfolded over time was, he believed, directed or governed by archetypes – or structures of universal reality. For a more detailed analysis of Jung's theories see Carl Gustav Jung, *Two Essays on Analytical Psychology*, The Collected Works of C.G. Jung Volume 7, London: Routledge, 1966; and Carl Gustav Jung, *Archetypes and the Collective Unconscious*, Abingdon and New York: Routledge, 1991.

[88] The same is true of information, thoughts or writings which exist in digitised form – an act of energy upon a physical medium is the only process which internalises (or transforms) these things.

[89] William Rueckert, 'Literature and Ecology: An Experiment in Ecocriticism' in Cheryll Glotfelty & Harold Fromm (eds.), *The Ecocriticism Reader*, p.108.

The crux of the thing is simply this: although energy, influence, experience or collective thought has *become* internalised, we should not so readily dismiss or forget the interactive process that has led to this internalisation. Indeed this process can only occur due to the interconnectedness of all things. For example (and this is but one example from many traceable pathways): for someone to process collective thought (consciously or not), for a thinker to think or a writer to write he must be alive, to be alive he must breathe, to breathe he must have air in his lungs and this breathable air is created by a process of photosynthesis, which is (as chemists Mary Archer and James Barber point out) 'the primary engine of the biosphere, essential to life.'[90] This process in turn is only possible by virtue of the Earth's position in and connection to the cosmos. John Muir, a pioneering ecologist and preservationist wrote almost a hundred years ago, '[w]hen we try to pick anything out by itself, we find it hitched to everything else in the universe.'[91]

Given this understanding, and the coming together of these ideas, the art of the writer is retained in the form of Tolkien's discerning and gifted 'gardener' who develops and nurtures the nascent and internalised thoughts of literary creation (the seed), and yet Glotfelty's interconnections come into view. Even Tolkien's remarks such as 'I was not inventing but reporting', '*The Lord of the Rings* was beginning to unroll itself' and 'thing seems to write itself' are suggestive of, not only the internalised experiences and memories of a lifetime 'watering' the seed of a story (and inducing all the self-directing power a seed contains), but also the coming together of external influences, ideas and energies – those of other writers, thinkers and older tales pouring energy onto 'the seed', causing the power of accumulated knowledge and literature to shine upon it like sunlight.

Indeed when we concede that the interconnections of the wider world of literature and other writers, thinkers and tales, along with an individual's internalised experiences, memories and anxieties all pour into and influence the creation of a single work, we may follow a line of literary works back into the past – and an interesting pattern emerges. If we agree that part of the

---

90 Mary Archer & James Barber, 'Photosynthesis and Photoconversion' in Mary Archer & James Barber (eds.), *Molecular to Global Photosynthesis*, London: Imperial College Press, 2004, p.1.
91 John Muir, *My First Summer in the Sierra*, New York: Mariner Books, 1998, p.145.

make-up of any work of literature is the life experience of the author, and for many the apprehension for the times in which he or she lives and writes (as it clearly was with Tolkien), *and* each author is influenced, to a degree, by the literature and philosophy of what has gone before, then it follows that the primary concerns of one writer for his time may be reflected in the work of another (consciously or not, implicitly or not) – as such 'a spirit of the age' or zeitgeist may emerge across literature which reflects the defining crisis of an age. Clearly Tolkien's work was received by a generation who were beginning to rise to face the environmental crisis in their midst – with many then and since making the implicit connection between the green dimension of his fiction and external reality. As Carpenter says of Tolkien's most famous work: '[i]ts implied emphasis on the protection of natural scenery against the ravages of an industrial society harmonised with the growing ecological movement, and it was easy to see *The Lord of the Rings* as a tract for the times.'[92] But, of course, Tolkien too was awakened to the dangers of machines, industry and the perils facing the green face of the world by those such as William Blake, William Morris and Samuel Butler. Indeed Tolkien may well have been alluding to 'the spirit of the age' when referring to the public (if not critical) embrace of *The Lord of the Rings*:

> I am indeed surprised at the reception of the 'Ring', and immensely pleased. But I don't think I have started any tide. I don't think such a small hobbitlike creature, or even a Man of any size, does that. If there is a tide (and I think there is) then I am just lucky enough to have caught it.[93]

We could go further, given the interconnected spheres of literature and ecology, and wonder if perhaps some organising will across creation, across nature itself sets such a zeitgeist in motion so that literature and philosophy may alert the human world, the agents of destruction, through its own channels of communication – to the dangers its activities are bringing to all manifestations of

---

92 The context of Carpenter's remark relates to the counter-culture movement that recognised and could identify with the green dimension of *The Lord of the Rings*. The ecological augury that radiates from its pages spoke clearly to counter-cultural sensibilities that first came to prominence in American colleges. The quote in context reads: 'Clearly there was much in Tolkien's writing that appealed to American students. Its implied emphasis on the protection of natural scenery against the ravages of an industrial society harmonised with the growing ecological movement, and it was easy to see *The Lord of the Rings* as a tract for the times' (Carpenter, *Biography*, p.230).
93 Tolkien, *Letters*, p.227.

life on the planet. The pursuit of that thought, however, is perhaps another book altogether!

(V) True Myth and Recovery

Certainly in terms of interconnectivity, Tolkien's assertion that all stories and myths are connected and intertwined on some vast 'Tree of Tales' suggests that he was very much alive to the concept of interconnectedness – if only at the level of suggesting that much of the make up of any 'original' work of fiction has come to the writer externally, and therefore literary creativity lies in not only what one may add, but in how 'received' components may be reshaped and retold anew. Indeed borrowing imagery from Sir George Webbe Dasent, Tolkien in 'On Fairy-stories' instantly transforms his 'Tree of Tales' into a 'Pot of Soup' in an attempt to further illuminate the concept: 'speaking of the history of stories and especially fairy-stories we may say that the Pot of Soup, the Cauldron of Story, has always been boiling. And to it have continually been added new bits.'[94] Clarifying the symbolism of the imagery, Tolkien tells us, 'by 'the soup' I mean the story as it is served up by its author or teller.'[95]

The implication here is that one tale is essentially another in disguise (at a profound level) and the craft is not, therefore, necessarily in the innovation but in the telling. Indeed returning to his 'Tree of Tales' analogy once more, Tolkien questions whether there is anything left to be added to the 'Tree' of storytelling, suggesting all the 'patterns' of creativity have already been taken, 'who can design a new leaf? The patterns from bud to unfolding, and the colours from spring to autumn were all discovered by men long ago.' Once he has made this remark, however, Tolkien instantly retracts it, 'that is not true. The seed of the tree can be replanted in almost any soil.'[96] Again this reference to a 'seed' suggests that any tale which arises from the 'soil' of a creative mind carries with it the self-propelling force of a thousand other tales, all of which are re-inventions and recreations of one 'great' tale.

---

94 Tolkien, *Tolkien Reader*, p.52.
95 Tolkien, *Tolkien Reader*, p.47.
96 Tolkien, *Tolkien Reader*, p.76.

In *The Hero with a Thousand Faces* Joseph Campbell also discusses this notion of a 'monomyth' (a term Campbell suggests was coined by James Joyce in *Finnegans Wake*), which has been continually 'reclothed' and retold. Moreover Campbell points to a fundamental and transferable structure which observably underpins many of the world's most enduring myths as he asks '[w]hat is the secret of the timeless vision? From what profundity of the mind does it derive? Why is mythology everywhere the same, beneath its varieties of costume?' Campbell, like Jonathan Bate much later, believed that myth permeated the history of human civilization because the construction of myth was necessary for humanity to begin to understand and make sense of the human condition. Furthermore Campbell offers that somewhere in the creation of myth and story lies the genesis of all cultural, religious and societal human activity:

> Throughout the inhabited world, in all times and under every circumstance, the myths of man have flourished; and they have been the living inspiration of whatever else may have appeared out of the activities of the human body and mind, it would not be too much to say that myth is the secret opening through which the inexhaustible energies of the cosmos pour into human cultural manifestation. Religions, philosophies, arts, the social forms of primitive and historic man, prime discoveries in science and technology, the very dreams that blister sleep, boil up from the basic, magic ring of myth.[97]

Whilst Tolkien would have agreed with much of the above (indeed it is interesting that both use the imagery of 'boiling'), on one vital point he would have undoubtedly disagreed: far from believing that some 'magic ring of myth' brought forth manifestations of religion, Tolkien believed, in one particular case, precisely the opposite. Tolkien firmly believed that one myth was truth – the story of Christ – and that all other myths (before or after) are merely representations of God's expression, filtered through the ages of humanity and thus distanced from truth but not devoid of it. Such was Tolkien's conviction to his ideas concerning 'true myth' that during a now celebrated early hour conversation with C.S. Lewis (and Hugo Dyson) on the matter, he succeeded in altering Lewis' theological viewpoint. A full account of the conversation which took place on Saturday 19th September 1931 may be read in Carpenter's *The Inklings* (here offered in edited form):

---

97 Joseph Campbell, *The Hero with a Thousand Faces*, Princeton: Princeton Press, 2004, p.3.

> Myths [said Lewis] are 'lies and therefore worthless, even though breathed through silver.'
> *No*, said Tolkien. They are not *lies*.
> [...] you look at trees, [Tolkien] said, and call them trees, and probably you do not think twice about the word. You call a star a 'star', and think nothing more of it. But you must remember that these words, 'tree', 'star', were (in their original forms) names given to these objects by people with very different views from yours. To you, a tree is simply a vegetable organism, and a star simply a ball of inanimate matter moving along a mathematical course. But the first men to talk of 'trees' and 'stars' saw beings. They saw the stars as living silver, bursting into flame in answer to the eternal music. They saw the sky as a jewelled tent, and the earth as the womb whence all living things have come. To them, the whole of creation was 'myth-woven and elf-patterned'. [...]
> Man is not ultimately a liar. He may pervert his thoughts into lies, but he comes from God, and it is from God that he draws his ultimate ideals. Lewis agreed [...] Therefore, Tolkien continued, not merely the abstract thoughts of man *but also his imaginative inventions* must originate with God, and must in consequence reflect something of eternal truth. In making a myth, in practising 'mythopoeia' and peopling the world with elves and dragons and goblins, a storyteller, or 'sub-creator' [...] is actually fulfilling God's purpose, and reflecting a splintered fragment of the true light. Pagan myths are therefore never just lies: there is always something of the truth in them.[98]

Upon first reflection Tolkien's comment that all 'imaginative inventions must originate with God' appears at odds with the parallels we have observed between Glotfelty's theory that literature is created as part of the maelstrom of 'energy, matter and ideas' and Tolkien's own claims (marked by their lack of religious allusion) that his creative work seemed able to demonstrate aspects of independence. There is a very distinct difference, however, between saying that the creative imagination *originates from God* and saying that it is *orchestrated by God*.

As a profoundly religious man Tolkien believed that all things including 'energy, matter and ideas' (and thus his own theories and Glotfelty's creative process) also originated from God. 'The story as it is served up by its author', however, was for Tolkien very different, and a matter of individual creation or 'sub-creation' as he termed it because it is creation under God. Moreover Tolkien considered, among all the genres of story that branched off from the 'Tree of Tales' or stewed in the boiling 'Pot of Soup', that fantasy was the purest form

---

98 Humphrey Carpenter, *The Inklings*, London: Allen & Unwin, 1978, p.43.

of sub-creation precisely because in fantasy, almost by definition, something new is created.

In Tolkien's view humanity's capacity to wield an imagination and to create flights of fancy outside of what is 'real' or what exists in reality most closely echoed divine creation. Tolkien tells us, 'in such 'fantasy' as it is called, new form is made; Faërie begins; Man becomes sub-creator.'[99] This realm of fantasy or as Tolkien terms it 'Faërie' is given form and is brought into existence by virtue of the human faculty to imagine, invent and envisage. Throughout 'On Fairy-stories' Tolkien goes to great lengths to point out that it is not merely the presentation of the fantastic or the 'unreal' which constitutes Faërie,[100] but more the sub-creation of a 'Secondary World' within the borders of which all that is seen and all that is encountered is offered as 'real'. To sustain this presentation of actuality or the 'real' in Faërie, the sub-creator must work what Tolkien calls an 'enchantment' upon all who enter the created realm. According to Tolkien this is more than simply the invocation of (as Coleridge suggested) the 'willing suspension of disbelief':

> What really happens is that the story-maker proves a successful 'sub-creator.' He makes a Secondary World which your mind can enter. Inside it, what he relates is 'true': it accords with the laws of that world. You therefore believe it, while you are, as it were, inside. The moment disbelief arises, the spell is broken; the magic, or rather art, has failed. You are then out in the Primary World again, looking at the little abortive Secondary World from outside.[101]

For Tolkien this human capacity for 'enchantment' and the sub-creation of a consistent and reasoned 'Secondary World', although derived from a divine source, casts humanity much like a lesser-form of the 'Valar' as possessed of great powers of creation which function largely independent of and distinguishable from the works of God, but which nonetheless contribute to, build upon and interconnect with the divine creation of the 'Primary World'.

'Fantasy is made out of the Primary World', Tolkien tells us, 'but a good craftsman loves his material, and has a knowledge and a feeling for the clay, stone

---

99 Tolkien, *Tolkien Reader*, p.49.
100 In 'On Fairy-stories' Tolkien offers his thoughts and explanations as to why certain genres of fiction are excluded from his understanding of what constitutes Faërie. These include traveller's tales, dreamscapes and beast-stories.
101 Tolkien, *Tolkien Reader*, p.60.

and wood which only the art of making can give.'¹⁰² The distinction here is that the 'material' of fantasy is created by God and the human sub-creator (who like God engages in 'the art of making') manipulates or crafts new form from what God has given. The environmental implications of these thoughts are located in Tolkien's sentiments that 'a good craftsman loves his material.' Thus this artistic re-forging of the primary world must promote a celebration and a preservation of God's creation – the natural world included. Trevor Hart takes up the point:

> Artistic making [...] departs freely, properly, and often from the constraints of whatever appears to be given in the world; but when it does so its end is never selfish, always being rooted in a delight in the world for its own sake and desiring nothing more than the world's own good.¹⁰³

Tolkien's theory of sub-creation becomes even more compelling from an environmental perspective when he suggests that fantasy, far from facilitating a retreat from the 'Primary World', actually allows one to see the world anew. This understanding of fantasy, of course, counters critical accusations (discussed in the introduction of this study and elsewhere) that Tolkien's work is essentially escapist. Indeed speaking specifically of *The Lord of the Rings*, Stephen R. Lawhead in *Reality and the Vision* discusses this 'twist' on the escapist tag: 'the best of fantasy offers not an escape away from reality but an escape to a heightened reality – a world at once more vivid and intense and real.'¹⁰⁴ Thus, according to Tolkien, the sub-creation of nature and natural phenomena in a 'Secondary World' can compel us to look at nature again, to '[see] things as we are (or were) meant to see them.'¹⁰⁵ The beauty and majesty of the 'secondary' natural world that so ornately radiates from the pages of Tolkien's work thus may illuminate and cast a reflection back to the natural wonder of our 'Primary World'. Tolkien refers to this 'illumination' – this 'seeing anew' as 'Recovery'.

The sub-creation of nature, therefore, in a secondary world promotes the 'recovery' of wonder for nature in the real world – engaging with sub-creations taken

---

102 Tolkien, *Tolkien Reader*, p.78.
103 Trevor Hart, 'Tolkien, Creation, and Creativity' in Trevor Hart & Ivan Khovacs (eds.), *Tree of Tales: Tolkien, Literature, and Theology*, Waco: Baylor University Press, 2007, p.52.
104 Stephen R. Lawhead, in Philip Yancey (ed.), *Reality and the Vision*, London: W. Pub Group, 1992, pp.35-36.
105 Tolkien, *Tolkien Reader*, p.97.

from the primary world, Tolkien suggests, helps us to 'clean our windows', that is to lose the indistinct focus of a familiar view in order that we may 'be freed from the drab blur of triteness or familiarity – from possessiveness.' Tolkien's contention here is that humanity has lost (is losing) its sense of wonder, and that the human need to name, catalogue and take ownership of the natural world has resulted in a universal, abstract view of all that is about us. In other words often we fail to value the natural world because we have become accustomed to it being there; we have named it and placed an abstract conception of it into our collective consciousness. 'This triteness' Tolkien tells us 'is really the penalty of 'appropriation'', thus in naming and mentally 'shelving' all that is about us: forests, seas, grasslands and clear blue skies we distance ourselves from how spectacular and precious these things are or, as Tolkien puts it, 'we laid hands on them, and then locked them in our hoard, acquired them, and acquiring ceased to look at them.'[106] We recall Tolkien's discussion with C.S. Lewis and Hugo Dyson (above) in which Tolkien warned of the dangers inherent in having a closed conception of 'trees' and 'stars'.

Indeed Tolkien makes it clear that it is in the representations of natural things that the realm of fantasy is truly brought alive: 'Faërie contains many things besides elves and fays, and besides dwarves, witches, trolls, giants, or dragons: it holds the seas, the sun, the moon, the sky; and the earth, and all things that are in it: tree and bird, water and stone, wine and bread, and ourselves, mortal men.'[107] Tolkien goes on to suggest that a story-teller (himself certainly included) may find a union with nature through the creation of a secondary world in which nature is spectacularly alive and vibrant: '[f]or the story-maker who allows himself to be 'free with' Nature can be her lover not her slave. It was in fairy-stories that I first divined the potency of the words, and the wonder of things, such as stone, and wood, and iron; tree and grass.'[108]

---

106 Tolkien, *Tolkien Reader*, p.77.
107 Tolkien, *Tolkien Reader*, p.38.
108 Tolkien, *Tolkien Reader*, p.78.

(VI) Closing Thoughts: The Power of Imagination

Taking his view that fantasy can facilitate a 'recovery' of wonder for the 'everyday' natural phenomena we have appropriated and taken for granted – we arrive at the supposition that Tolkien believed that literature was more than an idle pursuit undertaken for amusement or distraction but rather a means by which humanity could transfer and share ideas, passions and energy – the energy to foster new understandings, new wonder and even to bring about change. We surely need no convincing that impassioned and energized words contain the power to stir the world, negatively or positively. Tolkien believed that literature contained the same power. Indeed he believed that fantasy in particular contained the power to re-present the wonder and value of nature to a world that had begun to destroy the green face of its home.

Returning to Rueckert's essay 'Literature and Ecology: An Experiment in Ecocriticism' we find a similar understanding regarding the power of literature. 'A poem' Rueckert asserts 'is stored energy, a formal turbulence, a living thing, a swirl in the flow', but, as Rueckert points out, '[u]nlike fossil fuels, [poetry] cannot be used up.' In other words poetry (and thus literature) may be revisited ad-infinitum and reused as an endless reservoir of inspiration and reflection. Literature, like all artistic expression, is a storehouse that holds the passion and energy of the creative force which brought it into physical existence. 'In literature', Rueckert states 'all energy comes from the creative imagination. It does not come from language, because language is only one (among many) vehicles for the storing of creative energy [...] a painting and a symphony are also stored energy.'[109] Of course we must add experience and memory to the gathering swirl of energies which contribute to the creative imagination. It is when these energies are transferred, however, that imagination finds its true power. Rueckert, using the term 'poet' to signify what Tolkien would term the sub-creator explains:

> Energy flows from the poet's language centers and creative imagination into the poem and thence, from the poem (which converts and stores this energy) into the reader. Reading is clearly an energy transfer as the energy stored in the poem is released and flows back into the language centers and creative imagination of the readers.

---

109 Rueckert, 'Literature and Ecology', p.108.

Literature is thus 'active, alive and generative' as opposed to being 'inert' or as Rueckert puts it 'a kind of corpse upon which one performs an autopsy.'[110] The stored energy, passion and emotion of literature is thus passed from author to reader and re-absorbed or refashioned continuously into new expressions of the imagination – each, as Tolkien would assert, containing fragments of truth, and occasionally containing the power to secure real change in the physical world. Indeed Jonathan Bate offers us a specific example of how the transfer of poetic energy, independent of the author's intent (though reflective of his passions), brought about real environmental (and political) change. 'William Wordsworth' he writes 'could not have known that one effect of his writing on the consciousness of later readers would have been the establishment of a network of National Parks, first in the United States and then in Britain.'[111]

I have tried throughout this chapter to consider Tolkien's fiction and his theories on the creative imagination against some of the key ideologies, themes and works of modern ecocriticism. Of course, there is an implied tension in setting Tolkien's mythic works and his theories on the creative process against contemporary ecocritical understandings in that the green dimension of his fiction is but one avenue of critical concern. I contend, however, that environmental issues and green themes run in rich vein throughout almost every aspect of Tolkien's fiction, making his work not only exceptionally 'amenable' to ecocritical analysis but also, in my view, placing him amongst the most significant authors whose work may be regarded as green texts. Moreover his views on the power and capability of imagination to affect the physical world of nature, his ideas on the interconnection of all stories expressed as an organic 'Tree of Tales', his descriptions of a presence of other energies in his creative process (predictive of Rueckert's groundbreaking ecocritcal essay which speaks of imagination as 'a swirl in the flow' of existence), and most of all the ecological augury, the warning for the primary world which radiates from his major works like Carson's 'Fable For Tomorrow' cast Tolkien as one who may have expected the emergence of green literary theory or anticipated much of what we now understand as ecocriticism.

---

110 Rueckert, 'Literature and Ecology', pp.109-10.
111 Bate, *The Song of the Earth*, p.22.

Whether we accept that Tolkien, as a literary theorist and an author of fiction, anticipated environmentalism and aspects of modern green theory or not – there is no escaping the fact that Tolkien's fiction, and his views on the power of imagination to recover the wonder of nature, carried with them a deep embrace of nature. This embrace of nature was undoubtedly marked by Tolkien's apprehension that humanity's concern for the green face of the world was becoming lost among the wheels and cogs of more and more powerful machines, and that the wonder of the natural world was being sacrificed on the altar of progress. Tolkien, of course, would have believed such a sacrifice to have been an affront to God, as well as to nature, for God in Tolkien's eyes was the master creator, the master story-teller: the one to whom all humanity, all thought and all myth must some day return. Indeed in a letter to W.H. Auden, Tolkien declares 'to speak in literary terms, we are all equal before the Great Author.'[112]

---

112 Tolkien, *Letters*, p.215.

Conclusion

Mirrors of the Golden Wood

Even from his earliest experiments in imaginative literature, Tolkien's fiction can be characterised by the attendance of two major elements: fantasy and natural imagery. In one of his first attempts at verse, entitled 'Wood-sunshine', he depicts an enchanted forest that is alive with nature spirits:

> Come sing ye light fairy things tripping so gay,
> Like visions, like glinting reflections of joy
> All fashion'd of radiance, careless of grief
> O'er this green and brown carpet; nor hasten away,
> O! Come to me! Dance for me! Sprites of the wood,
> O! Come to me! Sing to me once ere ye fade![1]

These lines, written in July 1910, offer hints of thematic concerns that would later come to dominate his life's work. Across all his fiction Tolkien concerned himself with fantasy and the secondary world creation of aspects of natural wonder. Yet as remarkable and captivating as his natural scenes and depictions could be, they were almost always tinged with some unspoken sadness or troubled by a distant (even sometimes immediate) threat. In 'Leaf by Niggle', Niggle's own life's work, his elaborate and treasured painting of a tree, is taken from him by the autocratically-themed 'Inspector of Houses' and Niggle himself is taken away by another man 'dressed all in black'.[2] The elves in *Smith of Wootton Major* are ever-watchful of the natural landscapes of their kingdom, aware of the threat posed by the developments of humanity. Even in Tolkien's more jocular tales, natural elements are threatened and assailed by representations of power. In *Farmer Giles of Ham* for example the farmer of the title is forced, by circumstance, to face both a giant and a dragon, in part, to save the surrounding land from their apathetic attitude to it. Both of these creatures are associated with great strength and both use it recklessly to the

---

1 Humphrey Carpenter, *J.R.R. Tolkien: A Biography*, London: George Allen & Unwin, 1977, p.47.
2 J.R.R. Tolkien, *The Tolkien Reader*, New York: Ballantine Books, 1966, p.107.

detriment of the farmlands and countryside of Ham. Of the giant we are told, 'he brushed elms aside' and he is referred to as 'the desolation of gardens' who blindly does 'a great deal of damage in the woods'.³ The dragon Chrysophylax also, who like all Tolkien's dragons is possessed of a devious nature, is more concerned with accruing wealth than taking account of the damage he causes to the countryside. Janet Brennan Croft makes a similar point in relation to the tale: '[Tolkien's] concern with environmental themes and the depredations of war are also evident in the descriptions of the desolation of the well-ordered landscape wrought by the giant and the dragon.'⁴

But, of course, it is in the unfolding of his *legendarium* and his tales of Middle-earth that Tolkien's environmental themes are most pronounced. In the Third Age in particular, and the events chronicled in *The Lord of the Rings*, Middle-earth is under attack. The landscapes are yielding and the ground trembles under the force of a mechanised assault. Each realm within Middle-earth is under threat, even nature itself is losing the power to heal and restore the broken lands. Those such as Tom Bombadil, the elves and the ents whose power is tied to natural forces are in retreat or shudder as the agents of destruction move against the land. All of this, of course, both reflects and amplifies the environmental crisis of our own time and as such becomes an ecological augury that shows us something of ourselves and where we may be headed.

Indeed the environmental devastation we find in the barren grave-lands of Mordor may be viewed as a desert and the point of no return, a place where nature has been damaged and altered irreversibly – a scenario Bill McKibben warns us about for real in *The End of Nature*. The desolation of Mordor is absolute and it is on the move. We see it reflected and echoed in 'The Scouring of the Shire'. We recall Sam and Frodo's exchange as they cast eyes upon the desolation of Hobbiton and Bag End:

---

3 Tolkien, *Tolkien Reader*, p.127.
4 Janet Brennan Croft 'Farmer Giles of Ham' in *J.R.R. Tolkien Encyclopedia: Scholarship and Critical Assessment*, Michael D.C. Drout (ed.), New York: Routledge, 2006, p.197.

> 'This is worse than Mordor!' said Sam 'Much worse in a way. It comes home to you, as they say; because it is home, and you remember it before it was all ruined.'
> 'Yes, this is Mordor,' said Frodo.[5]

But we also begin to see it echoed in our own reality. We noted (in chapter three) Isaac Asimov's wife's exclamation when confronted with the environmental ruination caused by an oil refinery: 'There's Mordor.'[6]

Throughout this study I have considered the environmental themes and reflections that arise out of Tolkien's work against the thoughts and works of key ecologists and ecocritics, and contend that many of their philosophies, concerns and contentions are observable not only in the pages of Tolkien's fiction but also in his private contemplations on humanity's relationship with the natural world. Arguably the most influential ecologist whose work I have addressed is Paul B. Sears. His most renowned study *Deserts on the March* is a response to the Dust Bowl disaster, an ecological catastrophe in 1930s America caused by human error and mismanagement of soil. In the work Sears paints a picture of human arrogance and egotism that appears strikingly similar to the regime of and the war on creation waged by Sauron:

> [Man] has established a new order, with his own good as the criterion of it. He is attempting to rule the earth as a god might do, not only seeking what he needs, but manipulating all that is about him, supplying the conditions of life for the lower organisms which he uses, and combating those which are hostile with resources they do not have. He no longer accepts, as living creatures before him have done, the pattern in which he finds himself, but has destroyed that pattern and from the wreck is attempting to create a new one. That of course is cataclysmic revolution. We have seen something of what this entails in the way of hazards and failures. Soil has been exhausted or depleted, forests and grasslands destroyed, topography injured.[7]

The central struggle between forces of good and evil in *The Lord of the Rings* is undoubtedly a struggle for the land as much as it is anything else. Sauron's ultimate goal is absolute control. He will not share power, not even with nature. He knows also that those such as the elves draw strength from the earth and so he attacks Middle-earth itself. In destroying (or torturing) the landscape,

---

5 J.R.R. Tolkien, *The Return of the King*, London: HarperCollins, 1997, p.994.
6 Isaac Asimov, 'Concerning Tolkien' in *Magic: The Final Fantasy Collection*, New York: HarperPrism, 1996, p.155.
7 Paul B. Sears, *Deserts on the March*, London: Routledge & Kegan Paul, 1949, pp.137-138.

he begins to win his war against nature, and thus against the elves and the rest of creation. His single eye is symbolic of a narrow field of view, the blind pursuit of power, and a single intent to be a supreme lord over every other manifestation of life: wizard, hobbit, ent, tree or flower. He seeks to eradicate parity between the various beings and races, and impose a political regime, enforced and delivered by the One Ring, that is constructed against a hierarchy of power – with him at its zenith. He pulls those such as the Ringwraiths and even Saruman, vampire-like into his single vision. Saruman, losing sight of his purpose and 'under the spell' of Sauron and the Ring, sets himself up as another dark power. In the tower of Orthanc he, like Sauron, becomes a master of machines and engines.

Tolkien depicts Saruman, in particular, as a representation of ecologically unsound industry, or industry devoid of an ecological ethic. Indeed the two representations of mechanistic power in *The Lord of the Rings*, Orthanc and Barad-dûr, stand like giant factories, casting a shadow over the world about them, and pouring armies that have been 'produced' deep in their 'engine rooms' like pollution out across the land. They are thus emblems of ecological destruction and statements of intent that reflect the designs of Sauron and Saruman, or as Richard Mathews observes, 'the towers in Tolkien's tale stand as symbols of isolated powerful ambitions.'[8] Indeed both Sauron and Saruman oppose the Fellowship as a consequence of war, but they also oppose the *concept* of fellowship and the diversity it promotes.

Against these themes we have those such as Gandalf who teaches, guides, and stirs resistance against the gathering forces that threaten both the people and the land. Gandalf's power is in his wisdom. He values all life and the interrelatedness of creation. As Michael N. Stanton points out, his 'magic', like that of the elves, is associated with his love of nature: 'magic, as practised by Gandalf, seems to consist of using language as a tool to gather and concentrate and focus the ambient energies of nature [...] Thus what seems to be magic may be only (only!) a powerful sympathy with nature.'[9] Gandalf, who I have argued carries much of Tolkien's own worldview in *The Lord of the Rings*, acts

---

8 Richard Mathews, *Fantasy: The Liberation of Imagination*, New York: Routledge, 2002, p.72.
9 Michael N. Stanton, *Hobbits, Elves and Wizards: Exploring the Wonders and Worlds of J.R.R. Tolkien's The Lord of the Rings*, New York: Palgrave Macmillan, 2002, p.47.

as the catalyst which forges a union between the other characters and races in Tolkien's story. He brings once splintered energies and forces together, and with the help of Elrond shows them that they must abandon old grudges and prejudices in order to face the defining crisis of their time. This has clear implications for our reality – our world of divided nations that must come together to address environmental issues that threaten the entire globe. In Middle-earth Gandalf knows that individually those such as Aragorn, Gimli, Legolas and the company of hobbits would succumb to the regime of the Dark Lord – but together they stood a chance of resisting him.

Indeed amongst Tolkien's greatest strengths as a writer was his ability to create characters that could carry the weight of his tales. He imbued his characters with qualities, traits, passions and fears that reflected and bled into the overriding themes and struggles which propelled his narratives forward. For every force in Middle-earth there is a counter force, for every foe of the land who comes openly wielding weapons of environmental destruction we find a defender of the soil who finds strength in the earth itself. For every creeping shadow hungry for ever-greater power and domination of other wills we find a gentle heart who takes delight in even the most insignificant manifestation of life, and is ready to set power down in the pursuit of understanding. In this respect, as I have set out in chapters two and three, Tolkien creates positive and negative or adaptive and maladaptive environmental models, and cultures of opposition that are reflective of the main themes played out in his narrative.

Observable across all of his writings, both fiction and non-fiction, one of Tolkien's ecologically-themed concerns was clearly the respect of diversity. We see this represented in the positive models offered by those such as Gandalf and Tom Bombadil, in the coming together of the Fellowship, but also in the blended narrative perspective of elves, men, hobbits, spirits and trees, or as Verlyn Flieger puts it 'tales told by a variety of tellers'[10] that Tolkien himself offers. Indeed even nature itself is afforded a voice in Tolkien's work in the form of Tom Bombadil and Treebeard. Middle-earth also, of course, far from being

---

10 Verlyn Flieger, *Interrupted Music: The Making of Tolkien's Mythology*, Kent & London: Kent State University Press, 2005, p.49.

merely a stage or a setting upon which the action occurs, may be considered as a major player in the unfolding drama of the Third Age.

In the last chapter of this study I examined Tolkien's theories on the creative process, and the power of literature (in Tolkien's view fantasy in particular) to foster change or re-ignite wonder in the reader for the natural world. Tolkien's ideas on recovery represent the positive aspect of creating a secondary world where the very land and nature itself, in all its vibrant glory, is under siege. When Tolkien depicts the destruction of the Two Trees of Valinor in a frenzied attack by Morgoth and the spider Ungoliant, when he shows us the Shire under Sharkey where the natural beauty of the hobbits' home has been transformed to a spectre of industrialisation that covers the land, as the narrator puts it, with 'all its frowning and dirty ugliness',[11] we become aware of what has been lost and perhaps our minds may turn to what is at stake in our own world – the concept of recovery, as Tolkien understood it, is thus bound up with augury. We are shown the wonder and resplendent natural beauty of an 'enchanted' land and, in gazing into that mirror, we may find new wonder for the green face of our own world.

In a scene from *The Two Towers* Tolkien extends this idea of seeing anew and recovery even to the characters of a secondary world. As Frodo and the Fellowship first enter Lórien and the lands leading to the Golden Wood of Lothlórien, they are made to wear blindfolds as they reach the elven city. The wood elf Haldir removes Frodo's blindfold and Lothlórien is revealed to both Frodo and the reader:

> When his eyes were in turn uncovered, Frodo looked up and caught his breath. They were standing in an open space. To the left stood a great mound, covered with a sward of grass as green as Springtime in the Elder Days. Upon it, as a double crown, grew two circles of trees [...] At the feet of the trees, and all about the green hillsides the grass was studded with small golden flowers shaped like stars. Among them, nodding on slender stalks, were other flowers, white and palest green: they glimmered as a mist amid the rich hue of the grass. Over all the sky was blue, and the sun of the afternoon glowed upon the hill and cast long green shadows beneath the trees.

---

11 Tolkien, *Return*, p.993.

Tolkien's detailed description of the natural magnificence of Lothlórien reaches out beyond the Golden Wood to touch the sky, the sun and even the afternoon in which it is beheld. All natural facets of the world seem to come together to create an idyllic scene. Frodo of course, as a resident of the Shire, has encountered sublime natural beauty before and yet we are told: 'Frodo stood awhile still lost in wonder.'[12] Tolkien's understanding of recovery thus calls for a re-alignment of perception. John Clute and John Grant in *The Encyclopaedia of Fantasy* believe that this may be fantasy's principal function: 'It could be argued that, if fantasy (and debatably the literature of the fantastic as a whole) has a purpose other than to entertain, it is to show readers *how to perceive.*'[13]

It is clear from Tolkien's theory on recovery and the conviction with which he speaks of the realm of the imagination that he believed literature contained the power to effect change in the primary world. Given the breadth of and systematic adherence to green themes in Tolkien's fiction, and his specific allusion to nature with regards his theory on recovery perhaps Tolkien hoped that he, in some small way, could elicit some response in his readers or at least offer an implicit environmentally-themed warning. Indeed Joseph Meeker in *The Comedy of Survival* believed that literature, especially employed in the comic rather than the tragic mode, could aid in humanity's re-embrace of nature. In setting out the premise of his study he addresses some key questions:

> Human beings are the earth's only literary creatures [...] If the creation of literature is an important characteristic of the human species, it should be examined carefully and honestly to discover its influence upon human behaviour and the natural environment – to determine what role, if any it plays in the welfare and survival of mankind and what insights it offers into human relationships with other species and the world around us. Is it an activity which adapts us better to the world or one which estranges us from it? From the unforgiving perspective of evolution and natural selection, does literature contribute more to our survival than it does to our extinction?[14]

As a student and professor of literature, and as any cursory reading of 'On Fairy-stories' shows, Tolkien was very much aware of the tools of literary analysis, and given his views on recovery, he may well have asked himself the questions

---

12 J.R.R. Tolkien, *The Fellowship of the Ring*, London: HarperCollins, 1997, p.341.
13 John Clute & John Grant, *The Encyclopaedia of Fantasy*, London: Orbit, 1997, p.x.
14 Joseph Meeker, *The Comedy of Survival: Studies in Literary Ecology*, New York: Charles Scribner's Sons, 1974, pp.3-4.

Meeker raises above. Indeed, as I have contended, he may have anticipated green studies as a literary discipline. He certainly placed importance upon the imaginative representation of nature in works of literature and took account of a reader's possible reactions.

Although no supporter or exponent of transparent allegory, Tolkien's works nonetheless carry with them the anxieties of the twentieth-century – a time when humanity armed with new machines first began to threaten widespread ecological disaster. These anxieties and their inherent warnings lie just below the surface of Tolkien's fiction, reflected and played out in the plots and sub-plots of his unfolding narratives of machine versus nature, and dominion versus diversity. But it is worth restating that Tolkien's fiction is imbued with a multiplicity of themes and this book focuses on just one. Indeed as Tolkien, himself says '[t]here are other things more grim and terrible to fly from than the noise, stench, ruthlessness, and extravagance of the internal-combustion engine. There are hunger, thirst, poverty, pain, sorrow, injustice, death.'[15]

Moreover I make no attempt to cast Tolkien as an environmentalist who created fiction to impart a message. Rather he was a storyteller and a weaver of myth who imbued his tales with green themes and landscapes under threat – but these environmental aspects of his stories are primarily part of their respective tales. That Isengard becomes an industrialised force and destroys the surrounding forests and lands to feed its regime is part of the story, first and foremost. The reflective symbolism or applicability it has for our world is secondary.

Yet of course, as with any good story, we take something away with us. Tolkien's fiction gives us a moral universe where the freedom of choice to do right or wrong is the narrative driver. This atmosphere of moral dilemma is underlined in a scene when Éomer, in the time of his people's greatest peril, asks Aragorn, 'How shall a man judge what to do in such times?' to which Aragorn replies:

> As ever he has judged [...] Good and ill have not changed since yesteryear; nor are they one thing among Elves and Dwarves and another among Men. It is a man's part to discern them, as much in the Golden Wood as in his own house.[16]

---

15 Tolkien, *Tolkien Reader*, p.83.
16 J.R.R Tolkien, *The Two Towers*, London: HarperCollins, 1997, p.40.

Aragorn's response reaches out from the pages of the story and speaks to all humanity. Indeed his words seem to take account of the relationship between the spheres of imagination and reality – secondary and primary worlds. If we pursue this idea and determine that by 'Elves and Dwarves' Aragorn means fictional characters, and his reference to 'Men' alludes to the human race of the primary world, the statement becomes something like: 'good and evil are constant, that which you see reflected in a fictional world is no different to the evils you yourself face.' Furthermore if we take 'the Golden Wood' to be the realm of the imagination and one's 'own house' to be reality – the statement ends, 'the evils you identify in a fictional world are but reflections of the evils that are all around you in reality.'

Although I have allowed myself some 'poetic licence' in this interpretation of Aragorn's words, the fundamental sense remains. Indeed going one step further and applying this thought to Tolkien's fiction, with 'the Golden Wood' referring to Middle-earth, we must ask if we can see the evils of our own world, of our 'own house', reflected in the crisis of the Third Age and even in his wider work. I contend that we can. Tolkien's fiction holds a mirror up to reality and if we choose to look we may see, amongst other reflections, the environmental crisis facing our own reality.

With this, we are drawn back, not only to W.H. Auden's remark that Tolkien's world of Middle-earth reflects 'the only nature we know, our own' and that as such it should serve as both 'a warning and an inspiration',[17] but also the suggestion I made in the introduction to this book that the Mirror of Galadriel is the most indicative symbol that Tolkien's fiction is itself a mirror in 'the Golden Wood' of the imagination which has the power to show us 'things that were, and things that are, and things that yet may be.'[18] Indeed as Sam looks into Galadriel's Mirror he witnesses environmental devastation just as we see it across Tolkien's tales. But, as we noted above, Tolkien's work provides a moral universe in which there is always hope – and we hear Galadriel tell Sam (just as Tolkien seems to tell us): 'the Mirror shows many things, and not all have yet come to pass. Some never come to be, unless those that behold the visions turn aside from

---

17 W.H. Auden, 'The Hero is a Hobbit' in the *New York Times*, 31ˢᵗ October 1954.
18 Tolkien, *Fellowship*, p.352.

their path to prevent them.'[19] And, if we do see the environmental crisis of our own time reflected in Tolkien's fiction how should we respond? As individuals we have no 'Rings of Power' to destroy (though we may perceive them in the hands of others). Perhaps an answer may be found in the words of Gandalf, Tolkien's master-teacher and guide, who tells Frodo one fine spring morning at Bag End: 'All we have to decide is what to do with the time that is given us.'[20]

Finally, I'd like to end much as I began – with a personal account. Whilst on a visit to Oxford to examine Tolkien manuscripts at the Bodleian Library and give a talk at the Tolkien Society Conference in 2008, I had the great fortune of making the acquaintance of a very charming lady called Diana Willson. During our conversations about Tolkien she told me that her sister, Pamela Chandler, had taken Tolkien's photograph in an official capacity on more than one occasion. Tolkien, it seems, was rather reticent to allow himself to be photographed by interviewers or interested parties arriving without due warning with a photographer in tow. He much preferred to offer such callers an existing picture (only if they insisted that it was absolutely necessary) that had been taken at home by someone with whom he felt at ease. Pamela was one such person. Diana, now aware that I was interested in Tolkien's green themes and his love of nature, relayed one incident to me that her sister Pamela had mentioned involving Tolkien taking time to rescue a seedling that was struggling to grow amid the surrounding concrete. The sincerity of Tolkien's compassion for the well being of the little seedling had moved Pamela to such a degree that she made a note of it in her journal. Diana has very kindly permitted me to offer it here. It is quite a fleeting, unadorned entry which records Pamela's visit with Tolkien and his wife Edith in 1966. She writes: 'As we stepped back into the professor's study, he pointed out a tiny 'beech' seedling just peeping up through the step. He said 'Sad but that one won't be able to grow and must be moved."'[21]

I close my study with this account because it accurately conveys the authenticity of Tolkien's concern for natural phenomena. Even in private moments: away from the grand sweep of his Middle-earth narratives, removed from his letter writing and his theories on the power of imagination, he takes account of the

---

19 Tolkien, *Fellowship*, p.354.
20 Tolkien, *Fellowship*, p.50.
21 Entry sent via email by Diana Willson to Liam Campbell on October 28th 2008.

troubles of a tiny seedling that many others would stamp under their foot in the course of a busy day.

Afterword

Trouble with the Trees

Throughout this study I have drawn correlations and parallels between Tolkien's love of things that grow, his embrace of and concern for the natural world, and the environmental dimension of his fiction. One of the key concerns of this book has been to assert that the green aspects of Tolkien's work, the struggles between nature and machine – between defender and destroyer of the landscape – are reflections of not only the ever-gathering environmental crisis of the primary world, but also Tolkien's own ecological worldview. We recall that Tolkien declared in a letter to the *Daily Telegraph:*

> In all my works I take the part of trees as against all their enemies. Lothlórien is beautiful because there the trees were loved; elsewhere forests are represented as awakening to consciousness of themselves. The Old Forest was hostile to two-legged creatures because of the memory of many injuries. Fangorn Forest was old and beautiful, but at the time of the story tense with hostility because it was threatened by a machine-loving enemy [...] The savage sound of the electric saw is never silent wherever trees are still found growing.[1]

I discussed in chapter one how the contents of this letter (given the allusion to '[i]n all my works' and an 'electric saw') speak of Tolkien's concern for trees (and thus wider environmental issues) in both his fiction and the primary world. Referring to the sentiments expressed in this letter, however, and citing Tolkien's propensity to feature trees across the panorama of his fiction, Verlyn Flieger in 'Taking the Part of Trees: Eco-Conflict in Middle-earth', raises questions about the consistency of Tolkien's adherence to his declared position. Despite the traceable tide of environmental themes in Tolkien's work, and the apparent univocal nature of his green philosophy, Flieger suggests that '[t]he real picture [...] is not that simple' adding 'it is complicated, contradictory, and deserves more scrutiny.'[2] In

---

1 J.R.R.Tolkien, *The Letters of J.R.R. Tolkien*, edited by Humphrey Carpenter, London: HarperCollins, 2006, p.420.
2 Verlyn Flieger, 'Taking the Part of Trees: Eco-Conflict in Middle-earth' in George Clark & Daniel Timmons (eds.), *J.R.R. Tolkien and his Literary Resonances: Views of Middle-earth*, Westport: Greenwood Press, 2000, p.147.

pursuing such scrutiny Flieger's questioning of the uniformity or consistency of Tolkien's pro-tree/pro-environmental position (as represented in his fiction) centres primarily on the hostilities revealed in the interactions between the hobbits and the Old Forest relayed in the narrative of *The Lord of the Rings*. Before engaging with Flieger's commentary on, what she believes is, the contradictory nature of Tolkien's portrayal of these relations in the context of the wider environmental allusions observable in the Third Age, let us first briefly call these hostilities to mind.

Prior to the company led by Frodo even entering the Old Forest, at the outset of the Ring quest, we hear how it is a dark, intimidating and perilous place for the likes of hobbits to venture. Fredegar 'Fatty' Bolger, although not accompanying the party on their onward journey, still reacts with horror as the others resolve to pass the Hedge (the Shire/Old Forest border) and tread the forest's treacherous paths – his response sums up the prevailing hobbit perception of the dark wood: 'I am more afraid of the Old Forest than anything I know about.'[3] It is Merry's knowledge of the history and lore of the forest, as well as his experience of it as an occasional trespasser, however, that provides the most telling insights. As Frodo and company take their first steps into the forest, Fredegar's prophetic, parting warning 'I only hope you will not need rescuing before the day is out'[4] still ringing in their ears, Merry, acting as leader and guide, shares what he knows of the facts and legends concerning what is soon referred to as 'this abominable wood'.[5] Merry, although dismissing 'old bogey-stories' concerning the forest, nonetheless tells the others that 'the trees do not like strangers. They watch you.' He goes on to add '[t]hey do say the trees do actually move, and can surround strangers and hem them in.' It is the passage below, however, and the history recounted by Merry of an incident involving the hobbits and the burning of many trees, that provides the impetus for questions being asked regarding the evenness of Tolkien's representation of what we now term his green themes. Merry offers his travelling companions the following historical account:

---

3 J.R.R.Tolkien, *The Fellowship of the Ring*, London: HarperCollins, 1997, p.105.
4 Tolkien, *Fellowship*, p.107.
5 Tolkien, *Fellowship*, p.109. This comment is, strictly speaking, made by the narrator, although the narrator is reporting the thoughts which are swirling through Frodo's mind as his apprehension for the company's ever more perilous predicament increases.

> In fact long ago [the trees of the Old Forest] attacked the Hedge: they came and planted themselves right by it, and leaned over it. But the hobbits came and cut down hundreds of trees, and made a great bonfire in the Forest, and burned all the ground in a long strip east of the Hedge. After that the trees gave up the attack but they became very unfriendly.[6]

The tree-destroying actions of the hobbits detailed above are, according to Flieger, 'no less than what Saruman's orcs do to Fangorn.'[7] Moreover Flieger asserts that this incident at Buckland must be viewed as only part of a longer history of hostility or war between the hobbits and the Old Forest in which the 'well-ordered and well-farmed countryside',[8] and the agrarian landscape of the Shire has been made possible at the expense of the 'vast forgotten woods'[9] (of which now only the Old Forest remains). The implication being that the hobbits have systematically encroached upon and captured woodland in order to secure the land for themselves. This, Flieger states 'puts [Tolkien's] beloved Shire-folk in this one respect on a par with his orcs.'[10]

The crux of Flieger's point, made with reference to Tom Bombadil's words which describe how the trees are 'filled with a hatred of things that go free upon the earth, gnawing, biting, breaking, hacking, burning'[11] is 'that no matter who is doing the chopping, or for what purpose, the effect on the trees [...] will be the same, and it will be destructive.' In other words the hobbits' burning of hundreds of trees at the Buckland Hedge is, if dispassionately considered or viewed from the perspective of the trees, every bit as malicious as the orc foot soldiers of Saruman laying assault upon the trees of Fangorn in order to feed his war machine. Indeed, in Flieger's view, if we attempt to distinguish between the actions of the hobbits and those of Saruman's orcs on the grounds that the hobbits are defending their border from an encroachment of advancing trees and the orcs are insidiously destroying the trees of Fangorn in the pursuit of war, we are merely 'substitut[ing] motives for results.' This is precisely what Flieger accuses Tolkien of doing in his presentation of both scenarios:

---

6 Tolkien, *Fellowship*, p.108.
7 Flieger, 'Taking the Part of Trees', p.152.
8 Tolkien, 'Prologue' in *Fellowship*, p.17.
9 Tolkien, *Fellowship*, p.127.
10 Flieger, 'Taking the Part of Trees', p.150.
11 Tolkien, *Fellowship*, p.127.

> What we have here is not just an unreconciled contradiction: it is essentially a double standard: the chopping and burning of trees is presented as villainous when done by orcs in Fangorn, but when done by the hobbits in the Old Forest the same activities are not only made acceptable, they are necessary for 'a well-ordered and well-farmed' countryside.[12]

On the face of it Flieger would seem to be making a fair and considered point: objectively viewed, and understood in the context of Tolkien's wider environmental themes, the *purpose* for which trees are being cut down or destroyed in any given instance should be of little import – from the point of view of the trees – a destroyer is a destroyer, plain and simple. If we accept this premise, however, we must open the debate up beyond hobbits and orcs. Indeed if we turn our attention to Tom Bombadil, who is clearly in harmony with the natural world around him and who, as Flieger states 'understands the Old Forest if anyone does',[13] we should note that Bombadil has also created a hedge which keeps out the forest. As he arrives with the hobbits through the forest to his house, we are told that 'suddenly the trees came to an end' and '[t]he eaves of the Forest behind were clipped, and trim as a hedge.' Similarly, like the hobbits' 'well-ordered' lands, Bombadil's house is serviced by a 'well-tended'[14] path and is set in 'a flower garden' with a 'clipped hedge' where '[t]here was no willow-tree to be seen.'[15] Furthermore, although the narrator intimates that Tom's house is made 'of clean stone',[16] we are also told that within, lamps are 'swinging from the beams of the roof.' Presumably these beams are made of wood – if presumptions are questionable, however, there is nothing moot in the narrator's description of 'the table of dark polished wood'[17] which along with chairs and stools adorns Tom's main room. Indeed the likelihood is that Tom himself has been busy in the forest chopping at trees[18] and cutting wood; certainly he has carved out and tended an area that is free of trees and where the Old Forest has been 'hedged' out. Given

---

12 Flieger, 'Taking the Part of Trees', p.153.
13 Flieger, 'Taking the Part of Trees', p.151.
14 Tolkien, *Fellowship*, p.119.
15 Tolkien, *Fellowship*, p.126.
16 Tolkien, *Fellowship*, p.123.
17 Tolkien, *Fellowship*, p.121.
18 Perhaps it could be argued that Tom has not chopped down trees to make his furniture and/or beams but has had such things brought in from other places or given to him by someone like Farmer Cotton (with whom he is friendly). Either way Bombadil is taking part in a process which kills trees in order to facilitate his own comfort.

Flieger's premise we must ask if this spirit of the woods – this evocation of nature itself – who, in Flieger's words, 'understands the Old Forest if anyone does', is viewed by the trees as a destroyer, and if we, as readers, should question *his* orcish tendency of turning living trees into dead wood in order to satisfy a purpose.

The idea of viewing Bombadil, with all his pronounced pro-environmental virtues (discussed in chapter two) as an agent of natural destruction in Middle-earth, or as comparable to orcs in his treatment of forests and trees is plainly a misrepresentation of the character and indeed of Tolkien's work, and yet this is the direction in which Flieger's argument must inevitably lead us. We could, of course, go much further and begin to raise questions about many other characters, given their employment of wood, and ask how such wood was obtained. Where, for example, do the elves get their ready supply of bows and arrows? Or wood for their ornate dwellings? Given the elvish interconnection with nature and the woods they inhabit, do the trees allow the elves to take what they need? That would certainly seem to be the implication – and thus do trees make exceptions with respect to certain tree-destroyers? If this is the case (considered also with respect to Bombadil's use of wood) then even from the perspective of trees, not all chopping or felling of trees is viewed in the same light.

Clearly, to some degree, the circumstance and purpose which lies behind a given character or race's relationship and interaction with wood (and thus trees) must be taken into account. Patrick Curry in the 'Afterword' of *Defending Middle-earth: Tolkien Myth and Modernity* (second edition), in response to Flieger's assertions, offers a defence of the hobbits' actions against the trees of the Old Forest on these grounds:

> It has been suggested (by Verlyn Flieger) that Tolkien was confused, or at least inconsistent, on this subject; that from nature's point of view, there is no difference between, say, the hobbits of Bucklebury cutting back the Old Forest and Saruman turning Fangorn into fuel for his war-furnaces. Flieger also thinks Tolkien shrank from recognizing that civilization is necessarily locked into a war with nature. But this is a misunderstanding in a number of ways. Most obviously, as that example shows, it oddly fails to distinguish limited self-defence (the human right to which, when it is necessary, I do not deny) from gross exploitation finally resulting in complete destruction.

Curry goes on to suggest that Tolkien's presentation of the hobbits' relationship with the Old Forest reflects a more 'sensitive and sustainable use of nature, not for profit but for life',[19] namely *woodmanship*. Certainly I would, in principle, be in agreement with Curry that an inflexible interpretation of Tolkien's portrayal of interactions between 'things that go free upon the earth' and the trees of Middle-earth, which would hang all 'tree-destroyers' on a single hook, is in danger of ignoring the bigger picture and the prevailing climate of widespread environmental devastation that accompanies the rise of the Dark Lord and his servants. For example, can we really separate the onslaught of Saruman and the activities of his orcs at Fangorn from the wider war on nature and the regime being waged by Sauron? This regime, as discussed earlier, seeks to force nature itself into subjection – we recall that Sauron '*torture[s]* and destroy[s] the very hills',[20] and that he has succeeded in turning Mordor into a graveyard where nature is cast out and where nothing grows – certainly not trees. Saruman and his orc soliders are part of the same *premeditated* assault on nature; they are what we might term the engine room of Sauron's regime. Can we really say that the reactive hobbit strategy against the advancing trees at Buckland is on a par with an organised and calculated regime which devastates and subjugates all manifestations of life in its wake, and seeks final suppression of all other wills?

Indeed in terms of this 'bigger picture', Flieger's main contention, as outlined above, is that an orc attack on trees is no different to a hobbit attack and the wider context of the War of the Ring and the regimes of Sauron and Saruman (and thus issues of intentions and purpose) are of little concern to the trees or the sentient elements which represent them. Certainly the hostilities of the trees of the Old Forest and their general 'hatred of things that go free upon the earth, gnawing, biting, breaking, hacking, burning'[21] would seem to bear Flieger's line of argument out. I return to a discussion of these hostilities momentarily. But Flieger also cites Treebeard's remark to Merry and Pippin: 'I am not altogether on anybody's *side* because nobody is altogether on my *side*' as evidence that the trees (or those who speak for them) are unconcerned with

---

19 Patrick Curry, 'Afterword' in *Defending Middle-earth. Tolkien: Myth and Modernity*, 2nd edition, New York: Houghton Mifflin, 2004, p.155.
20 Tolkien, *Fellowship*, p.259; emphasis added.
21 Tolkien, *Fellowship*, p.127.

any notions of a wider context. And yet Treebeard *does* seem to be attentive to the crisis of the age – he states, '[t]here is something very big going on, that I can see.' Moreover he goes on to explicitly connect the fate of trees with the ascendancy of the dark power of Mordor:

> I used to be anxious when the shadow lay on Mirkwood, but when it removed to Mordor, I did not trouble for a while: Mordor is a long way away. But it seems that the wind is setting East, and the withering of all woods may be drawing near.[22]

Treebeard offers a direct link here between the final destruction of 'all woods' and the mechanistically-themed, insular, self-serving worldview and desire for power (at any cost) that is represented by the rise of the Dark Lord and those who serve him – and not the cumulative hostilities between 'things that walk free upon the earth' and their environments. Indeed it is worthy of note that Treebeard specifically states that the 'withering' or passing of the woods 'may be *drawing near*' (emphasis added). In other words such devastation may be imminent, and thus a casualty or a consequence of Sauron's (and by extension Saruman's) regime in the Third Age, rather than the end game of some long-drawn-out inevitability. Flieger, and later James G. Davis (in 'Showing Saruman as Faber: Tolkien and Peter Jackson'), however, both cite Treebeard's impassioned words to Pippin and Merry, as they and the ents begin their march on Isengard,

> 'Of course it is likely enough, my friends,' [Treebeard] said slowly, 'likely enough that we are going to our doom: the last march of the Ents. But if we stayed at home and did nothing, doom would find us anyway, sooner or later. That thought has long been growing in our hearts; and that is why we are marching now'[23]

as an acknowledgement from the ent that he is resigned to the fact that 'the withering of all woods' is unavoidable and inevitable in a more general sense. In other words Treebeard's remarks reference that, as Flieger puts it, '[t]o make a place for itself, humankind will tame a wilderness whose destruction and eventual eradication, however gradual, is at once an inevitable consequence and an irreparable loss.'[24] The 'humankind' Flieger refers to, would of course

---

22 J.R.R.Tolkien, *The Two Towers*, London: HarperCollins, 1997, p.461.
23 Tolkien, *Two Towers*, p.475.
24 Flieger, 'Taking the Part of Trees', pp.155-156.

be represented in Tolkien's fiction by *any* aggressor against trees or nature (including hobbits, men and dwarves) and not just the forces of Mordor and Isengard. Davis, citing and concurring with Flieger's sentiments adds '[t]he most reliable authority here is Treebeard, who knows that the ents and Fangorn are doomed.'[25] Flieger and Davis' interpretation of the significance of Treebeard's words suggests that his resignation to doom relates as much to the destruction of the trees of the Old Forest by the hobbits (and all other actions against trees) as it does to Saruman's assault on Fangorn – and as such it is a commentary on the general progressive destruction of woodland regions that must eventually consume all before it. A closer analysis of Treebeard's words and their context, I believe, reveals that this may not necessarily be the case.

Firstly we should acknowledge that the ents are marching directly on Isengard, and Treebeard has alluded to 'the withering of all woods' *expressly* in relation to Mordor. These two points of reference both underline a specific focus on the dark forces which have risen in the Third Age. Secondly Treebeard's comment regarding their march to war: 'it is likely enough […] that we are going to our doom […] But if we stayed at home and did nothing, doom would find us anyway' suggests that, in challenging Saruman, the ents are doing *something* to resist that which threatens them. Moreover Treebeard makes this remark in the context of 'the last march of the Ents' – it is *their* (the ents') fate he is referring to as opposed to the general fate of trees,[26] although the ent resistance clearly seeks to counter the regime of Saruman which, as Treebeard points out, has left 'wastes of stump and bramble where once there were singing groves.'[27] The words 'it is likely […] we are going to our doom' refers to the very real possibility that the ents could be, as Treebeard muses, 'hewn down, or destroyed by fire or blast of *sorcery*' (emphasis added) at Isengard. But, as he indicates, *if they fail to take action* 'doom would find [them]' – the ents are thus marching to try to make a difference in an age when dark forces have risen and threaten the trees and the very ecology of Middle-earth. More directly, if Treebeard and the ents believed that their (and

---

25 James G. Davis, 'Showing Saruman as Faber: Tolkien and Peter Jackson' in *Tolkien Studies* 5 (2008), p.65.
26 This allusion to the doom or final fate of ents also draws in the question of the disappearance of the entwives and the fact that, as a species unable to give life to new young in the natural manner, the ents are facing extinction as a race.
27 Tolkien, *Two Towers*, p.563.

the trees') doom would be delivered from the environmentally destructive and collective activities of hobbits, men and dwarves as much as it would from the regimes of Saruman (and Sauron), how could it possibly help their situation to march on Isengard and aid one side of the opposing forces in the War of the Ring over another?[28] Indeed Treebeard, referring to the possibility that the ents could meet their end in battle at Isengard, goes on to add 'we may help the other peoples before we pass away.'[29] Isn't this taking sides? Indeed we should ask why the ents would *want* to 'help the other peoples' if they are unconcerned with the wider context of the war or if they believed victory for either side would still bring ruination to the trees?

Also, when speaking of Saruman and his destruction of Fangorn, Treebeard refers to the wizard as 'a black traitor'.[30] And although this may refer to the fact that Saruman once walked in peace, with the leave of Treebeard, in Fangorn, it also seems to allude to the wider issue of Saruman's defection to the will of Mordor and the abandonment of his duty as an Istari wizard.[31] Indeed as Treebeard voices his contempt for the devastating effect Saruman's regime has had for the trees of Fangorn, he also takes account of what is driving the wizard's ecologically corrosive activity: 'I now understand what he is up to. He is plotting to become a Power. He has a mind of metal and wheels; and he does not care for growing things.'[32] All of Treebeard's remarks here refer to a state of mind and an underlying purpose. Saruman's desire to attain power and mastery over other wills, his predilection for machines, and his lack of regard for natural things (not just trees) are all taken into account in Treebeard's attempt to 'understand what [Saruman] is up to.' Also of note is that, in relation to the ents' march on Isengard, Treebeard takes further account of how such actions may aid the wider resistance against the

---

28 Perhaps it could be argued that the ents are seeking revenge on Saruman in particular for his 'crimes' against Fangorn – and are thus not, strictly speaking taking sides. This, however, does not allow for Treebeard's sentiment that he hoped the ent attack would 'help the other peoples.' Also Treebeard's words to Pippin and Merry regarding forces like those awake in the Old Forest, express a view that revenge constitutes a kind of evil and is evidence of a bad heart (Tolkien, *Two Towers*, p.457). It seems unlikely that with such a view Treebeard would march on Isengard primarily out of revenge.
29 Tolkien, *Two Towers*, p.475.
30 Tolkien, *Two Towers*, p.462.
31 In relation to Saruman's destructive regime against Fangorn, Treebeard states 'Wizards ought to know better' (Tolkien, *Two Towers*, p.474). In contrast to this, he refers to Gandalf as 'the only wizard that really cares about trees' (Tolkien, *Two Towers*, p.455).
32 Tolkien, *Two Towers*, p.462.

combined threat of Barad-dûr and Orthanc: '[i]f Saruman is not checked' he warns 'Rohan and Gondor will have an enemy behind as well as in front.'[33] Later, offering an insight into why the Entmoot has resulted in a march on Saruman's stronghold at Isengard, Treebeard explains 'it is the orc-work, the wanton hewing [of trees] without even the bad excuse of feeding the fires that has angered us.'[34] Here again there is a suggestion that the reasons *why* trees are being felled are taken into account. Indeed we recall that this sentiment is echoed in indignation by a hobbit (Farmer Cotton) in relation to Saruman/Sharkey's felling of trees in the Shire: '[t]here's no longer even any bad sense in it. They cut down trees and let 'em lie.'[35]

Given all of the above, we can say that qualitative judgements are being made by Treebeard, not only in relation to the underlying motives which may be driving the destruction of trees, but also in relation to the wider context of the ecological crisis that accompanies the struggles of the Third Age. So, in this analysis, is Treebeard lying when he says that he is 'not altogether on anybody's *side*'? Is it perhaps a contradiction in Tolkien's narrative? Well, no, neither is the case! The inclusion of the word 'altogether' removes the absolute exclusion of leaning to one side over another,[36] and although Treebeard acknowledges that no one, 'not even Elves', prioritise the fate of trees ('no one is altogether on my *side*'[37]), he is nonetheless clearly in alignment with the peoples of the Fellowship. The implication is that Treebeard has, to a degree, accepted that tree felling is inevitable – or at least he views the tree-felling activities of the free peoples of Middle-earth as a lesser evil. It is the needless and gratuitous felling of trees at the hands of an organised regime that has aroused so much anger and a stirring of the ents to war.

Returning to the question of the hostilities between the Old Forest and the hobbits (and all 'things that go free upon the earth'[38]), it is very clear from

---

33 Tolkien, *Two Towers*, p.463.
34 Tolkien, *Two Towers*, p.474.
35 J.R.R.Tolkien, *The Return of the King*, London: HarperCollins, 1997, p.989.
36 We should note also that this remark is made before the Entmoot, when Treebeard is not fully committed to involving the ents in what he views as affairs which 'mostly concern Elves and Men' (Tolkien, *Two Towers*, p.461). In the end game, however, the ents, in attacking Saruman, and stating they wish to 'help the other peoples' (Tolkien, *Two Towers*, p.475) are making a judgement as to who represents the greater environmental threat to trees.
37 Tolkien, *Two Towers*, p.461.
38 Tolkien, *Fellowship*, p.127.

Tolkien's narrative, and his commentary: '[t]he Old Forest was hostile to two-legged creatures because of the memory of many injuries',[39] that this forest cares little for the motives that may lie behind the destruction of trees. Here any destroyer of trees is an enemy and a legitimate target. As stated earlier this would seem to bear out Flieger's argument that there is no discrimination to be made, in terms of the perspective of the trees of the Old Forest, between one tree-destroyer and another. Strictly speaking, however, there is no evidence that this *is* the overriding perspective of the trees in the Old Forest. Bombadil's account[40] of the history and prevailing mood of the forest reveals that, although many of the trees were indeed filled with malice, Old Man Willow or 'the Great Willow' whose 'heart was rotten' was the predominant will and power, influencing and directing the other trees. We are told that he 'was cunning and a master of winds, and his song and thought ran through the woods [...] till it had under its dominion nearly all of the trees of the Forest.'[41] Indeed we later hear Treebeard say that trees such as Old Man Willow 'have bad hearts' and that this has '[n]othing to do with their woods.'[42] So the will of the Old Forest is directed by a single force categorised by both Treebeard and Bombadil as essentially malicious and thus unjustified in its arbitrary attacks on 'all things that go free upon the earth.' Moreover it is interesting to note that Treebeard, who as an ent is a protector of trees over other life forms, tells Merry that he and the other ents, if aware of the presence of a bad-hearted tree or 'dangerous parts' in a wood 'do what [they] can' to ' keep off strangers and the foolhardy.'[43] In other words they actively seek to counter the ill-will of trees such as Old Man Willow.

---

39 Tolkien, *Letters*, p.420.
40 Flieger states that Bombadil's (and thus Tolkien's) words to Frodo and company about the Old Forest and Old Man Willow are contradictory in that they first relay that Old Man Willow is consumed by hatred before immediately offering 'a legitimate reason for these dark thoughts, this hatred' (Flieger, 'Taking the Part of Trees', p.151), namely the destructive tendencies of 'things that go free upon the earth.' It should be noted, however, that this commentary is being supplied by Tom Bombadil who (as discussed in chapter two) seeks always to understand 'the other'. In other words he offers his account from both sides as part of the nature of his being.
41 Tolkien, *Fellowship*, p.128.
42 When making these remarks Treebeard specifically answers a question by Merry as to whether he is referring to the Old Forest – he answers 'Aye, aye, something like, but much worse. I do not doubt there is some shadow of the Great Darkness lying there still' (Tolkien, *Two Towers*, p.457). Indeed, although he seems to have roots in the ground, it is extremely plausible that Old Man Willow is a huorn – a tree-like being neither fully tree nor ent. Often the huorns were filled with great malice which they directed at tree-destroyers, particularly orcs. They took part in the assault on Isengard and the Battle of the Hornburg, but were under the direction of the ents.
43 Tolkien, *Two Towers*, p.457.

From the tree perspective of Treebeard then, the Old Forest's (more precisely Old Man Willow's) attack on Frodo and company (although the ent – and indeed Bombadil – understand the history feeding such an attack) is unjustified and viewed as an act of malice. The march on Isengard and the counter-attack on the orcs and Saruman, however, after due consideration at the Entmoot, is, in Treebeard's eyes, warranted and legitimate.

Tolkien's presentation of the hobbit hostilities with the Old Forest is, in my view, perhaps best understood, not as a parallel and (from an ecocritical perspective) contradictory version of the persistent orc attack on Fangorn, but rather a representation of what Joseph Meeker terms 'a ritual renewal of biological warfare'[44] between differing aspects of natural existence. The harsh reality is that the hobbits need land that is suitable for their survival. They need land that can be utilised for farming and adapted for living and the advance of the trees of the Old Forest represented a challenge to that, so the hobbits reacted. The extent and severity of their reaction is, however, a question of environmental ethics, and a representation of the balance between wilderness and civilization. And, although I have argued that the hobbit reaction is not analogous with the orc attacks, I believe, in terms of environmental ethics, their actions are certainly questionable – though many have been all too ready to absolve them of any wrongdoing.

Indeed whilst, as stated earlier, I agree, in principle, with Curry's defence of the hobbits' actions (understood in relation to the orc attack on Fangorn) I don't necessarily agree that the terms he uses to express what the hobbits *actually do* to the trees of the Old Forest (and the associated implication of the terms) are in keeping with the extent of their response to the perceived threat. Curry's employment of the phrase, '*limited* self-defence' (emphasis added) and the term 'woodsmanship' to account for (amongst other things) the cutting down and subsequent burning of *hundreds* of trees in a giant bonfire (set alight *in* the forest) hardly seems appropriate. It seems even less so when we consider that the provocation for this extreme hobbit reaction was an attack on the Hedge from some trees that, in Merry's words, 'came and planted themselves right

---

44 Joseph Meeker, *The Comedy of Survival: Studies in Literary Ecology*, New York: Charles Scribner's Sons, 1974, p.24.

by it, and leaned over it.'⁴⁵ Curry's rather lenient interpretation of the hobbits' actions and his association of these actions with 'human rights',⁴⁶ effectively absolves the hobbits of any ecological indiscretion and fails to adequately account for what would seem to be a gross overreaction and a large scale attack on the forest.⁴⁷ Although I make distinctions between the hobbits' move to reclaim and protect their borders and the orc participation in a regime that seeks total dominion over the natural world, there is no denying that what the hobbits do to the Old Forest is ecologically destructive. It is perhaps too tempting to become beguiled by the overriding depiction of hobbits as a race that is at one with nature, or as Flieger puts it '[i]t is easy to buy this vision of an idyllic rural world and an ecologically responsible species.'⁴⁸ In this I agree. Indeed we should note that after the hobbits cut down hundreds of trees, rather than attempt to use the wood in any constructive way, they elect to burn it as a warning to the remaining trees – risking the entire forest.

Davis likewise suggests that Curry (and others such as Dickerson and Evans) 'all are too eager to dismiss obvious problems between the hobbits and the Old Forest in order to portray the Shire as Tolkien's example of a perfect relationship with the environment.'⁴⁹ Although I concur with the underlying principle of Davis' sentiment (even if accusing Curry et al. of dismissing problems with hobbits is a little unfair) we should recall that Tolkien never intended hobbits to be 'perfect', or an example of a flawless society in any sense. '[H]obbits' he writes in 1954 'are not a Utopian vision, or recommended as an ideal in their own or any age.'⁵⁰ This, of course, extends, not only to the particulars of their society and their predominantly closed attitude to the wider world (discussed

---

45 Tolkien, *Fellowship*, p.108.
46 Curry, 'Afterword' in *Defending Middle-earth*, p.155.
47 One wonders if the hobbit reaction to the trees has been fuelled, in part, by the evil reputation of the Old Forest and the kind of 'old bogey stories' mentioned by Merry and feared by Fredegar Bolger – leading the hobbits to face the advancing trees like a Middle-earth version of villagers with torches marching to destroy the monster in their midst. Davis, however, asserts that the hobbits, in their severity, are like Saruman, attempting to establish mastery over the forest: 'the hobbits are making sure the Old Forest remains submissive […] [t]he burning of hundreds of trees in order to put the Old Forest back into its place is domination' (Davis, 'Showing Saruman as Faber', p.64). Indeed as discussed in the main text, I concur that the hobbits were exercising a measure of dominance over the Forest, but would qualify that by arguing it is more representative of a desire to protect themselves from a perceived threat than any notion of mastery or self-aggrandisement.
48 Flieger, 'Taking the Part of Trees', p.150.
49 Davis, 'Showing Saruman as Faber', p.64.
50 Tolkien, *Letters*, p.197.

in chapter five), but also to their environmental ethics. Indeed the incident at Buckland Hedge demonstrates that their version of environmentalism is far from ideal. Their parochial outlook prevents them from fully understanding the plight of others or from seeing things from a perspective other than their own. We recall Fredegar Bolger's words to the other hobbits 'I am more afraid of the Old Forest than anything I know about.' The narrator follows this declaration by adding 'Fatty Bolger had no desire to leave the Shire, nor to see what lay outside it.'[51] Indeed it is only by leaving the Shire that Frodo and company gain new perspectives on the world. Before meeting Tom Bombadil in the Old Forest they are less than sensitive to the woes of trees. As an act of bravado Frodo sings a song about the demise of the woods and Merry, although warning him of the dangers of singing the song whilst in the forest, adds '[w]ait till we get to the edge, and then we'll turn and give them a rousing chorus.'[52] When the hobbits fall in with Bombadil, however, he, in a very real sense, begins their education in environmental ethics. We recall that:

> [Bombadil] told them tales of bees and flowers, the ways of trees, and the strange creatures of the Forest, about the evil things and good things, things friendly and unfriendly, cruel things and kind things, and secrets hidden under the brambles. As they listened, they began to understand the lives of the Forest, apart from themselves, indeed to feel themselves as the strangers where all other things were at home.[53]

Note that as Bombadil explains to the hobbits 'lives [...] apart from their own' the narrator makes it clear that 'they began to understand.' This understanding continues as the hobbits experience the broken landscapes of Mordor (Frodo and Sam) and Isengard (Merry and Pippin) and witness, through their interactions with Gandalf, Treebeard, Quickbeam, Galadriel and others, what is at stake in the reckless destruction of the natural world. And, of course, this is why they react as they do as they return home in 'The Scouring of the Shire' episode to an industrial wasteland and uprooted trees. Indeed one could almost say that the hobbits have come full circle in that, by the time they reach the end of their adventures in *The Lord of the Rings*, they are not burning or chopping trees, they are in anguish over their loss:

---

51 Tolkien, *Fellowship*, p.105.
52 Tolkien, *Fellowship*, p.110.
53 Tolkien, *Fellowship*, p.127.

'[t]he trees were the worst loss and damage [...] and Sam grieved over this more than anything else', and they are planting and nurturing them: 'Sam planted saplings in all the places where specially beautiful or beloved trees had been destroyed [...] He went up and down the Shire in this labour.'[54]

What Curry, Dickerson and Evans, Flieger and Davis fail to fully acknowledge or represent in their discussions of hobbits, is that the hobbits are a people who are not stagnated in their attitudes to nature (like the orcs), but rather they are a people who are waking up to the concerns of other life forces and their *own* responsibility to Middle-earth. We, as readers, see this change, this awakening most vitally through the combined adventures of those such as Frodo, Sam, Pippin and Merry.

Although Old Man Willow may well be a huorn – a tree-like being rather than a tree – Flieger may be more right than wrong when she points out that 'the first real villain to be met with in *LR* is a tree' (abbreviation in original)[55] and thus Tolkien, in his presentation of Old Man Willow in particular, is inaccurate when he states 'in all my works I take the part of trees against all their enemies.'[56] But the overall consistency of the environmental dimension of his work is not compromised. In Tolkien's presentation of the hobbit interactions with the Old Forest, in relation to the orc attacks on Fangorn, we have not an 'unreconcilable contradiction'[57] in the overall presentation of Tolkien's green themes, but a reflection of the diversity and complexity *of* those themes. In his portrayals of the individual personalities and interactions of hobbits, forests, trees, wizards, elves, orcs and men, Tolkien offers us what Bombadil offers Frodo and the company of hobbits: tales of 'evil things and good things, things

---

54 Tolkien, *Return*, pp.999-1000.
55 Flieger discounts the Black Riders in this assertion since 'at this point in the narrative we have not met, but only seen and heard them' (Flieger, 'Taking the Part of Trees', p.148). Indeed she is correct to classify Old Man Willow as a villain since the reader, by virtue of the narrative design, feels an association and sympathy with the hobbits. And as Old Man Willow attempts to kill the hobbits: holding Frodo under water with a tree-root, enclosing Pippin and half-enclosing Merry in his trunk, he is just as much an enemy as the goblins who drag Bilbo and the company of dwarves through a crack at the back of a cave high on the Misty Mountains in *The Hobbit*, threatening to end their quest there and then.
56 Tolkien, *Letters*, p.420.
57 Flieger, 'Taking the Part of Trees', p.150.

friendly and unfriendly, cruel things and kind things, and secrets hidden under the brambles.'[58]

Finally, although this afterword has been concerned primarily with addressing issues raised by Flieger and others, regarding the consistency of Tolkien's presentation of the tree-destroying activities of hobbits and orcs, in terms of an apparent contradiction in the evenness of Tolkien's presentation of green themes, an altogether more striking episode in *The Lord of the Rings* involves one of his most environmentally positive characters – Gandalf. In the chapter 'A Journey in the Dark', the Fellowship, unable to pass over the snow covered mountain of Caradhras, set up camp on their way to Moria. Here, as night falls, they are assailed by a host of Wargs, and what Gandalf later calls 'no ordinary wolves'. In the ensuing battle Gandalf throws a burning branch from the camp fire into the air and, with an incantation in *Sindarin* elvish,[59] causes the flame to burn 'with a sudden white radiance'. The narrator then tells us: '[t]here was a roar and a crackle, and the tree above him burst into a leaf and bloom of blinding flame. The fire leapt from tree-top to tree-top. The whole hill was crowned with dazzling light.' The tree fire causes the wolf enemy to flee and the Fellowship are saved – we are subsequently told: '[s]lowly the fire died till nothing was left but falling ash and sparks; a bitter smoke curled above the burned tree-stumps [...] No trace of the fight remained but the charred trees and the arrows of Legolas lying on the hill-top.'[60]

Gandalf, it would seem, has set a large number of trees on fire, inflicting severe ecological damage to a tree-lined hill in order to secure his own and the Fellowship's safety – this from a character who states that his role in Middle-earth is to care for 'that [which] can still grow fair or bear fruit and flower.'[61]

This, however, in the same way that the hobbit burning of trees in the Old Forest is not, in my view, an inconsistency in Tolkien's presentation of the developing environmental sensibilities of hobbits, is not a contradiction in Tolkien's portrayal

---

58 Tolkien, *Fellowship*, p.127.
59 The incantation uttered by Gandalf is '*Nuar an edraith ammen! Naur dan i nqaurhoth!*' (Tolkien, *Fellowship*, p.291) which translates as 'Fire be for saving of us! Fire against the werewolf-host!' The reference to werewolf is consistent with Gandalf's remarks that these are 'no ordinary wolves', suggesting the wolves are supernatural and driven by a dark force.
60 Tolkien, *Fellowship*, p.291.
61 Tolkien, *Return*, p.742.

of Gandalf as a paragon of environmental ethics – nor is it an abandonment of Gandalf's own declared purpose and role in Middle-earth. As discussed in chapter three, Gandalf's role in Middle-earth is to oppose Sauron and the dark forces which have come to prominence in the Third Age, in the main, by stirring up native resistance against this menace. Gandalf is aware that all of creation, all forms of life must carry a burden of sacrifice in resisting the war on nature and the evil that threatens the world. In the same manner as he looks to those such as the hobbits for personal sacrifice, Gandalf, in necessity, must also call on the aid of eagles (Gwaihir), horses (Shadowfax) and, in the above scene, even trees, when danger arrives in the form of 'no ordinary wolves' (the inference being that these wolves are part of Sauron's regime). As previously noted (and underlined by Tolkien's own words on the matter[62]) Gandalf is reluctant to use his powers in anger and, as is the case with these 'werewolves', his magic is almost always set against other supernatural forces. No doubt faced with such a supernatural host of enemies, and without due cover or protection, Gandalf would have believed he had no choice but to call on his fire and the trees for assistance in order to defeat the host and advance the critical quest of the Fellowship and Ringbearer.

What is worthy of note, in terms of the scene above, is that Gandalf does not actually set the trees alight. The narrator emphasises that 'the tree above him burst into a leaf and bloom of blinding flame' and this spreads to the other trees. There is unquestionably a magic of sorts present in Gandalf's actions, but there is also a suggestion in the passage that the trees themselves sacrificially play a part in this flaming process as the Fellowship meets a point of crisis and Gandalf calls out for assistance. Certainly the phrase 'a leaf and bloom of blinding flame' is suggestive of natural power and the intrinsic energy of trees. Indeed we recall Michael N. Stanton's suggestion that Gandalf's magic 'consist[s] of using language as a tool to gather and concentrate and focus the ambient energies of nature' and that what we understand as Gandalf's magic may actually have its origins in 'a powerful sympathy with nature'[63] – in this case the coming together of the flame of Gandalf (who, we should recall, is referred

---

62 Tolkien, *Letters*, p.200.
63 Michael N. Stanton, *Hobbits, Elves and Wizards: Exploring the Wonders and Worlds of J.R.R. Tolkien's The Lord of the Rings*, New York: Palgrave Macmillan, 2002, p.47.

to by Treebeard as 'the only wizard that really cares about trees'[64]) and the 'leaf and bloom' that represents the natural energy of the trees themselves.

Whether we believe that the trees sacrificially come to the aid of the Fellowship or not, the trees here, like Frodo, Treebeard, Boromir, Théoden, the elves and even Gandalf himself, must, in a land where nature is at once so vibrantly alive and so under threat, play their part and carry some of the burden that comes with a unified resistance against the forces of darkness.[65]

---

64 Tolkien, *Two Towers*, p.455.
65 It is perhaps worth noting that on many occasions in the struggle against the forces of the Dark Lord, natural energy and phenomena, sometimes in harmony with benign magic, come to the aid of the Free Peoples of Middle-earth. One need only recall how the waters of the river at the Ford in Rivendell, in harmony with the enchantments of Elrond and Gandalf, rise in flood to see off the Ringwraiths that are in pursuit of an injured Frodo. Gandalf later tells Frodo that the river 'will rise in anger when [Elrond] has great need to bar the Ford' (Tolkien, *Fellowship*, p.218).

Bibliography

Works by J.R.R. Tolkien

Tolkien, John Ronald Reuel, *The Silmarillion*, edited by Christopher Tolkien, London: Unwin, 1977.

The Hobbit, 1st edition 1937, 4th edition 1981, London: HarperCollins, 1997.

The Lord of the Rings: The Fellowship of the Ring, 1st edition 1954, 2nd edition, revised impression, London: HarperCollins, 1997.

The Lord of the Rings: The Two Towers, 1st edition 1954, 2nd edition, revised impression, London: HarperCollins, 1997.

The Lord of the Rings: The Return of the King, 1st edition 1955, 2nd edition, revised impression, London: HarperCollins, 1997.

Unfinished Tales of Númenor and Middle-earth, edited by Christopher Tolkien, first published 1980, London: HarperCollins, 1998.

The Book of Lost Tales, Part One, The History of Middle-earth vol. 1, edited by Christopher Tolkien, first published 1983, London: HarperCollins, 2002.

The Book of Lost Tales, Part Two, The History of Middle-earth vol. 2, edited by Christopher Tolkien, London: George Allen & Unwin, 1984.

The Lays of Beleriand, The History of Middle-earth vol. 3, edited by Christopher Tolkien, first published 1985, London: HarperCollins, 2002.

The Treason of Isengard, The History of Middle-earth vol. 7, edited by Christopher Tolkien, first published 1989, London: HarperCollins, 1993.

The War of the Ring, The History of Middle-earth vol. 8, edited by Christopher Tolkien, first published 1990, London: HarperCollins, 1997.

Sauron Defeated, The History of Middle-earth vol. 9, edited by Christopher Tolkien, first published 1992, London: HarperCollins, 2002.

Morgoth's Ring: The Later Silmarillion The History of Middle-earth vol. 10, edited by Christopher Tolkien, first published 1993, London: HarperCollins, 2002.

The Peoples of Middle-earth, The History of Middle-earth vol. 12, edited by Christopher Tolkien, first published 1996, London: HarperCollins, 1997.

The Children of Húrin, edited by Christopher Tolkien, London: HarperCollins, 2007.

Smith of Wootton Major, edited by Verlyn FLIEGER, first published 1967, London: HarperCollins, 2005.

The Letters of J.R.R. Tolkien, edited by Humphrey CARPENTER, first published 1981, revised edition, London: HarperCollins, 2006.

The Monsters and the Critics and Other Essays, edited by Christopher TOLKIEN, first published 1984, London: HarperCollins, 1997.

The Tolkien Reader, New York: Ballantine, 1966.

Tree and Leaf, London: Unwin, 1964.

& Eric Valentine GORDON (eds.), *Sir Gawain and the Green Knight*, 1st edition 1925, 2nd edition revised by Norman DAVIES, Oxford: Oxford University Press, 1967.

Secondary Literature

ANDERSON, William, *Green Man: The Archetype of Our Oneness with the Earth*, San Francisco: HarperSanFrancisco, 1990.

ARCHER, Mary D. & James BARBER (eds.), *Molecular to Global Photosynthesis*, London: Imperial College Press, 2004.

ASIMOV, Isaac, *Magic: The Final Fantasy Collection*, New York: HarperPrism, 1996.

ATTFIELD, Robin, *Environmental Ethics. An Overview for the Twenty-First Century*, Cambridge: Polity Press, 2003.

AUDEN, Wystan H., 'The Hero is a Hobbit' in the *New York Times*, 31st October 1954.

'At the End of the Quest, Victory' in the *New York Times*, 22nd January 1956.

The Dyer's Hand and other Essays, New York: Vintage Books, 1968.

BACHMANN, Dieter, 'Words for Magic: *goetia*, *gûl* and *lúth*' in *Myth and Magic. Art According to the Inklings*, edited by Eduardo SEGURA & Thomas HONEGGER, Cormarë Series 14, Zurich and Berne: Walking Tree Publishers, 2007, pp. 47-55.

BAKER, David, 'The Pastoral: First and Last Things' in *Southern Review* 42.4 (2006), pp. 779-87.

BARSAM, Ara Paul, *Reverence for Life: Albert Schweitzer's Great Contribution to Ethical Thought*, Oxford: Oxford University Press, 2008.

BASSHAM, Gregory & Eric BRONSON (eds.), *The Lord of the Rings and Philosophy: One Book to Rule Them All*, Chicago and La Salle, Illinois: Open Court, 2003.

BATE, Jonathan, *The Song of the Earth,* London: Picador, 2000.

BAUCKHAM, Richard, *God and the Crisis of Freedom: Biblical and Contemporary Perspectives*, Louisville: Westminster John Knox Press, 2002.

BENVENUTO, Maria Raffaella, 'From *Beowulf* to the Balrogs: The Roots of Fantastic Horror in *The Lord of the Rings*' in *The Mirror Crack'd: Fear and Horror in JRR Tolkien's Major Works*, edited by Lynn FOREST-HILL, Newcastle upon Tyne: Cambridge Scholars Publishing, 2008, pp. 5-14.

BOOKCHIN, Murray, 'Toward an Ecological Society' in *Environmentalism: Critical Concepts,* edited by David PEPPER, Frank WEBSTER & George REVILL, New York and London: Routledge, 2003, pp. 31-41.

BOYENS, Philippa, 'The Appendices Part 3: From Book to Script: Finding the Story', *The Lord of the Rings: The Two Towers*, Dir. Peter JACKSON, DVD Extended Version: New Line Cinema, 2003.

BRABAZON, James, *Albert Schweitzer: A Biography*, 2nd edition, Syracuse: Syracuse University Press, 2000.

BRANCH, Michael P. & Scott SLOVIC (eds.), *The ISLE Reader: Ecocriticism, 1993-2003*, Athens and London: University of Georgia Press, 2003.

BURNS, Marjorie, 'Gandalf and Odin' in *Tolkien's Legendarium: Essays on the History of Middle-earth*, edited by Verlyn FLIEGER & Carl F. HOSTETTER, Westport, Connecticut: Greenwood Press, 2000, pp. 219-31.

Perilous Realms: Celtic and Norse in Tolkien's Middle-earth, Toronto: University of Toronto Press, 2005.

CALDECOTT, Stratford, *Secret Fire: The Spiritual Vision of J.R.R. Tolkien*, London: Darton, Longman & Todd, 2003.

CAMPBELL, Joseph, *The Hero with a Thousand Faces*, Princeton: Princeton University Press, 2004.

CAREY, John, 'Hobbit-forming: A Review of Humphrey Carpenter *J.R.R. Tolkien: A Biography*' in *The Listener* 97, 12th May 1977.

CARPENTER, Humphrey, *J.R.R. Tolkien: A Biography*, London: George Allen & Unwin, 1977.

The Inklings. C.S. Lewis, J.R.R. Tolkien, Charles Williams, and Their Friends, London: Allen & Unwin, 1978.

CARSON, Rachel, *Silent Spring*, London: Penguin, 2000.

CHANCE, Jane (ed.), *Tolkien's Art: A Mythology for England*, Lexington, Kentucky: University Press of Kentucky, 2001.

Tolkien the Medievalist, London and New York: Routledge, 2003.

& Alfred K. SIEWERS (eds.), *Tolkien's Modern Middle Ages*, New York: Palgrave Macmillan, 2005.

CHAPMAN, Jenny L. & Michael J. REISS, *Ecology: Principles and Applications*, 2nd edition, Cambridge: Cambridge University Press, 1999.

CLARK, George, 'J.R.R. Tolkien and the True Hero' in *J.R.R. Tolkien and his Literary Resonances: Views of Middle-earth*, edited by George CLARK & Daniel TIMMONS, Westport, Connecticut: Greenwood Press, 2000, pp. 39-51.

& Daniel TIMMONS (eds.), *J.R.R. Tolkien and his Literary Resonances: Views of Middle-earth*, Westport, Connecticut: Greenwood Press, 2000.

CLUTE, John & John GRANT, *The Encyclopaedia of Fantasy*, London: Orbit, 1997.

COMMONER, Barry, *The Closing Circle: Confronting the Environmental Crisis*, London: Cape, 1972.

Making Peace with the Planet, London: Gollancz, 1990.

COUPE, Laurence (ed.), *The Green Studies Reader: From Romanticism to Ecocriticism*, London: Routledge, 2000.

CROFT, Janet Brennan, 'Farmer Giles of Ham' in *J.R.R. Tolkien Encyclopedia: Scholarship and Critical Assessment*, edited by Michael D.C. DROUT, New York: Routledge, 2006, pp. 197-98.

CROWE, David M., *Oskar Schindler: The Untold Account of His Life, Wartime Activities, and the True Story Behind 'The List'*, Cambridge, Massachusetts: Westview Press, 2004.

CURRAN, Bob & Ian DANIELS, *Walking with the Green Man: Father of the Forest, Spirit of Nature*, Franklin Lakes, New Jersey: Career Press, 2007.

CURRY, Patrick, *Defending Middle-earth. Tolkien: Myth and Modernity*, London: HarperCollins, 1998.

'Magic vs. Enchantment' in *Journal of Contemporary Religion* 14.3 (1999), pp. 401-12.

'Afterword' in *Defending Middle-earth. Tolkien: Myth and Modernity*, 2nd edition, New York: Houghton Mifflin, 2004, pp. 151-59.

'Iron Crown, Iron Cage: Tolkien and Weber on Modernity and Enchantment' in *Myth and Magic. Art According to the Inklings*, edited by Eduardo SEGURA & Thomas HONEGGER, Cormarë Series 14, Zurich and Berne: Walking Tree Publishers, 2007, pp. 99-108.

DAVIS, James G., 'Showing Saruman as Faber: Tolkien and Peter Jackson' in *Tolkien Studies* 5 (2008), pp. 55-71.

DAY, David, *Tolkien's Ring*, London: Pavilion Books, 2001.

DEVAUX, Michael, 'Elves: Reincarnation' in *J.R.R. Tolkien Encyclopedia: Scholarship and Critical Assessment*, edited by Michael D.C. DROUT, New York: Routledge, 2006, p. 154.

DICKERSON, Matthew T., *Following Gandalf: Epic Battles and Moral Victory in The Lord of the Rings*, Grand Rapids, Michigan: Brazos Press, 2003.

& Jonathan EVANS, *Ents, Elves, and Eriador: The Environmental Vision of J.R.R. Tolkien*, Lexington, Kentucky: University Press of Kentucky, 2006.

DRENGSON, Alan & Yuichi INOUE (eds.), *The Deep Ecology Movement: An Introductory Anthology*, Berkeley: North Atlantic Books, 1995.

DROUT, Michael D.C. (ed.), *J.R.R. Tolkien Encyclopedia: Scholarship and Critical Assessment*, New York: Routledge, 2006.

DURIEZ, Colin, *J.R.R. Tolkien and C.S. Lewis: The Story of Their Friendship*, Stroud, Gloucestershire: Sutton Publishing, 2005.

ELGIN, Don D. *The Comedy of the Fantastic: Ecological Perspectives on the Fantasy Novel*, Westport, Connecticut: Greenwood Press, 1985.

ELLIS, Robert Leslie, James SPEDDING & John M. ROBERTSON (eds.), *The Philosophical Works of Francis Bacon*, Freeport and New York: Books for Libraries Press, 1970.

ELLWOOD, Robert S., *Frodo's Quest: Living the Myth in The Lord of the Rings*, Wheaton: Theosophical Publishing House, 2002.

FERN, Richard. L., *Nature, God and Humanity: Envisioning an Ethics of Nature*, Cambridge: Cambridge University Press, 2002.

FIMI, Dimitra, *Tolkien, Race and Cultural History: From Fairies to Hobbits*, Basingstoke: Palgrave Macmillan, 2009.

FLEMING, Rutledge, *The Battle for Middle-earth: Tolkien's Divine Design in The Lord of the Rings*, Grand Rapids, Michigan: Eerdmans Publishing, 2004.

FLIEGER, Verlyn, *A Question of Time: J.R.R. Tolkien's Road to Faërie*, London and Kent, Ohio: Kent State University Press, 1997.

'Taking the Part of Trees: Eco-Conflict in Middle-earth' in *J.R.R. Tolkien and his Literary Resonances: Views of Middle-earth*, edited by George CLARK & Daniel TIMMONS, Westport, Connecticut: Greenwood Press, 2000, pp. 147-58.

& Carl F. HOSTETTER (eds.), *Tolkien's Legendarium: Essays on the History of Middle-earth*, Westport, Connecticut: Greenwood Press, 2000.

Splintered Light: Logos and Language in Tolkien's World, 2nd revised edition, London and Kent, Ohio: Kent State University Press, 2002.

Interrupted Music: The Making of Tolkien's Mythology, London and Kent, Ohio: Kent State University Press, 2005.

'Smith of Wootton Major' in *J.R.R. Tolkien Encyclopedia: Scholarship and Critical Assessment*, edited by Michael D.C. DROUT, New York: Routledge, 2006, pp. 618-19.

FOREST-HILL, Lynn (ed.), *The Mirror Crack'd: Fear and Horror in JRR Tolkien's Major Works*, Newcastle upon Tyne: Cambridge Scholars Publishing, 2008.

FOSTER, Robert, *A Guide to Middle-earth*, Baltimore: The Mirage Press, 1971.

FULLER, Edmund, 'The Lord of the Hobbit: J.R.R. Tolkien' in *Understanding The Lord of the Rings: The Best of Tolkien Criticism*, edited by Rose A. ZIMBARDO & Neil D. ISAACS, Boston and New York: Houghton Mifflin, 2004, pp. 16-30.

GARRARD, Greg, *Ecocriticism*, London and New York: Routledge, 2004.

GARTH, John, *Tolkien and the Great War: The Threshold of Middle-earth*, Boston and New York: Houghton Mifflin, 2003.

GASQUE, Thomas J., 'Tolkien: The Monsters and the Critics' in *Tolkien and the Critics: Essays on J.R.R. Tolkien's The Lord of the Rings*, edited by Neil D. ISAACS & Rose A. ZIMBARDO, London and Notre Dame: University of Notre Dame Press, 1968, pp. 151-63.

GIDDINGS, Robert (ed.), *J.R.R. Tolkien: This Far Land*, London: Vision and Barnes & Noble, 1983.

GLOTFELTY, Cheryll & Harold FROMM (eds.), *The Ecocriticism Reader: Landmarks in Literary Ecology*, Athens and London: University of Georgia Press, 1996.

GORE, Al, *Earth in the Balance: Ecology and the Human Spirit*, New York: Houghton Mifflin, 2000.

HARGROVE, Gene, 'Who is Tom Bombadil?' in *Mythlore* 47.4 (1986), pp. 20-24.

HART, Trevor, 'Tolkien, Creation, and Creativity' in *Tree of Tales: Tolkien, Literature, and Theology*, edited by Trevor HART & Ivan KHOVACS, Waco: Baylor University Press, 2007, pp. 39-53.

& Ian KHOVACS (eds.), *Tree of Tales: Tolkien, Literature, and Theology*, Waco: Baylor University Press, 2007.

HARVEY, David, *The Song of Middle-earth: J.R.R. Tolkien's Themes, Symbols and Myths*, London: Allen & Unwin, 1985.

HONEGGER, Thomas, 'From Bag End to Lórien: the Creation of a Literary World' in *News from the Shire and Beyond – Studies on Tolkien*, edited by Peter BUCHS

& Thomas HONEGGER, 1st edition 1997, 2nd edition, Cormarë Series 1, Zurich and Berne: Walking Tree Publishers, 2004, pp. 59-81.

(ed.), *Reconsidering Tolkien*, Cormarë Series 8, Zurich and Berne: Walking Tree Publishers, 2005.

'Aelfwine (Old English 'Elf-Friend')' in *J.R.R. Tolkien Encyclopedia: Scholarship and Critical Assessment*, edited by Michael D.C. DROUT, New York: Routledge, 2006, pp. 4-5.

& Frank WEINREICH (eds.), *Tolkien and Modernity 1*, Cormarë Series 9, Zurich and Berne: Walking Tree Publishers, 2006.

& Frank WEINREICH, 'Introduction' in *Tolkien and Modernity 2*, edited by Thomas HONEGGER & Frank WEINREICH, Cormarë Series 10, Zurich and Berne: Walking Tree Publishers, 2006, pp. i-iv.

& Frank WEINREICH (eds.), *Tolkien and Modernity 2*, Cormarë Series 10, Zurich and Berne: Walking Tree Publishers, 2006.

HOOD, Gwyneth, 'Sauron and Dracula' in *Mythlore* 52 (1987), pp. 11-17.

HUNTER, John C., 'The Evidence of Things not Seen: Critical Mythology in *The Lord of the Rings*' in *Journal of Modern Literature* 29.2 (2006), pp. 129-47.

ISAACS, Neil D. & Rose A. ZIMBARDO (eds.), *Tolkien and the Critics: Essays on J.R.R. Tolkien's The Lord of the Rings*, London and Notre Dame: University of Notre Dame Press, 1968.

JACKSON, Peter, 'Appendices Part 1: From Book to Script' in *The Lord of the Rings: The Fellowship of the Ring*, directed by Peter JACKSON, DVD Extended Version: New Line Cinema, 2002.

JELLEMA, Rod, 'Auden, W.H.: Influence of Tolkien' in *J.R.R. Tolkien Encyclopedia: Scholarship and Critical Assessment*, edited by Michael D.C. DROUT, New York: Routledge, 2006, pp. 41-42.

JUNG, Carl Gustav, *Two Essays on Analytical Psychology*, The Collected Works of C.G.Jung Volume 7, London: Routledge, 1966.

The Structure and Dynamics of the Psyche, The Collected Works of C.G. Jung Volume 8, Princeton: Princeton University Press, 1981.

Archetypes and the Collective Unconscious, London: Routledge, 1991.

KERRIDGE, Richard & Neil SAMMELLS (eds.), *Writing the Environment: Ecocriticism and Literature*, London and New York: Zed Books, 1998.

KEYNES, Geoffrey (ed.), *The Complete Writings of William Blake with Variant Reading*, London: Oxford University Press, 1925.

Kocher, Paul H., *Master of Middle-earth: The Achievement of J.R.R. Tolkien in Fiction*, Harmondsworth: Penguin, 1974.

Kreeft, Peter J., *The Philosophy of Tolkien: The Worldview Behind The Lord of the Rings*, San Francisco: Ignatius, 2005.

Krueger, Heidi, 'The Shaping of Reality in Tolkien's Works' in *Tolkien and Modernity 2*, edited by Thomas Honegger & Frank Weinreich, Cormarë Series 10, Zurich and Berne: Walking Tree Publishers, 2006, pp. 233-72.

Larkin, Philip, *Collected Poems*, edited by Anthony Thwaite, London: Faber & Faber, 2003.

Larsen, Kristine, 'Shadow and Flame: Myth, Monsters and Mother Nature in Middle-earth' in *The Mirror Crack'd: Fear and Horror in JRR Tolkien's Major Works*, edited by Lynn Forest-Hill, Newcastle upon Tyne: Cambridge Scholars Publishing, 2008, pp. 169-96.

Lewis, Clive S., *C.S. Lewis: Essay Collection and Other Short Pieces*, edited by Lesley Walmsey, London: HarperCollins, 2000.

Light, Andrew, 'Tolkien's Green Time: Environmental Themes in *The Lord of the Rings*' in *The Lord of the Rings and Philosophy: One Book to Rule Them All*, edited by Gregory Bassham & Eric Bronson, Chicago and La Salle, Illinois: Open Court, 2003, pp. 150-63.

Lobdell, Jared (ed.), *A Tolkien Compass*, 1st edition 1975, 2nd revised edition, Chicago and La Salle, Illinois: Open Court, 2003.

Lovelock, James E., *Gaia: A New Look at Life on Earth*, Oxford: Oxford University Press, 1979.

The Revenge of Gaia: Why the Earth Is Fighting Back – and How We Can Still Save Humanity, London: Allen Lane, 2006.

Makdisi, Saree, *William Blake and the Impossible History of the 1790s*, Chicago: University of Chicago Press, 2003.

Manes, Christopher, 'Nature and Silence' in *The Ecocriticism Reader: Landmarks in Literary Ecology*, edited by Cheryll Glotfelty & Harold Fromm, Athens and London: University of Georgia Press, 1996, pp. 15-29.

Manlove, Colin N., *Modern Fantasy: Five Studies*, Cambridge: Cambridge University Press, 1975.

Mathews, Richard, *Fantasy: The Liberation of Imagination*, New York: Routledge, 2002.

Matthews, John, *The Quest for the Green Man*, Newton Abbot: Godsfield Press, 2001.

McKibben, Bill, *The End of Nature*, New York: Random House, 1989.

McKusick, James C., *Green Writing: Romanticism and Ecology*, New York: St. Martin's Press, 2000.

Meeker, Joseph, *The Comedy of Survival: Studies in Literary Ecology*, New York: Scribner, 1974.

Milbank, Alison, *Chesterton and Tolkien as Theologians. The Fantasy of the Real*, London and New York: T&T Clark, 2007.

Morton, Andrew H. & John Hayes, *Tolkien's Gedling 1914: The Birth of a Legend*, Studley, Warwickshire: Brewin Books, 2008.

Moseley, Charles, *J.R.R. Tolkien*, Plymouth: Northcote House Publishers, 1997.

Muir, John, *My First Summer in the Sierra*, New York: Houghton Mifflin, 1998.

Næss, Arne, 'The Shallow and the Deep, Long-Range Ecology Movement' in *The Deep Ecology Movement: An Introductory Anthology*, edited by Alan Drengson & Yuichi Inoue, Berkeley: North Atlantic Books, 1995, pp. 3-10.

— & George Sessions, 'Platform Principles of the Deep Ecology Movement. A Summary' in *The Deep Ecology Movement: An Introductory Anthology*, edited by Alan Drengson & Yuichi Inoue, Berkeley: North Atlantic Books, 1995, pp. 49-53.

Nash, Roderick, 'The Greening of Religion' in *This Sacred Earth: Religion, Nature, Environment*, edited by Roger S. Gottlieb, London and New York: Routledge, 1996, pp. 194-229.

Noel, Ruth S., *The Mythology of Middle-earth*, Boston and New York: Houghton Mifflin, 1977.

O'Neill, Timothy R., *The Individuated Hobbit: Jung, Tolkien and the Archetypes of Middle-earth*, Boston: Houghton Mifflin, 1979.

Parham, John (ed.), *The Environmental Tradition in English Literature*, Aldershot: Ashgate, 2002.

Pearce, Joseph, *Tolkien: Man and Myth*, London: HarperCollins, 1999.

Peat, F. David, *The Blackwinged Night: Creativity in Nature and Mind*, New York: Perseus Books, 2000.

Pepper, David, Frank Webster & George Revill (eds.), *Environmentalism: Critical Concepts*, London: Routledge, 2003.

Peterson Del Mar, David, *Environmentalism*, Harlow: Pearson, 2006.

PLANK, Robert, 'The Scouring of the Shire: Tolkien's View of Fascism' in *A Tolkien Compass*, edited by Jared LOBDELL, 1st edition 1975, 2nd revised edition, Chicago and La Salle, Illinois: Open Court Publishing, 2003, pp. 105-13.

RISSIK, Andrew, 'Middle-earth, Middlebrow' in *The Guardian*, 2nd September 2000.

ROBERTS, Jeremy, *Oskar Schindler: Righteous Gentile*, New York: Rosen Publishing, 2000.

ROGERS, Deborah W. & Ivor A., *J.R.R. Tolkien*, Boston: G.K. Hall, 1980.

ROSEBURY, Brian, *Tolkien: A Critical Assessment*, London: St. Martin's Press, 1992.

RUECKERT, William, 'Literature and Ecology: An Experiment in Ecocriticism' in *The Ecocriticism Reader: Landmarks in Literary Ecology*, edited by Cheryll GLOTFELTY & Harold FROMM, Athens and London: University of Georgia Press, 1996, pp. 105-23.

SALE, Roger, *Modern Heroism: Essays on D.H. Lawrence, William Empson and J.R.R. Tolkien*, Berkeley and Los Angeles: University of California Press, 1973.

SEARS, Paul B., *Deserts on the March*, London: Routledge & Kegan Paul, 1949.

Where There Is Life, New York: Dell Publishing, 1972.

SIEWERS, Alfred K., 'Tolkien's Cosmic-Christian Ecology' in *Tolkien's Modern Middle Ages*, edited by Jane CHANCE & Alfred K. SIEWERS, New York: Palgrave Macmillan, 2005, pp. 139-53.

SHIPPEY, Tom A., *The Road to Middle-earth*, 1st edition 1982, 3rd edition, London: HarperCollins, 2005.

J.R.R. Tolkien: Author of the Century, London: HarperCollins, 2000.

'New Learning and New Ignorance: Magia, Goeteia, and the Inklings' in *Myth and Magic. Art According to the Inklings*, edited by Eduardo SEGURA & Thomas HONEGGER, Cormarë Series 14, Zurich and Berne: Walking Tree Publishers, 2007, pp. 21-46.

SIDERIS, Lisa H., *Environmental Ethics, Ecological Theology, and Natural Selection*, New York: Columbia University Press, 2003.

SPIRITO, Guglielmo, 'Speaking With Animals: A Desire that Lies Near the Heart of Faërie' in *Tolkien's Shorter Works. Essays of the Jena Conference 2007*, edited by Margaret HILEY & Frank WEINREICH, Cormarë Series 17, Zurich and Jena: Walking Tree Publishers, 2008, pp. 17-35.

STANTON, Michael N., *Hobbits, Elves and Wizards: Exploring the Wonders and Worlds of J.R.R. Tolkien's The Lord of the Rings*, New York: Palgrave Macmillan, 2002.

SULLIVAN, C.W., 'Tolkien the Bard: His Tale Grew in the Telling' in *Tolkien and His Literary Resonances: Views of Middle-earth*, edited by George CLARK & Daniel TIMMONS, Westport, Connecticut: Greenwood Press, 2000, pp. 11-20.

TENNYSON, Alfred, *Selected Poems*, edited by Christopher B. RICKS, London: Penguin, 2007.

TRESCHOW, Michael & Mark DUCKWORTH, 'Bombadil's Role in *The Lord of the Rings*' in *Mythlore* 25.1-2 (2006), pp. 175-96.

TYLER, J.E.A., *The Complete Tolkien Companion*, London: Pan Books, 2002.

VARNER, Gary R., *The Mythic Forest. The Green Man and the Spirit of Nature*, New York: Algora Publishing, 2006.

WHITE JR., Lynn, 'The Historical Roots of Our Ecological Crisis' in *The Ecocriticism Reader: Landmarks in Literary Ecology*, edited by Cheryll GLOTFELTY & Harold FROMM, Athens and London: University of Georgia Press, 1996, pp. 3-14.

WHITE, Michael, *Tolkien: A Biography*, London: Abacus, 2004.

WHITMORE, Timothy C. & Jeffrey A. SAYER, 'Deforestation and Species Extinction in Tropical Moist Forests' in *Tropical Deforestation and Species Extinction*, edited by Timothy C. WHITMORE & Jeffrey A. SAYER, London: Chapman & Hall, 1992, pp. 1-14.

(eds.), *Tropical Deforestation and Species Extinction*, London: Chapman & Hall, 1992.

WILCOX, Miranda, 'Exilic Imagining in *The Seafarer* and *The Lord of the Rings*' in *Tolkien the Medievalist*, edited by Jane CHANCE, London and New York: Routledge, 2003, pp. 133-54.

WILLIAMS, Raymond, *The Country and the City*, London: Hogarth, 1993.

WILSON, Colin, *Tree by Tolkien*, London: Covent Garden Press, 1973.

WILSON, Edmund, 'Oo, Those Awful Orcs' in *The Nation* 182.15, 14th April 1956.

WOOD, Ralph C., *The Gospel According to Tolkien: Visions of the Kingdom in Middle-earth*, Louisville: Westminster John Knox Press, 2003.

YANCEY, Philip, (ed.), *Reality and the Vision*, London: W. Pub Group, 1992.

ZIMBARDO, Rose A. & Neil D. ISAACS (eds.), *Understanding the Lord of the Rings: The Best of Tolkien Criticism*, Boston and New York: Houghton Mifflin, 2004.

Index

The index is arranged in standard format – one point of clarification may, nonetheless, avoid any possible uncertainty: on occasion page numbers related to specific entries (or sub-categories therein) may appear as consecutive pages (i.e. 87, 88, 89, as opposed to 87-89), these refer to successive mentions where the entry in question is not discussed in a continuous fashion across the pages.

A
Ackerman, Forrest J. 75
The Adventures of Tom Bombadil 93
Ainulindalë 113-14
Ainu(r) 63, 64-65, 68, 78, 184
Aiwendil (see also Radagast) 170
Alatar 127
Alf (King of Faery/elf-king) 195-96
alliance 133, 149, 150
Anderson, William 93
Andreth 175
Angband 54
angel(s) 63, 64, 70-71, 109-10, 114-15, 116, 157, 160, 170
Animal Farm 15
animal(s) 34-35, 87, 168, 169
animism 115, 116, 166
applicability 24, 37, 103, 130, 212, 250
appropriation 102-03, 238, 239
Aragorn 17, 131, 186, 247, 250-51
Archer, Mary 231
Arda (the Earth) 64, 67, 78, 85, 90, 143, 188
Ariosto 6-7
Arwen 17, 62
Asimov, Isaac 145, 245
Athrabeth (Finrod ah Andreth) 175
Atlantis-dream, Númenor 27
atomic bomb 55
Attfield, Robin 112, 113, 120
Auden, W.H. 5, 6, 7-8, 13, 25, 208, 241, 251
augury 3, 20, 21, 25, 70, 112, 137, 164, 174, 197, 201, 240, 244, 248
Aulë 65, 88-89, 90, 96, 116
Austin, Mary 203
automobile/motor-car 28, 37, 71, 216, 219

B

Bacon, Francis 160
Bag End 42, 44-45, 129, 131, 136, 137, 244, 252
Baggins, Bilbo 121-23, 129, 131-32, 137, 138, 148, 149, 217, 218
Baggins, Frodo 25, 30, 41-43, 44-45, 67, 74, 81, 83-84, 87, 89, 90, 92, 94, 96, 101, 111, 121, 129-31, 132, 136, 138, 143, 148, 149-50, 155, 165, 180, 181, 183, 191, 205, 218, 219, 223, 244-45, 248-49, 252, 256, 266, 268, 269, 272
Baker, David 215, 219
Bakshi, Ralph 74
Balrog 41, 134, 135, 210, 223
Barad-dûr 43, 99, 246, 264
Barber, James 231
Barr, Donald (critic) 6
Barrow-wights 41, 74, 75, 77
Bate, Jonathan 24, 39, 198, 210-11, 216, 217, 234, 240
Bauckham, Richard 167-69
Benvenuto, Maria Raffaella 134
Beorn 78, 158
Beren and Lúthien 17
Bible, 12, 64, 113, 164, 167, 168
Bill the pony 169-70
Birmingham 29, 30-31, 38, 56, 58, 60
Black Riders (see Nine Black Riders)
Blake, William 28, 29, 173, 174, 203, 204, 219, 232
Blue Wizards (Alatar and Pallando) 127
Bombadil, Tom 22-23, 73-96, 109, 116, 120, 133, 134, 146, 165, 174, 178, 212, 257, 259, 265-66, 268, 269
    as Aulë 89-90
    as nature under threat 22, 83-87, 90, 95, 99, 107, 128, 198, 244
    as the Green Man 90-96, 170
    as voice of nature 78, 87, 176, 199, 247
    function for the plot 74, 78-83
    model of ecological ethics 76, 80, 83, 96, 259
    nature spirit/genius loci 75, 78, 83, 85, 88-91, 93, 95, 106, 115, 181
    origin 23, 74, 75, 90-91
    power of his voice 77-78, 105, 107
    renunciation of power 79-80, 83, 88-89, 94, 95, 96, 98, 100, 103, 107, 128, 187
    resistance to the One Ring 81-83, 85, 92, 103, 107
    The Adventures of Tom Bombadil 93
Bookchin, Murray 51-52
Boromir 119, 135, 148, 272
botany (early tuition) 31
Boyens, Philippa 95

Brabazon, James 122
Branch, Michael 202
Bree 74, 222
Brontë, Emily 179
Brothers Grimm 134, 154
Brown Wizard (see also Radagast) 170
Buckland 217, 257, 260, 268
bulldoze/bulldozing 1, 136, 140, 143, 193
Burns, Marjorie 99, 184-85
Butler, Samuel 53, 71, 232
Bywater 42, 49, 217

C

Campbell, Joseph 151-52, 234
capitalism 46, 51, 102, 147, 216
Caradhras, Mount 125, 179, 180, 270
Carpenter, Humphrey 8, 20, 29, 30, 32, 61, 156, 177, 223-24, 232, 234
Carson, Rachel 201, 204-13, 240
    A Fable for Tomorrow 201, 204-13, 240
The Catcher in the Rye 8, 15
Celeborn 88
Celtic mythology 177-79, 182, 183-84, 185
Chandler, Pamela 252
Chance, Jane 20, 132, 149
Chant, Joy 203
Cherryman, A.E. (critic) 6
The Children of Húrin 69
Children of Ilúvatar (elves and men) 65, 159, 162-63
Christ (Jesus) 181, 182, 234
Christianity/Christian belief/Christian doctrine/Catholicism 1, 21-22, 35, 57, 58, 59, 60, 62, 64, 68, 70, 109, 112-18, 120, 145, 147, 153, 159, 163-70, 171, 172-73, 176, 177, 178, 180-82, 190, 197
The Chronicles of Thomas Covenant 203
Chrysophylax (dragon) 244
Círdan 135
Clare, John 29, 203
Clark, George 137
Clute, John 249
Coleridge, Samuel 203, 236
Commoner, Barry 24, 33, 40, 221, 229-30
corruption/corrupted 1, 37, 43, 51, 69, 81, 82, 89, 96-97, 107, 123, 124, 128, 140, 141-42, 145, 149, 208-09

cosmology (in Tolkien's fiction) 75, 90, 109,110, 114, 116, 128, 153, 156, 162-63, 165
Council of Elrond 2, 82, 85-86, 88, 97, 111, 188, 208, 210
counter-culture 8-9, 10
Crankshaw, Edward 177
creation myth (see also cosmology) 63-70, 113-16, 153, 159, 163, 165
creative process 151, 201, 220-33, 235, 240, 248
Croft, Janet Brennan 244
Crowe, David M. 44
cultures of opposition 22, 71, 73, 96, 149, 247
Curunír (see also Saruman) 127
Curran, Bob 91
Curry, Patrick 20, 24, 52, 75, 115, 139, 148, 173, 179-80, 192, 218, 259-60, 266-67, 269

D

Daniels, Ian 91
Dark Lord/dark lord 23, 28, 41, 77, 88, 99, 109, 110, 111, 118, 130, 134, 143, 145, 150, 193, 247, 260, 261
darkness vs. light 134, 141, 149
Dasent, George Webbe 233
Davis, James G. 47, 50, 70, 261-62, 267, 269
Day, David 97, 104, 148
The Day of the Triffids 203
death (see also mortality) 43, 44, 51, 206, 207
    as a theme 1, 53, 121, 138, 175, 181, 187, 189, 190
    in Tolkien's fiction 38, 54, 86, 111, 121, 138, 142, 154, 156-57, 180-81, 189, 190, 227
    in the primary world 54, 198, 203, 227, 250
    of Tolkien's father 29, 58
    of Tolkien's mother's (the lasting effect of her passing on Tolkien) 59-62
Deep Ecology 35
defeat 37, 77, 85, 86, 104, 111, 139, 271
Denethor 111-12, 117, 118-19, 135
desolation (environmental) 18, 38, 42, 85, 139, 144, 180, 185, 207, 220, 244
destruction/destructive 18, 22, 27, 33, 34, 36, 37, 39, 41, 44, 46, 48, 51, 54-55, 56-57, 70, 71, 79, 81, 82, 97, 99, 101, 107, 111, 118, 136, 137, 140-41, 144, 146, 148, 151, 152, 156, 180, 196, 197, 199, 204, 214, 232, 244, 246, 247, 248, 257, 259, 261-63, 264-65, 267, 268
detractor(s) (of Tolkien) 4, 213
devastation (environmental) 34, 38, 41, 43, 44, 45, 50-51, 52, 53, 69, 70, 86, 100, 101, 125, 130, 137, 140, 144, 146, 165, 185, 189, 193, 197, 204, 207, 209, 244, 251, 260, 261

Devaux, Michael 190
Dickerson, Matthew 21, 45, 67, 73, 75, 112-14, 118, 130, 217, 267, 269
Donaldson, Stephen 203
Dracula 142
dragons 28, 31, 115, 162, 194, 235, 238, 243-44
    as analogous to bomber planes 54
Duckworth, Mark 78, 81-82
Duino Elegies 157
Duriez, Colin 102-03, 116, 148
dwarves 131, 133, 134, 150, 158, 159, 162, 179, 210, 238, 250-51, 262, 263
Dyson, Hugo 234, 238

E

Eä (the World) 64-65, 88
Eärendil 67
Earth 21, 24, 29, 34, 35, 63, 64-69, 78, 85, 99, 112, 115, 143, 158, 159, 162-63,
    167, 179, 188, 189-90, 193, 209, 231
ecocentric 117, 120, 121, 165, 172, 173, 176-177, 178, 181, 184
ecocritical canon 202-04
ecocriticism/green themes 2, 3, 13, 20-21, 23-24, 29, 34, 129, 131, 152, 176, 180,
    201-04, 205, 211, 220, 221, 226-27, 228-29, 230, 239, 240, 249, 250, 252, 255,
    256, 269-70
ecocritics 20, 24, 201-02, 204, 211, 221
ecosphere 23, 40, 150, 153, 176, 221
ecotheology 2, 62-63
Edain of the Túatha Dé Danann (Celtic Myth) 184
Eden/Edenesque 68, 183, 216
Elbereth 62, 195
Elgin, Don D. 20, 199, 202, 203
Eliot, T.S. 19, 54
Ellwood, Robert S. 110
Elrond (see also Council of Elrond) 81, 126, 131, 133, 153, 188-89, 208, 210, 247
elves (see also Children of Ilúvatar) 44, 62, 64, 65, 81, 114, 115, 116, 133, 134, 149,
    150, 152, 153-79, 235, 238, 247, 250-51, 259, 264, 269, 272
    as a flawed race 127, 147, 154, 187, 188, 193, 197
    as a race that is passing from the world 146, 155, 156, 159, 181, 182, 185-86
    as an aspect of humanity 157, 159, 161, 186-89
    as interconnected with nature and their environment 23, 146, 153, 155, 178,
        181, 186, 187, 188-91, 193, 196, 197, 244-46
    as metaphysically sundered from humanity 157, 159, 161, 175, 187, 188, 197
    as nature lovers 154, 163, 165, 173, 174, 177, 182, 183, 185, 186-87, 189, 192,
        197, 246
    immortality 154, 155, 156-57, 175, 176, 184, 188-90, 197

in *Father Christmas Letters* 194-95
　　in *Roverandom* 194
　　in *Smith of Wootton Major* 194, 195-97, 243
　　reincarnation 184, 190-91, 223
enchantment (vs. magic) 191-93, 236
engine(s) 1, 39, 50, 51, 54, 56, 103, 141, 191, 216, 246, 250, 260
England/English/Englishness 8, 15, 28, 29, 30-31, 48, 53, 75, 154, 178, 195, 201, 206, 212, 213, 214, 217, 218-19, 224
ent(s) 2, 39, 102, 103, 124, 135, 150, 162, 174, 176, 178, 199, 221, 244, 261-64, 265
Entmoot 264, 266
Éomer 104, 250
Eregion 193, 210
Eru (see Ilúvatar) 63
escapism, Escape 8, 11, 16-19, 53, 213, 216, 237
Evans, Jonathan 21, 45, 67, 73, 75, 112-14, 118, 130, 217, 267, 269
evil (see also good vs. evil) 6, 37, 41, 43-46, 52, 53, 54, 55, 56-57, 63, 68-71, 76-77, 82, 97, 109, 111, 120-21, 123-25, 126, 128-29, 130, 133, 134, 136-39, 140-48, 149, 161, 164, 172, 188-89, 193, 206, 209-10, 245, 251, 264, 268, 269, 271
exploitation 51, 80, 82, 83, 94, 102, 107, 118, 119, 121, 126, 165-66, 168, 198, 259
Ezekiel, Book of 167

F

Fall (the Fall) 1, 68, 69, 164
Fangorn 1, 36, 66, 101, 124, 179, 180, 255, 257-58, 259-60, 262-63, 266, 269
fantasy 19-20, 105, 130, 179, 184, 192, 197-99, 203, 216, 218, 235-39, 243, 248, 249
Faramir 133
Farmer Cotton 46, 49-50, 264
　　as spokesperson for Tolkien 46-47
Farmer Giles of Ham 243
Farmer Maggot 30, 100, 217
Father Christmas Letters 194
Fawcett, H. l'A. (critic) 6
Fëanor 67, 153, 160
Fellowship 132-33, 134, 150, 161, 169, 179, 183, 186, 192, 193, 210, 246, 247, 248, 264, 270-72
Fimi, Dimitra 56-57
Finrod 175
Finwë 160
First Age 69, 70, 175, 189, 223
Firstborn and Followers (see also Children of Ilúvatar) 154, 159
Fleming, Rutledge 100, 101

Flieger, Verlyn 20, 174-76, 187, 195-96, 247, 255-56, 257-62, 265, 267, 269, 270
flower(s) 30, 55, 76, 112, 117, 118, 121, 155, 162, 183, 185, 196, 205, 246, 248, 258, 268, 270
foreshadowing 125
Forestry Commission 34, 36
Saint Francis of Assisi 168-71
free will 68-69, 129, 168, 250
Friends of the Earth 34
Fuller, Edmund 75

G

Galadriel 24-25, 62, 81, 146, 155, 251
   Mirror of Galadriel 24, 155, 251
   Phial of Galadriel 67
Galdor 2, 85, 89, 111, 146
Gamgee, Sam 25, 41-43, 44-45, 49, 67, 74, 81, 132, 146, 149-50, 155, 169-70, 174, 191, 205, 207, 217, 218, 244-45, 251, 268-69
Gandalf 22, 44, 63, 64, 81, 82, 84-85, 88, 89, 96, 97-99, 153, 180, 210, 222, 272
   as emissary of the Valar 109-11
   as guide/activist 23, 124-25, 128-33, 141, 149-52, 246, 252, 271
   as steward of Middle-earth 111-22, 150-52, 159
   carrying Tolkien's worldview 120, 121, 122, 131, 137-38, 148, 151, 246
   contrasted to Sauron 23, 109, 126, 136, 149, 150, 271
   environmentally aware/protector of natural phenomena 23, 109, 110, 111-18, 119-21, 126-27, 128, 131, 133, 135-37, 143, 146, 147, 149-51, 159, 164, 168-71, 174, 246, 247, 268, 270-71,
   his moral code 97, 125, 130, 137-38
   his reputation 122-23
   his wisdom 98, 109, 111, 125-26, 132, 135-36, 140, 148, 149, 246
   parallels with Albert Schweitzer 120-22, 138, 169, 171
   parallels with St. Francis of Assisi 170-71
   reticent to use powers in anger 121, 135-36, 140, 150, 271
   role in Middle-earth 109, 110, 120, 122-25, 131-32, 134-35, 150-52, 271
   spiritual nature of 109-11, 114, 116-17, 118, 124-25, 138, 139, 145, 151, 152, 170, 181
Garrard, Greg 129, 202, 204-06, 211, 213, 215, 217
Garth, John 17
Gasque, Thomas J. 73
Genesis, Book of 113, 164
genetic engineering 18, 103
Gift of Ilúvatar (mortality of men) 188, 189
Gimli 149, 179, 186, 193, 247
Glorfindel 85, 88, 223

Glotfelty, Cheryll 24, 180, 202, 221, 228-29, 231, 235
God
   in the primary world 21, 59, 61-63, 64, 69, 112-13, 114, 117, 163-64, 166-69, 171-72, 224-25, 234, 235-37, 241
   in Tolkien's fiction (see also Ilúvatar) 63, 65, 67-68, 75, 102, 114, 115, 162-63, 173, 181
Goldberry 62, 76, 94, 115, 165
Golden Wood 185, 191, 243, 248-49, 250-51
Golding, William 8, 203
Gollum (see also Smeagol) 81, 89, 98, 121, 124, 130, 138, 207
Gondor 102, 111-12, 118-19, 175, 181, 264
good vs. evil 68-69, 79, 121, 125, 137-38, 141, 149, 161, 245, 250-51
Gothic tales 134, 142
Grant, John 249
The Grapes of Wrath 15
grass/grasslands 20, 37, 42, 66, 100, 116, 121, 122, 144, 155, 165, 170, 183, 207, 227, 238, 245, 248
Great Chain of Being (scala naturae) 160
Green Dragon (inn) 207
Green Man 90-96, 170
Greenpeace 34, 139, 145
Green, Peter (critic) 5-6
Greer, Germaine (critic) 11, 16
Grey Wanderer (see also Gandalf) 110, 169
Grey Wizard (see also Gandalf) 109, 170, 171
grief 189, 190, 195, 243
Gwaihir 168, 169, 271

H

Haldir 248
Hardy, Thomas 203
Hargrove, Gene 88-89, 90, 95, 223
Hart, Trevor 64, 113-15, 182, 237
Harvard 8
Herbert, Frank 203
hero(es) 137, 151-52, 198, 234
heroic 6, 8, 19, 45, 60, 62, 132, 137, 152
The Hobbit 18, 78, 122-23, 131-32, 137, 140, 152, 158, 220, 223
Hobbiton 30, 42, 47, 49, 55-56, 205, 217, 244
hobbits 8, 41, 42-45, 47, 55, 57, 74, 76-78, 80-81, 84-85, 93, 94, 101, 105, 119, 122-23, 128, 130-32, 133, 134, 135, 138, 139, 149-50, 153, 159, 201, 205, 206-08, 212-13, 222, 246, 247, 248, 256-60, 262, 263, 264, 266-70, 271
   as a pastoral ideal 213-19, 220

as identification figures 45
home/homelands 19, 21, 29, 41-46, 58, 76, 84, 101, 131, 183, 194, 196-97, 207, 214, 219, 239, 245, 248, 252, 261, 262, 268
Honegger, Thomas 13
Hood, Gwyneth 142-43
humanity (as men) in Middle-earth 153, 158-62, 163-64, 175-76, 187, 197-98, 199, 251
Hunter, John C. 218
huorn 269

I

Ilbereth (Christmas elf) 195
Ilúvatar (see also the Gift of Ilúvatar) 63-65, 67, 75, 78, 110, 159, 162-63, 181, 188, 189
imagination 2, 4, 5, 15, 27, 28, 29-31, 54, 56, 93, 114, 154, 157, 173-74, 179, 195-96, 220, 221, 222, 225, 235, 251
    power of imagination 172, 173, 222, 236, 239-41, 249, 253
    realms of the imagination 174, 195, 236, 238, 249, 251
incorruptible 82, 210
industry/industrialisation 1, 3, 9, 18, 20, 28, 29, 30, 38-39, 41, 42, 46-47, 48-50, 52, 53-54, 55-57, 69, 70, 73, 92, 98-99, 100, 104, 105, 107, 125, 130, 139, 140-41, 143, 145, 147, 174, 185, 189, 191, 208, 213-14, 215, 217, 219-20, 232, 246, 248, 250
    Industrial Revolution 56, 57, 215, 219
inspiration 25, 33, 36, 64, 192, 225, 234, 239, 251
interconnectedness/interconnectivity/interconnection(s) 3, 23, 33, 51, 63, 66, 100, 117, 119, 120, 146, 150, 153, 154, 158, 187, 189, 191, 196, 211, 221, 229, 231-32, 233, 236, 240, 259
interrelatedness 23, 66, 67, 110, 221, 229, 246
Ireland/Irish 1, 178, 184
Isengard 2, 28, 37-39, 41, 43, 73, 86, 99, 107, 125, 141, 185, 192, 207, 220, 250, 261-64, 266, 268
Isildur 89, 149, 188, 208
Isis (ancient Egyptian goddess) 94
Istari 75, 99, 101, 109, 111, 124, 126-28, 170, 263
Ithryn Luin (see also Blue Wizards) 127
Ivy Bush (inn) 207

J

Jackson, Peter 4, 74, 95, 139, 203
Jacobson, Howard (critic) 11
Jeffreys, Susan (critic) 11, 16
Jesus (see Christ)

joy 5, 6, 92, 173, 174, 243
Joyce, James 10, 15, 19, 234
Jung, Carl Gustav 225-26, 229
justification/justify 14, 51, 97, 104, 113, 121, 179, 180, 198, 214, 265-66

K

Kelvar 128
Keneally, Thomas 43
Kerridge, Richard 131
king(s) 65, 77, 79, 119, 123, 141, 175, 195
kingdom(s) 27, 68, 77, 111, 117, 142, 169, 183, 184, 185, 243
King Edward's School 58
King of the Valar (see also Manwë) 65
Kocher, Paul H. 20
Kortirion among the Trees (poem by Tolkien) 154-55
Krueger, Heidi 16

L

The Land of Little Rain 203
landscape(s)
    in the primary world 1-2, 29, 38, 53, 56, 61, 75, 89, 100, 103, 105, 137, 140-41, 144, 145, 220
    in Tolkien's fiction 16, 18, 22, 23, 36, 37-38, 39, 41, 42, 53-54, 70, 73, 75, 82, 85, 86, 100, 106, 107, 111, 117, 125, 126, 128, 131, 136, 138, 139, 140, 143, 145, 151, 165, 178-81, 183-85, 189, 191, 192, 193, 197, 208, 209, 219, 220, 243, 244, 245, 250, 255, 257, 268
Lang, Andrew 31
languages (early tuition and appreciation) 31
Larkin, Philip 207
Larson, Kristine 143
Láthspell 123
Lawhead, Stephen R. 237
Leaf by Niggle/Niggle 33, 36, 174, 227-28, 243
    as reflective of Tolkien's views on the creative process 227-28
Lee, Harper 15
legendarium (Tolkien's myth cycle) 1, 15, 64, 75, 110, 113, 153, 155-57, 158, 161, 162, 175-77, 179, 182-83, 184, 194, 195, 222, 244
Legolas 88, 149, 186, 193, 247, 270
Lewis, C.S. 6-7, 199, 203, 234-35, 238
Light, Andrew 20, 42, 77, 176
light from an invisible lamp 182
literary establishment 4, 7, 8, 10, 13, 14, 20
living world 62, 119, 128, 149

Index   295

Lobdell, Jared 90, 125
Lord of the Flies 8
The Lord of the Rings 1, 22, 24, 38, 43, 44, 70, 73, 78-80, 81, 83, 87, 89, 92-95, 96,
    109, 116, 123, 126, 134, 136, 140, 143, 148, 149, 151, 152, 161, 175, 191, 192,
    201, 205-13, 216, 219-20, 232, 237, 244-46, 248, 256, 268-69, 270
    adaptations of 4, 74, 75-76, 95, 139, 203
    as a contemporary work 6-7, 15-19, 25, 27, 52, 70, 102, 105-06, 204, 220, 232
    critical reception of 4-10, 232
    evolution/writing/publication of 6, 27, 36, 39, 73-74, 79, 132, 205, 213, 222-32
    not engrained in the education system 15
    popularity of 4, 5, 8-9, 10-15, 139, 232
    spiritual climate in 173, 181-82
Lord of Waters (see also Ulmo) 69
Lórien 161, 192, 193, 248
Lóthlorien 21, 36, 66, 70, 146, 155, 183, 185-86, 191-92, 248-49, 255
Lotho 57, 218
Lucifer 64
Luke, Gospel of 164

M

machine(s), The Machine 1, 2, 28, 36, 43, 49, 54, 55, 56-57, 68, 69, 71
    age of/rise of the machine 3, 18, 21, 22, 27-28, 29, 47-48, 52-55, 70-71, 92,
        105-06, 137, 141, 147, 172, 214, 219, 232, 241, 250
    as 'Mordor-gadgets' 55, 71
    first war of the machines 54
    in Tolkien's fiction 1, 2, 18, 22, 28, 36-37, 39, 47-49, 50-51, 52-54, 70-71, 96,
        100, 103, 105, 141, 147, 148, 179, 186, 193, 246, 250, 255, 257, 263
magic 18, 52, 103, 104, 105, 115, 135, 140, 141, 148, 149, 184, 186, 193, 195, 213,
    271
    magic vs. enchantment 191-93, 246
Maia(r) 75, 81, 88, 89, 95, 96, 97, 99, 109, 110, 116, 145, 150, 151, 170, 208
Maid Marian (as counterpart to Goldberry) 94
malevolence/malevolent 37, 68, 69, 96, 130, 146, 151, 152, 208
malignancy/malignant 38, 69, 89
Manes, Christopher 160
Manwë 65, 66, 116, 139, 146, 195
Mathews, Richard 246
Matthews, John 91-95
McKibben, Bill 24, 86-87, 244
Meeker, Joseph 198-99, 202, 249-50, 266
Melkor (see also Morgoth) 63, 208
men (in Tolkien's fiction) 47, 65, 77, 97, 115, 122-23, 127, 134, 141, 149, 150, 153,
    154, 156-59, 161-63, 175, 182-83, 187-90, 196, 199, 247, 250-51, 262, 263, 269

Merry (Meriadoc Brandybuck) 1, 41, 43-44, 46, 74, 100, 124, 132, 218, 219, 256, 260, 261, 265, 266, 268, 269
Middle-earth 1, 8, 9, 14, 24, 45, 63, 64, 77, 89, 154, 55, 164, 175, 194, 196, 221, 223, 252, 269, 270
   as a character 153, 179-81, 197-98
   ecology/environmental devastation in 2, 3, 16, 22, 34, 37, 39, 41, 42, 44, 54, 66-67, 68, 69, 70-71, 73, 75, 78, 82, 84-86, 88, 99, 101-02, 103, 106, 111-12, 116-17, 120-21, 123, 125, 127-28, 133, 136, 138, 139, 140-44, 146, 147, 149-50, 151, 153, 158, 165, 169-70, 176, 178-79, 180-81, 183-84, 186-87, 189, 192, 193, 197-98, 206-07, 208, 209, 220, 244-45, 247, 259, 260, 262-63, 264
   free peoples 2, 84, 106, 111, 121, 128, 133, 149, 210, 264
   history 64, 67, 73, 96, 158, 175, 176, 189, 193, 194, 223
   not a 'never-never' land 158
   reflective of the primary world 2, 19, 47, 52, 73, 76, 106, 130, 139, 141, 144, 146-47, 158-59, 182, 189, 247, 251
   spiritual climate of 68, 70-71, 113-115, 116-17, 180-83
   war/crisis in 2, 22, 23, 36-37, 41, 44, 47, 54, 69, 72, 73, 74, 80, 82, 84-86, 97, 99, 101-02, 103, 106, 109-12, 122, 123, 124-25, 128, 131, 133-34, 135, 136, 138, 139, 140-44, 146, 147, 149-50, 151, 152, 160-61, 165, 180-81, 186, 189, 193, 197-98, 206-07, 208, 209-10, 220, 244-45, 247, 259, 262-63, 264, 271
Milbank, Alison 102
Minas Tirith 118, 142
Mirkwood 180, 261
Mitchison, Naomi 79, 124, 141, 178, 209
Mithrandir 152
mithril 210
modernity/modern age/modern 3, 11, 13, 15, 17-21, 25, 28, 32, 33, 35, 39, 41, 45, 47-48, 50, 51-52, 53, 55, 56, 57, 62, 70, 71, 87, 91, 103, 106, 109, 113, 116, 120, 147, 160, 166, 174, 201, 203, 204, 211, 213, 217, 226, 240-41
The Monsters and the Critics 134
Mordor 21, 28, 37-38, 41, 43, 45, 46, 50, 55, 71, 85, 86-87, 111, 125, 130, 134, 140-45, 149, 174, 180, 185, 207, 220, 244-45, 260-62, 263, 268
Morgan, Father Francis Xavier 59-60
Morgoth 23, 28, 53, 54, 63-64, 66, 68-70, 96, 102, 139, 143, 145, 147, 149, 160, 174, 208, 248
Moria 133, 134, 135, 169, 210, 270
Morris, William 232
mortality (see also death) 1, 68, 69, 153-54, 175, 187-90, 238
Moseley, Charles 222-23
Muir, John 203, 231
Music of the Ainur (see also creation myth) 63-64
My First Summer in the Sierra 203

myth/mythology 3, 19, 23, 27, 29, 31, 63-64, 67, 68, 70, 71, 75, 79, 91, 113-15, 116, 125, 134, 142, 143, 151, 153, 154, 157-60, 174-76, 177-85, 188, 195, 197, 210-11, 221, 225, 227, 228, 233, 234-35, 240, 241, 250
    Celtic myth 177-85
    monomyth 151, 234
    mythology for England 178, 224
    true myth 224, 233-35

N

Næss, Arne 35
Narnia 6
Narya (Ring of Fire) 135
Nash, Roderick 169, 171
natural energy 70, 84, 85, 181, 272
natural world 2-3, 18, 19, 21-22, 27, 29, 31, 33, 37, 39, 41, 51, 54, 57, 59, 60-63, 65-67, 69-70, 75-76, 77, 80, 93-94, 98, 102, 107, 113, 115, 118, 120, 128, 137, 146, 148, 154, 163-65, 167, 169, 171, 173, 177, 178, 180, 187, 189, 193, 197, 204-05, 221, 237-38, 240-41, 245, 248, 255, 258, 267-68
nature
    nature in Tolkien's fiction 2, 22, 23, 37-38, 65, 66-67, 69, 70-71, 75-77, 78-80, 83-87, 89-90, 94, 95, 99, 107, 111, 115, 117, 128, 142-43, 146, 147, 153, 155, 161, 162-63, 165, 174, 176-78, 180, 182, 184, 185, 186-88, 189, 191-92, 196, 197-98, 199, 205, 218-19, 220, 237-38, 241, 243, 245-46, 247, 248, 249-50, 252, 255, 259-60, 267, 269, 271-72
    nature in the primary world 1, 3, 21, 22, 28, 29, 33, 36, 39, 60-63, 66-67, 69, 70, 77, 80, 83-87, 91-92, 95, 112-113, 120, 130, 138, 156, 163, 164, 165-67, 168-69, 172-73, 180, 185, 197-98, 199, 201, 201, 206, 211, 215, 219, 229, 232, 237-38, 239-40, 241, 244, 249-50, 252, 259-60
    nature under threat 1, 2, 22, 23, 32, 34, 37-38, 39, 70, 71, 83-87, 88, 90, 95, 99, 107, 111, 128, 130, 142-43, 146, 147, 165-66, 174, 189, 195, 196, 198, 199, 219, 220, 240, 241, 244-46, 248, 250, 255, 259-60, 262, 271-72
nature and memory of Tolkien's mother 59-62
nature and religion 58, 61-62, 67, 68, 112-13, 115-16, 164-73, 176-77, 178, 180, 183, 197-98, 201, 235, 237, 241
nature vs. human society 1, 39-41, 51, 71, 86-87, 95, 98, 105-06, 143-44, 163, 165, 166, 174, 198, 232, 238, 241, 243, 245, 259, 261
Nazgûl 41, 88, 134
Neave, Jane 32, 35
Nenya (Ring of Adamant) 191
Nienna 66
Nine Black Riders/Black Riders 44, 74, 126, 134, 141
Nineteen Eighty-Four 15
Nine Walkers 133

Noel, Ruth S. 75
Noldor 147, 160
non-human 3, 21, 23, 34, 35, 120, 150, 153, 157-61, 162, 163-65, 166, 170, 172, 174, 176-77, 179-80, 184, 190, 197-98, 199, 202-04, 211
Númenor 27, 127, 175, 181

O

Old Forest 36, 74, 83, 93, 105, 165, 179, 219, 255-60, 262, 264-67, 268, 269-70
Old Man Willow 66, 74, 77-78, 83, 84, 105, 265-66, 269
Old Mill 47, 55-56
Olórin 139, 152
One Ring 18, 67, 74, 80-83, 85, 89, 96-99, 102, 103, 107, 119, 129-30, 140, 142, 150, 151, 188, 193, 208, 210, 246
    as a machine/technology 53, 71, 148, 191
    as a symbol of the will to power 41, 90, 96-97, 98, 99, 140, 148
    having a will of its own 89-90
On Fairy-stories 19, 28, 71, 102, 191, 196, 228, 233, 236, 249
orcs 4, 77, 99, 103, 126, 174, 209, 257-58, 259, 260, 264, 266-67, 269, 270
Orodruin's fire 208
Orthanc 43, 99, 102, 104, 126, 246, 264
Orwell, George 15
Osiris (ancient Egyptian god) 94
Otherworld (Celtic Myth) 177, 178-79, 184, 196
Owen, Wilfred 54
Oxford 6, 8, 37, 55, 75, 78, 83, 91, 145, 190, 212, 252

P

Palantir 102
Pallando 127
pantheism 63, 172
pastoral tradition 201, 213-20
Pearce, Joseph 4, 10, 16, 53, 224
philology (Tolkien as philologist) 3, 8, 31, 89
philosophy/philosopher(s) 1, 9, 16, 20, 21-22, 35, 51, 71, 122, 132, 138, 158, 163, 164, 167, 169, 170-71, 173, 190, 212, 232, 234, 245, 255
photosynthesis 51, 231
Pippin (Peregrin Took) 1, 41, 43-44, 74, 84, 100, 118-19, 124, 132, 183, 192, 217, 218, 260, 261, 268, 269
Plank, Robert 105
plant(s) 34, 35, 36, 51, 82, 87, 93, 120, 125
polls (Waterstone, Channel Four, Folio Society, BBC, Mori) 10-12, 14
pollution 20, 48, 49-50, 51, 54, 68-70, 86, 87, 103, 139, 142-43, 144-45, 167, 246
popularity (of Tolkien's works) 4, 8-10, 12, 13, 14-15, 139

power 18, 37, 39, 52-53, 54, 63, 65, 66, 70, 79, 80, 83, 85, 94, 96, 104-05, 116, 121, 124-25, 137, 140, 145, 149, 151, 154, 163, 169, 171, 172, 193, 231, 251
    regimes of power 20, 41, 43, 49, 53, 54, 69, 73, 86, 97-98, 99, 100-03, 107, 109-11, 117, 127, 130, 135-36, 139, 143, 147-48, 152, 166, 168, 204, 208, 209, 220, 243, 245, 246, 261, 265
    the will to power 2, 22, 38, 52, 69, 81, 82, 89-90, 96, 99, 100, 118-19, 124, 126, 140-42, 145-46, 148, 165, 208, 209-10, 246, 247, 261, 263
    the power of nature 23, 39, 65, 67, 69, 71, 77, 78, 85, 87, 89, 99, 105, 107, 142, 144, 146, 153, 154, 162, 188, 191-92, 197-98, 236, 244, 246, 271
Powers of the World (see also Valar) 65, 162
Primary World 1, 15, 19, 21, 36-37, 47, 50, 53, 64, 105, 156, 159, 174, 180, 181, 190, 196-97, 199, 236-38, 240, 249, 251, 255

Q

Queen of the Earth (see also Yavanna) 65
Quest(s) 7, 19, 67, 74, 79, 81, 91, 124, 137, 146, 217, 256, 271
Quickbeam 268

R

Radagast 126-28, 170
realm(s) 48, 119, 134, 141, 146, 174, 183-85, 193, 195, 196, 244
    of the imagination 174, 195, 236, 238, 249, 251
Recovery (Tolkien's theory) 19-20, 21, 233, 237, 239, 241, 248-49
The Red Fairy Book 31
Rednal 59-60, 61
reincarnation (see elves) 184, 190-91, 223
Return of the Native 203
Revelation, Book of 167
Rhetoric 5, 46, 104-05, 214
Ringbearer 74, 129, 271
Rings of Power 141-42, 154, 193, 197, 252
Ringwraiths 88, 134, 141, 142, 183, 206, 246
Rissik, Andrew (critic) 12, 16
Rivendell 70, 84, 146, 170, 183, 185, 186, 188, 208, 210, 219, 223
Robin Hood (as Green Man) 94
Rogers, Deborah and Ivor 195
Rohan 121, 123, 180, 264
Romanticism and green themes 29, 203, 215, 219
Rosebury, Brian 18, 20, 27, 30, 54, 62, 115, 157
Roverandom 194
Routledge (The New Critical Idiom Series) 201-02
Rueckert, William 24, 34, 230, 239-40

S

Sackville-Bagginses 217, 218
sad/sadness 2, 43, 100, 126, 183, 243, 252
Sale, Roger 18
Salinger, J.D. 15
Sandyman, Ted 47-48, 49, 55, 57, 218
Sarehole 29-31, 38, 55, 58-59, 60-61
Sarehole Mill 29, 55-57
Saruman (see also Sharkey) 2, 22, 23, 37, 39, 41, 43, 44, 47, 70, 96-107, 109, 111, 121, 127, 128, 135, 140, 148, 149-50, 153, 174, 212-13, 257, 259, 260, 261, 262-63, 264, 266
   as a 'little Sauron' 99, 125
   his voice 104-05, 107
   love of machines 2, 38, 48, 51, 53, 70, 100, 103, 107, 146, 191, 263
   pursuit of power 2, 51, 53, 69, 96-99, 100, 101-02, 103, 107, 117, 124, 125, 126, 191, 246, 263
Sauron 18, 22, 43, 44, 52, 53, 89, 97, 99, 106, 109, 110-11, 116, 117, 118, 120, 124-25, 126, 127, 129, 131, 132, 134, 135-36, 139, 168, 174, 188, 191, 193, 206, 212, 263
   against nature 2, 23, 37-38, 41, 69, 70, 85-86, 111, 125, 128, 133, 136, 137, 140-48, 151, 152, 245-46, 260, 261
   as Ringmaker/machine-maker 89, 96, 148, 193, 210, 246
   contrasted to Gandalf 23, 109, 126, 136, 149, 150-51, 271
   lord of machines 52, 141
   Lord of the Rings 85
   not pure evil 52, 89, 145, 146, 208-09
   pursuit of dominion over Middle-earth 69, 86, 96, 111, 121, 130, 140, 146, 151, 245-46
Sayer, J.A. 33
Schindler's Ark 43
Schindler's List 43
Schweitzer, Albert 120-22, 138, 171
Scouring of the Shire 28, 41-52, 70, 105, 149, 206-07, 244-45, 268
Sears, Paul B. 24, 71, 143, 245
seasons/seasonal 76, 93, 195
   autumn 76, 205, 233
   spring 41, 92, 205-06, 213, 233, 248, 252
   summer 30, 59, 144, 195, 207
   winter 144, 161, 195
Secondary World(s) 21, 22, 36, 46, 64, 70, 114, 115, 139, 157, 159, 160, 164, 165, 169, 176-77, 181, 190, 196-97, 212, 224, 236-38, 243, 248, 251
Second Music (afterlife) 188
Sessions, George 35

Index   301

Shadowfax 168, 169, 271
Shakespeare, William 75, 154, 203
Sharkey 41, 46-52, 55, 57, 105, 130, 141, 149, 180, 208, 248, 264
sharpening effect 44-45
Shelob 67
Shippey, Tom 10, 12-13, 14, 16, 17-18, 20, 45, 48-49, 51, 52, 75, 83, 88, 103-104,
    106, 115, 154, 157
Shire (see also Scouring of the Shire) 25, 44, 49, 55, 56, 100, 134, 180, 249, 256-
    57, 267, 268, 269
    environmental devastation in 41, 42-43, 45-47, 49-52, 57, 70, 105, 130, 141,
        185, 206-07, 208, 248, 264
    in the pastoral tradition 55, 201, 214-20
    pastoral idyll under threat 205-08
    real world inspiration for 30
    Sauron becomes aware of 44, 130
Shirriff 216, 218
Siewers, Alfred K. 178-79, 184
Síndarin (elven language) 178, 270
Silmaril(s) 67, 160
The Silmarillion 54, 63-69, 78, 113-14, 140, 141, 155, 156-58, 159, 160-61, 173,
    175, 177, 181, 184, 189-90, 194
sin 55, 68, 181
Sir Gawain and the Green Knight 91
Sirion 70
Slovic, Scott 202
Smeagol (see also Gollum) 81
Smith of Wootton Major 174, 194, 195-96, 243
sorcery 54, 103, 104-05, 141, 209, 262
sorrow 59-60, 189, 195, 250
Spielberg, Steven 43-44
Spring, Howard (critic) 6
Stanton, Michael N. 63, 165, 187, 193, 246, 271
Steinbeck, John 8, 15
stewardship 62, 112-13, 116-17, 118-20, 150, 159
Stimpson, Catherine 213
Stormcrow 123, 152
Straight, Michael 30, 156, 187
sub-creation 67, 114, 162, 191, 196, 235-37, 239
Suffield, Beatrice 60
Suffield, John (Tolkien's maternal grandfather) 58
Sullivan, C.W. 53
supernatural 135, 151-52, 184, 206, 208-09, 271

T

Taggard, David 139, 145
technocrat(s) 18, 22, 70, 100, 139
technology 1, 3, 28, 39, 47-50, 51-52, 54-55, 56-58, 69, 70, 98, 100-01, 103, 107, 130, 137, 138, 141, 145, 147, 149, 154, 166, 171, 172, 174, 191, 193, 197, 214, 234
technosphere 40-41
The Tempest 203
Tennyson, Alfred 77
Tess of the D'Urbervilles 203
Theocritus 214
Théoden 117, 123, 272
Third Age 2, 23, 25, 43, 70, 71, 72, 109, 111, 116, 120, 123, 124, 127, 128, 130, 131, 133, 134, 142, 147, 149, 151, 155, 168, 175, 181, 182, 188-89, 197, 208, 220, 223, 244, 248, 251, 256, 261, 262, 264, 271
Thoreau, Henry David 203
Thorin Oakenshield 131
To Kill a Mocking Bird 15
Tolkien, Arthur 29, 58
Tolkien, Christopher 54, 69, 137, 175, 184, 212
Tolkien, Edith 252
Tolkien, Hilary 29, 30, 59
Tolkien, John Ronald Reuel
    and religion 1, 3, 21-22, 29, 35, 58-65, 69, 70-71, 109, 112-18, 137, 147, 153, 160, 163-65, 166-67, 169-73, 176-77, 178, 180-83, 190, 195, 197, 198, 201, 224-25, 234-35, 241
    anticipating ecocriticism/green studies 23-24, 158, 180, 220, 226, 228, 240-41, 249-50
    anticipating extent of future environmental issues 2, 3, 39, 54, 71, 87, 137, 144, 171, 174, 212
    as a contemporary writer 13-20, 24, 25, 27, 41, 51-52, 70, 251
    as a storyteller 3, 6, 22, 27, 45, 79, 102, 203, 212, 238, 250
    as an environmentalist 3, 21, 22, 29, 34, 35, 121, 158, 163, 166-67, 170, 250, 255
    critical reception 4-10, 53, 74, 203, 213-14, 232
    defender of nature 3, 21, 32-34, 36, 62, 166, 252-53
    distrust of machines 3, 21, 27, 28, 29, 37, 48, 49-50, 52-55, 56-57, 71, 92, 105-06, 137, 141, 147-48, 172, 214, 220, 232, 241, 250
    early years 28, 29-32, 46, 55, 58-61, 156, 177
    environmental anxieties 1, 3, 13, 15, 18, 20-21, 24, 27-28, 29, 32-33, 36-37, 53-54, 61, 71, 86, 87, 92, 103, 105-06, 112, 128, 131, 137, 138-39, 140-41, 147-48, 197, 199, 204, 214, 219, 220, 232, 238, 241, 244, 250, 255
    experiences of war 17, 54, 155

Index 303

love of trees 22, 29, 31, 32-33, 34-35, 46, 173-74, 255
not a Luddite 28, 54-55, 56-57, 71, 172
Tolkien, Mabel 28, 31, 58-62
Tolkien, Michael 60
Tolkien Society 11-12, 252
Toynbee, Philip (critic) 4
treachery/treacherous 81, 99, 101, 126, 256
tree(s) 2, 27, 28, 30, 42, 62, 66, 115, 117, 120-21, 156, 166, 213, 228, 233, 235, 238
   have enemies 3, 32-37, 46
   in Tolkien's fiction 20, 33, 34, 36-37, 42, 46, 66-67, 76-77, 86, 88, 93, 100, 101, 116, 117, 125, 126, 150, 154-55, 158, 162, 165, 174, 179, 185, 191, 192, 196, 205, 207, 219, 227, 243, 246, 247, 248, 255-72
   Tolkien's love of 22, 29, 31, 32-33, 34-35, 46, 173-74, 255
Tree and Leaf 33, 222
Treebeard 1-2, 48, 61, 66, 79, 87-88, 89, 95-96, 100-01, 124, 164, 221, 260-64, 265-66, 268, 272
   as voice of nature 38, 176, 199, 247
   as the Green Man 95, 170
Tree of Tales 228, 233, 235, 240
Treschow, Michael 78, 81-82
Two Trees (of Valinor) 66-67, 248
Túatha Dé Danann (Celtic Myth) 184
twentieth century 3, 8, 10-20, 36, 42, 47, 52, 56, 143, 250
twenty-first century 14, 47, 144
Tyler, J.E.A. 101-02, 110-11, 122-23, 124, 128
tyrant(s)/tyranny 2, 79, 82, 101, 142, 147, 208

U

Uin (great whale in Tolkien's fiction) 194
Ulmo 65, 66, 69-70, 115-16, 146
Ulysses 10, 15, 19
Undying Lands 70, 96, 115, 153, 154, 158, 161, 175
Ungoliant 67, 69, 174, 248
unnatural creations 39, 69, 103, 141, 146
Unwin, Camilla (Rayner's daughter) 62-63, 171
Unwin, Rayner 62, 219
Unwin, Stanley 7, 177

V

Vala(r) 65-67, 69, 75, 88-89, 95, 109-10, 114, 115-16, 122, 126, 139, 146, 161, 162-63, 174, 195, 236
   as the 'Powers of the World' 65, 162

Valinor 66, 67, 160, 248
Varda 62, 116
victory 77, 86, 98, 138, 263
Völuspá 134

W

Walden 203
Waldman, Milton 1, 147, 157, 175
Walmsley, Nigel (critic) 9-10
Warg(s) 270
warn/warning 7, 15, 25, 28, 33, 37, 38, 61, 64, 70, 77, 84, 86, 102-03, 130-31, 137, 139, 145, 167, 174, 186, 196-97, 204, 210, 212, 227, 238, 240, 244, 249, 250, 251, 252, 256, 264, 267, 268
War of the Ring 2, 44, 67, 117, 260, 263
Warwickshire/Warwick 31, 55, 156
water 37, 42, 65, 66, 69, 76, 77, 105, 111, 115-16, 150, 167, 192, 207, 238
    water pollution 20, 48, 49, 57, 69-70, 144, 167, 207
Weinreich, Frank 13
Welsh (language) 177-78
White Jr., Lynn R. 113, 115, 160, 165-69, 173, 198
White, Michael 138
White Wizard (see also Saruman) 48-49, 50, 73, 98, 101, 125
Whitmore, T.C. 33
Wilcox, Miranda 189
wild/wilderness 2, 76, 87, 95, 100, 140, 167, 196, 261, 266
wildlife 38, 117, 127
Williams, Charles 203
Williams, Raymond 214-16, 217
Willson, Diana 252
Wilson, Edmund (critic) 4-5, 12, 16
wizard(s) 41, 44, 48-49, 50, 73, 98-99, 101-02, 105, 109, 110, 111, 113, 122, 125, 126-27, 132, 137, 152, 170, 171, 194, 246, 263, 269, 272
wood(s)/woodland 1-2, 38, 48, 61, 76, 83-84, 92, 101, 115, 116, 121, 140, 152, 176, 179, 180, 183, 185, 191, 205-06, 237, 238, 243, 244, 248-51, 256, 257, 258-59, 261-62, 265, 267, 268
Wood, Ralph C. 3, 57, 62
Wood-sunshine (poem) 243
Wordsworth, William 29, 203, 204, 240
World (see also Eä) 64-65, 88
World War One (the Great War) 17, 18, 52, 54, 155
World War Two 18, 52, 53, 54, 137-38, 212
Wormtongue, Gríma 123
Wuthering Heights 179

Wyndham, John 203

Y
Yale 8
Yavanna 65-66, 115-16, 146

Z
Zaillian, Steven 44
zeitgeist 232
Zimmerman, Morton Grady 75

Walking Tree Publishers

Walking Tree Publishers was founded in 1997 as a forum for publication of material (books, videos, CDs, etc.) related to Tolkien and Middle-earth studies. Manuscripts and project proposals can be submitted to the board of editors (please include an SAE):

Walking Tree Publishers
CH-3052 Zollikofen
Switzerland
e-mail: info@walking-tree.org
http://www.walking-tree.org

Cormarë Series

The *Cormarë Series* has been the first series of studies dedicated exclusively to the exploration of Tolkien's work. Its focus is on papers and studies from a wide range of scholarly approaches. The series comprises monographs, thematic collections of essays, conference volumes, and reprints of important yet no longer (easily) accessible papers by leading scholars in the field. Manuscripts and project proposals are evaluated by members of an independent board of advisors who support the series editors in their endeavour to provide the readers with qualitatively superior yet accessible studies on Tolkien and his work.

News from the Shire and Beyond. Studies on Tolkien
Peter Buchs and Thomas Honegger (eds.), Zurich and Berne 2004, Reprint, First edition 1997 (Cormarë Series 1), ISBN 978-3-9521424-5-5

Root and Branch. Approaches Towards Understanding Tolkien
Thomas Honegger (ed.), Zurich and Berne 2005, Reprint, First edition 1999 (Cormarë Series 2), ISBN 978-3-905703-01-6

Richard Sturch, *Four Christian Fantasists. A Study of the Fantastic Writings of George MacDonald, Charles Williams, C.S. Lewis and J.R.R. Tolkien*
Zurich and Berne 2007, Reprint, First edition 2001 (Cormarë Series 3), ISBN 978-3-905703-04-7

Tolkien in Translation
Thomas Honegger (ed.), Zurich and Jena 2011, Reprint, First edition 2003 (Cormarë Series 4), ISBN 978-3-905703-15-3

Mark T. Hooker, *Tolkien Through Russian Eyes*
Zurich and Berne 2003 (Cormarë Series 5), ISBN 978-3-9521424-7-9

Translating Tolkien: Text and Film
Thomas Honegger (ed.), Zurich and Jena 2011, Reprint, First edition 2004 (Cormarë Series 6), ISBN 978-3-905703-16-0

Christopher Garbowski, *Recovery and Transcendence for the Contemporary Mythmaker. The Spiritual Dimension in the Works of J.R.R. Tolkien*
Zurich and Berne 2004, Reprint, First Edition by Marie Curie Sklodowska, University Press, Lublin 2000, (Cormarë Series 7), ISBN 978-3-9521424-8-6

Reconsidering Tolkien
Thomas Honegger (ed.), Zurich and Berne 2005 (Cormarë Series 8),
ISBN 978-3-905703-00-9

Tolkien and Modernity 1
Frank Weinreich and Thomas Honegger (eds.), Zurich and Berne 2006 (Cormarë Series 9), ISBN 978-3-905703-02-3

Tolkien and Modernity 2
Thomas Honegger and Frank Weinreich (eds.), Zurich and Berne 2006 (Cormarë Series 10), ISBN 978-3-905703-03-0

Tom Shippey, *Roots and Branches. Selected Papers on Tolkien by Tom Shippey*
Zurich and Berne 2007 (Cormarë Series 11), ISBN 978-3-905703-05-4

Ross Smith, *Inside Language. Linguistic and Aesthetic Theory in Tolkien*
Zurich and Berne 2007 (Cormarë Series 12), ISBN 978-3-905703-06-1

How We Became Middle-earth. A Collection of Essays on The Lord of the Rings
Adam Lam and Nataliya Oryshchuk (eds.), Zurich and Berne 2007 (Cormarë Series 13), ISBN 978-3-905703-07-8

Myth and Magic. Art According to the Inklings
Eduardo Segura and Thomas Honegger (eds.), Zurich and Berne 2007 (Cormarë Series 14), ISBN 978-3-905703-08-5

The Silmarillion - Thirty Years On
Allan Turner (ed.), Zurich and Berne 2007 (Cormarë Series 15),
ISBN 978-3-905703-10-8

Martin Simonson, *The Lord of the Rings and the Western Narrative Tradition*
Zurich and Jena 2008 (Cormarë Series 16), ISBN 978-3-905703-09-2

Tolkien's Shorter Works. Proceedings of the 4th Seminar of the Deutsche Tolkien Gesellschaft & Walking Tree Publishers Decennial Conference
Margaret Hiley and Frank Weinreich (eds.), Zurich and Jena 2008 (Cormarë Series 17), ISBN 978-3-905703-11-5

Tolkien's The Lord of the Rings: Sources of Inspiration
Stratford Caldecott and Thomas Honegger (eds.), Zurich and Jena 2008 (Cormarë Series 18), ISBN 978-3-905703-12-2

J.S. Ryan, *Tolkien's View: Windows into his World*
Zurich and Jena 2009 (Cormarë Series 19), ISBN 978-3-905703-13-9

Music in Middle-earth
Heidi Steimel and Friedhelm Schneidewind (eds.), Zurich and Jena 2010 (Cormarë Series 20), ISBN 978-3-905703-14-6

Liam Campbell, *The Ecological Augury in the Works of J.R.R. Tolkien*
Zurich and Jena 2011 (Cormarë Series 21), ISBN 978-3-905703-18-4

Margaret Hiley, *The Loss and the Silence. Aspects of Modernism in the Works of C.S. Lewis, J.R.R. Tolkien and Charles Williams*
Zurich and Jena, forthcoming

Rainer Nagel, *Hobbit Place-names. A Linguistic Excursion through the Shire*
Zurich and Jena, forthcoming

The Broken Scythe. Death and Immortality in the Works of J.R.R. Tolkien
Roberto Arduini and Claudio Antonio Testi (eds.), Zurich and Jena, forthcoming

Christopher MacLachlan, *Tolkien and Wagner*
Zurich and Jena, forthcoming

Renee Vink, *Tolkien vs. Wagner*
Zurich and Jena, forthcoming

Constructions of Authorship in and around the Works of J.R.R. Tolkien
Judith Klinger (ed.), Zurich and Jena, forthcoming

Tolkien's Poetry
Julian Morton Eilmann and Allan Turner (eds.), Zurich and Jena, forthcoming

Beowulf and the Dragon

The original Old English text of the 'Dragon Episode' of *Beowulf* is set in an authentic font and printed and bound in hardback creating a high quality art book. The text is illustrated by Anke Eissmann and accompanied by John Porter's translation. The introduction is by Tom Shippey. Limited first edition of 500 copies. 84 pages.
Selected pages can be previewed on: www.walking-tree.org/beowulf
Beowulf and the Dragon
Zurich and Jena 2009, ISBN 978-3-905703-17-7

Tales of Yore Series

The *Tales of Yore Series* grew out of the desire to share Kay Woollard's whimsical stories and drawings with a wider audience. The series aims at providing a platform for qualitatively superior fiction with a clear link to Tolkien's world.

Kay Woollard, *The Terror of Tatty Walk. A Frightener*
CD and Booklet, Zurich and Berne 2000 (Tales of Yore Series 1)
ISBN 978-3-9521424-2-4

Kay Woollard, *Wilmot's Very Strange Stone or What came of building "snobbits"*
CD and booklet, Zurich and Berne 2001 (Tales of Yore Series 2)
ISBN 978-3-9521424-4-8

www.ingramcontent.com/pod-product-compliance
Lightning Source LLC
Chambersburg PA
CBHW070916180426
43192CB00037B/1270